THE FUTURE
IS FOREIGN

I0061681

THE FUTURE IS FOREIGN

Women and Immigrants
in Corporate Japan

Hilary J. Holbrow

ILR PRESS
AN IMPRINT OF
CORNELL UNIVERSITY PRESS
ITHACA AND LONDON

Copyright © 2025 by Cornell University

All rights reserved. Except for brief quotations in a review, this book,
or parts thereof, must not be reproduced in any form without permission
in writing from the publisher. For information, address Cornell University Press,
Sage House, 512 East State Street, Ithaca, New York 14850.
Visit our website at cornellpress.cornell.edu.

First published 2025 by Cornell University Press

Librarians: A CIP catalog record for this book is available from the Library
of Congress.

ISBN 9781501784347 (hardcover)
ISBN 9781501784354 (paperback)
ISBN 9781501784378 (pdf)
ISBN 9781501784361 (epub)

GPSR EU contact: Sam Thornton, Mare Nostrum Group B.V., Mauritskade 21D,
1091 GC, Amsterdam, NL, gpsr@mare-nostrum.co.uk.

*This book is dedicated to Kazumi Ikeda,
who has enriched my understanding of Japanese
society by sharing her stories and friendship.*

Contents

Figures

Note on Transliteration and Names

This book uses modified Hepburn transliteration, with roman letters to indicate long vowels, rather than macrons. Place names (e.g., Tokyo) or other words that are familiar to English speakers are represented as they usually are in English.

Names are printed in the standard English order, with family name last. Survey and interview respondents, and others whom I encountered and observed as part of my fieldwork are referred to by pseudonymous first names. Colleagues in Japan who facilitated the research are referred to by their real names.

THE FUTURE
IS FOREIGN

INTRODUCTION

The area around Tokyo Station is the beating heart of "Japan Inc.," a district of glass office towers, five-star hotels, and high-end shops, intersected by wide boulevards lined with gingko trees. Amid the humdrum bustle of office workers, coiffed and made-up young mothers sipping tea and window-shopping, and tourists striking out for the Imperial Palace, the simple and sometimes stark urban design emanates an aura of power and money.

Although anyone can wander into the lobbies of the office towers, to reach the office floors, visitors must clear lobby reception. Some companies, in a performance of efficiency and tech savvy, place electronic terminals where visitors can contact their counterparts inside and print out a scannable barcode. Others project tradition and hospitality, with welcome desks staffed by elegantly uniformed women who greet visitors and place phone calls to their hosts in an impeccably mannered, gracefully choreographed routine. All the while, employees stream in and out to the sounds of arrhythmic beeping from the electronic gates to the elevator banks.

For the visitor, this aura of power and money is heightened inside the private realms within the glass office towers, where it combines with a heady sense of elevation above the masses outside. Meeting rooms in the towers offer panoramic views of the city stretching out to the horizon, or overlook the lush greenery of the imperial palace grounds just a few blocks away. Employees, however, do not often enjoy such views from their desks. Everyday workspaces are large, crowded floors on which teams work nearly elbow to elbow around numerous rectangular desk blocks, each with a manager at the head. The working floor hums with the sound of quiet conversations, shuffling papers, and the tippy-taps of dozens or hundreds of computer keyboards.

During my fieldwork for this study of changing inequalities in Japanese firms, I commuted almost every day to Marunouchi—literally "inside the circle"—as the neighborhood sandwiched between Tokyo Station and the Imperial Palace grounds is called. Rising up the escalator into the granite-finished lobby of the ShinMaru building, where the Canon Institute for Global Studies (CIGS) generously offered me desk space, I never failed to feel the frisson of being *at the center of things*. For the first, and perhaps the last, time in my life I wore nice slacks, a blazer, and makeup every single day.

The mystique of working for a large firm is powerful in Japan.[1] More than half of all college graduates aspire to employment in a large firm, and for men graduating from elite national universities, the percentage is as high as 80 percent.[2] Employment in a large, well-known company marks you as a person worthy of respect.[3] It testifies that you not only are smart and persistent, having most likely passed the gauntlet of "examination hell" to gain admittance to one of Japan's most prestigious universities but also have leapt the successive hurdles of essays, personality tests, aptitude exams, and interviews that large firms use to screen for the most capable candidates.[4] The firms headquartered in the Marunouchi district are the epitome of this dream of working for a big, important company.

Seven of the twelve firms where I conducted my research are headquartered in Marunouchi; the other five are located in other major business hubs in central Tokyo. Despite this geographic prestige, the employees I surveyed and spoke with did not, for the most part, hold powerful jobs. Although some of my informants led teams, or wielded at least some influence over executive decision-making, respondents were either rank-and-file employees or midlevel managers, and their work could be tedious and mundane. Their salaries were comfortable, not exorbitant. The symbolic cachet of work "inside the circle," however, was widely acknowledged. Hideki, a Japanese man in his mid-twenties, jokingly mentioned his *oote byou* (big company sickness), a fixation on working for a large firm. Although he felt no particular interest in the industry or even the firm in which he was employed, he was content because it met his desire to be working *in Tokyo* "in a skyscraper at the company headquarters." According to another employee in her mid-thirties, Emi:

> If you're working for a small company, your company has zero "name value." There's no way you can work together with companies listed in the first section of the Tokyo stock exchange [where large companies with top market capitalization are listed], unless you have some sort of

personal connection. But this firm has firm-level connections, long-standing connections, so we can work with those type of companies. We can take on those type of big jobs.

Despite these employees' relatively undistinguished positions within their firms' hierarchies, working for a large firm still confers status.[5]

Beyond prestige, work "inside the circle" comes with other inherent advantages. Because these companies often handle multiple areas of business, or work closely with other companies across industries, informants also described a wealth of opportunities to learn and grow. Xinyan told me: "Basically, I do any kind of research to corporate strategy. Macroeconomics, of course. But also politics, economy, and society. And, industry research, energy, real estate, food . . . the scope is very broad. . . . I learn things every day. Every single day, I gain new knowledge, new points of view, meet new people. Every day is new." Whereas in smaller firms, employees might find themselves doing the same tasks day in and day out, the scope of business at a larger firm means employees always have some way to stretch themselves.

Although rich learning opportunities and daily immersion in an environment redolent of power, wealth, and influence make elite Tokyo firms a highly desirable place of work, for white-collar workers, it offers even more: the chance to move even closer to the center of the circle. Far more than in small and midsize companies, employees can expect their compensation to increase over the course of their careers. What many white-collar employees value even more than income growth, however, are the opportunities for upward mobility, and the chance to hone their skills and expand their impact. Describing his hopes for his future career, Takeshi (age 29) said: "I want to change things. It's my strong desire to make this a good company, a company with a global presence, a company that's fiscally strong. I have a lot of ideas. As long as my job lets me do that, I'll be satisfied." Whether or not Takeshi, a rank-and-file employee, can achieve these dreams is an open question. But what elite firms offer is an arena in which employees like him can make the attempt.

This wide scope stands in contrast to smaller firms at which the career ladders are less established or absent. Emi, who had previously worked for a smaller company, described starkly how lacking her opportunities for advancement had been there: "At my old company, it was just me and my boss. . . . [A]fter I entered as the most junior person, no one came in under me for three or four years. All the positions were static. You can't see a future for yourself. It's like, 'it's always going to be like this.'" After two years in her current, much larger firm, Emi was not confident that she would be able to advance, but as she said, "at least the [career] system is laid out for you."

This is the scene of this study: Elite firms with a global reach, at which all employees can bask in the reflection of money and power, and at which a few can obtain it for themselves. From the 1950s through the 1990s, there was a simple prerequisite: You had to be a Japanese man. Profound demographic, social, and legal changes, however, are putting pressure on firms to increase opportunities for Japanese women as well as for workers with roots outside Japan. In this book, I ask whether this new era is indeed opening up room for members of these historically absent, excluded, or marginalized groups to obtain greater parity with Japanese men in the rarified world of elite Japanese business. Who is getting ahead? Who continues to be held back? And why?

Making It to the Top in Historical Perspective

To contextualize the pressures facing powerful Japanese firms to create greater opportunities for members of formerly absent and excluded groups, it is necessary to understand these groups' status in relation to large firms before 1990.

Although many elite firms of the high-growth era, particularly those in the service sector, hired women in large numbers,[6] they notoriously relegated female employees to the periphery. Before the 1990s, women employed in large companies worked almost exclusively as "smiling receptionists and clerical assistants."[7] Companies hired women fresh out of high school, junior college, or, more rarely, university, and employed them to answer phones, type documents, make photocopies, and serve tea.[8] The vast majority of women ended their employment with large firms when they married or became pregnant, both because firms' policies or informal norms demanded it, but also because few women wanted to continue working.[9] Women who remained with large employers in their thirties and beyond were rare and were pitied by their coworkers for "having" to work, either because of their failure to marry or their husbands' failure to provide adequately for their families.[10] Writing in 1979, Rodney Clark bluntly declared, "Japanese companies do not promote women."[11] Exceptions to this rule were few and far between. In 1989, women held just 2 percent of section chief (*kachou*) positions.[12]

Although large, prestigious companies at least *hired* women, employment of immigrants or non-Japanese ethnics in these firms was virtually zero.

Before 1945, hundreds of thousands of colonial subjects of Japan's East Asian empire had come to Japan, in many cases as forced-labor conscripts for large Japanese mining and manufacturing firms. The majority of these subjects came from the Korean peninsula, and one estimate puts their numbers at around

2.4 million in the mid-1940s.[13] After Japan's defeat in 1945, most prewar and wartime-era migrants returned to the Korean peninsula, but around a quarter remained in Japan. Stripped of Japanese citizenship by the San Francisco Peace Treaty of 1952, they and their children settled in Japan as a permanent, noncitizen ethnoracial minority. These colonial-era migrants and their descendants are referred to as Zainichi Koreans (literally, "Koreans in Japan").

In the high-growth period, poverty, discrimination, and the small size of the Zainichi community relative to Japan's rapidly expanding population precluded representation in large Japanese firms. First, the hardship and poverty among the first generation of Zainichi Koreans meant that few second- and third-generation Koreans could acquire the elite educational credentials that would qualify them for white-collar jobs in prestigious companies.[14] Second, large firms openly refused to hire Koreans, even for blue-collar jobs.[15] Third, given that Zainichi Koreans accounted for just 0.6 percent of the population in 1970, even in the absence of poverty and discrimination, their numbers in large firms would necessarily have been small.[16]

Apart from Zainichi Koreans, virtually no other outsiders could have even been considered for employment in large companies. Unlike Germany, which responded to labor shortages in the 1950s and 1960s by authorizing bilateral guestworker agreements with other countries, postwar Japan relied largely on internal migration from rural areas to fill labor needs. With a small, poor, and excluded Zainichi population, and no ongoing migration to speak of, the Japan Inc. of the high-growth era was a thoroughly Japanese enterprise, not only at the top but also at the bottom.

Pressure for Change

External circumstances, however, have made large firms' marginalization and exclusion of all but Japanese men far less tenable than in the past.

Japan's astonishing economic growth of the 1960s and 1970s occurred during a time when the population was growing and urbanizing, and when access to education was expanding. Even after excluding the female half of the population from consideration, and even in the absence of immigration, large companies had their pick of talent for white-collar jobs among Japanese men alone. This situation was not to last.

Japan's demographic turnaround over the past fifty years has been dramatic. Birthrates fell rapidly in the postwar era, dipping permanently below replacement levels of 2.1 children per woman in 1973.[17] As a result of below-replacement fertility and limited immigration, the working-age population (usually counted

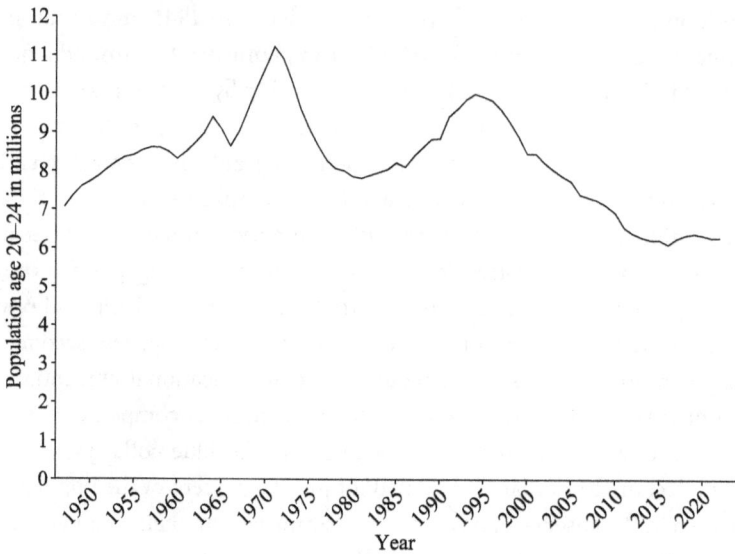

FIGURE I.1. Japan's population, age 20–24, 1947–2022. Calculated from Ministry of Internal Affairs and Communications, "Jinkou suikei no kekka no gaiyou" [Summary of population estimation results]; Ministry of Internal Affairs and Communications, "Nenrei (5sai kaikyuu oyobi 3kubun), danjo betsu jinkou (kakunen 10gatsu 1tachi genzai)—soujinkou taishou 9nen–heisei 12nen" [Total population by age-group (5-year and 3-category) and sex (as of October 1 annually), 1920–2000]; Ministry of Internal Affairs and Communications, "Nenrei (5sai kaikyuu oyobi 3kubun), danjo betsu jinkou (kakunen 10gatsu 1tachi genzai)—soujinkou 2000nen–2020nen" [Total population by age-group (5-year and 3-category) and sex (as of October 1 annually), 2000–2020].

as those between the ages of 15 and 64), peaked in 1995. When I began my field-work in 2015, it had already fallen by 11 percent, and it is projected to fall by an astonishing 48 percent off its peak by 2070.[18]

Decline in the number of young labor market entrants is even starker. The population of 20- to 24-year-olds, depicted in figure I.1, peaked in 1971. This was followed by a second, lower peak in 1995, as the children of postwar baby boomers came of age. By 2015, the size of the prime age-group for labor market entry had already shrunk by 45 percent compared with 1971 levels and was 12 percent lower than it had been in 1947.

This transition from exponential growth to exponential decline is novel. Economically and politically troubled nations, such as Ireland in the 1840s through the 1950s and much of Eastern Europe from the 1990s onward, have also lost population, often through outmigration. Regions within nation-states or

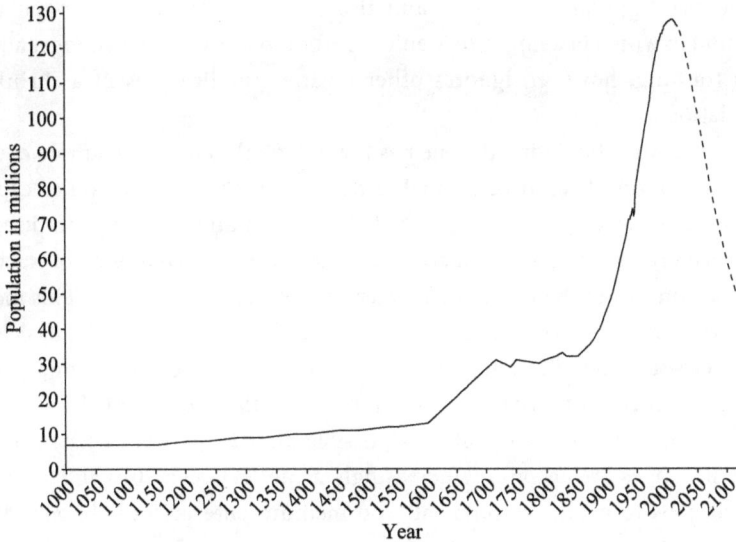

FIGURE I.2. Japan's actual and projected population, 1000–2115. Calculated from Ministry of Internal Affairs and Communications, "Nenrei (5sai kaikyuu oyobi 3kubun), danjo betsu jinkou (kakunen 10gatsu 1tachi genzai)—soujinkou taishou 9nen–heisei 12nen" [Total population by age-group (5-year and 3-category) and sex (as of October 1 annually), 1920–2000]; Ministry of Internal Affairs and Communications, "Nenrei (5sai kaikyuu oyobi 3kubun), danjo betsu jinkou (kakunen 10gatsu 1tachi genzai)—soujinkou 2000nen-2020nen" [Total population by age-group (5-year and 3-category) and sex (as of October 1 annually), 2000–2020]; Ministry of Internal Affairs and Communication, "Wagakuni ni okeru soujinkou no choukiteki suii" [Our country's long-run population trends]; National Institute of Population and Social Security Research, "Nihon no shourai suikei jinkou (Heisei 29nen suikei)" [Japan's future estimated population (2017 estimate)].

empires have always experienced population booms and busts. But nationwide population decline for a powerful, wealthy country is truly unprecedented.[19]

Long-run population projections (figure I.2) show nearly all of Japan's modern population expansion vanishing over the course of the next century. Almost universally, this demographic reversal is perceived as a slow-moving catastrophe. Japanese demographers have created a "doomsday clock" counting down the hypothetical days, hours, minutes, and seconds until the number of children reaches one.[20] Media reports refer to population decline in apocalyptic terms as a "looming crisis," a "new population bomb," and a "death cross."[21] A *Washington Post* headline refers to Japan as a "dying country."[22]

Academics highlight the social and fiscal costs of an inverted population pyramid in which tax-supported seniors outnumber tax-paying younger adults. This framing, however, ignores other positive implications of a shrinking population.

Specifically, population decline has the potential to usher in a more equitable distribution of resources. As labor becomes scarcer in relation to capital, workers gain leverage to bargain for better wages and working conditions.[23] Furthermore, as long as population decline outpaces economic contraction, each person can in theory attain a larger slice of the economic pie. This means that demographic decline can spark what sociologist Richard Alba has called "non-zero-sum mobility": in theory at least, a shrinking society permits people to improve their circumstances without making others worse off.[24]

If this non-zero-sum mobility is possible anywhere, it is in Japan, where labor shortages are becoming increasingly acute. Between 2010 and 2021, the ratio of jobs to applicants in small and medium enterprises ballooned from three jobs to every applicant, to almost ten.[25] Because large firms are more desirable places of employment, labor shortages are less severe—at firms with more than three hundred employees, jobs-to-applicants ratios have hovered just under one. Nonetheless, 41.5 percent of large firms say they lack sufficient labor power.[26]

This shortage places tremendous pressure on firms—even those that attract relatively large numbers of applicants—to change how they evaluate (potential) workers. As Gary Becker has pointed out, discrimination by ascriptive characteristics comes at a cost to employers, who have to pay higher wages to workers from the "preferred" category.[27] When the working-age population shrinks, the cost of discrimination increases correspondingly. Moreover, the number of workers in preferred categories may not be sufficient to fill all the most desirable jobs.[28] Consequently, a declining population increases pressure on all firms, including elite firms, to expand the pool of workers they choose to hire, train for leadership, and promote.[29] And workers, regardless of background, are better positioned to demand treatment that is both fair and generous.

Changes to employment and immigration law since the high-growth era also buttress economic pressures for Japanese firms to diversify whom they hire and promote. In 1974, Chong-sok Pak, a second-generation Zainichi Korean, won a court case against Hitachi. Hitachi had rescinded its offer of employment after learning that Pak, who applied under the Japanese name he used in daily life, was a Korean citizen. The Yokohama district court ruled this as ethnic discrimination. This precedent, as well as extensive activism by Zainichi Koreans, has made it less acceptable for firms to turn down job applicants on the basis of nationality.[30]

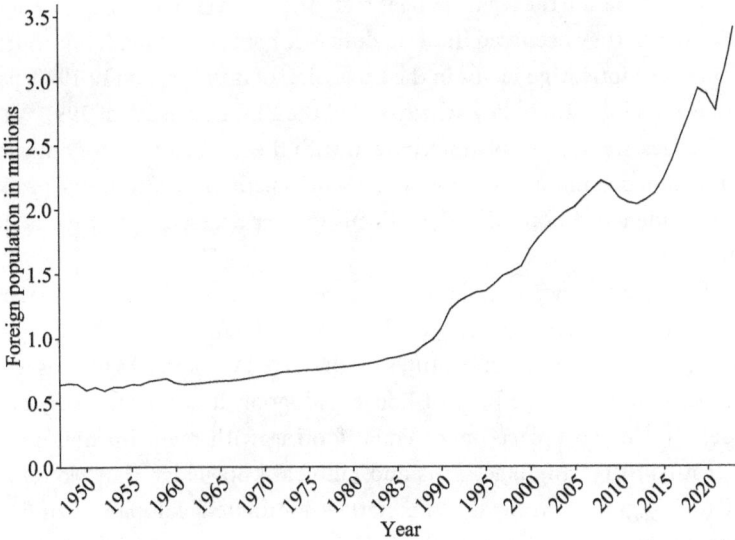

FIGURE I.3. Japan's foreign citizen population, 1947–2023. Calculated from Ministry of Justice, "Zairyuu gaikokujin toukei (kyuu touroku gaikokujin toukei) toukeihyou" [Statistics on resident foreigners (formerly statistics on registered foreigners)].

Revisions to Japan's visa policies and border control laws implemented in 1990 have brought increasing numbers of non-Japanese citizens to Japan, as shown in figure I.3. These revisions dramatically expanded the types of visas available, and created a new pathway to permanent residency for foreign citizens. Post-1990 immigrants and their children—often called "newcomers" to distinguish them from groups with origins in the colonial era—have benefited from the legal restrictions on employment discrimination ushered in by "oldcomer" activists.[31]

Gender employment law has also evolved. In response to feminist activism and international pressure, Japan passed the Equal Employment Opportunity Law (EEOL) in 1985.[32] This law required companies merely to "endeavor" to offer equal opportunity to women, and it had limited impact.[33] However, revisions passed in 1997 and implemented in 1999 strengthened the law to prohibit gender discrimination in hiring, job assignments, and promotions outright.[34] Since the early 1990s, policymakers have also adopted increasingly generous provisions for parental leave and subsidized childcare, which facilitate women's continuous labor force engagement.

Although activism has been important to the passage of these laws banning or mitigating historical practices of marginalization and exclusion, we cannot analytically separate the legal changes from the broader demographic environment in which they occurred. Indeed, domestic concerns about labor shortages were a major motivating factor in the expansion of immigration in 1990, parental leave and childcare policy schemes, and the EEOL revision of 1997.[35] These legal changes are thus deeply intertwined with the impersonal economic forces of population decline, and they work in tandem with direct economic pressures to give women and non-Japanese citizens greater access to prestigious, high-paying jobs.

At the same time, population decline does not eliminate barriers to advancement for members of outsider groups. First, workers from outsider groups may not be perfect substitutes for preferred workers. As long as women continue to shoulder the bulk of household labor, it is difficult for them to compete in the workplace on an equal footing with men. Immigrants may lack host-country language skills and cultural knowledge that would allow them to integrate seamlessly into native-dominated companies and work groups. Second, even if outsiders' productivity exactly matches that of preferred workers, insiders' beliefs about the relative capabilities and moral worth of members of outsider groups—what Michèle Lamont has called "symbolic boundaries"—do not evaporate in the face of economic forces or legal changes.[36]

These tensions—between demographic pressures for greater workplace inclusion, on one hand, and between structural and cultural barriers to outsider group members' advancement, on the other—form the backdrop for the analyses in this book. We know that, over the past three decades, demographic and legal changes have exerted ever-greater pressure on firms to move away from the exclusionary practices of the past. But to what extent are those pressures changing the reality on the ground? Faced with countervailing forces, can any outsiders in elite business take advantage of the momentum generated by population decline? Who is best positioned to do so, and why?

The Argument

In this book, I examine outcomes for four different outsider groups—Japanese women; women and men from other Asian countries, predominantly East and Southeast Asia; and men from Europe, North America, and Oceania, which I refer to in shorthand as the West. I show that, descriptively, gender penalties vastly outstrip ethnoracial or region of origin penalties. Women, regardless of national origin, earn far less than men and are less likely to advance to management. By contrast, despite their historical absence from large Japanese firms,

Asian immigrant men experience relatively modest wage gaps with Japanese men; and, anomalously, Western immigrant men earn more.[37]

These patterns are puzzling. Why, despite intense political and demographic pressure to expand women's workplace opportunities, do women continue to fare so poorly? Why, despite Japan's reputation as a xenophobic country, do immigrant men fare so well? I demonstrate that conventional explanations—which focus on women's and immigrants' violation of "ideal worker norms"—fall short in accounting for patterns of advantage and disadvantage in elite workplaces. I advance a novel explanation for changing patterns of stratification, contending that the demography of low-status jobs is critical to the construction of symbolic boundaries and the (re)production of inequality.

Conventional accounts of inequality in the Japanese workplace locate the source of white-collar women's and immigrant workers' disadvantage at the intersection of firms' expectations for workers, and the workplace behaviors of women and immigrants. Firms have historically dictated that employees work long hours, socialize extensively after work, eschew vacation and leave, and cede control of their career paths to the employer. Because women shoulder the bulk of reproductive and household labor, the narrative asserts, they are unable (or unwilling) to meet employers' demands, and their careers suffer. For immigrants, by contrast, the gap lies in immigrants' imperfect linguistic and cultural assimilation to the Japanese workplace. Because immigrants do not consistently adhere to expected cultural patterns of workplace behavior, the logic goes, employers perceive them to be flawed substitutes for Japanese workers and evaluate them unfavorably.

In this book, however, I challenge these narratives in several ways. First, employer expectations and practices associated with both immigrant and women's disadvantage, such as long work hours or expectations of long-term commitment to one employer, have moderated since the high growth era. This is consistent with theoretical predictions that employers may grant concessions to workers to better attract and retain labor in an era of population decline; it also suggests that, for both women and immigrants, structural barriers to advancement are lower than in the past.

Perhaps even more critically, however, women who "work like men" and immigrants who "work like Japanese" fare little better (and in some cases, worse) than their counterparts who violate ideal worker norms. Tellingly, Asian immigrant women's ambition and commitment to work exceeds that not only of Japanese women but also of Japanese men. Yet Asian women's earnings and access to promotion is, at best, on par with that of Japanese women. In addition, although Western men are far less acculturated than Asian men, their workplace outcomes are superior. These findings cast doubt on claims that women's and immigrants' violation of ideal worker norms are the primary reasons for their disadvantage.

I argue that, as elite firms' employment practices have evolved, the locus of women's and immigrants' disadvantage has shifted. In the past, firms' employment practices worked "automatically" against outsiders in a rules-based fashion; today, however, disadvantage arises primarily from discretionary decisions by human resource officials and managers. Compared with the recent past, then, managers' beliefs about workers' capabilities and potential matter far more for their outcomes.

In this environment of high managerial discretion, the symbolic boundaries and status hierarchies people draw between demographic groups are a critical determinant of how members of the different groups will be treated. I show that negative gender stereotypes about women remain pervasive, despite women's growing visibility in management and management-track jobs. In contrast, negative ethnoracial stereotypes about Asians are more unstable, and on teams with the largest shares of Asian workers, Japanese coworkers abjure the negative stereotypes so ubiquitous in the broader society.

Why are gender biases so stable, whereas ethnoracial biases are subject to greater disruption? I argue that it is women's persistent overrepresentation in low-status and irregular jobs that reinforces perceptions of women's lower worth and capabilities. Although, numerically speaking, women in the sample firms are more likely to work in management-track jobs, women remain "the face" of low-status clerical and irregular jobs in many elite firms. Because coworkers in many firms see predominantly women when they "look down" the organizational hierarchy, they continue to associate female gender with mundane, undervalued tasks. In turn, this shapes how all women are perceived and treated, regardless of their job titles. Consistent with this perception, gender inequality among management-track workers is approximately three times greater in firms where support staff are predominantly women. Furthermore, in such firms, women on the management track feel far less valued by their managers. Thus, women's overrepresentation in clerical and irregular jobs remains a major driver of inequality in elite firms, but through its indirect effects on how all women are perceived, rather than its direct impact on clerical and irregular workers' wages.[38]

By extension, immigrant men's advantage may stem in part from their *absence* from the bottom of organizational hierarchies. Unlike women, Asian immigrant men are never "the face" of low-status jobs within elite firms; furthermore, because of Japan's restrictions on migration for low-paid work, longstanding negative stereotypes about Asians find little echo in the daily lives of Japanese white-collar workers outside the office. Thus, the absence from the bottom may give Asian men a symbolic tailwind that enhances Asian immigrant men's opportunities to achieve parity with their Japanese counterparts, despite their historical exclusion from elite settings. Neither Japanese nor Asian immigrant women, in contrast, escape the omnipresent gender status hierarchy, buttressed as it is by Japanese women's concentration in low-status jobs.

These results have profound implications for how stratification orders in Japanese firms will change under pressure of demographic decline. They suggest that, despite the small numbers of immigrant men in Japan today, as individuals, they stand to receive a disproportionate share of the opportunities and resources freed by a shrinking population.

Why Study Elite Firms

For several reasons, both theoretical and practical, I concentrate my study of changing stratification on large, elite firms. First, firm size (far more than industry or occupation) is the critical determinant of material rewards in the Japanese labor market.[39] In cases in which the pot of resources to be distributed is greater, so too is the potential for inequality. In addition, larger inequalities are easier to detect, both for the people who experience them and for outside observers. For example, among workers, an annual wage gap of $20,000 might be readily visible in the clothes they wear, the vacations they take, and the cars they drive. A wage gap of $2,000 or $200 is less obvious. In statistical research, the smaller a difference relative to overall dispersion of the data, the larger the sample size required to identify it. Thus, a study of large firms is best suited to assessing whether stratification occurs.

Second, large companies have long hired women in relatively high numbers, and over the past twenty years, these companies have also been at the forefront of hiring foreign workers. Consequently, relative to Japanese employees, foreign workers are overrepresented in large firms.[40] Studying large firms, then, is a strategic choice designed to understand most effectively how foreign workers are being integrated into white-collar employment in Japan and to assess how the outcomes for immigrants compare with those of similarly qualified Japanese women.

Moreover, at a theoretical level, although large firms represent less than 1 percent of all firms in Japan, they constitute a significant, and growing, share of the employment landscape.[41] As of 2021, 31 percent of all nonagricultural employees work in companies with at least five hundred workers.[42] Hence, stratification patterns within large firms are of increasing importance to inequality in the broader society.

Third, the unparalleled prestige associated with white-collar employment in a large firm—particularly those "inside the circle" that are the focus of this study—imbues what happens there with added significance. For workers, employment and advancement within these firms gives social standing, with potential impacts on how group members are perceived and treated far beyond the workplace. For both Japanese women and immigrant workers, career-track employment and advancement in a large firm is potent evidence that they have "made it" by conventional metrics of success. Similarly, the visibility of these prominent firms makes them targets of imitation. Whether these firms relegate outsiders to the periphery, or increasingly permit them to approach the center, whatever these central firms do is likely to diffuse among other companies with aspirations for expansion and growth.[43] In sum, large firms' disproportionate influence—on both the lives of workers and the behavior of other firms—makes them a critical site in which to illuminate changing patterns of stratification.

Site Selection

I began this research in summer 2013, interviewing human resources (HR) managers at large firms, whom I connected with both through cold calls and through introductions from acquaintances. Despite their busy schedules, HR managers were usually receptive to requests for interviews and were willing to share at least some of the challenges they faced in hiring and managing labor market outsiders. At the same time, to a man (and they *were* all men), the HR professionals I spoke with expressed a commitment to meritocratic ideals. Their aim, they told me, was to hire and promote the most talented employees, irrespective of gender or national background. This marks a stark contrast from discourse on gender in the high-growth era, when women's relegation to peripheral roles was accepted as only natural and right. It also evoked, however, the well-known gap in organizations everywhere, between the way things work *in principle* and the way things work on the ground. When I arrived in Japan in 2014 for a fifteen-month research stint, I committed to a bottom-up approach, emphasizing worker outcomes and experiences rather than HR narratives.

I also felt it was important to situate outsider workers *in context*, particularly the context of their places of employment. I decided on this approach for two reasons. First, without knowledge of the insider experience, it is impossible to know whether outsiders are treated equally. Hence, I hoped to survey and interview outsider and insider employees *within the same firms*, to permit apples-to-apples comparisons among various groups.

Second, this approach has the added benefit of permitting a "crowdsourced" measurement of firms' rules, procedures, and informal practices. These contextual features of the workplace are a critical source of stratification.[44] As the early HR interviews illustrated, however, HR officials are motivated to portray their firms in a positive light, and their narratives of formal policies may correspond more closely to what is perceived to be desirable than to on-the-ground organizational routines.

Early interviews with foreign employees, which I also undertook in 2013, additionally illustrated a hazard of understanding the work environment solely through outsiders' perspectives. Precisely because they are outsiders, foreign employees are often uncertain about what company HR policy is, let alone whether it is enacted according to principles laid out in HR manuals. In 2013, a Taiwanese game developer I spoke with told me he thought that starting salaries probably were lower for foreign employees, but he could not be certain. When I asked a US man working for a large finance company how his company determined compensation, he told me, "I believe, I guess it depends on per year, your evaluations and how you do. To get that yearly raise. I believe. Again, a lot of the stuff in training just goes over my head for the most part. I'm like, oh, they'll tell me again eventually. I don't really need to know that right now."

Faced with sanitized HR perspectives and the outright confusion of outsider employees, I decided that asking both outsider and insider employees to report anonymously on relevant firm-level practices represented a desirable middle ground. Together, insider and outsider accounts of day-to-day practices at their places of employment could offer a telling, and triangulated, look at organizational environments and their effects on stratification.

Obtaining Research Access

Given these considerations, I hoped to select firms as research sites and to collect data through surveys and interviews with workers employed in the selected firms. But this plan came within a hairsbreadth of crashing to the ground.

During my time as a Fulbright scholar in 2014 and 2015, colleagues at Sophia University and at CIGS, a think tank, agreed to sponsor my stay. I spent the first few months refining my survey instrument, with the generous support of colleagues at both institutions, who served as the first survey testers. My efforts to recruit firms, however, proved futile. Although HR managers were happy to talk to me directly, the same HR managers would not consider allowing me to conduct research directly with workers. Understandably so: The worker surveys and interviews I proposed to conduct could expose wage inequality, employee dissatisfactions, and biases. Naturally, many firms were reluctant to run that risk.

Finally, through the mediation of my CIGS host, Jun Kurihara, Akinari Horii, special adviser to CIGS and former assistant director of the Bank of

Japan, agreed to listen to my research pitch. After months of painstaking and fruitless outreach to firms, I presented a six-minute pitch to Horii-san. He agreed to help.

Horii-san asked the managing director of the Japan Association of Corporate Executives (JACE), Kiyohiko Ito, for assistance. Ito-san was clear that JACE regularly received requests for research, which it routinely declined. Because this request was mediated by CIGS and by Horii-san, Ito-san assented and assigned a JACE staff member, Natsuko Kasahara, to help with implementation. Ito-san also pointed out that firms might be more willing than usual to go along with the survey because I was a US researcher: In the 1980s, US researchers were practically banging down the door, but since then, US interest in Japanese business had become a rare, and perhaps more desirable, commodity.

Kasahara-san's strategy for implementing the research was for JACE to send a request to the chief executive officers (CEOs) of more than two hundred firms that were members of its diversity committee. I requested that firms select at least two teams, and grant research access to every member of these teams, regardless of regular or irregular employment status, gender, or national origin. I used team-based sampling to facilitate apples-to-apples comparison among employees, and Kasahara-san suggested requiring participation from no more than two teams to minimize the burden on participating firms. I elected to request only teams that included foreign workers to ensure that these foreign workers, a tiny minority of all white-collar workers in large Japanese firms, would be represented in the sample. Of the two hundred firms JACE contacted with my research request, twelve firms miraculously agreed to participate. Staff from each CEO's office contacted me directly and put me in touch with the HR personnel. HR selected the target teams, and distributed the survey link to members of these teams.[45] Upon conclusion of the survey, I provided a summary of the results to the HR departments, but no one at the target firms had access to the individual-level data collected through the survey.

Overview of the Survey

The survey collected four types of individual-level data: information on organizational policies, practices, and norms (as understood by the respondents); attitudinal data on satisfaction with various aspects of the work environment; information about employees' position in the workplace (e.g., work content, type of employment relationship, level of supervisory authority, compensation, and the like); and demographic background (e.g., gender, country of birth, education level, tenure, age, language abilities, and parental status). The survey also included a series of four experimental vignettes designed to test attitudes toward Chinese, Korean, and Western/Anglo foreign workers.

I drafted the original version of the survey in English. Then, with a multilingual team of experts, I translated the survey into Japanese and Mandarin Chinese. Following the principles of iterative, team translation, a native speaker in each of the target languages first drafted a translation.[46] Then, other translators and subject matter experts reviewed the target language drafts in reference to the original English survey, flagged areas in which the meaning was inconsistent across languages or scanned poorly in the target language, and suggested revisions. Next, an adjudicator fluent in the source and target languages reviewed the queries and suggestions, and determined which wording was most appropriate. Translators then reviewed the new drafts in relation to the original, followed by a subsequent round of adjudication. In addition to myself, five native Japanese speakers worked on translation and revision of the Japanese survey, and six native Mandarin speakers worked on the Chinese version, including two fluent in Japanese who reviewed the Mandarin version in relation to the Japanese draft. I also relied on my colleagues at CIGS, who repeatedly user-tested the survey.

I collected survey data from the firms between January 2015 and April 2015. The firms sent the survey to 909 employees, and 539 employees completed the survey, for a response rate of 59 percent.

Table I.1 lists the firms included in this study. All firms are referred to by pseudonyms throughout the book. Although none is foreign owned, several

TABLE I.1. Industry and response rate by firm

COMPANY	INDUSTRY	NO. SURVEY RESPONDENTS	NO. EMPLOYEE INTERVIEWS	RESPONSE RATE
Upstore	Consumer services	32	2	100.0
Asahi	Manufacturing	43	0	100.0
FuturaCorp	Business services	35	1	49.3
Kaneda	Consumer services	50	3	78.7
Hamabe	Consumer services	30	0	100.0
Takematsu	Business services	81	2	77.9
Dazan	Consumer services	27	1	81.8
Cyatec	Business services	37	3	100.0
Henderson	Business services	142	1	35.0
Maruyama	Manufacturing	23	1	50
Pixisa	Manufacturing	29	1	100.0
Green Elm	Business services	10	0	71.4

have non-Japanese names, and I assigned pseudonyms accordingly. Because all of the firms are prominent establishments, I list industry only in the broadest possible terms to preserve anonymity. All firms have more than one thousand employees, and eight have more than five thousand.

Qualitative Data Collection

To further contextualize and deepen the survey data, I also used a variety of other information sources. As described, in 2013, I conducted interviews with a snowball sample of foreign white-collar workers, including men from China, Taiwan, India, and various English-speaking countries, and women from mainland China, Taiwan, and Central Asia. I also spoke with HR managers at five large firms that hire foreign workers, attended seminars and meetings for HR professionals managing diversity, met with career counselors at universities and language schools, attended career fairs and networking events for foreign students and professionals, and held discussions with academics researching foreign workers and female workers in Japan. Because this book focuses on the JACE firms, I refer to these only in cases in which they help to provide general insight into the white-collar working environment in Japan. Nonetheless, that early phase of research provided background knowledge that informs the findings shared in this book.

As for the JACE firms, I collected further information through publicly available sources, such as the firms' websites and the government database on which large firms are required to report various metrics of gender (in)equality. In a few cases, I also had informal follow-up conversations with HR personnel. I only pursued these conversations when the opportunity presented itself organically, usually through chance meetings at events or through spontaneous introductions by people who did not know I was already conducting research at these firms. I did not systematically request such meetings because of the burden it would place on the already very busy staff at the firms. In all instances, it was the CEO who committed to participation in the research and then delegated the work of implementation to HR departments or other staff. I did not want to put staff in a position in which they felt pressured to go beyond the initial commitment made by their CEOs. Thus, although I provided all firms with summary reports of the survey findings, I did not discuss these results further with HR personnel.

The survey asked individual respondents to submit an email address if they would be willing to participate in a follow-up interview. More than two hundred employees submitted email addresses. Scheduling interviews, however, was not an easy matter. Some employees were concerned about confidentiality and ultimately decided they were not comfortable with an interview. Others were transferred to new units within their firms, sometimes in geographically distant locations. Others reported being too busy, never responded, or had forgotten about completing the survey and did not understand why they were being contacted. Ultimately, of those who submitted email addresses, my Japanese research assistant and I were able to reach and schedule interviews with fifteen respondents in nine firms. These include five interviews with Japanese men, one with a Japanese woman, three with women from China or Taiwan, three with men from China or Taiwan, two with men from Western countries, and one with a third-generation ethnic Japanese raised abroad by second-generation immigrant parents. In some cases, where country of origin could potentially identify interviewees to others at their firm, I change or omit mentions of that specific country. To further protect interviewees' identities, I do not link individual interviewees to specific firms—I identify interviewees either as "an employee of XYZ firm" or by a pseudonym consistent with their ethnic background, but never simultaneously by both.

The interviews took place between July and December 2015. I conducted interviews with non-Japanese employees on my own, using either Japanese or English. Because I asked about sensitive topics around working with non-Japanese, I employed a Japanese research assistant, Fumiya Uchikoshi,

TABLE I.2. Interviewees at the sample firms

PSEUDONYM	GENDER	AGE
Liling	F	30s
Yuanyuan	F	30s
Chaoxiang	M	20s
Xinyan	F	30s
Derek	M	30s
Hugo	M	30s
George	M	20s
Dawen	M	20s
Wei	M	20s
Masato	M	40s
Hideki	M	20s
Shouichiro	M	30s
Emi	F	30s
Yuichi	M	40s
Takeshi	M	20s

who contacted the Japanese interview candidates and conducted their interviews. Interviews took place in coffee shops, in private meeting rooms at CIGS, or in one case in a closed meeting room at the respondent's place of employment.

Thirteen interviews were audio recorded and transcribed. Two respondents refused recording. For these respondents, I took handwritten notes during the conversation, and immediately afterward typed up a detailed summary of the interview, along with quotes I had written down verbatim in my notes. These interviews were semistructured, and I asked employees to elaborate on their survey responses, their day-to-day work tasks and environment, their experiences of being treated fairly or unfairly in the workplace, and their attitudes toward working with Japanese and non-Japanese employees.

Finally, I observed the work environment at CIGS, where I was an international research fellow. As a fellow, I did not have any formal duties or receive compensation. CIGS staff, however, provided considerable administrative support for my research. My cubicle neighbors became friends and reliable sources of advice and material help with moving to, and living in, Tokyo. Almost daily, an assortment of coworkers took the elevators down to the extensive underground shopping area beneath the ShinMaru building to purchase bento lunches, which we ate together in the breakroom alongside more frugal staffers who brought lunches from home. Occasionally, I participated in afterhours *nomikai* (drinking parties) with coworkers. My observations gleaned from these experiences were casual, not systematic, but nonetheless they inform my analyses of the data collected through more formal methods.

Outline of the Book

The rest of the book is laid out as follows. Chapter 1 introduces the reader to the work environment in elite Japanese firms today, and how it is changing in an era of population decline. It elucidates what the sample firms expect of workers, how they assess workers against these expectations, and what workers receive in return. In doing so, this chapter highlights the importance of managerial discretion in shaping employees' careers and sets the scene for the exploration of inequality and its causes in the rest of the book.

Chapter 2 acquaints the reader with the immigrant workers in the sample firms, and investigates how they fare in terms of pay and promotion relative to Japanese employees. This chapter shows that gender is a sharper axis of inequality than is immigrant background; immigrant men tend to fare relatively well, whereas among women, both native Japanese and Asian immigrants alike fall to the bottom of the stratification hierarchy, despite Asian women's high levels of ambition.

Chapter 3 investigates the reasons for women's enduring disadvantage in promotion and pay. It shows that even women in historically male management-track jobs earn far less than their male counterparts. It argues that women's continued overrepresentation in support jobs fuels devaluative beliefs that women are best suited to routine work and assistant-type tasks and that these symbolic boundaries in turn influence how managers assign tasks to subordinates, perpetuating the gender pay gap for workers regardless of job track.

Chapter 4 probes the relationship between acculturation and Asian immigrants' career trajectories. It highlights the considerable pressure Asian employees face to acculturate to the Japanese work environment. It also shows, however, that while meeting these acculturative expectations improves job performance, it does not necessarily result in Asian workers' attaining parity with Japanese coworkers. It argues that this counterintuitive pattern emerges because acculturation occurs in tandem with small acts of discrimination, the impact of which accrue gradually over the course of Asian workers' careers.

Chapter 5 examines which symbolic boundaries may play a role in Asian employees' disadvantage. It demonstrates that discourses of Asian criminality, while widespread in the broader culture, are muted but not absent in elite firms. Moreover, such discourses are less prevalent on the teams with the highest shares of Asian coworkers. This implies that symbolic boundaries toward Asians are more unstable than those toward women. Moreover, they receive little reinforcement in the white-collar workplace, providing Asian immigrant men greater opportunities to attain parity with Japanese men than women of any background.

Chapter 6 dives into the puzzling question of Western men's earnings advantage in the sample firms. Although they are less acculturated than Asian immigrants of both genders, on average, they earn more than Japanese men. This chapter grapples with possible objective reasons for Western men's success, but finds no evidence to support rules-based reasons why Western men earn more than others. Moreover, it shows that Japanese and other Asian respondents recommend more generous rewards for hypothetical Western men than for either Asian or Japanese men. These findings indicate that symbolic boundaries privileging whites and/or Westerners are persistent and contribute to enduring economic advantage for Western men who find jobs in elite firms.

The book concludes with a discussion of the implications of the findings for the future of stratification in elite firms, in Japanese society more broadly, and in other countries facing population decline.

Contributions and Importance

This book is the first to assess quantitatively how immigrant workers fare in white-collar employment through a comparison with closely matched Japanese coworkers. As Japan's population shrinks and immigration increases, this fills a critical gap in our understanding of who can thrive "inside the circle" of elite workplaces and demonstrates that gender persists as a far sharper axis of disadvantage than immigrant background in this context.

Through this analysis, the book advances understanding of what it means to be an immigrant in Japan. Japan is commonly described as an ethnonationalist society, indicating that, to be widely accepted as "Japanese," one must be of Japanese parentage, hold Japanese citizenship, and demonstrate total cultural and linguistic fluency.[47] This, combined with Japan's low share of immigrants compared with many other wealthy countries, is sometimes taken to indicate that Japan is unusually racist or xenophobic in international comparison.[48] This book demonstrates, however, that economic advancement is not contingent on being defined as "Japanese." Immigrant men from both Asia and from the West fare nearly as well, or indeed better, than Japanese men in elite workplaces. Ethnonationalism does not, therefore, indicate that immigrant background is a universal axis of exclusion and disadvantage across all of Japanese society. Other aspects of identity—most notably, in the context of elite firms, gender—are far more salient for immigrants' outcomes than their status as non-Japanese, despite the ubiquity of ethnonationalist discourse.

This book also offers new insight into the sources of persistent gender inequality. Although previous research has thoroughly explored the structural barriers to women's advancement in elite firms, the findings in this book suggests that the mechanisms sustaining these inequalities are evolving.[49] Although structural barriers remain significant, discretionary decisions by managers and HR personnel, and the attitudes and symbolic boundaries that underpin these decisions, exert a growing influence as firms respond to government pressure to dismantle structural hurdles to women's advancement.

Furthermore, this book proposes a new way to think about the ways in which organizations, and society at large, (re)construct symbolic boundaries. A large body of research stresses how outsiders' absence from the top of organizational hierarchies produces beliefs that members of outsider groups are less capable and worthy.[50] Indeed, this argument has profoundly influenced the Japanese government's gender equity policy in its emphasis on increasing women's managerial representation as a tool to mitigate gender inequality more broadly. I argue, however, that outsiders' overconcentration in low-status, subordinate roles at the *bottom* of organizational hierarchies is at least, if not more, important in shaping how group members are viewed.

Finally, in highlighting the demography of low-status jobs' importance to the creation of symbolic boundaries, status beliefs, and the distribution of workplace resources, the book sheds light into the question of who is likely to benefit most from demographic decline more broadly, both in Japan and beyond.

Japan's continued restrictions on immigration for the purposes of low-paid work suggest that, unlike in many other countries, immigrants are unlikely to become "the face" of low-status jobs in the near and medium term. It is possible, therefore, that this will consolidate the relative advantage of immigrant men in white-collar work, not just in elite firms, but across the broader economy, as the population continues to contract.

Japan's demographic trajectory is important not because it is distinct, but because it is a forerunner to other powerful economies. Among the world's ten largest economies in 2021, five—China, Germany, France, Italy, and South Korea—already have shrinking working-age populations.[51] Three others—the United States, Canada, and the United Kingdom—are projected to grow, but, absent immigration, would also be facing declines in the number of working-age adults.[52] In the next two to three decades, many of the most economically powerful countries will have lost as large a proportion of their peak working-age population as Japan has today—South Korea by 2035, followed by Italy in 2040, Germany in 2045, and China in 2050.[53]

Japan's economic ascent of the 1960s and 1970s presaged the rapid growth of many other Asian economies. Nearly 40 percent of the world's population now lives in countries with below-replacement birthrates.[54] As a bellwether of demographic decline, Japan is once again blazing a trail, this time not only for its Asian neighbors but also for wealthy countries around the world poised to follow in Japan's demographic footsteps. By examining who is reaping the rewards of demographic decline in Japan, and why, we can shed light on how inequalities will evolve in other countries with shrinking populations.

INSIDE THE CIRCLE

Change and Continuity in Elite Japanese Firms

Japanese firms' "peculiar" employment arrangements have long fascinated Western observers. Beginning in the 1950s and continuing through the 1980s, hundreds if not thousands of US journalists and scholars attempted to distill from firms' human resource practices the "secret sauce" to Japan's rapid economic growth and to sell it to a US public looking nervously over its shoulder at an encroaching rival. Many Japanese, too, were eager to identify the cultural recipe of distinctly successful management practices to polish Japan's international image and restore a national pride battered by World War II. In the 1990s, however, Japan entered a new era of slow growth. As Japan's economic trajectory leveled off, "Japanese-style employment" lost its luster in US eyes. The very same human resource practices, such as long-term employment and earnings that rise with seniority and age, once lauded as the secret to Japan's economic stardom, now drew Western audiences' attention primarily as risible exemplars of inefficiency and stagnation.[1] Criticism from without and soul-searching from within Japan increasingly prompted calls for "reform" and "liberalization" that would transform employment in Japan Inc. for the twenty-first century.

Current depictions of Japanese firms—and of the successes and failures of efforts to transform them—largely fall into two categories: the neoliberal and the neoclassical models of Japanese employment. The former perspective holds that companies have fundamentally restructured their approach to employment, making it more precarious and exploitative for all workers, even the most privileged. The latter perspective portrays changes to employment practices as predominately surface level and symbolic, suggesting that core practices have remained fundamentally unchanged since the high-growth era.

In this chapter, I elucidate employment practices at the sample firms and assesses them against these two models. I explore the sample firms' expectations of their workers; employees' perceptions of their obligations to their employers; and firms' reward, evaluation, and promotion practices. I show that, in the elite firms in the sample, the strong commitments that firms made to core workers in the high-growth era remain largely intact. Workers are confident in their job security and reasonably anticipate their earnings will increase with age. But even as these commitments hold fast, companies' demands on employees have lessened: Work hours are shorter, expectations for after-hours socializing have decreased, and workers are free to seek more lucrative or satisfying employment elsewhere. This combination of continued stability *and* greater flexibility is inconsistent with both the neoliberal and neoclassical perspectives on Japanese firms. It does align, however, with theoretical predictions that population decline and labor scarcity can push firms to offer concessions to workers and improve work conditions.

At the same time, other elements of employment relations remain relatively unchanged: Firms and managers retain a great deal of control over workers' careers, and although women are present in management and management-track jobs in far greater numbers than in the past, gender inequality in pay remains stark.

Classical Postwar Employment Practices

Perhaps the most storied facet of "Japanese employment relations" is so-called lifetime or permanent employment. In its most iconic form, lifetime employment means that companies hire entry-level employees straight out of high school, university, or graduate school, and employ them until they retire, formerly at age 55 but more recently at age 60 or 65, depending on the firm.[2]

This form of employment emerged in the late 1940s and early 1950s and was solidified in the 1960s and 1970s during the era of high growth.[3] Traditionally, lifetime employment entails a bargain between employer and employee. White-collar employees cede control over their *career paths*, such that employers can transfer workers to different positions with little regard for employee preferences. Employees also sign over their *time* to the employer, working long hours as required by business demands.[4] In return, employers offer rock-solid job security. They refrain from firing even the most incompetent employees, although they may shunt them to the side, placing them in unimportant, out-of-the-way posts.[5]

Under classical lifetime employment, male employees could count on steady wage growth.[6] In the 1950s, firms tied such wage increases explicitly to age, but by the 1960s and 1970s, many firms moved to ability or job grade systems. As "ability" was perceived to increase with age, however, in practice the change did not significantly alter the age-wage curve.[7]

Without the "stick" of dismissal to impel performance in the lifetime employment model, companies have relied on the "carrot" of promotion to successively higher ranks of management. Promotion to the highest levels of the firm hierarchy—board member or even company president—is a very tasty carrot. Not only is each level of management more highly paid than the last, but the few who reach the uppermost job levels are the only employees allowed to work beyond the company's standard retirement age, significantly boosting lifetime earnings.[8]

Some observers have characterized promotion in the classical postwar employment model as age-based *rather than* merit-based.[9] This view is mistaken. Rather, firms specify an age floor for promotion to management, usually in the mid-thirties. Among employees qualified by virtue of age, firms choose those they deem to be the most suitable for promotion. Because the number of posts at each level of management is smaller than the one before it, competition intensifies at each step.[10]

The promotion age floor dovetails with the lifetime employment system. If employees were promoted rapidly at a young age, the overall wage burden on the company would increase. Delaying promotion also means the time in which all younger employees are in the running for a promotion is longer, further spurring performance.[11]

In the classical postwar employment mode, firms also worked to cement long-lasting employer-employee relationships emotionally, notably by investing in company retreats and facilitating extensive after-hours socializing in bars and restaurants. Ethnographic studies of Japanese business in the high-growth era describe employees going out together several times a week, cultivating emotional bonds that further enmesh them in the firm.[12]

Accounts from the 1960s and 1970s suggest that changing jobs was seen as not merely foolhardy but morally dubious as well. Thomas P. Rohlen, who conducted ethnographic research in a large Japanese bank in the 1960s, notes, "When someone quits or is fired there is the strong implication that the relationship has failed. A general feeling exists that both parties must share responsibility for its failure. As a rule both suffer some loss of reputation because of it."[13] Rodney Clark, drawing on research in a manufacturing firm, reports that

"Marumaru workers of all ages interpreted events as if lifetime employment was normal and right, and exceptions to it [as] due to pressure of circumstance or moral deficiencies."[14]

Male employees' commitment to their firms under classical lifetime employment is thus buttressed in several ways: economic incentives, including a limited job market for those beyond the entry level; age/seniority wage and promotion ladders that make it difficult for midcareer job changers to advance; employees' feelings of loyalty, obligation, and belonging; and social mores that deprecate job change as deviant and risky.[15]

Firms' commitment to lifetime employment in the 1960s and 1970s was supported and reinforced by judicial decisions that made it increasingly difficult to fire workers except to stave off bankruptcy, by the strong sentiments of employees, and by firms' economic incentive to recoup investments in worker training.[16]

Women's workplace roles diverged sharply from those of men, however. Many large firms, particularly in service industries, hired young women as office assistants and receptionists. Companies expected, and often required, these women to quit upon marriage and childbirth. This high-turnover, low-wage pool of female labor increased firms' labor cost flexibility. In doing so, it allowed them to deploy greater resources toward training, age-wage increases, and advancement for men. Thus, in the classical postwar employment model, firms' relegation of women to the periphery enabled and upheld the institutions of long-term employment for a core workforce of regular, male employees.[17]

At the same time, even for men, the concept of "permanent" or "lifetime" employment as *the* quintessential employment pattern was also more a marketing slogan or national branding exercise than it was an accurate depiction of reality. Core male employees at large firms sometimes changed jobs, particularly in their twenties, when their opportunities for good employment in other prestigious firms were greatest. Smaller firms also could not guarantee the same predictable wage increases with age, or offer promotion as widely, and male workers at such firms changed jobs (or were laid off) without apparent moral qualms.[18]

Nonetheless, it is indisputable that Japanese employees of the 1960s and 1970s, particularly Japanese men in white-collar jobs in elite firms, were much less mobile than their US counterparts.[19] Although the ideal US career associates moving on with moving up, the same cannot be said in Japan.[20] Moving up in large Japanese firms has historically been associated with staying put, working one's way up the corporate ladder within one firm. That said, I refer to human resource practices and typical individual paths among male, white-collar workers at large firms as "long-term employment" rather than

"permanent" or "lifetime" employment. "Long-term employment" acknowledges that labor mobility has occurred, albeit at low levels, even among white-
collar workers in large firms, throughout the postwar period.

The Neoliberal Employment Model

We can think of the period from the late 1950s until the late 1980s as the era of
the *classical Japanese employment model*. How, then, has the employment
landscape evolved since then? Two main schools of thought explain how to
conceptualize Japanese employment from the 1990s onward.

The first is what I term the *neoliberal employment model*. This model represents a stark departure from the past. Scholars working in this tradition argue
that, following the bursting of Japan's bubble economy in 1991, firms—including
those at the pinnacle of the employment hierarchy like those in the sample—
ripped up the implicit contract of long-term employment.[21] Firms' behavior
under this employment model features three pillars: greater willingness to lay
off core employees; substitution of regular employees with irregular workers
with low pay and little job security; and the introduction of performance management systems that delink earnings and age even for regular workers.

Seika shugi—that is, "results-based" assessment and decision-making—is at
the heart of this model.[22] In the classical model, firms' moral obligation to core
workers demanded that they maintain their employment at all costs, whereas
in the neoliberal model, companies are thought to freely dismiss even core
workers in service to their bottom lines.[23] In addition, neoliberal firms rely
increasingly on irregular workers.[24] These workers are attractive to firms
because they are cheaper and easier to dismiss, and allow firms, at least in theory, to respond more nimbly to changing market conditions.

In addition to changing the relationship between workers and firms, neoliberalism and *seika shugi* are also said to have changed what firms value about
employees as well as how they reward it. In the classical assessment model,
firms evaluate core workers primarily based on their inputs, particularly dili-
gence and teamwork.[25] Under *seika shugi*, in contrast, performance evaluation
places a greater weight on outputs, such as the volume of sales an employee
generates. In turn, performance on these metrics is tied more explicitly to
short-term outcomes, such as annual bonuses and raises.[26]

Critics charge that the neoliberal turn has dramatically diminished workers'
economic security.[27] For one, *seika shugi* changes the locus of control over performance. Under classical performance management models, performance lies
fully within a worker's command: Workers may choose to slack off or to exert
themselves. In contrast, under *seika shugi*, even if workers do their utmost,

forces beyond their control may undercut what they can accomplish. Key clients may defect or go bankrupt; investments may languish. Consequently, employees may experience unpredictable wage fluctuations; steady and guaranteed increases are a thing of the past.

Critics also argue that that *seika shugi* has intensified competition among workers. In the classical employment model, white-collar, male workers enjoyed a relatively high "lifestyle floor": Even the most feckless man could anticipate a secure future, as long as he got a decent job out of high school or college. In contrast, in the neoliberal regime, critics allege, the costs of "losing" the competition for career advancement are far higher, ranging from stagnant earnings to the terrifying possibility of dismissal. To avoid this terrifying prospect, critics say, employees in the neoliberal regime must put in *continuous*, intensive effort, perpetuating and even exacerbating the classical-era tendency to work long hours.[28]

These changes are also said to have weakened workers' sense of belonging in the workplace. Without the guarantee of a long-term job, workers feel no obligation to remain with their employer. Furthermore, nonproductive bonding activities, such as drinking together after hours, are less appealing to employees, because they find themselves in zero-sum competition with their coworkers—and indeed are less encouraged by employers as well, because these activities do not produce short-term economic "results."[29]

In the neoliberal model of employment, gender inequality persists, but it does so through new bureaucratic mechanisms. For example, firms hire women in irregular jobs, keeping their wages low and periodically forcing them out of their jobs regardless of marital or parental status.[30] In addition, the focus on "results" works to women's disadvantage, given that women's outsize share of household labor makes them less available to put in the continuous, intensive effort the neoliberal firm demands.

Anne Allison has argued that these changes have ushered in a bleak new era of precarity and insecurity. In her account, companies and the government have "dismantled" the postwar social bargain that companies will "take care of" core male workers.[31] She sees little hope of firms expanding access to the most desirable jobs to Japanese women or non-Japanese. Instead, the shrinking benefits of white-collar employment in large firms continue to become concentrated in the hands of a smaller and smaller number of middle-age Japanese men.[32]

The Neoclassical Employment Model

The neoliberal employment model implies radical, and for workers, deeply destabilizing, change in Japanese white-collar workplaces. In contrast, the neoclassical model largely portrays continuity. Proponents of the neoclassical model argue that most of the iconic practices of the classical era, including long-term employment, slow promotion, long work hours, extensive after-hours socializing, and marginalization of women, persist in big white-collar workplaces.[33]

In the neoclassical model, however, firms must adopt new strategies to maintain old patterns. For example, following years of criticism of Japan's long work hours, in 2018, the government passed "work-style reform" legislation, designed to penalize companies that require excessive overtime. The neoclassical model suggests that companies circumvent oversight mechanisms and continue their previous practices sub rosa, for example by discouraging overtime reporting while assigning employees the same amount of work as before.[34] This type of "symbolic compliance" to changing legal and social norms is at the heart of the neoclassical model.[35]

Another domain in which scholars argue that symbolic compliance defines firms' approach to employment is in their treatment of women. As with overtime, government leaders increasingly portray gender inequality as an embarrassing social problem.[36] Therefore, if firms wish to appear legitimate, they must demonstrate at least some efforts toward women's empowerment. Scholars using the neoclassical lens, however, argue that firms' efforts are superficial at best and that their underlying aim is to maintain men's advantage. Examples of symbolic compliance in this domain include hiring women into irregular rather than regular jobs; establishing a clerical track for regular workers, with little to no opportunity for promotion, and staffing this supposedly gender-neutral track almost entirely with women; allowing women to remain in the workforce after having children, but counting parental leave against them in decisions about advancement; and promoting a few women onto corporate boards or the upper echelons of management, but otherwise relegating women to the sidelines.[37] These two models of contemporary employment in Japanese firms—the neoliberal and the neoclassical—provide a structure within which we can analyze and understand the firms in this study. Do they closely adhere to one model or the other? Do some firms follow one and others another? Or do all firms represent a hybrid of the two models? Finally, what firm characteristics do not fit well in either model? Table 1.1 shows a list of domains, and the predictions the two models generate for each domain. In the following section, I use both qualitative and quantitative data to consider how the twelve study firms conform to or diverge from these frameworks.

Because the focus of classical studies of Japanese business is on core male employees, these predictions and the attendant analyses focus primarily on Japanese men, with some attention given to women's roles and opportunities.

As table 1.1 illustrates, the two models largely agree that firms marginalize women, although the neoclassical model suggests that, because of symbolic

TABLE 1.1. Neoliberal and neoclassical predictions about Japanese firms

DOMAIN	NEOLIBERAL PREDICTIONS	NEOCLASSICAL PREDICTIONS
Firms' commitments to core male workers		
Age-wage increases	No	Yes
Long-term job security	Low	High
Age of promotion to management	<35 years (for select high performers)	>35 years
Core, male workers' commitments to firms		
Work hours	≥ Classical-era hours	= Classical-era hours
After-hours socializing	Very little	Extensive
Control of career	Individual responsibility	Ceded to firm
Firms' treatment of women		
Gender wage inequality	High	High
Women in management	Low	Some
Women in management track	Low	Low

compliance, some women may make it to the managerial ranks. Both models agree, however, that firms are likely to keep women off the management track, employing them either as irregular workers, or as regular workers on the non-promotional clerical track. Otherwise, the models generate largely opposing predictions. While the neoliberal perspective faults Japanese firms for changing too much, the neoclassical model highlights stagnation and failure to change.

Taking Care of Workers in a "Demi-Meritocracy"

Turning first to the question of the age-wage profiles, the neoliberal model predicts that older men are not likely to earn more than younger ones. Because firms use results-based performance management, high-performing young workers might receive high wages, whereas underperforming older workers might receive lower wages. In contrast, the neoclassical model would expect wages to rise with age, as they did in the classical era. To examine which pattern applies, figure 1.1 plots annual earnings by age for Japanese men in regular, management-track employment.[38] Because the companies in the sample demonstrate two distinct age-wage profiles, the two profiles are plotted with separate lines.

Figure 1.1 shows that, in all the sample firms, early-career wages for Japanese men in regular, management-track jobs start at around 2–3 million yen annually. At FuturaCorp and Takematsu, workers in their thirties and beyond

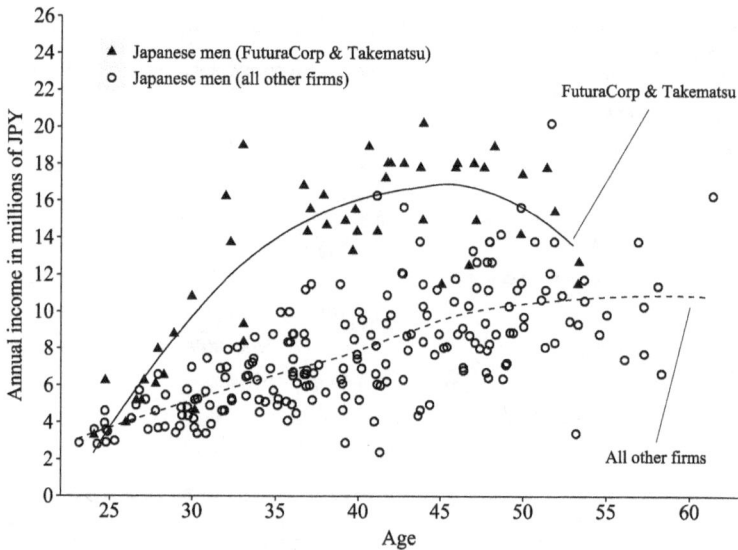

FIGURE 1.1. Annual earnings by age among Japanese men in regular management-track jobs. Calculated from author's survey data.

earn very high wages. A typical worker in his forties earns around 16 million yen per year, placing him well above the 99th percentile in male earnings in Japan (about 9 million yen annually).[39] In the other ten firms, the relationship between age and earnings is less steep than in FuturaCorp and Takematsu, but nonetheless, a typical 45-year-old male regular worker earns about 8 million yen per year, placing him at about the 98th percentile of male earnings in the Japanese economy as a whole.

Two workers report anomalously low wages: One man in his forties and one man in his fifties earn under 4 million yen. More commonly, however, although the wage ceiling is perhaps three times higher, men in regular employment can expect to earn *a minimum of* 5 million yen a year by age 40, and of 6 million yen by age 50. These are still very generous wages is the context of the broader employment landscape, in which the 90th percentile for male earnings is about 5.3 million yen,[40] underscoring the elite character of the sample firms. At least in these firms, age continues to be associated with significantly higher wages, consistent with the neoclassical model.

Neoclassical employment practices also persist with regard to age at promotion. As described previously, during the high-growth era, the earliest a typical male employee in a large firm might expect a promotion to management was in his mid-thirties. Table 1.2 displays the age of the youngest

TABLE 1.2. Age-based promotion by firm

COMPANY	AGE OF YOUNGEST MANAGER	AVERAGE AGE OF MANAGERS	NO. MANAGERS
Upstore	48	53.6	5
Asahi	40	46.8	10
FuturaCorp	38	46.5	4
Kaneda	43	47.3	14
Hamabe	38	48.7	7
Takematsu	32	45.5	18
Dazan	47	51.0	3
Cyatec	30	38.7	7
Henderson	28	44.5	21
Maruyama	42	47.0	2
Pixisa	52	56.5	4
Green Elm	37	43.8	6

manager, and the mean age of all managers in the samples from all twelve firms. (Here a manager is defined as someone who supervises a team of at least six subordinates.) Three firms have managers younger than 35: Takematsu, Cyatec, and Henderson. The average age of managers, however, is older than 40 everywhere but Cyatec. Thus, on the whole, the ages of managers in the sample indicate that these companies remain reluctant to promote employees at a young age.

On paper, however, the firms in this study have adopted neoliberal performance management practices popularized since 1990s, including relying on output to assess performance and tying pay to short-term performance. Among Japanese men in regular employment, 94 percent of respondents report that their firms evaluate their individual performance. Of these, 81 percent say their managers evaluate performance in relation to specific targets or goals. Typical goals include things like achieving revenue targets, controlling costs, meeting deadlines, or acquiring certifications. Moreover, respondents report that evaluations are linked with short-term pay. Some 82 percent say that the performance evaluation has a moderate or large influence on their annual raise, and 89 percent report that it has a moderate or large influence on their biannual bonuses. In sum, despite the persistence of the classical age-wage curve, these firms rely heavily on the bundle of neoliberal practices associated with more intense competition and greater insecurity.

How do firms maintain a traditional age-wage curve in light of the newer emphasis on "results"? One way they achieve this is through the continued reliance on age as a criterion for promotion, as illustrated previously. As in the classical model, older workers earn more because more of them have reached the management ranks. Even workers who do not obtain management-tier positions, however, still see their wages rise. As in the past, companies continue to set a baseline for wage increases and bonuses based on job grade and rank. Employees at many different firms echoed this point. One employee at Henderson described the process thus:

> **Respondent**: I don't know if I should say this, but even if you're not really working hard, you can still earn a pretty good salary.
> **Interviewer**: My impression is that your company is meritocratic [*seika shugi*], but you're saying that's not the case?
> **Respondent**: At Henderson, I'd say it's more of a . . . demi-meritocracy [*puchi seikashugi*].
> **Interviewer**: Demi-meritocracy?
> **Respondent**: That's right. The best way to put it is, if you do a good job, you do get recognized for that. But if you don't [perform well], if you don't really do *anything*, it doesn't go the other way. No one's salary really gets reduced. . . . [T]he understanding is, you might get a lot more, or you might get a little more.

An employee at Cyatec also emphasized how wages inevitably increase with age:

> **Interviewer**: So, the system is officially merit-based, right?
> **Respondent**: Right, the policy is that [your pay] is based on your current abilities, your current skills, and your current results. But, as I said earlier, there's a reluctance to cut pay. So, your pay might be flat, or it might go up a little [in the event of poor performance].
> **Interviewer**: So, because pay never goes down, as time passes, it increases no matter what?
> **Respondent**: Yes. Effectively, it's an age-based wage system [*nenko joretsu*].

A Kaneda employee agreed, concluding that because companies dependably raise wages across the board and never claw money back, "even geezers who do absolutely nothing are getting 10 million."

De facto seniority wage increases are not the only way in which firms counteract the inequalities of competition and meritocracy. In addition, managers also massage performance evaluations. A Cyatec manager said:

> On paper, I get evaluated. And I'm also in a position where I evaluate others. We've been updating our performance evaluation system for the past ten years or so. The standards for evaluation are specified in detail. So that aspect is legitimate and reasonable [*datou*]. And when

I evaluate people, of course I have to give them feedback. But it's difficult to give an evaluation that is too low or too high. So, that's where there's some manipulation.

This pressure to avoid "extreme" performance scores at Cyatec is but one strategy in firms' toolboxes to equalize performance assessments. Takematsu takes a different approach. Unlike Cyatec, Takematsu grades performance "on a curve." Only the top 5 percent of performers can earn the top evaluation score. Nonetheless, a Takematsu employee denied that this generated intense competition. She noted: "There's also a somewhat Japanese-style element to [the performance evaluation]. Trying to balance things out. Adjustments. Like, 'this year it's your turn [to get a strong evaluation].'" According to this employee, you are unlikely to get a high evaluation two years in a row, because next year, it would be someone else's "turn."

A Kaneda employee described yet another type of egalitarian adjustment. In his account: "Every year, there's a unit-level adjustment process. For example, this year they might decide that everyone in our unit is going to get an A grade, and next year everyone will get a B grade. Or so I hear. So even though it's supposedly an individual evaluation, in fact no one's getting evaluated at all. . . . [I]t's ludicrous to suggest everyone's [actual performance] is identical."

Thus, despite systems that seem harsh and competitive on their surface, companies "take care of" average and below-average employees in various ways. These companies' adoption of "results-oriented" performance management appears to be a classic case of symbolic compliance, in which on-the-ground practices diverge sharply from official policies.

Of course, because the wage data include only current employees, they cannot show the ultimate penalty: getting laid off. Yet employees did not appear concerned. Interviewees never spontaneously brought up the possibility, and when prompted, they responded dismissively. As Dawen told me, "Getting laid off or fired? That would never, ever happen." Masato described how poor performance did not place employees at risk: "Let's say we're having a problem with someone. We have incentives to work with that person to train them, and to somehow address those issues. That makes this an easy company to work at." Hideki complained bitterly about having to make nice with "stupid" coworkers. But even his "extreme" proposed solution to the problem of his "worthless" coworkers employed the classic strategy of relegating them to a distant and "shabby" department.

In sum, despite claims by some scholars that market-driven, neoliberal employment practices have diffused broadly, important elements of the classical postwar employment model persist in elite firms, such as those in the sample. Core male employees at these firms are all but guaranteed to rise to the top of the Japanese earnings pyramid, because wages increase predictably with age, and because of leveling influences on performance evaluations. Of course, the system does create winners and losers. The highest paid men in their forties and fifties may earn two or three times the annual income of their lowest paid peers. But being a "loser" in these elite firms is still a sinecure, not an impecunious humiliation.

Not Your Dad's Showa-Stinking Company

These elite firms continue to rely on classical employment practices, including age floors for promotion, wages that increase with age, and high levels of job security for core employees. In the classical model, male workers were expected to do many things in return: work long hours, demonstrate loyalty to their firm by sticking with one employer, and cede control over their career paths. As I will show, however, although the classical commitments firms make to workers remain largely intact, this is not a two-way street. Workers' commitments to firms are considerably looser than the neoclassical model suggests.

In the high-growth era, male employees worked long hours and spent their off-hours drinking and socializing with each other. This was a hugely important part of postwar business culture. As Rohlen notes: "A man who would not or could not drink is at a great disadvantage in the achievement of leadership: not to drink means to be unable to utilize the drinking party to win the affection of followers, to solidify the group, and to improve office morale in general."[41] During the high-growth era, the typical salaryman might work ten-hour days during the week, work a half day on Saturday, and join his fellows for after-hours drinks two or three times per week.[42]

Close friendships formed in drinking groups transformed long days in the office to a shared challenge among comrades, but they also left little time for family, community, or private pursuits. This was part and parcel of the bargain whereby workers received job security but relinquished their time to company, hesitating not only to go home at the end of standard working hours but also to take their entitled vacation days.

Compared with descriptions of high-growth era firms, the core male employees in my sample go out relatively little with coworkers, feel free to take vacation for personal reasons, and work shorter hours.

Consider the firm-level data in table 1.3 on workers' use of time and on their attitudes. According to classic accounts of large Japanese firms, working more than fifty hours a week is par for the course. Of the twelve firms in the sample, working hours for Japanese men exceed fifty only in Asahi. (It is perhaps

TABLE 1.3. Control of workers' time by firm

COMPANY	WORKING HOURS[a]	SOCIALIZING AFTER HOURS[b]	STAYING LATER OFFERS BRIGHTER FUTURE[c]	TAKING VACATION REFLECTS POORLY[d]	MISSING A WEDDING IS EXPECTED[e]
Upstore	45.5	2.3	26.9	38.5	15.4
Asahi	51.0	1.4	16.1	29.0	22.6
FuturaCorp	41.9	3.0	11.1	14.8	14.8
Kaneda	45.9	2.5	11.9	31.0	28.6
Hamabe	40.5	1.2	7.7	30.8	19.2
Takematsu	47.2	2.9	24.2	28.8	21.2
Dazan	43.9	0.8	4.0	8.0	4.0
Cyatec	40.2	1.5	25.0	29.2	4.2
Henderson	38.5	1.5	36.4	28.0	14.4
Maruyama	45.9	2.6	35.7	28.6	0.0
Pixisa	44.3	1.9	13.6	31.8	4.5
Green Elm	45.0	3.4	0.0	0.0	16.7

[a]Average weekly working hours for Japanese male regular employees.
[b]Average number of times Japanese male regular employees socialized with coworkers or clients outside of work hours in the past month.
[c]Percent of Japanese respondents who believe someone who stays after hours will have a brighter future in the company than someone who does the same amount of work during business hours.
[d]Percent of Japanese respondents who agree that their supervisor would think poorly of an employee who takes vacation at a busy time to attend a friend's wedding.
[e]Percent of Japanese respondents who think an employee should miss a friend's wedding if it means taking vacation at a busy time.

no coincidence that no Asahi workers responded to my requests for an interview—they were all too busy working!) More typically, core male employees work around forty-five hours a week.[43]

Interviewees with long-term perspectives on working conditions in Japan agreed with the conclusion that employees work fewer hours than in the past. For example, an employee at Henderson (where working hours are shorter than at any other firm in the sample) lamented the conditions at his previous employer, which he derided as "stinking of Showa," referring to the "bad old ways" of the 1970s and 1980s. He said:

> **Respondent**: [At my old company], we had a lot of time-wasting meetings, and were expected to stay at work if our colleagues were still there. I had basically no free time. I stayed at work until midnight or 1 a.m. every day. And went into work on Saturdays and Sundays, too. I half ruined my health. So that's when I started to think about [changing jobs]. . . . Here, even on late nights, we can leave for the evening at 8 or 9 p.m.

Interviewer: That's quite early, isn't it.

Respondent: That's right. Way earlier than before. Also, there are days when we can go home at 5 o'clock. And there are days when I'm on a deadline, staying at work till 10 or 11. I consider those practically all-nighters. That's when I'm trying to finish a report or something. But that's something I decide on my own, because I've chosen what standard of quality I want to reach. To achieve that [standard], I have to stay late. I do it of my own volition, because it can't be helped.

In Pixisa, working hours are longer than at Henderson, on average, but a Pixisa employee said:

The work day starts at 8:30 a.m. But today, I came right before 9, and that's just fine. No problem at all. And as for leaving time, the work day ends officially at 5:20, but it's fine to leave early. We can do as we please. In exchange, the expectation is that we properly complete the work we're assigned, and make sure we keep channels of communication open. As long as we do that, everything else is up to us.

But companies have not eradicated the notorious culture of face-time, in which employees are expected to spend long hours in the office, whether or not they have work to do.

A Cyatec employee shared his experience:

Respondent: [My coworkers] pay attention to what time you come into the office, and whether you stay late. If you go home on the early side, your evaluation will go down.

Interviewer: So, it's more about how long you spend at work, not about what you produce?

Respondent: That's right. In my last unit, if you're just sitting there doing nothing but staring at your screen, people would say, "I see you're working hard!" and you'd get a really high evaluation. But it's more difficult for people who clear off their desk and go home early. So, you finish up your work, and then you sit there, just waiting for an hour or 30 minutes. You can't go home.

This perspective, however, is in the minority. In the survey, I asked respondents to assess who would have a brighter future in the firm: someone who arrives early and stays late, or someone who completes the same tasks within regular business hours and goes home at the official closing time. As shown in table 1.3, relatively few respondents in any firm say that employees who spend more time in the office will have a brighter future. The majority of Japanese respondents think that either the more efficient employee would have a brighter future or that there would be no difference between them. This was true at Cyatec as well, where only 25 percent of Japanese respondents agree that staying long hours is a better career strategy.

Moreover, the degree of overtime required, whether to complete tasks or signal commitment and eagerness, is modest in relation to the past. The Cyatec employee quoted previously complained of staying thirty minutes or an hour late, not until late at night. A Kaneda employee also noted:

> I think [overtime expectations] have gotten much better. It's not absolutely compulsory. But everyone's still sitting there at 5 or 6 p.m. If you want to leave earlier, you can't. If you do, someone might say, "What, leaving already?" . . . Our official workday ends at 5, but the only people who leave at 5 are contract employees. Mostly its 7 or 8 o'clock. Actually, in my department at least, it's ok to leave around 7, even if your boss is still there. But if you leave at 5 or 6, people will tell you, "*You're* leaving early!"

Considering that workers often have long commutes, even forty to forty-five hours of work would make it difficult for employees to, for example, drop off or pick up children from daycare. But on the whole, working hours in these firms are considerably shorter than what was typical in the high-growth era. Although the focus on "results" still incentivizes employees to work beyond normal hours, as in the case of the Henderson employee quoted earlier, in these firms, the pressure for "results" is less acute than the informal expectations and peer influence of an earlier era.

After-hours drinking and socializing is also less common than in the past. Classical accounts describe male workers drinking together two or three times a week, a minimum of eight times per month. Only 18 percent of Japanese men in regular employment, however, report socializing five or more times in the last month, and nowhere is the average greater than three times a month.[44]

At Cyatec, where the number of monthly social events falls around the average within the sample firms, an employee said, "You know, it's really not like you see in a textbook, or in a manga. Like, let's go golfing, that kind of extreme stuff. It's a work environment where you can say, 'I'm not really into that kind of thing.' I don't like going out. You can just lie low, and no one bothers you." In keeping with this, this employee reported no after-hours socializing in the past month.

A Kaneda employee also noted that drinking with government stakeholders was no longer legitimate. He said: "It's important to have good relations with regulators. But it's not like we go with them to pantyless shabushabu, or give them gifts of wine. That's completely off the table in this day and age. It's probably not okay to socialize outside of work in any way. We just have to show we're trustworthy."

Intriguingly, it was often foreign employees who emphasized the importance of after-hours socializing for getting ahead. When I asked Chaoxing what is necessary to advance in his firm, he said:

> Well, the first thing is, accumulate seniority. That's one. The second is, get your certifications. It has to be the same certifications as Japanese employees get. And the third thing is, immerse yourself in the Japanese people's delicate world of interpersonal relationships. Go golfing. Go golfing with Japanese colleagues. Do whatever's expected at drinking parties with your boss. If you don't do those things, getting promoted is difficult.

Another foreign respondent also remarked that if you turned down too many invitations to drinking parties, executives would be less likely to remember you, putting you at a disadvantage. Even Chaoxing goes out with coworkers only one or twice a month, however. So, although drinking together with coworkers may still play an important function, as with work hours, core male workers' time investments in after-hours socializing have fallen.

Reduced working hours and after-hours socializing have reshaped relationships between salarymen and their families. In the "bad old days of Showa," salarymen were conspicuously absent from family life. In contrast, 62 percent of the married Japanese men in the sample eat dinner with their families at least several times a week. For male employees, the private sphere has expanded, and the depth of their involvement in the firm has shrunk.

But perhaps more striking is the degree of normative change. In every firm, only a minority of employees believe that their boss would think poorly of someone who takes vacation at a busy time for an important life event (see table 1.3). And the share of employees who think that an employee should actually refrain from taking vacation in this situation is even smaller. Not only do employees spend less time working and with coworkers, but they no longer see the extensive demands of the past as reasonable.

This normative change extends to the "loyalty to the firm" so vaunted in studies of Japanese firms in the high-growth era. As described earlier, job change during the high-growth era was seen as morally dubious as well as economically risky. However, my interviewees considered job change a pragmatic matter, not a moral one.

Takeshi, whose company was about to send him to study abroad for two years, told me that if he changed jobs within five years of coming back, he would need to repay his study abroad tuition and living expenses. But he did not plan to repay this with his long-term loyalty:

> I guess I'm still planning to be here seven years from now. But after that, I can't honestly say. . . . [S]even years from now, the Olympics will be over. I really can't imagine what the situation will be then. Of course, emotionally, I know that this is the company where I've built my career. But, the people at the top will have changed by then, the environment will be completely different, and my motivation could change, too. So, I'm undecided. But I'm not strongly committed to working here my whole life.

Masato was similarly matter-of-fact. He said, "Since I entered the company, every three years I think if I want to stay on here. My philosophy is, first, I'll try it for three years, and then I'll think about the next three years."

Respondents also rarely worried about how coworkers might react if they did want to change jobs. Chaoxing said, of the possible reactions:

> HR personnel might criticize you [for leaving the company]. But the people you actually work with probably would not. The reason is that people's consciousness is changing. It's your life. Everyone under-stands that. When I entered the company, that first week I had a meeting with the *buchou* [department head]. What the *buchou* told me was, if the company doesn't suit you, it's fine to quit. It's fine to change jobs. He was very clear.

At the same time, informants also acknowledged that coworkers might view job changers askance. But they mostly shrugged this off.

> **Takeshi**: People might [criticize job changers behind their backs]. . . . But someone might change jobs for all sorts of reasons. Maybe their evalu-ation isn't good, or maybe there's something than they want to achieve, and they're changing jobs to do that. I think it's pathetic for people to criticize someone who's changing jobs to make a better future for themselves.
>
> **Interviewer**: So [the criticism] wouldn't bother you [if you wanted to change jobs]?
>
> **Takeshi**: Only to the extent that I would think, "Too bad for them."

Similarly, Masato said: "If someone quits, people will criticize them. It doesn't bother me at all though. Of course, I'd still keep in touch, meet up for drinks with them, share information. But I think a lot of people would dislike it. . . . [I]f they go to a rival company, people consider that a betrayal . . . but as

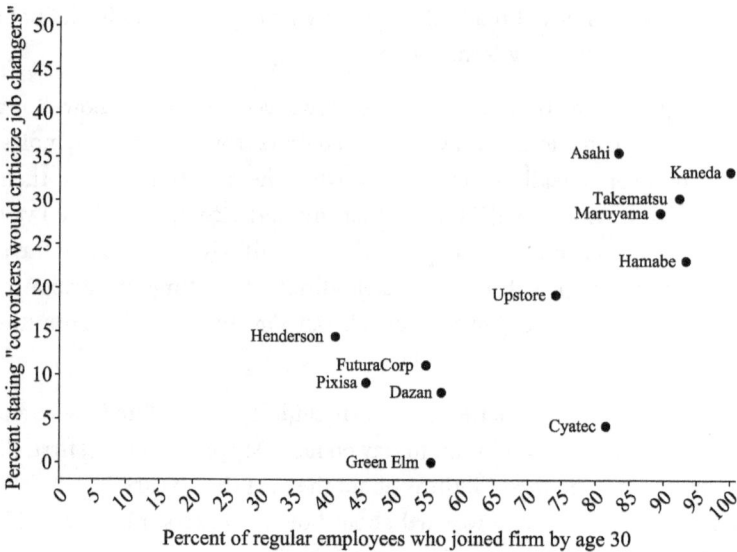

FIGURE 1.2. Job change norms among Japanese employees. Calculated from author's survey data.

far as the company's policy, this isn't a company that will point the finger at you for changing jobs. If you want to come back, you can."

Hugo anticipated perhaps the harshest reaction from coworkers. "If you leave," he said, "coworkers might say, 'Oh, so you think you're better than us?' or 'You are making a mistake.'" He added, "If there is a good, personal reason for changing jobs, not just a higher salary, people can probably accept and understand it." Like Masato, Hugo noted that changing jobs did not mean severing ties with the firm completely. He also said, "It is possible to return if you leave. In that sense, maybe it is permissive. I know one guy who left, and I know for a fact that he could come back if he wanted."

These patterns thus reveal several major breaks with the past: Many employees see job change in positive, or at least neutral, terms; few feel constrained by the moderate persistence of social norms that discourage job change; and firms are more willing to welcome workers back after they have worked elsewhere.

Importantly, weakened moral constraints on job change are common among all companies in the survey. As shown in figure 1.2, several of the firms—generally the older ones with Japanese names—do the bulk of their hiring at the entry level, as estimated by the share of employees who joined the firm before age 30. Others, usually younger firms, rely more on midcareer hiring. A strong relationship exists between the share of entry-level hiring and the likelihood that employees believe coworkers would criticize someone who was quitting to work at a different firm. Even at the firms where traditional entry-level hiring predominates, however, only a minority of Japanese respondents think that their coworkers would criticize job changers.

For example, a Japanese employee at one of the traditionally-minded firms denied having any particular loyalty to his company. He said, "The only reason I work here is because they offered me a job. I didn't get any other job offers." In particular, if he was transferred to a unit where he was uninterested in the work, he said, he would have no qualms about changing jobs. "The experiences I've gained are certainly useful," he said, "but I think I might be able to leverage that career experience even better at another company."

A non-Japanese employee in one of the traditional firms said, "of course, the mainstream, the majority of employees here came in as new graduates." But, she added, "If someone is leaving, we throw a party for them to say 'best of luck'. . . . [T]here's not any discomfort with that."

Although employees have always changed jobs, in studies from the 1960s and 1970s, white-collar workers describe coworkers' job changes as unsettling and problematic. In contrast, the employees in this study view job change positively and permissively. This does not mean that the labor market in Japanese firms has remade itself along Anglo-American lines. In the survey sample, 56 percent of the male, Japanese, regular employees worked continuously for the same employer. Although a significant minority of employees believe their coworkers would criticize a job changer, the normative constraints on job change are demonstrably looser than in the past.

Across these three areas of worker commitment—work hours, after-hours socializing, and loyalty to an employer—both the neoclassical and the neoliberal models fit poorly. In contrast to neoclassical models, employee commitments to the firm have been much reduced. Work hours are shorter, after-hours socializing is less, and employees feel considerable freedom to change jobs. Although these lower amounts of socializing are, on the surface, consistent with neoliberal predictions, the valence to workers is positive, not negative. Rather than feeling as though they have little connection to coworkers because they do not go out together, they experience these reductions as an increase in free time for leisure and family.

Job Placement and Limits to Autonomy

In one important area, however, employee autonomy has not increased in the sample firms. In the classical model of employment, large, white-collar firms transfer employees between jobs and units with little regard to specialty or employee preference. The firms in this study closely adhere to this model.

The experience of my colleagues at CIGS mirrored that of the employees in the twelve firms I studied. Unlike researchers, who were employed directly by the Canon Institute, administrative staff at CIGS were posted there temporarily by Canon Global. After working for several years at the think tank, they would return to headquarters or be posted elsewhere. Like many large firms, Canon posts new employees in sales roles to learn the business from the bottom up as well as to an gain understanding of customer perspectives and appreciation for the value of persistence. Several of my CIGS coworkers humorously recalled their early days at Canon, going door to door and attempting to convince proprietors of small firms to sign leases for Canon photocopiers and printers, largely without success.

Like my CIGS colleagues, employees in the twelve study firms described the heavy hand of companies in career placement. Xinyan said: "It's fundamental to the management track that the company decides where you go. So if the company says 'go to the US' or 'go to China,' you can't refuse. . . . That's the rule." This often results in undesirable placements. Dawen, who had hoped for a job in logistics or accounting but ended up in insurance, said bitterly: "Most of the time, you get the opposite of what you want. . . . I do not understand the thinking of Japanese HR [human resources] personnel."

The employees in the sample had varied careers. Some older employees had worked continuously on one product, or in one functional area, such as HR. Many mature employees had meandering careers, however, taking them from logistics to marketing to business strategy, or from aviation to foreign currency exchange, the president's office, and survey research. Often, but not always, these transfers took them far afield. Although some had worked their whole careers in Tokyo, many had done stints in other parts of Japan, or in Korea, China, Southeast Asia, the Middle East, Europe, or North America.

Xinyan noted that, through these circuitous career paths, employee preferences had played *some* role: "They do of course pay some attention to employee requests. . . . We write a career plan every year. Maybe they won't take your request right away, but if you write every year that you want to go to the US, eventually you'll probably get a chance." Some companies, like Pixisa, also give employees opportunities to apply to work on special projects, but this is not a regular occurrence. Even this practice shows the heavy hand of companies, which may or may not eventually bestow a desirable job placement.

Japanese as well as foreign employees acknowledge the heavy hand of the company in career paths. As shown in table 1.4, large majorities of Japanese employees in every company in the sample report that their firms would likely

TABLE 1.4.   Control over workers' careers by firm

COMPANY	STATE THEIR COMPANY WOULD PRIORITIZE EMPLOYER NEEDS OVER EMPLOYEE WISHES IN JOB PLACEMENT (%)	STATE EMPLOYEES SHOULD ACCEPT THAT THEY MAY NOT GET THE JOB PLACEMENTS THEY DESIRE (%)	NO. JAPANESE RESPONDENTS
Upstore	80.8	92.3	26
Asahi	77.4	93.5	31
FuturaCorp	74.1	74.1	27
Kaneda	88.1	92.9	42
Hamabe	88.5	80.8	26
Takematsu	89.4	86.4	66
Dazan	84	88	25
Cyatec	95.8	83.3	24
Henderson	72.7	71.2	132
Maruyama	100	85.7	14
Pixisa	86.4	81.8	22
Green Elm	83.3	100	6

ignore employee preference for placement if they conflict with HR priorities and that this is simply something that employees need to accept. Yuichi, who was unhappy in his current placement, exemplified this view, saying, "I see this as my fate. I can't change it."

This fatalistic attitude does not mean that Japanese employees are happy with their lack of autonomy, or even as passive as Yuichi's comment suggests. Takeshi explained that placement was critical to promotion chances at the firm, because promotion is more likely for employees in some units than in others. He complained, however, that HR decisions around placement were utterly opaque: "If it works out that you get placed in a unit [where people are less likely to get promoted], you've lost your chance at promotion. . . . That certainly breeds discontent." Even Yuichi, who described his undesirable placement as "fate," also said he was actively lobbying for a placement where he would be able to generate revenue and make sales.

Thus, although employer control over employees' time has relaxed, and normative constraints around job change have weakened, employers continue to retain extensive control over workers' career paths within the firm.

Managerial Control over Employees' Careers

Because HR departments allocate employees to units, HR is often, in the words of an employee at Upstore, "powerful and feared." In the context of long-term employment with a single firm, employees' direct managers also exert considerable—and often unpredictable—control over workers' careers. In the context of these elite firms, managerial control takes two main forms: work assignments and performance review.

In large firms, employees rarely have job descriptions. Units are jointly responsible for undertaking certain business operations, but under the umbrella of a given unit, it is managers who assign specific objectives or projects to employees. When HR posts a new employee to a unit, that person may take over the tasks of the person they replace, but managers may also reallocate work according to employees' perceived interests and abilities. The extent to which a manager assigns an employee high-value and value-added work—work that is thought of as important, can produce valued "results," teaches new skills, and is visible to others—is an important determinant of employees' career trajectories. Of course, the availability of high-value-added work depends on the unit and, by extension, on HR decisions about job postings. But managerial discretion over work assignments also critically shapes employees' careers.

The second way in which managers influence subordinates' careers is through performance evaluation. The firms in the sample vary in how they conduct performance evaluations. At Takematsu and Cyatec, for example, employees write a self-evaluation, and managers write an employee evaluation. Managers and employees discuss these, and following the discussion, managers assign final performance scores for every person on the team. At Kaneda, immediate managers assign scores to their subordinates, and higher-level managers review and adjust the scores for everyone in the department. At Henderson, employees self-evaluate, and managers evaluate subordinates, and both submit their reports to a committee composed of HR personal and senior departmental managers. The committee adjudicates and generates a final evaluation, after seeking additional input from managers if a discrepancy exists between the two. Thus, despite differences in the formal process, in every firm, managers' assessments are critical in shaping employee evaluations, and along with this, employees' chances for promotion.

Although managers' evaluations influence workers' outcomes in many national contexts, in Japan, low labor mobility magnifies their impact.[45] In a high-mobility labor market, workers regularly "escape" the effects of poor reputation or performance review by changing jobs. Not so in a context of long-term employment, in which HR retains career-long records of performance, and coworkers and managers may have memories of an employee that stretch back decades. Hence, firms' continued adherence to the long-term employment model gives added weight to managers' employee evaluations.

Employees universally emphasized that managers could make or break this process. Hideki put this with characteristic bluntness, saying, "I think [the evaluation process] is fair. Well, actually, whether it's fair or not depends on your boss. To give an extreme example, if your boss sucks, then the system goes to shit."

In general, employees raised two main ways the managers idiosyncratically influence evaluation: through managers' *interpretation* of the rules and through managers' *implementation* of the rules.

As organizational scholars have long recognized, in highly bureaucratized systems, firms may delineate formal rules, but all rules inevitably spawn gray zones where individuals either must, or can, exercise discretion in implementation.[46] In the case of performance evaluation, this means that despite proliferating guidelines, managers' evaluation priorities—their individual interpretation of the rules—vary. As Yuichi said: "There are ten axes on which we're evaluated. But, what those axes are change over time. And then there's the question of how your evaluator interprets the evaluation matrix, and which axes they consider the most important. That part is not specified."

In other words, in Yuichi's case, the sum or average of the evaluation subscores did not have a consistent relationship with the overall evaluation. Because different managers assign different weight to the various criteria, even someone with the same quantitative scores on the matrix might get a different final grade, depending on which axes their manager considers most important.

Shouichiro likewise described the importance of discerning a manager's specific priorities rather than conforming to some universal standard of performance: "What is your boss looking for? Is it someone who's going to go out and earn a lot of money [for the company]? Or someone who's going to be able to train other staff really well? Different bosses will have different ways of thinking about it. So you have to figure out your boss's unspoken needs, and match yourself to that."

Managers also vary in the importance they place on facetime as a facet of evaluation. Some managers adopt a "butts-in-seats" mentality, valuing overtime for the sake of overtime, or encouraging drinking together after hours as a demonstration of team spirit. Chaoxiang, quoted earlier, thought that drinking with his boss was absolutely critical for his promotion chances. Dawen noted that when he left on schedule, his grade decreased. Through this variable interpretation of the rules and application of different evaluation standards, managers wield considerable power over their subordinates.

Beyond these idiosyncratic variations in evaluation standards, managers also differ in whether they follow formal procedure *at all*.

> **Masato**: Feedback depends on the person. I've always received feedback, and given it to my subordinates. But there are some managers in my current unit who don't.
>
> **Interviewer**: So it's optional?
>
> **Masato**: Well, it is company policy that we are supposed to do it. But, in terms of implementation, there're people who do and people who don't. And it seems like maybe there are more who don't.

Yuichi encountered similar variation: "The system is, your boss meets with you in-person to give feedback. That's required. But, if the question is, does everyone actually do it, the answer is no." He added that, because of the direct relationship between evaluation grades and the size of his biannual bonus, he could extrapolate what his grade must have been by comparing the size of his bonus to the average for all employees of the same rank, which the company shares with employees.

Emi described how her company, on paper, has a 360-degree performance evaluation system. In this system, managers evaluate subordinates, and subordinates evaluate managers. But, she had never actually evaluated her manager, nor did she know anyone who had.

Takeshi reported that, although his company also expects managers to give employees feedback, "My [old] boss never really offered feedback. . . . Basically, he said 'This is your grade, please sign your name here.'" In his current unit, however, managers give feedback twice a year, as required by company policy.

Firms' failure to consistently apply policy extends managerial power over employees' careers. It also foments considerable distrust among employees. Only 4 percent of Japanese men in the sample believe information their company provides about performance evaluations or career opportunities all or nearly all the time. In contrast, 56 percent believe it half the time or less.

Because managers exercise considerable discretion in evaluation, and indeed in whether they adhere to formal evaluation processes at all, respondents agree that their boss is the single largest player in the promotion process. Emi said: "Your relationship with your boss is probably 70 or 80 percent of the promotion decision. Even if you have the right performance record, without the right relationship, you sink any chance of promotion."

Shouichiro deemphasized the importance of relationships per se as the prime factor in promotion, putting it at "only 30 percent." But, bosses still play a critical role, he said, because "After all, it's your boss who decides about your promotion. Or at least, your boss, meeting with people at that same level. So there's how he evaluates you. And then there's whether he's willing to push your candidacy."

When asked what it takes to get ahead at his firm, Takeshi said: "Become a 'boss's pet.' It's not the official policy, but as I'm telling you about this, I realize it's true. . . . Stick to him like glue."

Masato expressed similar sentiments, saying that "At our company, [getting ahead] is all about your relationship with your boss. He's the one who evaluates you directly."

Thus, although worker commitments are reduced and worker autonomy is greater in many domains, in the areas of career direction, employers still hold the reins. In the case of job placements, the HR department is responsible, but individual managers also play a hugely decisive role in workers' careers.

Gender Inequality

For men, firms' classical-era commitments to workers remain strong. Male regular workers experience wage progression and feel secure in their jobs. At the same time, the demands that firms place on men, including work hours, expectations for after-hours socializing, and normative prohibition against changing jobs have all loosened. If anything, then, conditions for male workers in these firms have improved, compared with typical conditions in the high-growth era, in contrast to neoclassical predictions that they have stayed largely the same and to neoliberal predictions that they have deteriorated. But what about women? As we saw earlier, both models predict persistent gender inequality, and, in particular, women's relegation to less desirable clerical-track or irregular jobs.

To examine conditions for women, figure 1.3 plots Japanese women's earnings by age, alongside the trend lines for Japanese men's earnings. Because both neoclassical and neoliberal models of employment cast women's overconcentration in irregular employment or clerical-track jobs as major sources of gender inequality, figure 1.3 includes all Japanese women, regardless of job category. The figure reveals stark levels of gender inequality.

Although some women are high earners, illustrated by the points positioned above the black trendlines for men, the gray trendlines for women reveal vast discrepancies between the typical woman's earnings and those of men in regular, management-track jobs. Moreover, the gender gap is not merely a relic of historic practices, as it appears even among employees in their twenties.

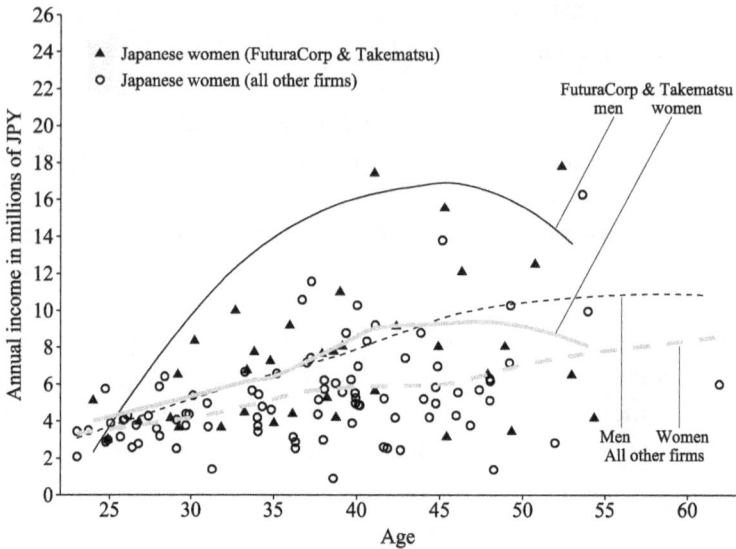

FIGURE 1.3. Annual earnings by age among Japanese women, compared with earnings among Japanese men in regular management-track jobs. Calculated from author's survey data.

These persistent, high levels of gender inequality are consistent with both the predictions of the neoliberal model and those of the neoclassical one.

Table 1.5 further investigates women's concentration in poorly paid irregular and clerical-track positions by comparing women's share of management-track jobs to their share of the sample. If women's share of management-track jobs is considerably less than their overall share, this indicates women's concentration in other forms of employment. Surprisingly, however, the results fail to support this prediction. In the great majority of the firms, the shares are relatively close, indicating that most women work in positions that, at least on paper, offer generous pay and opportunities for advancement available to core male workers. Only in three firms (i.e., Hamabe, Takematsu, and Dazan) are women notably underrepresented on the management track.

Thus, as was the case in firms in the high-growth era, gender inequality is high in the sample firms. It appears, however, that gender inequality is driven primarily by disadvantage *between* women and men working in core jobs, rather than by women's outright exclusion from such positions, as in the past. In light of the findings on managerial discretion, this result suggests that the behaviors of individual managers may be a larger contributor to women's exclusion than in the classical era, when women's positions were, by definition, temporary and lacked opportunities for advancement.

TABLE 1.5.   Women's representation by firm

COMPANY	WOMEN RESPONDENTS (%)	WOMEN'S REPRESENTATION ON MANAGEMENT TRACK (%)
Upstore	31.3	25.9
Asahi	27.9	25.0
FuturaCorp	40.0	35.5
Kaneda	24.0	17.9
Hamabe	23.3	13.3
Takematsu	35.8	15.4
Dazan	66.7	28.6
Cyatec	35.1	37.0
Henderson	26.8	28.6
Maruyama	30.4	31.6
Pixisa	34.5	37.5
Green Elm	30.0	33.3

Neoliberal and Neoclassical Models in the Broader Economy

Both neoliberal and neoclassical perspectives take a critical view of Japanese employment. In the former, workers are insecure, disconnected, and exploited. In the latter, core male workers at least enjoy job security, but they do so at the cost of ceding control over their time and careers to the firm.

Although the neoliberal and neoclassical perspectives on Japanese employment have been used to characterize elite firms, these models were developed to describe a much broader employment ecosystem. How typical—or atypical— are the sample firms' changes and continuities relative to other workplaces in the economy at large? In the sample firms, workers note that they feel confident of continued employment and observe that even low performers enjoy steady wages that grow with age. Concurrently, workers have seized greater control over their time: Work hours have moderated, after-hours socializing and drinking no longer monopolize male workers' private lives, and employees feel free to seek alternative employment. In sum, core male workers enjoy continued security *and* greater, if not unlimited, autonomy. Despite women's increased representation in core jobs, however, gender inequality in pay remains pervasive. Various nation-level statistics offer some clues as to whether these trends find echo outside the exclusive echelons of top-tier employers, and thus they permit an assessment of the strengths and weaknesses of the models as heuristics for employment in the broader economy as well as in the sample firms.

Undeniably, as name-brand, highly recognizable companies "at the center of the circle," the sample firms are in some ways exceptional. In particular, remuneration for the Japanese men in the sample is well beyond what an average salaryman might expect. Beyond this, however, the changes in these elite firms and those in the broader economy share many commonalities, although the trends are less pronounced outside the rarified world of elite firms.

As in the sample firms, many metrics highlight persistent, and even growing, job security or stability in the broader economy. One such measure is the share of the working-age population in regular employment. As described earlier, regular employees enjoy strong legal protections from dismissal. Thus, the share of the working-age population in regular employment is a reasonable measure of whether access to these protections is rising or falling over time.

Between 1988 and 2020, the size of the prime working-age population (ages 25–54) fell from 53 million to 48 million. Over the same period, the number of prime working-age adults in regular employment grew, from 34 million to 36 million. Thus, even in the presumed heyday of long-term employment, only 48 percent of working-age adults held regular jobs, compared with 55 percent in 2020.[47]

Of course, this period is also characterized by a massive expansion in irregular employment, from 7 million employees in 1988 to 21 million employees in 2020. It is, however, misleading to suggest this represents an unravelling of the social contract. The economy has added irregular new jobs at a rapid clip; but as the stability in the number of regular employees over the past three decades underscores, these irregular new jobs have supplemented rather than replaced regular jobs. Moreover, irregular jobs are overwhelmingly staffed by people who were unlikely to be in the labor market at all during the high-growth era—particularly women and adults age 55 and older. More central is the fact that, for prime-age workers, access to regular employment, with the attendant job security, has *expanded* rather than contracted since the late 1980s.

Another measure of stability is the rate of involuntary dismissals, which remain rare; between 2008 and 2022, the share of employed persons leaving their job because of "employer priorities," which include transfers to subsidiaries, as well as layoffs, has hovered around 1 percent, with the exception of 2009, when it "leaped" to 2 percent.[48]

National wage surveys also show that the relationship between age and earnings has remained remarkably unchanged over the past three decades. Like the elite salarymen in the sample, ordinary white-collar male employees can still expect to earn more in their forties and fifties than in their twenties and thirties, across both small and large employers.[49] In sum, although the employees at the sample firms are indisputably privileged relative to the average white-collar employee in terms of the magnitude of their earnings and benefits, the underpinning logics of job stability and wages that increase with age do not set them apart from white-collar workers generally.

With regard to attitudes toward and opportunities for job change, the sample firms are also representative of national trends. The number of voluntary job changers continues to increase, reaching its highest levels ever in 2019, whereas involuntary job change has fallen. Workers are also more likely to move from irregular to regular work than in the past.[50] Overall rates of voluntary mobility, however, are much higher among workers at smaller firms than at the large ones in the sample, in part because workers may have to change jobs to achieve upward mobility as small firms, whereas large firms offer a career ladder through the internal labor market.

With regard to work hours, conditions in the sample firms are more favorable than those in the economy at large, but work hours for full-time employees are falling in firms of all sizes—in 1996, full-time employees worked an average of 2,050 hours annually. By 2019, this figure had dropped to 1,980 hours. Assuming fifty weeks of work a year, this represents a decline of about 1.5 hours per week. Thus, although the five- to ten-hour reductions in weekly working hours the study respondents describe far exceed the national average, the trendline in the broader economy mirrors that of the sample firms.[51] Use of paid vacation is also increasing in firms of all sizes, although as with work hours, change is more dramatic in the largest firms, likely because large firms are more likely to command the resources necessary to redistribute work by increasing the number of employees.[52]

As for gender inequality, the sample firms are typical of large firms in that gender gaps in pay are wide. Small and midsize firms demonstrate gender inequality as well, but for women, employment in a large firm is associated with a much smaller pay advantage than it is for men.[53] Consequently, gender gaps in pay are largest in larger firms, and this trend is even more pronounced in the elite firms in the sample.

Returning to the predictions of the neoliberal and the neoclassical models, the neoliberal model holds up poorly, both in the sample firms and in the economy at large. There is little evidence of a rising tide of precarity and an unravelling of the institutions that offered many workers financial stability during the high-growth era.

Assessing the neoclassical model is more complex. In the sample firms, its predictions of business as usual fail in several ways: Core male workers' hours have fallen significantly; after-hours socializing with coworkers is less common than in the past; normative restrictions on job change have loosened; and women are increasingly incorporated into the sample firms in management-track jobs. At the same time, the model correctly identifies that many firms engage in "symbolic compliance" to changing norms: for example, firms have adopted quantitative performance management systems, but they implement them in ways that increase earnings with employee age; more and more women work on the management track, but gender inequality in pay remains high. In addition, although attitudes toward job change have become more permissive, HR and managers retain considerable influence over the direction of workers' careers through job rotations and task assignment. Moreover, work hours in the broader economy have moderated to a far lesser degree in than in the sample firms.

The neoclassical model thus offers a far better heuristic for understanding the labor market than the neoliberal model, but it also overlooks some key changes, particularly in elite firms such as those in the sample. As discussed in the introduction, in an era of population decline, attracting and retaining workers has become increasingly challenging. The working-age population, especially those who are entry-level age, has declined precipitously. In theory at least, labor shortages can shift the balance of power in the workplace in favor of workers. Changes in the sample firms and in the broader economy, whereby core male workers retain the securities of the past while also garnering greater flexibility and self-determination, are not necessarily solely attributable to population decline, but they are consistent with theoretical predictions that a shrinking population can lead to better work conditions. The neoclassical model, although accurate on many counts, obscures these important changes.[54]

As the investigation of pay, promotion, and job stability among Japanese men shows, in elite firms, there are plenty of spoils to go around. Despite their adoption of splashy performance management systems that in theory link pay more closely to workers' output, even underperforming men receive high salaries simply by showing up. Even as the security of the past persists, worker autonomy and flexibility have increased.

At the very least, these changes hold the potential to make workplaces more equitable for white-collar women and immigrant workers. Even if companies of the high-growth era had considered women as long-term members of the workforce, the long work hours and extended after-hours drinking would have weighed heavily in men's favor in the competition for advancement within the firm. Today, employees' reduced commitments to their employers make the ideal worker model easier for women to reach. Of course, even the more moderate work hours and after-hours expectations of the present day still pose barriers for women in the workplace. Even if regular overtime extends "only" until 7 or 8 p.m., or if after-hours drinking happens "only" a few times a month, it is still challenging to combine this model with regular household tasks, such as collecting children from daycare, supervising homework, and preparing meals. In contrast to the past, however, filling the "care gaps" with assistance from family members, friends, neighbors, or paid childcare is now at least within the realm of possibility for some women.

For foreign workers and women alike, increased opportunities for interfirm labor mobility also improve their chances of making it big in Japanese business. Although changing jobs is socially accepted for *Japanese men*, firms have less reason to discriminate against Japanese women and foreign workers in pay, training, and promotion, based on the assumption that they may quit to raise a family or go back to their home countries. In general, then, increased worker autonomy stands to benefit those for whom the more rigid expectations of the past were untenable.

Other practices still create daunting barriers to women and immigrants' career trajectories in elite firms. Because they are more likely to be in dual-career marriages, women and foreign workers may need to decline transfers to distant locations. Foreign workers may also eventually need to return to their home countries, for example to care for aging parents, but they have no guarantee that their firms will post them there. The heavy hand of the firm in job placement is inconvenient for all workers regardless of gender or nationality. Although Japanese men also bear these costs, they may be more challenging for women and foreign workers to shoulder.

In addition, managers' extensive discretion in performance evaluation may work in favor of low-performing Japanese men, who benefit from "equity adjustments" in performance evaluations. By contrast, bias and prejudices against female and foreign workers may lead to lower average evaluations, regardless of real performance. Studies in Western countries show that when evaluation processes are opaque and evaluators not held accountable, gender, ethnic, and racial biases are more likely to affect evaluation. As described by Yuichi, evaluations inevitably take on a "qualitative" and "emotional" tenor, in spite of the proliferation of goal-setting and quantitative performance metrics. This creates ample room for stereotypical beliefs about outsiders to color managers' evaluations, and with them, outsiders' opportunities for advancement.

Overall, these changes in employment practices are shifting the mechanisms driving exclusion and inclusion. Structural barriers at the level of firm policy, such as outright exclusion of women from the management track, or work hour demands that are impossible for caregiving women to meet, are lower than in the past, but by no means gone. At the same time, however, considerable scope for exclusion remains in individual-level processes, such as managerial discretion over employees' work assignments and advancement opportunities.

(IN)VISIBLE INEQUALITIES

Foreign Workers' Place in Elite Firms

Quietly poised to take notes, around forty young human resource employees sat two to a desk in seminar room overlooking the Tokyo skyline. At the front of the room, an HR consultant, whom I will call Kiyoshi, strode to the podium. Fixing us with a hawklike stare, he confidently assured us that he was distinctly well-positioned to offer solutions to what he called one of the most pressing issues of twenty-first century HR management in corporate Japan: the challenge of integrating "global talent."

Global talent is a common shorthand for non-Japanese white-collar workers. Unlike Japanese women, who have long composed a critical, yet marginalized, segment of the workforce in elite firms, foreign workers' presence in these settings is relatively new. Before 1990, vanishingly few non-Japanese worked at elite firms. Those who did were usually hired in Western Europe or North America, transferred to Japan for a few years of training, and then sent to work in subsidiaries or branch offices of Japanese firms in their home countries.[1] The very existence of Kiyoshi's seminar points to a sea change in corporate Japan, whereby companies not only can, but, in the face of demographic pressure, also *must* open their doors to foreign workers in greater numbers. In 2010, 26 percent of large Japanese companies reported that they hired at least one foreign white-collar worker that year; by 2019, the percentage had more than doubled to 53 percent.[2]

As we have seen, work conditions for Japanese men in elite firms have improved since the high-growth era. To core male workers, these firms offer continued stability alongside greater autonomy and flexibility. Even as more women enter core jobs, gender inequality remains deeply entrenched. As firms increasingly incorporate non-Japanese workers, will they be able to attain parity with Japanese men? Or will their outcomes be similar to, or even worse than, those of Japanese women?

Compelling arguments can be made on both sides of this question. On one hand, as domestic markets shrink, Japanese firms increasingly need staff who can lead expansion in foreign markets. Foreign workers' ability to fill this strategic niche may position them to reap the rewards of population decline.[3] On the other hand, Japanese firms are notorious for their strong insider cultures, and for their close identification with narratives of Japan's purported racial and cultural homogeneity.[4] Indeed, these essentializing narratives featured prominently and disturbingly in Kiyoshi's seminar, in which he characterized Japanese as conflict-averse "island people," and Chinese, Koreans, and Americans as culturally similar to each other but deeply different from Japanese, as outspoken and aggressive "continental people." As cultural and ethnic outsiders, therefore, foreign workers may land at the bottom of the stratification hierarchy in Japanese firms, despite pressures of population decline.

This chapter introduces the foreign workers in the sample by gender and region of origin and positions them against the backdrop of growing white-collar migration to Japan. Drawing on respondents' own perspectives, on research from Japan, and on research on elite employment contexts in the United States, it identifies several possible patterns for integration into the firms, and compares workers' outcomes to these stylized models.

This analysis of respondents' perceptions of their opportunities, combined with earnings and job placement data, reveal that although Asian women often see a bright future for themselves in Japanese firms, in fact they fare little or no better than do Japanese women. By contrast, immigrant men, including those from both Asian and Western countries, attain outcomes similar to or better than those of Japanese men. In sum, despite Japan's reputation for xenophobia, and a long history of almost complete exclusion of noncitizens from the white-collar workplace, gender remains a far sharper dividing line than ethnicity or region of origin.

White-Collar Foreign Workers in Japan

In most wealthy countries, companies must demonstrate that they tried and failed to hire a host country national for a white-collar position before offering the job to a noncitizen.[5] Not so in Japan. Following 1990 revisions to border control policy, firms are legally free to offer jobs to white-collar workers with foreign citizenship as long as they can plausibly describe their duties as fitting under the broad umbrella of the "specialist in humanities and international services" or "technical" visas. The range of occupations permitted under these two visa categories is extensive, ranging from insurance, marketing, graphic design, and translation to engineering, programming, and life sciences research.[6]

Human resource (HR) professionals at large firms told me that when they wish to offer a job to a noncitizen, it is easy to secure one of these visas. They submit the required paperwork documenting the prospective hire's job content, salary, and educational background to the Ministry of Justice, and the guarantee of employment at a prestigious firm smooths a path for rapid approval.[7]

Despite the relative lack of bureaucratic hurdles, companies did not embrace noncitizen hiring in large numbers during the first decade following reform. As shown in figure 2.1, growth in white-collar work visa holders accelerated only after 2004, when the population of Japanese age 20–24 fell below the previous postwar nadir of the late 1970s and early 1980s. Although growth slowed and slightly reversed following the Lehman Shock, and again during the COVID-19 pandemic, since the 2012, the dominant trend is of exponential increase.

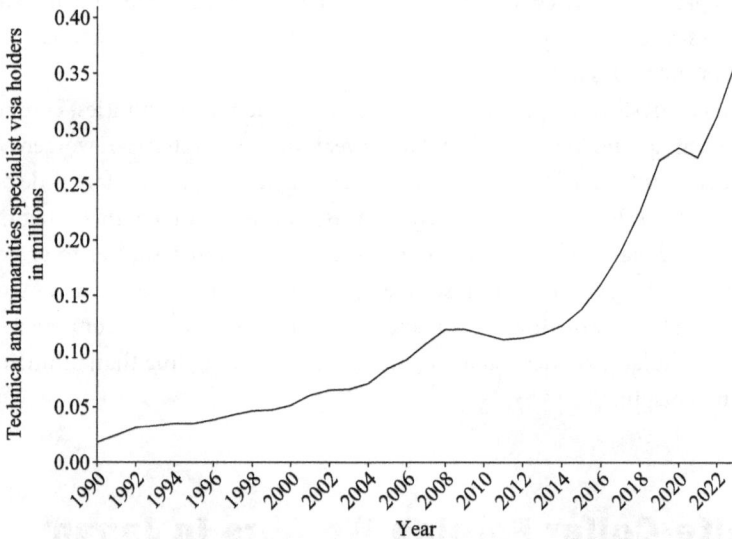

FIGURE 2.1. Technical and humanities specialist visa holders, 1990–2023. Calculated from Ministry of Justice, "Zairyuu gaikokujin toukei (kyuu touroku gaikokujin toukei) toukeihyou" [Statistics on resident foreigners (formerly statistics on registered foreigners)].

Postreform white-collar workers are different from those of the prereform period in three main ways. First, many first arrived in Japan as students at Japanese language schools and universities, giving them greater proficiency in Japanese language and culture than hires from abroad in the prereform period.[8] Second, other East Asian countries, especially China and Taiwan, rapidly surpassed Europe and North America as the leading source countries for white-collar migration.[9] In 2015, 83.7 percent of technical and humanities specialist visa holders were from Asian countries, and more than half of these hailed from China and Taiwan. Only 15.5 percent were from North America, Europe, or Oceania. The final difference for postreform white-collar workers is that they enjoy a legal path to long-term settlement. As part of the 1990s reforms, the government created a new visa for permanent residency. In theory at least, naturalization was an option for foreign residents even prereform. Naturalization requires immigrants to renounce their natal citizenship, however, a step that gives many migrants pause.[10] Permanent residency, on the other hand, now available to noncitizens with at least ten years consecutive residence, offers full labor market access without severing immigrants' legal relationships to their countries of origin.[11] In recent years, the government has approved around thirty thousand applications for permanent residency a year.[12] About one-third of the total noncitizen population of Japan are permanent residents.[13]

Successive Liberal Democratic Party (LDP) governments have repeatedly denied that Japan has an "immigration policy."[14] A growing gap exists, however, between this official narrative and the reality on the ground. Visa reform of 1990 legalized new types of foreign worker migration and permitted long-term settlement for more categories of foreign residents; market pressures associated with population decline and globalization are now spurring companies to make use of these visas in ever greater numbers. Even without further policy revisions or official acknowledgment, Japan's transformation into an immigrant receiving country is well underway.

Foreign Workers and Immigrants in Elite Firms

Most studies of foreign workers in Japan define Japanese and non-Japanese by citizenship. To acknowledge the reality that Japan has already become a country of immigration, my approach differs. I define a foreign worker as anyone who does not speak Japanese as their native language. This definition includes noncitizen foreign workers, immigrants who have taken Japanese citizenship, and second- or 1.5-generation immigrants whose mother tongue is not Japanese. It excludes Japanese citizens born and raised outside Japan who speak Japanese as their native language, children with at least one foreign parent who were born in Japan and grew up speaking primarily Japanese, and "oldcomers," such as Zainichi Koreans, whose first language is almost always Japanese.[15]

Using this definition, this sample includes 441 native Japanese and 98 non-Japanese respondents. Of the non-Japanese, 75 percent are from other Asian countries (predominantly East Asia, followed by Southeast Asia), 22 percent from Western countries (i.e., Europe, North America, and Oceania), and 2 percent from Latin America.[16] This composition broadly mirrors that of white-collar work visa holders, albeit with a slight underrepresentation of Asians and over-representation of Westerners, which likely reflects Western workers' relatively larger presence in elite firms as compared with all white-collar work environments.[17] For both practical and theoretical reasons, I use these broad region of origin groupings to understand variation in foreign workers' experiences and outcomes.[18] Detailed birth country tabulations appear in table 2.1.

Like white-collar foreign workers generally, many of the foreign survey respondents are "educationally channeled migrants."[19] Chaoxiang is a typical case. After completing high school in China, he enrolled in language school in Japan, and after two years, he gained admission to a top-ranked Japanese university. As a third-year university student, he participated in the annual recruitment process for large Japanese businesses, undergoing the same grueling rounds of essays, personality testing, and interviews as Japanese applicants.[20] He received multiple job offers and chose his company because he believed in its potential for overseas expansion, a mission to which he hoped to contribute. He entered the firm immediately after graduation at age 25, slightly older than many of his Japanese *douki* (contemporaneous entry-level hires), as a result of

TABLE 2.1.   Birthplaces of survey respondents by region of origin

JAPANESE (N = 441)		ASIANS (N = 74)		WESTERNERS (N = 22)		OTHER (N = 2)	
BIRTHPLACE	N	BIRTHPLACE	N	BIRTHPLACE	N	BIRTHPLACE	N
Japan	435	China	43	Anglophone countries	17	Latin America	2
Outside Japan	6	Southeast Asia	10	Western Europe	3		
		South Korea	7				
		Japan	6	Japan	2		
		Taiwan	5				
		Other Asia	3				

his earlier stint at language school. Like Chaoxiang, 54 percent of the foreign respondents received all of their higher education in Japan, usually at prestigious private universities, such as Doshisha or Meiji University, before finding employment at a Japanese firm.

Yuanyuan illustrates a different mode of educationally channeled migration. After graduating from a university in Taiwan, she held a job there for a few years, in which she worked with Japanese clients, and became interested in moving to Japan. In her mid-twenties, she quit her job in Taiwan to enter an English-language master of business administration (MBA) program in Japan, where she also began studying Japanese. Because some firms classify new master of arts (MA) and MBAs as entry-level job applicants, postbaccalaureate programs are a strategic way to "reset the clock" and rejoin the entry-level labor pool. After receiving her MBA, Yuanyuan landed a job at her current company. Unlike Chaoxiang, she completed the interview process mostly in English, although she reported that her Japanese language skills had improved by leaps and bounds since she began working for her firm three years earlier.

Although Yuanyuan's Japanese was not as fluent as is typical among respondents who received all of their higher education in Japan, most respondents who completed only part of their higher education in Japan also spoke very good Japanese. Xinyan, for example, studied Japanese in college in China, worked for a Japanese firm in China to save money before matriculating in a Japanese masters' program, and then found a job in Japan. Derek, an American, also studied Japanese in college, came to Japan on the Japan Exchange and Teaching (JET) program, married a Japanese woman, and then entered an MBA program while working full time as an in-house translator for a major bank; following completion of his MBA, he landed a midcareer job at his current firm. Like their counterparts who attended higher education exclusively in Japan, members of this group graduated from brand-name educational programs at famous universities. Respondents who, like Yuanyuan, Xinyan, and Derek, received their undergraduate degrees abroad but their advanced degrees in Japan, compose 20 percent of the foreign sample. Together the two types of educationally channeled migrants account for approximately three-quarters of the foreign respondents.

The remaining respondents fall into one of three categories: childhood arrivals, early-career arrivals, and midcareer arrivals. Eleven non-Japanese respondents came to Japan as children or were born in Japan to at least one foreign parent. Nine of the eleven have roots in East Asian countries, and seven are permanent residents. All attended high school in Japan and went on to Japanese higher educational institutions. Almost all members of this group are fluent or near-fluent in Japanese, reflecting a long period of acculturation as children, teenagers, and young adults.

TABLE 2.2.   Arrival pathways of foreign workers by region of origin

	ASIANS (N = 74)		WESTERNERS (N = 22)		OTHER (N = 2)	
	%	N	%	N	%	N
Childhood arrivals	12.2	9	9.1	2		
Young adult arrivals with all Japanese higher education	56.8	42	40.9	9	100.0	2
Young adult arrivals with some Japanese higher education	21.6	16	18.2	4		
Early-career arrivals educated outside Japan	6.8	5	27.3	6		
Midcareer arrivals educated outside Japan	1.4	1	4.5	1		
Unknown	1.4	1				

The sample also includes eleven early-career arrivals. Wei, a Taiwanese man, fits this pattern. Wei moved with his family from Taiwan to an English-speaking country when he was a child. He attended university and graduate school in his new home. After graduation, he moved to Southeast Asia, where he worked for two years as an engineer. He connected with Japanese HR staff at a local career fair, and received a midcareer, nonmanagerial job offer to work in Japan when he was 26 years old. Wei never studied Japanese formally, and communicates with coworkers exclusively in English. Like Wei, members of this group, as well as childhood arrivals or educationally channeled migrants, are less likely to speak Japanese, but the majority nonetheless has strong Japanese language skills acquired on the job.

The final group consists of only two respondents, both of whom attended schools outside Japan and arrived in Japan past the age of 30 years old. Both worked for their current company in Europe and came to Japan on short-term contracts. They do not speak Japanese beyond basic greetings, and they conduct their work entirely in English. Both plan to return to their home countries.

From these five arrival paths, we can glean several things about the foreign workers. Despite their stellar credentials, we should not think of these respondents as "expats" or "foreign executives" who have parachuted to positions at the top of Japan's employment hierarchy on the strength of accomplished careers abroad.[21] Most of these workers initially arrived as educationally channeled migrants and have invested considerably in earning local degrees and completing Japanese language training. Moreover, almost universally, even those without local degrees began their Japanese careers in entry-level or early-career jobs. Many of these have since committed decades of their lives to building careers from the bottom up. Indeed, most respondents profess a strong commitment to either settling in Japan (22 percent of respondents), or living cross-culturally between Japan and their home countries (41 percent of

TABLE 2.3. Foreign workers' Japanese language skills and migration intentions by arrival pathway

	CHILDHOOD ARRIVALS	YOUNG ADULT ARRIVALS WITH ALL JAPANESE HIGHER EDUCATION	YOUNG ADULT ARRIVALS WITH SOME JAPANESE HIGHER EDUCATION	EARLY-CAREER ARRIVALS EDUCATED OUTSIDE JAPAN	MIDCAREER ARRIVALS EDUCATED OUTSIDE JAPAN
Advanced Japanese language skills (%)	90.9	79.3	85.0	63.6	0.0
Stay intentions					
Intend to settle permanently in Japan (%)	36.4	17.0	20.0	36.4	0.0
Intend to live transnationally between home country and Japan (%)	45.5	43.4	40.0	36.4	0.0
Unsure or intend to leave Japan (%)	18.2	39.6	40.0	27.3	100.0

respondents).[22] Sixty-seven hold white-collar work visas, twenty-nine hold spousal visas or permanent residency, and two have naturalized. Reflecting the ten-year wait for naturalization, most work-visa holders are 30 years old or younger. Older respondents are much more likely to have either permanent residency or a spousal visa that offers nearly the same rights.

Despite the Japanese government's denials, it is difficult to contest that at least some of the foreign workers in this study are likely to settle permanently in Japan as immigrants.[23] The distinctions, however, between a presumably temporary "foreign worker" or "migrant" and a presumably permanent "immigrant" are porous and dynamic. Intentions to stay evolve over the life course. Non-Japanese who never intended to settle in Japan may change their minds and vice versa. In recognition of the fact that permanent settlement is a legal option for the non-Japanese in the sample and that some, but certainly not all, are likely to take advantage of this pathway, I use the terms *foreign worker*, *immigrant*, and *migrant* interchangeably when referring to non-Japanese study participants.

"Concerned Uncertainty": Immigrant Workers' Perceptions of Opportunities

The declining working-age population and the increased importance of overseas markets to Japanese firms' financial vitality have forced open the doors of elite firms to foreign workers, who are now deeply enmeshed in the corporate environment described in chapter 1. In this environment, are immigrant workers marginalized? Or do they get a shot at equality with Japanese men?

As a relatively recent presence in elite firms, foreign employees themselves are generally uncertain about the answers to these questions. As Dawen pointed out, "There are not very many foreign workers at this company. And most of us are just in our first three years. Will we be treated equally going forward? It's hard to say."

Chaoxiang echoed this sentiment, explaining:

> I'm still young. So it's normal that I haven't been promoted yet. But at this company, there's a Chinese woman who's been working here for about 20 years. And she still has the same job title as I do. She's been working hard for this company for 20 years. And she's an unmarried woman. But she hasn't been given a position commensurate with that [level of dedication to the company]. But maybe the company will change. It's a matter of 10 or 20 years, after all. So I think I might end up in a slightly higher rank than she has. But since we're talking about something 10 or 20 years in the future, I just don't know.

Naturally, Japanese employees also face uncertainty about promotion prospects, but for foreign workers like Chaoxiang and Dawen, those uncertainties are magnified by the specter that their national origin might hold them back. At the same time, not all respondents thought this was likely. Faced with the same scenario as Dawen and Chaoxiang, Xinyan put a positive spin on it:

> [In this industry], companies started hiring foreign workers around ten years ago. In ten years, you don't reach the leadership level. So, with that in mind, it's natural [*atarimae*] that there isn't a single foreign employee, or foreign woman employee in upper management. Actually, it isn't zero. There's one Chinese man . . . but when it's my generation's turn, 10 or 15 years down the road, I expect there will be more. It's a matter of time. . . . I expect the company to follow the policy of equality. . . . I don't feel it's a big handicap to be a foreigner, to be a woman. I'm still young, and not of the age to be promoted. I think my future is pretty bright.

Overall, however, Xinyan was more optimistic than other immigrant workers in the sample. Chaoxiang, for example, argued that Japanese workplaces are ill-equipped to treat foreign workers fairly. Leaning in and becoming animated, he asked rhetorically,

> Recently, you hear a lot about "empowering women" [*josei katsuyou*], right? [Japanese employers] haven't even figured out how to effectively

use *their own* women in the workplace. How do you think they're going to be able to use foreign workers? I have serious doubts about that. First, you need to figure out how to empower women properly. *Then* you can think about foreign workers. It's a step-wise process. Empowering foreign workers is going to take a long time.

Dawen, Chaoxiang, and Xinyan are all examples of educationally channeled migrants, and they were both eloquent and personable in Japanese. Respondents with lower levels of Japanese language skills, in contrast, were more likely to highlight their struggles operating in the Japanese cultural and linguistic context. Yuanyuan, who attended an English-language MA program before landing her job, felt ambivalent about her promotion prospects. She said, "I'm a foreigner so I have several disadvantages in terms of the language and the culture. Even though I try, still there is some gap. I would say the gap is smaller compared to two or three years ago when I started working here. But still I feel there is some disadvantage."

George, a Latin American man, was not sure if he would be promoted, but he argued, "If we put aside things like language, I think I have the same opportunities for promotion as a Japanese man." Derek also thought it would be unlikely for him to attain a prominent position in his firm, grumbling sarcastically, "In terms of non-Japanese, [getting promoted] is no problem, just as long as you can do everything exactly like a Japanese person."

These responses illustrate many migrants' shared experiences *as foreigners*. This shared experience is usually, but not always, characterized by concern about prospects for upward mobility, which immigrant workers fear may be limited because of their foreign background, because of their limited linguistic and cultural fluency, or both.

Beyond the Foreigner-Japanese Divide

The discursive divide between "foreigners," on one hand, and "Japanese," on the other, is often strongly demarcated in elite workplaces. Kiyoshi's seminar, in which he contrasted a supposed shared culture of Chinese, Koreans, and Americans, with that of Japanese, is an example *par excellence* of this demarcation. It was not only Japanese who highlighted this divide, as I discovered in my interview with Liling, a Chinese woman working in HR, who had also participated in Kiyoshi's diversity training. As someone who was tasked with overseeing and assessing the role of other foreign employees in her company, I was curious to what extent Kiyoshi's rather sweeping generalizations resonated with her. To my surprise, she enthusiastically endorsed his take, saying, "Basically I agree with him. I think he has it right."

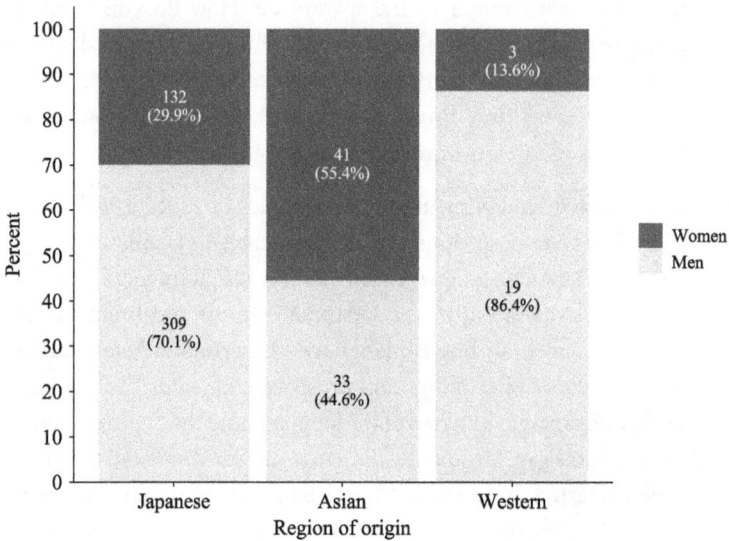

FIGURE 2.2. Respondent gender by region of origin. Calculated from author's survey data.

Despite foreign workers' shared experiences, and the frequency with which workers in elite firms invoke the foreigner-Japanese divide, neither preclude even more significant *variation* in migrants' experiences associated with other aspects of their identities. As intersectionality theory highlights, complex, multiple identities, including gender and nation or region of origin, compound and shape lived experience in nonadditive ways.[24] To what extent do other aspects of identity figure into foreign respondents' assessments of their opportunities?

As figure 2.2 illustrates, the gender composition of both Asian and Western workers is quite different from that of Japanese. Women represent about 30 percent of the Japanese respondents, which is typical of elite firms' gender composition. Relative to this, women are overrepresented among the Asian respondents and underrepresented among the Western respondents. How do the Asian women see themselves fitting in, in what we saw in chapter 1 remains a highly gender-unequal environment?

Typical of the sample at large, the Asian women interviewees are highly ambitious; Liling, for example, aspired to find work at foreign company, and she spent evenings and weekends studying English to make herself a more competitive candidate for these jobs. Xinyan expected to work her way to up the senior ranks of management within her current firm. Yuanyuan was eager to make a big impact by expanding her company's marketing initiatives within Asia.

None of these women expressed concern that their gender would hold them back. Xinyan, as quoted earlier, was confident in a bright future and felt that her strong performance and skilled relationship-building would be rewarded fairly. Both Liling and Yuanyuan harbored fears that, as foreigners, they would not be accorded the same opportunities as Japanese men. But neither worried that gender posed a major barrier.

These women's relative inattention to gender does not indicate that the topic is taboo. Both Xinyan and Yuanyuan mentioned experiences of sexual harassment, including unwanted sexual advances at *nomikai* (drinking parties) and groping on the train. Yuanyuan said, "After drinking alcohol, sometimes Japanese guys become more aggressive. Maybe they are so belligerent they try to touch you." After several unpleasant experiences at *nomikai*, Yuanyuan said, she began to plan lunch dates with coworkers for networking, rather than joining evening parties where drinking was inevitable. In this way, she believed she could render it a surmountable annoyance rather than a serious threat to her career.

The three interviewees are by no means outliers, either in their ambition or in their confidence in their opportunities. Among survey respondents under age 35, 52 percent of Asian women describe opportunities for promotion as either "absolutely critical" or "very important" to their overall job satisfaction, compared with just 32 percent of Japanese women and 43 percent of Japanese men.[25] As for the likelihood of promotion, 37 percent of Asian women and 38 percent of Asian men under age 35 assess their promotion chances as either good or certain. This contrasts to large gender difference among Japanese respondents, with 55 percent of Japanese men but only 29 percent of Japanese women selecting either good or certain.

Both the interviews and the surveys therefore suggest that although Asian men and women see themselves as falling somewhere in between Japanese men and Japanese women in the stratification hierarchy, Asian women are relatively sanguine about gender barriers, and they see disadvantage as stemming primarily from their status as foreigners rather than from their status as women. In sum, the Asian women, perceived the oft-emphasized foreigner-Japanese divide to have greater relevance to their opportunities than the gender unequal employment environment.

Although Asian women minimize gender barriers and highlight the foreigner-Japanese divide, respondents did allude to other sources of variation in the immigrant experience, namely a possible advantage for Western men compared with Asian men and women. George, who is Latin American of Japanese descent, groused that "Western-looking" foreigners, by virtue of their physical differences from Japanese, are highly visible within his firm. "Without them even trying, the people at the executive level will grab them," he said, enhancing their possibilities for promotion.

Hugo, a white European man, inadvertently reinforced the point. He related at length how, as the "first" and indeed "only" foreigner at his firm, he had been able to make a "unique impact." But it is clear from the survey data that his company had been actively recruiting Chinese and other Asians for more than a decade before he was hired. Liling had worked for the same company for six years compared with his two, albeit on a different team. Even Hugo's *own* team had three more senior employees from Asia. Hugo's pride in his status and accomplishments as the "only" foreigner highlight the same special visibility and attendant advantage that irked George.

Not every Western man was as oblivious to these differences as Hugo. Derek, a white American man, acknowledged that his position in his firm was different than those of his Asian coworkers, noting: "It's so much easier for us. There're all these stereotypes about Asians." Despite this admitted privilege, however, Derek felt that his inability to "do things exactly like a Japanese person" would continue to hold him back. With these perceived limitations, Derek spoke longingly of moving to an American or European firm where he felt his opportunities would be improved.

On the whole, foreign employees' subjective evaluations of their chances in Japanese firms are characterized by uncertainty. Many, but not all, suspect their chances of promotion are lower than those of Japanese men, because of their imperfect acculturation, their nation or region of origin, or both. But these are tentative conjectures, not solid convictions. As for differences among the various immigrant groups, Asian women are relatively unconcerned about the prospect of gender-based exclusion, and they express equal confidence in their promotion opportunities as did Asian men. At the same time, some respondents also indicate that employers see Western men as "special," leading to greater opportunities relative to other immigrants, if not in comparison to Japanese.

Past Research

How do these three interview themes—white-collar foreign workers' disadvantage relative to Japanese men; Asian women's ability to transcend at least some of the gender barriers Japanese women face in elite firms; and Western men's advantage relative to Asians—align with or diverge from previous research in Japan and elsewhere?

In the United States and Canada, immigrant status is a source of disadvantage in white-collar employment. White-collar employers are less likely to call back immigrants who apply for entry-level jobs; are less likely to recommend them for hiring after interviewing them; and offer lower raises after adjusting for performance.[26] Employers justify the lower success rates of immigrants in callbacks and hiring with concerns about language skills and "cultural fit."[27] In other words, considerable evidence shows that this (perceived) lack of acculturation, as well as racial or ethnic bias, holds back white-collar immigrants, even in countries with long histories of immigrant settlement.

Research on immigration in general, and on white-collar foreign workers in particular, is less developed and conclusive in the Japanese context. This literature falls into four broad categories: qualitative studies; quantitative studies using convenience samples, often from opaquely constructed internet panels; more rarely, quantitative studies using a systematic sampling strategy; and studies based on administrative and government data.[28] As a tool for understanding stratification in white-collar contexts, however, the literature is in its infancy. Quantitative studies either use samples that are too heterogenous to illuminate the white-collar experience, lack a closely matched native comparison group, or both. Despite these drawbacks, the literature makes clear that, as in other national contexts, the typical nonnative worker's position in the Japanese labor market is inferior to that of the typical native worker. Specifically, compared with Japanese workers, foreign workers cluster in irregular work, for which pay, benefits, and opportunities for advancement are markedly worse.[29]

Whether this pattern holds true within elite, white-collar firms remains an open question. On one hand, older accounts suggest that foreign white-collar men are more likely to work in irregular positions than Japanese men.[30] In addition, in a 2008 survey, 45 percent of firms with foreign employees reported using foreign regular employees differently than Japanese employees, suggesting informal segregation.[31] Newer studies, however, paint a different picture. They highlight firms' increased appetite for employing foreign men on regular career tracks, and for using them in the same way as Japanese employees.[32] These studies are impressionistic and lack convincing data to back both claims of job-type segregation in the past and those regarding greater integration in the present.

To a greater degree than quantitative studies, qualitative studies focus on the experiences of foreign workers in white-collar jobs. Like the respondents in this study, informants often lament the fact that their imperfect acculturation impedes their upward mobility.[33] Indeed, Japanese employers' top complaint about foreign workers is their imperfect language skills, followed by their incomplete cultural and social adaptation.[34] Although immigrants' unfamiliarity with host country norms, culture, and language is a barrier to their advancement in US firms as well, scholars generally assume that elite Japanese firms demand an even higher degree of acculturation.[35] In sum, like the interviewees, and like the US-focused literature, the Japan scholarship suggests that foreign workers will not be as successful in the workplace as Japanese men.

In contrast to the concordant predictions on immigrant disadvantage, the literature offers divergent hypotheses as to Asian immigrant women's ability to circumvent gender barriers. At the entry level, little evidence indicates that Asian immigrant women in Western countries are disadvantaged in callbacks or job offers relative to Asian men, although Asian immigrants of both genders are disadvantaged relative to native-born whites.[36] Relative to their presence at lower levels of organizational hierarchies, however, Asian women are severely underrepresented in leadership in elite US firms.[37] Both white, native-born women, and immigrant Asian men fare better in leadership representation.[38] Scholars term these penalties associated both with immigrant status and with gender as "double jeopardy" and argue that, as a result, immigrant women (and women of color) fall to the bottom of stratification hierarchies in white-collar contexts.[39]

In the Japanese context, some scholars suggest that Asian women avoid "double jeopardy."[40] Unlike Japanese women, employers speak of Asian women as driven and career-oriented.[41] Qualitative researchers report that Asian women claim to evade some of the gendered norms and expectations that bind their female Japanese colleagues and successfully secure "opportunities not even available to Japanese male employees" thanks to their ability to work cross-culturally.[42] At the same time, quantitative research consistently shows that Asian women working in Japan earn less than Asian men.[43] On balance, the Japan-focused research suggests that, rather than falling at the bottom of the hierarchy as in the United States and other Western countries, Asian immigrant women may have higher attainment than Japanese women, although they may still be disadvantaged compared with immigrant and native men.

Regarding Western immigrant men's relative position, the literature from the United States and other Western countries highlights the importance of acculturation for immigrants' labor market success.[44] In Japan, Westerners tend to be less acculturated than immigrants of other regional backgrounds.[45] The implication of the US literature for the context of elite firms in Japan is thus that, by dint of their lower levels of acculturation, Western immigrant men should fall below Asian immigrant men in the stratification hierarchy.

The literature on contemporary Japan also suggests that outcomes for Western men and Asian men relative to Japanese men will be similar. This was

TABLE 2.4.   Predicted stratification orders by research basis

PLACE IN STRATIFICATION ORDER	PREDICTIONS BY RESEARCH BASIS		
	RESPONDENTS' SUBJECTIVE ASSESSMENTS	RESEARCH ON JAPAN	RESEARCH ON US WHITE-COLLAR FIRMS
1	Japanese men	Japanese men	Japanese men
2	Western men	Asian men/ Western men	Japanese women
3	Asian men/Asian women	Asian women	Asian men
4	Japanese women	Japanese women	Western men
5			Asian women

not always the case. In the early 1990s and before, the small number of organizations that hired Western men screened them more leniently and compensated them more handsomely than they did male Japanese employees.[46] Although other scholars have found that employers and coworkers bestow special attention on Westerners, particularly white, Western men, they also argue that Western men are no longer able to convert their "special" status into higher returns in mainstream, white-collar workplaces.[47] Quantitative research has also failed to demonstrate an advantage for Western men over Asian men, although sample heterogeneity prevents apples-to-apples comparisons between the two groups.[48] As such, the Japanese literature on the contemporary period suggests that Western immigrant men experience a penalty associated with foreign status close to that of Asian men.

Table 2.4 depicts the simplified predictions of the relative employment outcomes for native and immigrant men and women in elite Japanese firms as implied by previous research and the subjective accounts of respondents in the sample.

The respondents in this study recount a stratification order that is similar, but not identical, to that described in the existing literature on white-collar foreign workers in Japan. First, Asian immigrant women in the sample do not perceive a gender disadvantage compared with immigrant men, although some suspect they face penalties as non-Japanese. Second, in contrast to the prevailing consensus in the literature that immigrant men's outcomes do not vary by ethnicity or region of origin, some respondents suspect that Western men are advantaged relative to other immigrants, even as they face hurdles related to imperfect acculturation. The predictions from the US literature diverge still more widely, with immigrants (most notably, immigrant women), landing at the bottom of the stratification order, below native-born women as well as native-born men.

Analytic Plan

To refine our models of gender and ethnic stratification within elite firms and to determine which groups, if any, are reaping the benefits of demographic decline to obtain parity with Japanese men, I next analyze the quantitative data collected through the survey. First, I examine the descriptive characteristics of the groups in question to see how they compare to Japanese men on various metrics. Next, I explore the likelihood of having become a manager among those age 35 and older (the youngest age at which one might typically become a manager) for members of the different groups.[49] Finally, as a more precise measure of how firms value employees of various backgrounds, I model respondents' annual incomes using two-level hierarchical linear models with random effects for firms. Random effects models are appropriate when data have a two-level structure, in this case individuals nested within firms. This modeling strategy adjusts for the fact that workers within a firm are more likely to have similar incomes than individuals from different firms. The models assess how income levels vary by gender and region of origin after adjustments for firms' varying levels of pay and other respondent characteristics, such as age.

I calculate annual income by multiplying respondents' self-reported income from the previous month by twelve and adding the amount of bonus respondents reported for the past twelve-month period. Results of the income analyses appear in millions of yen, which is roughly equivalent to ten thousands of dollars.[50] The analyses include all Japanese men, Japanese women, Asian men, Asian women, and Western men. They exclude Western women and Latin American men, for whom there are too few individuals to draw meaningful conclusions.[51]

The first model adjusts only for the curvilinear association between age and earnings. The model results thus demonstrate whether employees of the various groups earn more or less than same-age Japanese men in the same firms.

In addition to age, the second model also adjusts for human capital—specifically respondents' levels of education, tenure, and number of languages spoken. This adjustment reveals how employers value workers of different backgrounds after accounting for premiums for education, tenure, and language skills.

These models are parsimonious and include relatively few adjustment variables. They do not, for example, adjust for job category, occupation, or supervisory authority, because they are intended to assess the *overall* positioning of foreign and Japanese workers in the sample firms, regardless of cause. In the descriptive tables, however, I include measures of job category (management track, clerical track, and irregular job) to aid in interpreting the modeling results.[52] I examine the relationship between job categories and earnings further in chapter 3.

Stratification by Gender and Region of Origin

Table 2.5 shows the age, tenure, education levels, language skills, and job categories of the relevant groups. Unsurprisingly, most of the outsider groups are younger and have shorter tenures than Japanese men.

For Japanese women and Japanese men, the differences in average age and tenure are relatively small, at only three years. The small size of this gap highlights two features of the changing employment landscape in elite Japanese firms. First, women's average tenures are increasing, both because of generous parental leave that allows women to remain employed after having children, and because an increasing number of women forgo marriage and childrearing. Second, although labor mobility remains low overall, elite firms hire some regular employees at the midcareer level. Among the interviewees, both Emi and Shouichiro were midcareer hires to regular, management-track positions. These higher rates of midcareer hiring are reducing men's tenures, even as women's tenures increase, narrowing gender differences in age and tenure, compared with the past.

TABLE 2.5. Human capital by gender and region of origin

	JAPANESE MEN (N = 312)		JAPANESE WOMEN (N = 129)		ASIAN MEN (N = 33)		ASIAN WOMEN (N = 41)		WESTERN MEN (N = 19)	
	MEAN OR %	SD	MEAN OR %	SD	MEAN OR %	SD	MEAN OR %	SD	MEAN OR %	SD
Age	40.5	8.9	37.6	8.6	33.2	8.0	31.6	6.3	40.6	7.8
Tenure	12.1	9.5	9.4	8.5	6.4	8.2	3.6	4.1	6.5	8.1
Number of past employers	0.7	1.0	1.1	1.2	0.5	0.8	0.6	0.8	2.4	1.5
Education										
Below BA/BS	6.7		15.5		3.0		0.0		0.0	
BA/BS	71.5		72.9		63.6		46.3		42.1	
MA/MS	17.9		10.1		30.3		39.0		31.6	
MBA/JD/PhD	3.8		1.6		3.0		14.6		26.3	
Language skills										
One advanced language	72.4		64.3		12.1		7.3		36.8	
Two advanced languages	25.3		34.1		33.3		48.8		31.6	
Three advanced languages	2.2		1.6		54.5		43.9		31.6	
Job category										
Regular, management track	81.4		58.9		84.8		70.7		73.7	
Regular, clerical track	6.4		17.1		9.1		17.1		5.3	
Irregular	12.2		24.0		6.1		12.2		21.1	

For Asian men and women, age and tenure gaps with Japanese men are larger. This is predominantly attributable to the fact that hiring foreigners was extremely rare in the past. Although four of the firms hired foreign workers before 1990, many only began to hire foreigners after 2000 or even 2010; 70 percent of Asian respondents were hired between 2010 and 2015. Foreign workers' tendency to change jobs at a higher rate than Japanese workers, however, is a perennial complaint by Japanese HR managers. A higher attrition rate may also contribute to foreign workers' shorter tenures; however, because the survey does not capture responses from people who have left the firms, we cannot be certain of its relative impact.

Western men's age and tenure patterns are notably different from any of the other groups. Although their average age is similar to that of Japanese men, their tenures are much shorter, reflecting the fact that they have changed jobs considerably more often than employees of any other background.

Perhaps the most striking feature of the descriptive statistics is the high degree of educational attainment of the sample overall and of foreign workers in particular. In 2010, about 36 percent of all Japanese men ages 25–55 were college graduates.[53] As table 2.5 shows, both Japanese men and women in the sample far exceed this rate of college completion, reflecting the elite character of the sample firms. Even compared with the high levels of attainment among Japanese respondents, the qualifications of the foreign employees shine. About one-third of Asian men, and more than half of Asian women, hold an advanced degree, as do half of Western men.

In terms of language capability, too, the foreign employees' skills are impressive. Whereas most Japanese employees speak only one language—Japanese—to an advanced level, most Asian employees speak two or even three languages well (usually Japanese, the language of their home country, and, in the case of a third language, English). In terms of linguistic capabilities, Western men are somewhat less accomplished than their Asian counterparts. They are more likely than Asian employees (but less likely than Japanese) to be monolingual, in all cases in English, and they are less likely to speak Japanese well.

Foreign workers' high qualifications reflect the barriers they face to enter Japanese firms. Whether because firms hold foreign workers to a higher standard than Japanese, or because foreigners educated abroad must "reset the clock" by obtaining a second degree in Japan to secure access to entry-level job opportunities, the end result is that foreign employees' credentials exceed those of Japanese. Despite Xinyan's claim that "everything is equal," the head-to-head comparisons of foreign workers and Japanese workers' qualifications suggest foreigners have to do more than Japanese to reach the starting line in these elite Japanese firms.

TABLE 2.6. Percentage of respondents age 35 and older who are managers

	MANAGER (%)	TOTAL N
Japanese men	33.0	224
Japanese women	12.4	81
Asian men	44.4	9
Asian women	0.0	11
Western men	53.3	15

Firms, however, are not simply relegating outsiders to peripheral roles. In every outsider group, the majority of respondents hold regular management-track jobs, suggesting considerable access to opportunities for upward mobility. Indeed, consistent with many foreign employees' subjective sense that their opportunities are better than those of Japanese women, foreign employees of all backgrounds are *more* likely than Japanese women to be in management-track jobs.

With the caveat that most foreign workers are relatively young, as was the case with all the interviewees, some have reached 35, the age at which they may first be considered for promotion to management. Table 2.6 compares the share of managers among employees age 35 and older in all five groups. This comparison provides an initial look at whether foreign employees' relatively strong representation in management-track jobs translates to managerial jobs.

Strikingly, table 2.6 shows that Asian and Western men are *more* likely to be managers than even Japanese men. The data also reveal, however, a sharp disjuncture by gender. Compared with a third of Japanese men, only 12 percent of Japanese women are managers, and not a single Asian woman is a manager. These results fly in the face of Asian women's optimistic assessment of their position. Their complete absence from management suggests that, despite Asian women's star-studded credentials and skills, they experience significant disadvantage compared with Japanese men and perhaps with Japanese women as well. In sum, table 2.6 suggests an environment in which gender is a larger barrier to opportunity than nationality or region of origin. To investigate this possibility further, I next model respondents' income, conditional on age (model 1) as well as on their human capital (model 2).

Modeling results appear in table 2.7. Model 1 predicts that a Japanese man at age 38 (the mean age of all employees in the sample) would earn 8.2 million yen, compared with just 5.9 million yen for a Japanese woman of the same age—a gender wage gap of 28 percent or 2.3 million yen. Asian women's estimated wage gap with Japanese men is smaller, but still very large at 1.5 million yen, or 18 percent.

TABLE 2.7.   Regression of human capital on annual earnings

	MODEL 1			MODEL 2		
	BETA		SE	BETA		SE
Region of origin and gender[a]						
Japanese women	−2.3	***	0.3	−2.1	***	0.3
Asian men	−0.6		0.6	−1.3	*	0.6
Asian women	−1.5	**	0.5	−2.4	***	0.6
Western men	2.2	**	0.8	1.8	*	0.8
Age	0.5	***	0.1	0.2		0.1
Age*age	−0.0	*	0.0	0.0		0.0
Tenure				0.3	***	0.1
Tenure*tenure				−0.0	***	0.0
Education[b]						
BA/BS				1.7	***	0.5
MA/MS				1.9	**	0.6
MBA/JD/PhD				2.9	***	0.8
Advanced language skills[c]						
Two advanced languages				1.1	***	0.3
Three or more advanced languages				1.9	***	0.5
Constant	−6.8	**	2.3	−3.2		2.6
Model information						
Observations	525			525		
Number of firms	12			12		

***p <0.001, **p <0.01, *p <0.05
Note: All models are from HLM with random effects for firms.
[a]Reference category is Japanese men.
[b]Reference category is below BA/BS.
[c]Reference category is one advanced language.

Asian men demonstrate a small wage gap with Japanese men that does not reach statistical significance. This suggests either that Asian men achieve parity with Japanese men, or that if they are disadvantaged in wages, the magnitude of that disadvantage is small compared with that for women. Perhaps most surprisingly, however, Western men outearn Japanese men by a predicted 2.2 million yen.

Model 2 further adjusts for human capital. It demonstrates that respondents with BAs enjoy an earnings premium relative to those with education below a bachelor of arts, and specialty professional degrees, such MBAs, JDs, and PhDs carry a higher premium still. Moreover, consistent with prior research that foreign language skills are valuable in the Japanese labor market, respondents who speak two or three advanced languages earn more than monolingual respondents.

The gender gap between Japanese women and Japanese men barely shrinks compared with the previous model. In other words, although we know from the descriptive statistics that Japanese women are younger, have shorter tenures, and are less likely to hold higher degrees than Japanese men, these factors do very little to explain the gender pay gap, which is estimated at 2.1 million yen or 24 percent. Japanese women's somewhat lower human capital does not account for the gender gap among native employees.

Furthermore, once we add these human capital measures, the disadvantage for Asian women grows dramatically to 2.4 million yen, or 28 percent. This means that, once we compare Asian women with Japanese men who have the same skills, they are just as disadvantaged, if not more so, as Japanese women.

After adjustments for human capital, Asian men also demonstrate a wage disadvantage compared with Japanese men. Model 2 predicts that Asian men earn 1.3 million yen (15 percent) less than Japanese men. This too is a sizable wage gap, although it pales beside the larger wage gap that both Asian and Japanese women experience.

Finally, the experience of Western men is markedly different from those of the other outsider groups. Although Western men have greater language skills and higher levels of education than Japanese men, their wage advantage observed in model 1 does not disappear after accounting for these factors in model 2. Compared with Japanese men with the same qualifications, Western men still earn 1.8 million yen (21 percent) more.

Reconciling Subjective and Objective Measures of Stratification

Asian men and women are often uncertain about their prospects in these elite firms, concerned but not sure that their lack of acculturation or their foreign background will impede access to opportunities. These quantitative results shed light into the deeper causes of this uncertainty. As described earlier, Asian men obtain surface-level parity, or near parity, with Japanese men by dint of strong educational backgrounds and strong language skills. The inequalities that are apparent after accounting for skill, however, are likely more difficult for Asian men to detect in casual and observational experience, compared with *outright* inequalities with a typical Japanese, male employee of the same age.

Figure 2.3 illustrates this phenomenon. In this figure, Asian men's unadjusted incomes are plotted as points, and we can compare these to the smoothed age-wage curve for Japanese men. To the extent that Asian men observe inequality, the information that appears on this chart is more visible in everyday life than the adjusted figures calculated through a regression

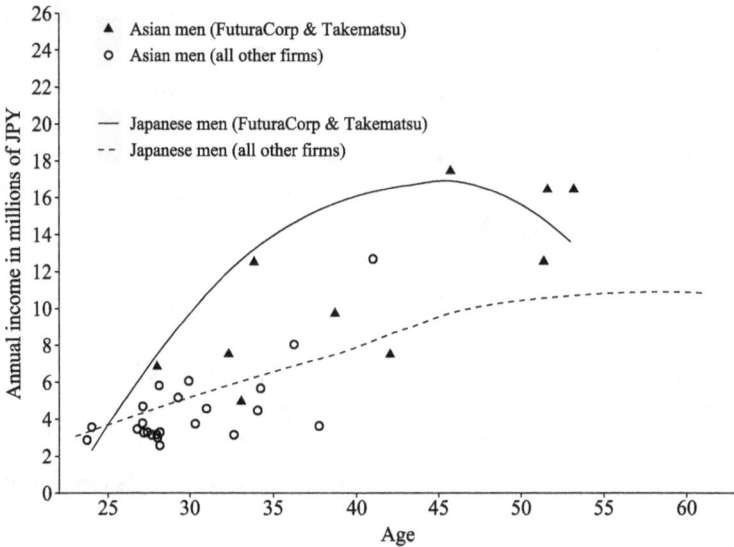

FIGURE 2.3. Annual earnings by age among Asian men, compared with earnings among Japanese men in regular management-track jobs. Calculated from author's survey data.

analysis. If surface-level inequality were present and widespread, the points for Asian men would systematically fall below the smoothed average for Japanese men. Indeed, the majority of Asian men's points do fall below the smoothed average, but the trend is equivocal: Around a third of Asian men's incomes fall above the line.

Because Asian men have higher levels of education, and more valuable language skills than Japanese men, we can see this near equality as a product of overachievement. Because both the overachievement and the inequality are difficult for respondents to observe directly, respondents express their assessments of inequality as uncertainty.

Reconciling Asian women's assessment of their opportunities in these elite firms with the reality of the income data is more complex. Figure 2.4 illustrates Asian women's clear disadvantage in unadjusted earnings, compared with Japanese men. The points for Asian women are obviously clustered below the lines, although a handful of Asian women do exceed the male average in earnings. Although Asian men arguably achieve equality with Japanese men through overachievement, Asian women definitively do not. This sample does not include a single Asian women working as a manager, and adjusting for skills, predicted earnings for these women are even lower than those of

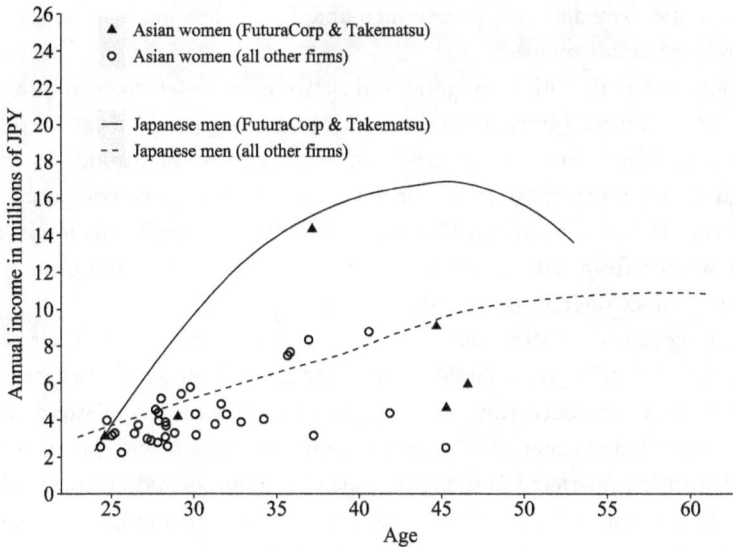

FIGURE 2.4.   Annual earnings by age among Asian women, compared with earnings among Japanese men in regular management-track jobs. Calculated from author's survey data.

Japanese women. Why, then, are Asian women not more pessimistic than Asian men about their opportunities?

As we saw previously, Asian women are highly ambitious and eager for promotion. In elite firms, however, gender inequality is frequently attributed to women's lower motivation for advancement. Where this narrative predominates, Asian women may believe that their ambition will be enough to overcome gender penalties, even though the earnings data show this to be a false hope.

A second reason for Asian women's misplaced optimism may be that, compared with Japanese women and Asian men, Asian women have less access to information that would make inequalities apparent. As discussed in chapter 1, informal socializing after work is a critical source of intelligence on how on-the-ground company practices differ from official policy. Asian women are the least likely of all the groups to go out drinking with coworkers. Among those under age 35, for whom uncertainty about promotion is the highest, 73 percent of the Asian women under age 35 go out with coworkers fewer than three times a month, compared with 55 percent for Japanese men, 58 percent for Japanese men, 57 percent for Asian men, and 60 percent for Japanese women. As a result, Asian women are likely to be less informed than other groups about the opportunities available to Japanese men and, hence, less likely to notice their own relative disadvantage.

Compared with both immigrant and native men, Asian women also have less access to formal information channels. Managers are critical gatekeepers to opportunity and sources of information, but Asian women under 35 report spending only 6 percent of their working time with managers, compared with 10 percent for Asian men and 17 percent for Japanese men.[54] This too isolates Asian women from critical sources of information about pay and promotions and may reduce their awareness of inequality.

Turning last to Western men, we see that, like Asian women, their actual outcomes also differ considerably from their assessments. For Western men, however, this difference runs in the opposite direction. The Western men I interviewed thought that, at best, they were treated equally with Japanese men and that their imperfect knowledge of Japanese language and business culture might hold them back. On average, however, Western men in the sample earn considerably *more* than Japanese men, both overall and compared with those with similar qualifications.

This earnings advantage is not universal. Just as there are Asian women who do better than Japanese men, there are also Western men who do worse, as illustrated in figure 2.5. But overall, many Western men outearn comparable

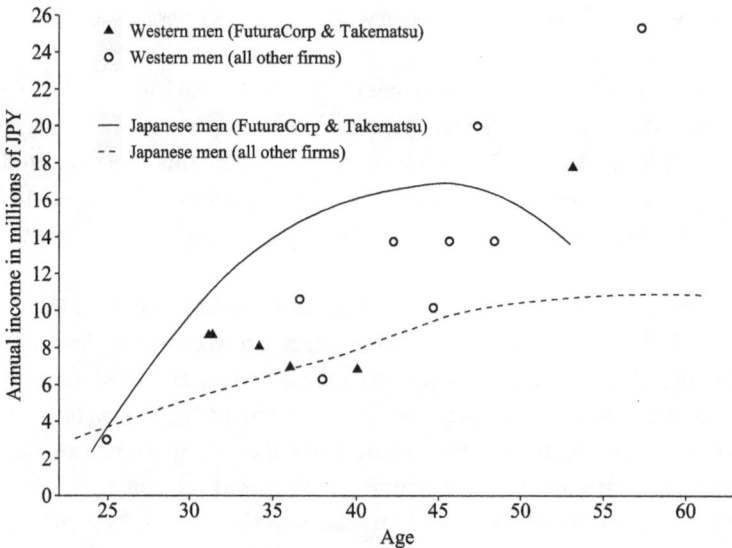

FIGURE 2.5. Annual earnings by age among Western men, compared with earnings among Japanese men in regular management-track jobs. Calculated from author's survey data.

TABLE 2.8.   Income stratification among sample respondents (not adjusted for skill)

PLACE IN STRATIFICATION ORDER	RESPONDENT GROUP
1	Western men
2	Japanese men/Asian men
3	Asian women/Japanese women

Japanese men, and to a considerably degree. The data bear out George's insight that Western-looking immigrant men receive special treatment that gives them access to superior career opportunities, advantaging them not only in relation to Asian immigrant men but also to Japanese men.

This chapter has shed new light on the question of how Asian and Western immigrants, historically almost entirely absent from elite Japanese firms, are being incorporated into the existing stratification order.

On average, native-born Japanese men and immigrant men from Western and Asian countries fare better than native-born Japanese women and Asian women. Table 2.8 depicts a simplified model of this observed stratification order (unadjusted for skill) for comparison with the predictions drawn from the literature in table 2.4.

As this table shows, gender is a far sharper dividing line in the context of elite firms than is region of origin. In many ways, this is a surprising finding. A large popular discourse in Japan paints the country as ethnoracially and culturally homogeneous.[55] Pointing both to this discourse, and to Japan's unusually restrictive policies on refugees or labor migration for low-paid work, some scholars have characterized Japanese society as uniquely xenophobic or racist.[56] The influence of this discourse also infuses literature on white-collar foreign workers in Japan, which emphasizes Japanese firms' impossibly high expectations for foreign workers' acculturation.[57] Moreover, evidence from the United States shows that, even in a country with a much deeper tradition of large-scale immigration, nativity is a more significant source of disadvantage in white-collar workplaces than gender. In sum, there are powerful reasons to belief that foreigners might fall at the bottom of the stratification hierarchy in elite firms.

And yet, foreign background does not consign immigrant workers to marginality. Although the sample firms prefer highly acculturated foreigners, whatever imperfections remain in their acculturation do not, on balance, bar them from upward mobility or equality with same-sex peers once they have obtained employment in this milieu. Indeed, immigrant men from Western countries outearn even Japanese men, and Asian men are at parity or near parity with Japanese men, whereas Asian women are either at or above parity with Japanese women, before accounting for human capital.

This does not mean that immigrant background never carries a penalty. Indeed, net of skills, Asian men earn less than Japanese men, and Asian women perhaps earn less than Japanese women. This implies that Asian men and women must work harder than their Japanese coworkers to achieve the same results. In other words, Asian immigrants do face disadvantage, likely because of some combination of imperfect acculturation and ethnoracial discrimination. The ethnic/nativity penalties are modest enough that Asian men and women do often overcome them through overachievement and superior skills.

Gender-associated penalties are significantly steeper. Unlike ethnic penalties, the majority of Asian and Japanese women do not surmount them through overachievement. This gender gap is particularly striking among Asian women, who are not only highly ambitious but also more likely to hold an advanced degree than members of any other group. In spite of this, and in spite of their strong language skills, their outcomes are at best only modestly better than those of Japanese women, before skill adjustments.[58] Even this is arguable, as not a single Asian women holds a management role. After skill adjustments, Asian women's earnings may even be lower than those of Japanese women.

There has been some debate as to whether Asian women in white-collar jobs experience "double jeopardy" (i.e., penalties associated with both their gender and their foreign origin or ethnicity), which lands them at the bottom of the status hierarchy.[59] These results illustrate the limitations of the double-jeopardy metaphor as a heuristic for Asian women's experiences in elite Japanese firms. Certainly, absent adjustments for skill, Asian women fare about the same, or perhaps modestly better than, Japanese women. As such, they avoid the fate of immigrant women in elite work environments in the United States, who are unambiguously situated at the bottom of the stratification hierarchy. Perhaps in a technical sense, Asian women may thus be said to avoid double jeopardy. At the same time, Japanese women's workplace outcomes are so poor that achieving parity with them is somewhat of a pyrrhic victory. The huge gender penalty that affects both Japanese and Asian women dwarfs any benefits Asian women accrue from high motivation and skills. The defining feature of Asian women's experiences is thus not whether they evade the strictures of double jeopardy, but that they, like their Japanese women coworkers, remain caught in an invisible "gender trap."

Western men's advantage is also largely invisible, at least to Western men. Although some respondents acknowledged that Western men have an advantage *relative to other foreigners*, neither of the Western men I interviewed broached the possibility that they might be at an advantage relative to Japanese men. Among the survey respondents, only one out of eighteen Western men (6 percent) think their pay is high "relative to their contributions," compared with 16 percent of Japanese men; only two Western men (11 percent) think their pay is high "relative to their peers in this firm," compared with 12 percent of Japanese men. Western men's inaccurate assessments of their place in the stratification order is perhaps not too surprising. As scholars have long noted, "privilege is invisible to those who have it."[60] This points to limitations in existing studies that accept Western immigrant men's claims of disadvantage at face value.

These disparate findings on stratification outcomes underscore the importance of an intersectional approach to understanding immigrants' place in the stratification order. All too often, studies lump all foreign workers together, regardless of national origin or gender.[61] Critically, this approach elides the fact that gender is a far sharper dividing line than foreign origin. Like Japanese women, Asian women face an enormous, often invisible, gender penalty. Second, among men, foreign origin is not universally a source of disadvantage. Although Asian men achieve equality or near equality through overachievement, Western men earn more than even their Japanese counterparts, net of qualifications.

These results have important implications for questions about which outsider groups are best positioned to take advantage of labor market opportunities in elite firms associated with population decline. First, and perhaps most important, the data indicate that all outsider groups have greater opportunities to "reach the center" than in the past. For much of the postwar period, elite Japanese firms hired native women exclusively in temporary and peripheral roles, and excluded non-Japanese entirely. In contrast, in an era of declining population, these elite firms are hiring Japanese women and immigrants of both genders. Moreover, firms are not relegating members of outsider groups exclusively to less advantageous jobs, whether as regular workers on the clerical track, or as irregular workers. Compared with the past, outsider groups' path to "the center of the circle" has opened to a remarkable degree. That path is far more open to men than to women, however. Conditional on employment in an elite firm, male groups universally fare better than female groups, regardless of nativity or region of origin. In other words, immigrant men stand to benefit disproportionally from the spoils of population decline within elite firms.

THE LONG SHADOW OF THE SECRETARY

Gender Inequality in a "Gender Progressive" Climate

> **[Our company] continues to support women's advancement, creating a work environment where the strengths of employees with ability and drive can be fully unleashed!**
>
> —Press release of participating firm

> **[We] believe that bringing women's perspective to management is crucial to our organization's growth, and are committed to cultivating women leaders.**
>
> —Website of participating firm

Popular discourse in both Japan and the United States describe motherhood as the Rubicon of a woman's professional life, ushering in harsher discrimination, and placing competing demands on women's time.[1] One survey in Japan found that two in five married women had experienced either "maternity harassment" or "childrearing harassment"—adverse workplace treatment related to pregnancy and motherhood.[2] In both Japan and the United States, motherhood penalties in pay contribute significantly to overall gender inequality in the workplace. It was, therefore, with considerable anxiety that I embarked on my fieldwork. I was pregnant, and almost exactly midway through my stay in Tokyo, I gave birth. Would my colleagues accept me as a "serious" researcher?

As it happened, as a visitor with few fixed obligations to others, it was easy for me to downplay my pregnancy. I disclosed it with studied casualness, letting those around me know that "by the way," I was having a baby. My intermittent absences for prenatal appointments, the weeks when I was absent after giving birth, and the two days a week I stayed home to watch my baby were unobtrusive because I often had research-related reasons to be out of the office. Although I shared enjoyable lunchtime conversations with young mothers on the Canon Institute for Global Studies (CIGS) staff about pregnancy and childrearing, many interlocutors, particularly men and single women, seemed relieved to collude with my pretense that there was nothing to see here.

After giving birth, without the obvious physical reminder of a large pregnant belly, it became easier to elide my parental status in most work situations—with one exception. Because I was nursing, I needed a place to pump breastmilk at the office. My own desk space, a cubicle in a central area with several other junior researchers, was out of the question. The obvious option was the tiny, darkened "relaxation rooms" with lounge chairs on the recreation floor shared by all workers in the building. These had their own downsides, however. At any given time, they stood a fair chance of being fully occupied by napping salary-men. In addition, using them involved trekking to the recreation floor, waiting in line, and filling out a use request, a time-consuming process that I would need to repeat several times a day. At the same time, I suspected that these rooms were far superior to the facilities a typical nursing mother might have access to at work. Full-time employed women usually take long maternity leaves. Returning to the workplace within six months of giving birth is rare in any Japanese employment context; and new mothers who return to work within a year of giving birth are far more likely to be in irregular jobs or to work for small companies.[3] "Don't insist on a private room," advised one website for new mothers who needed to pump at work. "Assure your boss that a corner with a curtain will be sufficient."

It was therefore with some trepidation that I broached the topic of a more convenient place to pump to one of the young mothers on the CIGS office staff. A day or two later, she had worked out a solution. Handing me a key to an unused private office and then showing me the room, she said conspiratorially, "But if there's a conference going on back here, you'll have to use the relaxation rooms. You can't let any of the old men (*ojisan-tachi*) catch you back here!" I did not ask to what extent this arrangement had or lacked official authorization, and my colleague always privately warned me a few days before conferences so that I could avoid the space. Although I often chuckled to myself during the many cumulative hours I spent in that room that, "I guess motherhood is the route to the corner office after all!" the guilty sense of sneaking around never entirely dissipated. These physical and logistical demands of pregnancy, child-birth, nursing, and childcare kept gender at the forefront of my mind, even as I and others sidestepped the topic through strategic silences and evasions.

This silence extended to other areas, such as the gender composition of the CIGS workforce. Typical of many Japanese firms, at CIGS, the administra-tive staff were relatively gender balanced. More prestigious research positions were almost all men, however, and leadership was exclusively male. Like the demands of motherhood, men's overwhelming predominance in leadership in Japanese organizations is also often cited as a central driver of gender inequality in Japanese firms.[4] In day-to-day office life, however, this was accepted as a natural fact of life and met with little comment.

The interpersonal silence I encountered around issues of gender contrasted sharply with the public discourse and stances of the sample firms. These firms are, quite literally, the posterchildren of longstanding government efforts to decrease gender inequality in corporate Japan.[5] Eleven of the twelve firms prominently feature efforts to promote women on their career or corporate social responsibility web pages. Eight firms have received awards for woman- or family-friendly policies from the Ministry of Health, Labor, and Welfare. Executives from these companies regularly participate in government working groups and public panels on women's advancement.

The disjuncture between the firms' public positions as champions of gender equality, on one hand, and the persistence of stark gender inequities in pay and strategic gender silences, on the other, presents a fascinating tension. Why, despite firms' public endorsements of female advancement, government encouragement, and the economic pressures of population decline, do women continue to fall to the bottom of the economic hierarchy? Why are women not able to capture a larger share of the economic pie?

This chapter explores the bases of the gender wage gap. It first introduces the narratives that white-collar employees and academics have crafted to explain gender inequality in elite Japanese firms. Next, it tests whether these explanations—which focus on women's segregation into less remunerative job categories and on differences in male and female work habits—convincingly account for the sizable gender pay gap in the sample firms. To the contrary, it shows that these factors contribute relatively little to the pay gap. This bolsters the argument made in chapter 1 that gender inequality increasingly occurs *among* management-track workers as a result of managers' discretionary decisions. It moreover highlights the need for a deeper investigation of the symbolic boundaries—the beliefs about differences in men's and women's abilities and characteristics—that drive managers' discriminatory decision-making.

Policymakers, business leaders, and academics often locate the organizational source of negative attitudes about women workers in two places: employers' expectation that employees prioritize paid work above all else, and women's underrepresentation in management. Because women shoulder a larger share of household labor than men, the thinking goes, managers suspect women of lacking the commitment expected of an "ideal worker." Further, because few women hold managerial positions, managers doubt women's capacity for leadership. These explanations imply a two-part strategy for reducing gender bias. If employers curtail their expectation of long work hours for all employees, it no longer follows that (most) men will better fit employers' ideal worker model than (most) women. And if more women rise to the upper echelons of management, this will undercut assumptions that women lack leadership skills.[6] I argue, however, that this diagnosis of the problem and its implied solutions are, at best, incomplete. For one, in its emphasis on women's underrepresentation at the top of organizational hierarchies, this narrative overlooks women's overrepresentation in undervalued roles as a potential driver of bias. More fundamentally, however, these arguments about organizational sources of gender bias have relatively little empirical support. They are a product of "hope and logic" rather than of rigorous social scientific evidence.[7]

This chapter exploits variation across the twelve firms in the sample in work hours, women's representation in management jobs, and women's representation in subordinate jobs to test the implications of these accounts of the organizational sources of gender bias and gender inequality. If long work hours, low female managerial representation, or female overrepresentation in subordinate jobs affects gender attitudes and treatment of women, we would expect greater gender equality in firms in which work hours are shorter, women hold higher shares of managerial jobs, and support jobs are male dominated or gender balanced.

I find strong support only for the hypothesis that female overrepresentation in low-status roles matters for attitudes and treatment. Women in firms in which all or almost all assistants are women experience a gender gap almost three times as large as in firms in which they are not all or almost all assistants, even if these women hold management-track positions. In addition, women in these firms are far less likely than men to feel that their managers consistently value their contributions.

These findings imply that conventional explanations for the gender pay gap—both those emphasizing individual-level factors, such as initial job category and work habits, and those focused on organizational factors, such women's absence from management—cannot account for the persistence of gender inequality in elite firms. The results suggest that organizational factors, particularly symbolic boundaries between men and women, endure not because of women's absence from the top of organizations, but because of their place as "the face" of undervalued, low-status support roles. Because firms' interventions have focused nearly exclusively at the top, both gender bias and gender inequality can persist strongly even in progressive firms.

Mismatches Between Firms' Expectations and Women's Work Patterns

The gap between median male and female earnings among full-time workers in Japan is 22 percent, almost double the Organization for Economic Co-operation and Development (OECD) average of 11.7 percent.[8] Notoriously, the

World Economic Forum ranks Japan 120 out of 156 countries in its Global Gender Gap Index, more similar to Saudi Arabia and Yemen than to wealthy postindustrial societies, such as the United States or Germany.[9] Although the international media and even Japan's own government cite these figures as unacceptable, this longstanding issue has been deeply resistant to change.[10] As we have seen in earlier chapters, the gender gap in the context of the study firms is even larger than in the economy more broadly.

Scholarship on the gender pay gap in white-collar work environments in Japan has described it largely as the result of two related phenomena: (1) the mismatch between firms' expectations for "ideal workers" and women's labor market behaviors over the life course; and (2) the resulting overrepresentation of women in irregular or clerical-track jobs.[11] The general stance of the literature is that mismatches between expectations and women's labor market choices were more severe during the high-growth era but persist strongly today.

During the high-growth era, it was all but impossible for women to fulfill the ideal of long-term commitment to a single employer. Employers argued that training and promoting women was inefficient, because women would inevitably quit their jobs to focus on domestic duties.[12] As companies could and did *require* women to resign upon marriage or pregnancy, this argument was a self-fulfilling prophecy: Regardless of individual preference, most women were de facto limited-term workers, and they almost never were able to accrue the training or seniority necessary to advance. These practices manifested in the dramatic "M-curve" in female labor force participation rates. As shown in figure 3.1, labor force participation dropped off sharply among women in their late twenties and early thirties, as they left jobs to marry and have children, and rose moderately among older women, who reentered the labor force, usually in smaller firms and or part-time jobs, as their children grew older.[13]

Beginning in the mid-1980s and continuing to the present day, legal reforms have made these practices impossible to sustain. Contemporary employment law forbids companies to treat women disadvantageously because of marital or parental status; it also mandates paid parental leave.[14] Furthermore, as the working-age population shrinks, firms face considerable economic pressure to use women's talents more fully. As a result of the intertwined forces of legal change and population decline, the incompatibility between long-term employment, firms' treatment of women, and women's labor market supply has moderated. Women now can and do remain in the labor force throughout their working years. As of 2020, the notorious M-curve had almost disappeared. This reflects both a rise in the number of women who do not have children as well as an increase in mothers' likelihood of remaining in the workforce.

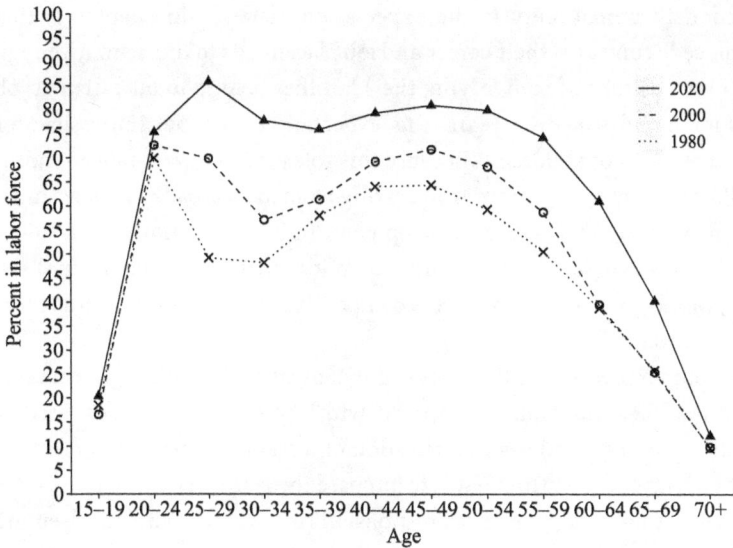

FIGURE 3.1. Women's labor force participation rates by age, 1980–2020. Data from Gender Equality Bureau, "Josei no nenrei kaikyuu betsu roudouryokuritsu no suii" [Changes in female labor force participation rate by age-group].

Not only are women able to remain with the same employer long term but also, even if they do switch jobs, the taboo against job change is not as strong as it was in the past, as we saw in chapter 1. Thus, in theory at least, a major facet of the incompatibility between firms' expectations for (ideal) workers and women's working patterns no longer stands in the way of gender equality.

At the same time, scholars argue that many other female work patterns run counter to firms' ideal worker model. The first of these is new mothers' use of legal parental leave entitlements. This entitlement grants one or both parents paid leave until the baby's first birthday, or second birthday if daycare is not available. The great majority of mothers, however, take leaves of at least twelve months, whereas most fathers either do not take leave or take only a few days.[15] Compared with the pregnancy bars of the past, this system is advantageous to women. Women do not have to seek new employment after childbirth, and they do not lose the benefits of their seniority. Nonetheless, firms and coworkers see (erroneously, as anyone who has cared for a newborn knows) a long parental leave as a "career blank"—a period during which the leave taker is not accumulating new skills.[16] This causes mothers to fall behind men and childless women in the race for promotion and, scholars argue, contributes to the persistence of the gender wage gap.[17]

A second incompatibility is the expectation, detailed in chapter 1, that employees cede control of their career and job placements to the firm. Although there is a long history of men leaving their families behind to take distant job postings for months or even years, this expectation is all but impossible for primary caretakers of children.[18] Because this role almost always falls to mothers, companies may refrain from transferring women as broadly as they transfer men, hampering their career development. In addition, mothers are more likely to turn down such posts if offered. Without these developmental job transfers, women with children are less competitive for promotion, and as such, receive lower wages.[19]

Work hours represent the third area of incompatibility. Although demands for face time have moderated compared with the high-growth era, leaving "early" (i.e., by 5 or 6 p.m.) is still a violation of workplace norms. But one parent must pick up children from daycare, prepare their dinner, and so on. As it is mothers who usually take on these responsibilities, women with children are less likely to receive paid overtime, and, as with parental leave, over the course of their careers, they accumulate less experience and are less competitive for lucrative promotions.[20]

Finally, childcare responsibilities also mean that mothers are less available to socialize and drink with coworkers after the end of the workday. This was the case among my coworkers at CIGS. When there was an "official" party of some kind, some mothers would plan childcare in advance so they could participate, but some did not have spouses or parents who could pick up their children. Mothers could never participate in spur-of-the-moment plans to grab drinks or dinner after work. Unlike overtime work in the office, there is no direct link between pay and after-hours socializing. This time is off the books. As an important, and longstanding, element of business practices, after-hours socializing is key to building one's network and tacit knowledge of the workplace, and women's relative lower rates of participation thus inhibit gender equality in pay and promotion.[21]

Although most of these areas of incompatibility apply largely to mothers, scholars argue they affect childless and unmarried women as well.[22] Childless women may turn down developmental job transfers and limit work hours, in anticipation of inevitably falling off the fast track when they have children. Further, even the most ambitious single women may limit after-hours socializing to avoid sexual harassment or unpleasant rumors.[23] In sum, scholars argue, women pragmatically "lean out" and reduce the time and effort at work from early in their careers.[24] Human resources (HR) managers generally agree, giving "women don't want to be promoted" as one of their most common answers to why women's share of management is low.[25]

Tracking and Job Segregation

These explanations for the gender gap focus predominantly on the behaviors of women and their divergence from company expectations and male work habits. But scholars also highlight the behavior of firms in channeling women into less lucrative tracks from the point of hire. The first of these channels is irregular work, which often carries no long-term job security, few benefits, and low pay with little wage growth.[26] In the broader labor market, 68 percent of irregular workers are women.[27]

The second channeling mechanism is the tracking system many large firms implemented after the passage of the first Equal Employment Opportunity Law (EEOL) in 1985. The EEOL discouraged firms' historical practice of hiring women exclusively for "women's' jobs" (i.e., as assistants and receptionists). Following the ban on explicitly sex-segregated hiring, many firms established ostensibly gender-neutral "managerial" and "clerical" tracks. Like "women's track" employees of the past, however, clerical-track employees engage primarily in support work and are ineligible for promotion to management.[28] Job placements under this new system are not as sex segregated as those of the high-growth era, and not all firms use the tracking system. Among firms that do, however, the association between track and gender is strong. Management-track jobs are male dominated in more than 80 percent of firms, and the clerical track is female dominated in 64 percent of firms.[29] Employers justify this difference as an inevitable result of women's preferences and labor market supply patterns. Because women want to "lean out," employers claim, it makes sense to place them in positions for which expectations for work hours and developmental job transfers are lower; this not only saves on training costs but also meets women's needs and (lower) aspirations.[30] At the same time, this pattern indisputably contributes to gender wage inequality. A survey of 394 firms found, for example, that at workers' peak earning year (age 55), the average monthly salary of a clerical-track employee with a college degree was only 55 percent of that of a management-track employee with identical education.[31]

Faith in "Rational" Explanations for the Gender Gap

In general, my respondents shared the view that gender inequality is the inevitable result of gender differences in behavior and performance. For example, considering gender inequality in her firm, Emi argued:

> In terms of the system, there's no difference [in how men and women are treated]. Like, this position has to go to a man . . . or, this job has to

go to a woman. As far as the system goes, it's completely open. That said, there's the question of whether you meet certain performance expectations. And that's up to the individual. In terms of performance, men are more likely to have that drive. There are a lot more women who just say, "I'm fine in my current position." So, in the end, it's not really about the system, it's about individual attitudes [toward work].

Xinyan agreed: "The company doesn't care whether you are a man or a woman, whether you are foreign or Japanese. They treat you exactly the same. Of course, some differences might emerge at the promotion stage, like, if you want to have a child, or whether or not you've got stamina. But the company's system is fair."

Other research indicates that this is the majority view among employees. In a separate project conducted in 2021, I resurveyed more than one thousand employees at Henderson. Because promotion is the largest determinant of wages, I asked employees if they think that men and women are treated equally in promotion decisions.[32] Some 70 percent report either that treatment is fair or that women are advantaged, either because Henderson's policy is to proactively increase women's share of management, or because employees do not feel women are *sufficiently penalized* for shorter work hours and long parental leaves. In sum, in this elite context, most employees rationalize and naturalize gender inequality.

At the same time, a sizable minority does perceive injustice in firms' treatment of women. As quoted in the previous chapter, Chaoxiang commented on a senior, unmarried female colleague who had been working at the firm for twenty years and had never received a promotion. Unlike Xinyan and Emi, Chaoxiang felt "saddened" by this, feeling the firm had unfairly passed her over, despite her tremendous sacrifices to the firm. Chaoxiang, however, was the only interviewee to express concerns about unfairness. Xinyan's and Emi's view—that whatever the differences, they occurred because of men's and women's choices and behaviors—are far more common.

Despite the broad consensus among academics, and the majority opinion among employees, direct evidence for the view that "rational" work habits and initial job category account for the gender gap is limited. First, the explanation of gender inequality focused on gender differences in work habits indicates that women "lean out" either because of family responsibilities or in anticipation of having such responsibilities. This dismisses the growing number of women who remain single and focus on their careers.[33] Although on average, women work shorter hours and take longer parental leaves than men, in individual-level studies of earnings, information about most of the relevant work habits, such as use of parental leave or participation in after-hours socializing, is not usually available.[34] This makes it difficult to assess claims that men and women vary as extremely in their work habits within the same workplaces, and whether individual-level differences in habits correspond to individual-level differences in earnings.

The evidential lacuna also extends to the issue of initial job category. Individual-level data on earnings collected from national representative samples, such as the Basic Survey on Wage Structure, the General Social Survey, and the Social Stratification and Social Mobility Survey, do not include information on track status. Other prominent studies of earnings with linked employer-employee data also fail to include track status as a variable.[35] The linked employer-employee studies amply document that women are promoted more slowly than men within the same firms. Although authors attribute this to track status, this hypothesis remains speculative, as track status is not recorded.

In sum, the narrative about work habits and track status is consistent with aggregate patterns of gender inequality, work habits, and job segregation. The strength of employees' and academics' belief in this narrative, however, does not reflect a deep and conclusive body of evidence at the individual level.

Interrogating the Consensus View

In my study, I had a unique opportunity to interrogate the consensus view, both because the survey collected information on work hours, and because, more uncommonly, it collected data on frequency of after-hours socializing, employees' motivations for advancement, track status, and job rotation history. The data do not include information on parental leaves. However, among regular employees, almost all women who give birth and who do not drop out of the work force take leaves of a year or longer, and we can assume that this is true of most mothers in the sample. [36]

The analyses break down the sample by gender, but not region of origin or immigrant status, because, as discussed in chapter 2, both Asian and Japanese women experience significant disadvantage relative to men.

As shown in table 3.1, gender differences in job category and work habits follow expected patterns. At the same time, however, these gender differences are not as prominent as the consensus narrative would suggest.

First, contrary to the popular image that most women in white-collar firms are clerical-track or irregular employees, the majority of women in this sample are in management-track jobs.[37] Women are overrepresented among irregular workers and among regular workers on the clerical track, but not exceedingly so.

TABLE 3.1. Job and family characteristics by gender

	MEN (N = 357)		WOMEN (N = 173)	
	MEAN OR %	SD	MEAN OR %	SD
Job category				
Management track	80.7		62.4	
Clerical track	7.0		16.8	
Irregular job	12.3		20.8	
Job transfer outside the Kanto area	22.1		10.4	
Work hours	43.8	8.6	42.2	8.4
After-hours socializing (times per month)	2.0	1.7	1.6	1.6
Has children	54.3		16.8	
Compensation critically important	18.8		9.8	
Promotion opportunities critically important	10.1		6.4	

Job transfer histories also follow the expected gendered pattern, but once again, the gender differences are not extreme. Respondents reported up to five most recent job postings, including the city and country of each posting. Sizable majorities of both men and women reported no job postings outside the Kanto region (Tokyo and its surrounding prefectures), although the share of men who had distant transfers, at 22 percent, is about double that of women at 10 percent.[38]

In terms of work hours and after-hours socializing, women's habits are only minorly different from those of men. Women work just 1.6 hours less than men on a weekly basis, and socialize only slightly less than men do. Third, the great majority of women in the sample do not have children.

Finally, I identified gender gaps in ambition, as assessed by the share of respondents who say that compensation or promotion opportunities are "critically important" to their job satisfaction. Men are about twice as likely as women to select both of these, but the great majority of *both* men and women are not hyperfocused on either compensation or promotion opportunities.

Of course, these measures have limitations as well. They capture work habits at only one point in time, and even in this snapshot, these metrics may miss elements of work habits.[39] Nonetheless, they cast doubt on the consensus narrative. If most women are "leaning out," either because of low aspirations or household responsibilities, women's behaviors would differ far more from men's.

A second way to assess the narrative is through regressions of earnings, using hierarchical linear models (HLM) with random effects to adjust for firms' differing levels of pay. As discussed previously, aggregate data seemingly support the narrative that job category and work habits explain the gender gap. But these data offer a rare opportunity to investigate the relationship between individual-level behaviors and pay. If, in modeling the relationship between work habits and job categories and earnings, the estimated gender gap narrows considerably, this supports the consensus narrative. If it does not, this illustrates that gender inequality persists sharply even for women who adopt male work habits and work in management-track jobs.

All the models adjust for various individual-level factors known to influence earnings, including age, tenure, and education, as well as random effects for firms. Model 2 adds work hours, female parental status, and frequency of socializing to estimate the gender gap after taking work habits into account; model 3 adds job category and whether the employee has experienced a distant job posting. Because we are interested in the full magnitude of women's disadvantage after accounting for work habits and job category, and promotion is one of the main ways firms increase employee salaries, the models do not adjust for level of supervisory authority.[40] Hence, the coefficients for women can be interpreted as the magnitude of female disadvantage arising in both the promotion and pay setting stages of employment.[41] Model results appear in table 3.2.

Model 1 estimates the gender pay gap at 1.9 million yen, or 24.5 percent. Model 2 estimates the gender pay gap separately for women with children and women without, as well as adjusting for work habits. The gender pay gap is 1.6 million yen (or 21.3 percent) for women without children, and 1.8 million yen for mothers (23.4 percent). As shown in table 3.1, men and women's work habits are, on balance, quite similar. What slight differences exist do little to explain, at the individual level, why women's wages are so much lower than men's.

Model 3, which includes job category and transfer history, as well as work habits, produces similar results. The wage gap for women without children is 1.4 million yen (18.8 percent) and 1.7 million yen (22.4 percent) for those with children. In sum, huge gender gaps persist. Contrary to the popular narrative, women's and men's different work habits, companies' track placement of workers, and men's greater propensity to accept (or be offered) distant job transfers do not explain the large gender gap in pay.

Although these models cannot account for all individual-level differences in work attitudes and behaviors that influence how companies pay and promote their employees, they do indicate that gender inequality in this context occurs primarily within, rather than between, employment tracks. Moreover, in demonstrating persistently high levels of gender inequality between women without children and men, after adjustments for work habits, the results also imply that discretionary treatment of women and men by the firm is a far more important determinant of gender inequality at these elite firms than is women's failure to adhere to ideal worker norms.

TABLE 3.2.   Regression of work habits and job category on annual earnings

	MODEL 1			MODEL 2			MODEL 3		
	BETA		SE	BETA		SE	BETA			SE
Women	−1.9	***	0.3							
Parental status[a]										
Women without kids				−1.6	***	0.3	−1.4	***		0.3
Women with kids				−1.8	**	0.6	−1.7	**		0.6
Age	0.2		0.1	0.2		0.1	0.2			0.1
Age*age	0.0		0.0	0.0		0.0	0.0			0.0
Tenure	0.2	***	0.1	0.3	***	0.1	0.2	***		0.1
Tenure*tenure	0.0	***	0.0	0.0	***	0.0	0.0	***		0.0
Education[b]										
BA/BS	1.9	***	0.5	1.9	***	0.5	1.3	**		0.5
MA/MS	2.2	***	0.6	2.1	***	0.6	1.5	**		0.6
MBA/JD/PHD	3.7	***	0.7	3.7	***	0.7	3.0	***		0.7
Weekly work hours				0.0	*	0.0	0.0	*		0.0
After-hours socializing (monthly)				0.3	***	0.1	0.3	***		0.1
Job category[c]										
Regular, clerical track							−1.6	***		0.4
Irregular							−0.6			0.4
Any postings outside Kanto region							0.5			0.4
Constant	−3.2		2.6	−6.9	**	2.7	−5.4	*	***	2.
Model Information										
Observations	530			530			530			
Number of firms	12			12			12			

*** *p* <0.001, ** *p* <0.01, * *p* <0.05
Note: All models are from hierarchical linear modeling (HLM) with random effects for firms.
[a]Reference category is men, regardless of parental status.
[b]Reference category is below BA/BS.
[c]Reference category is regular, management-track jobs.

In other words, the "ideal worker" logic of gender inequality has become what Irene Padavic calls a "hegemonic narrative." Padavic and coauthors define a hegemonic narrative as "a pervasive, status-quo-preserving story that prevails despite countervailing evidence."[42] As described in chapter 1, most men in the sample do not work extremely long hours—just 20 percent work fifty hours or more—but the share of women who work fifty hours or more, 15 percent, is only slightly less. Moreover, the great majority of women in the sample do not have children. Like men with part-time or stay-at-home spouses, these women also have limited household responsibilities to draw them away from work.

The consensus narrative in academic writing and among the employees elides these significant *similarities* between women and men's work habits within elite firms, and, in doing so, exaggerates the importance of individual work habits in driving the gender pay gap.

The limited explanatory power of the conventional explanation for gender inequality points to the importance of managers' discretionary decisions in shaping gender inequality. These include, as we saw in chapter 1, decisions about how to allocate work, how to evaluate subordinates' performance, and ultimately, whether or not to support an employee's promotion.

Discretionary Decisions and Women's Disadvantage

In the context of long-term career building in elite firms, supervisors' discretionary decisions about work assignments have particularly weighty consequences for workers' careers. Although HR posts workers to particular units or job rotations, within units, it is the manager who allocates projects and tasks. Evaluation, job rotation, and promotion all depend on workers' achievements; but workers' achievements occur within the confines of the projects and tasks their supervisors assign. Receiving an important or valued task assignment is, therefore, the foundation of an upwardly mobile career.

Although it has received relatively little attention in the literature compared with work habits or job category, a few scholars have noted that women lose out in work assignments. Hiroki Sato, for example, observes that managers do not "train and nurture" their female staff as assiduously as their male staff.[43] Ulrike Schaede, too, remarks that managerial-track women tend to get less important assignments than men.[44]

Interviewees in my study did not mention differential task assignments, arguably because most of them inaccurately attribute gender inequality to men's and women's work habits. The follow-up study at Henderson, however, backs up the intuition that work assignments may hold a key to gender inequality in an environment in which more women work on the management track. In open-ended responses about whether and how the company treats men and women differently, Henderson employees repeatedly touched on differential task or project assignments. A 34-year-old women still working at the entry level pointed out, "Women don't get to act as lead on major accounts." Several respondents mentioned "hot jobs," referring to projects with high visibility and potential for accomplishment, and lamented that managers were unlikely to seat women in these plum posts.

These reports of unequal task assignment do not indicate that men and women are engaged in fundamentally different occupations. Indeed, although management-track men in the sample are more likely to report "sales" as their main job function than are management-track women, other gender differences in management-track respondents' primary work content are minimal.[45] Rather, unequal task assignment occurs at a much more fine-grained level; for example, managers might assign women working in financial analysis more routine administrative tasks than their male counterparts; they might charge women with analysis of sectors seen as less promising; they might choose men over women to serve as project leads, and so on.

Gender inequities in task or project assignment, and gender differences in job rotations or unit placements are likely to mutually reinforce each other. Even though HR departments are increasingly willing to transfer women to far-flung locations, because managers assign women lower-value tasks, women are less likely establish track records that recommend them to HR for promising, developmental job rotations. Moreover, even after women's work accomplishments are taken into account, it is doubtful that HR decisions about rotations are entirely free of gender bias. Furthermore, even when HR posts women to units that offer a fast track to promotion, managers are still less likely to assign women less highly valued tasks. A women manager in her forties succinctly summarized these concerns: "It's not that men are advantaged in promotions. It's that the opportunities they're given prior to the promotion stage are greater."

In combination with the limited explanatory power of the consensus model of gender inequality, these comments suggest that gender differences in work assignments *within job tracks* are an increasingly important, and often overlooked, source of gender inequality in elite firms. Because managers and HR officials make decisions about work and unit assignments on a discretionary basis, this suggests the need for deeper investigation of the beliefs and biases—what Michèle Lamont calls symbolic boundaries—that influence these discretionary decisions, and the origins of these beliefs.[46]

Biases Against Women Employees

The problem of workplace gender bias has drawn increasing attention from policymakers in recent years. Although the government once embraced and promoted a "separate spheres" gender ideology as a tool for economic growth,[47] in an era of population aging and decline, the government now identifies "rigid gender roles" as a barrier to women's labor force participation and to women's ability to support themselves financially over longer and longer lifespans. As of

2022, policy documents therefore assert the need to "weaken" or even "dispel" gender stereotypes.[48]

As part of the initiative to loosen rigid gender roles, the government conducted a survey in 2021, asking more than ten thousand respondents about encounters with gender stereotypes in their everyday lives, and whether they agree with the stereotypes.[49]

The findings of the government survey mirror the large body of qualitative and anecdotal evidence about gender stereotypes in the workplace. We can divide these into two general categories. First, a constellation of related beliefs holds that women should raise children and men should concentrate on paid work. Approximately half of respondents endorsed the statement that men should financially support their families. About a third endorsed the statement that mothers should not do "important" work while their children are young.

The second set of beliefs maintains that, independent of parental status, men's skills and personalities suit them for "high-value" work, while women's skills and personalities befit them better for "routine" work.[50] Between a third and a quarter of women report encountering stereotypical beliefs that men are more suited for leadership, that men are better negotiators, that women are more emotional, or that assistant-type work should be done by women. Relatively few respondents (a quarter or less), however, endorse these views.

The Organizational Origins of Stereotypes

Social scientists describe stereotypes like these as "socially constructed." This means that the beliefs do not reflect fundamental, unchanging characteristics of the groups in question. Rather, such stereotypes simplify and justify patterns of social organization *within a given* institutional and cultural context.[51] For example, as shown in figure 3.1, in the 1980s a large share of women dropped out of the labor market during their childrearing years. While this might naively be ascribed to women's "natural" desire to care for their young children, it is also a product of particular institutional circumstances, including firms' refusal to retain women employees after marriage, and a dearth of childcare providers. Attributing the status quo to essentialized, inherent characteristics of women (and men) obscures its institutional origins, which are the product of human choice, exercise of power, and historical coincidence.

In the case of gender stereotypes in Japanese workplaces, scholars and the government have primarily pinned the blame on two organizational features: long work hours (and associated ideal worker norms), and women's absence from management.[52]

The link between long work hours and gender stereotypes is intuitive. In cases in which managers equate excellence with long work hours and round-the-clock availability, it seems logical that mothers' "short" work hours disqualify them from important or difficult work.[53] If managers could define excellence in other ways, the argument goes, the belief that it is inappropriate or inefficient to assign mothers (or potential mothers) high-value tasks might fade.

Faith in this organizational mechanism for attitudinal change is implicit in the 2018 Work-Style Reform legislation. Through this legislation, the government promises to dissipate the "pervasive, commonsense understanding that long work hours are a badge of pride."[54] In doing so, the law explicitly aims to diversify the routes toward upward mobility in organizations and implicitly attempts to undercut the logic justifying mothers' and women's exclusion from high-value work.

The link between women's managerial representation and gender stereotypes originates in the research of Western management scholar Rosabeth Moss Kanter. Kanter has noted that, in a firm that had very few women managers, these women were isolated and faced intense, critical scrutiny. Kanter attributes these negative attitudes to women's "token" status in management and argues that they would fade if women's managerial representation grew beyond 15 percent. In later decades, status construction theorists generalized Kanter's argument, highlighting how we tend to attribute greater status and ability in socially valued tasks to members of groups who already have more power and resources.[55] Many scholars, drawing on Kanter's study and status construction theory, have since argued that women's representation in management is a key determinant of how all women are perceived in the workplace and have advocated for women's managerial advancement as a tool for reducing stereotypes and achieving gender equality.[56] Kumiko Nemoto has applied this logic specifically to large Japanese firms, to argue that, if women held a higher share of managerial jobs, this would demonstrate women's true capabilities and reduce negative stereotypes.[57]

This logic infuses many of the Japanese government's signature efforts to address gender inequality. Although bringing more women into management is now primarily associated with Shinzo Abe, it was the Koizumi government that, in 2003, established the goal of filling 30 percent of managerial roles in private firms with women by 2020.[58] Abe's more famous "womenomics" proposals were largely a continuation and, to a lesser extent, an expansion of the gender policies of past administrations, built on recommendations issued by major business groups and government bodies from the 1990s. These included a recommitment to the 30 percent target for female managerial representation, which later was extended to "as soon as possible before 2030").[59] Recommendations also included corporate governance reform that encourages companies to bring on at least one female board member and requests that large companies establish "positive action plans" to promote female career advancement and publish the share of women in management on a searchable government website.[60]

During the period of my research in 2014 and 2015, these initiatives were just coming into effect. Because the proposals drew so heavily from business groups' recommendations, they were not novel in the corporate world. Half of the sample firms had established "positive action" plans for women's employment before 2014, when the practice received the imprimatur of law, and some had plans dating as far back as the 1990s and early 2000s.

At Pixisa, for example, the HR director spearheaded an effort to place women in management beginning in 2013. With the support of upper-level management, he asked each unit director to recommend at least one woman for promotion to team lead. These women participated in management training and were duly promoted. The process was not easy. Not only did a few of the (male) managers initially decline to select female candidates, but some of the women candidates protested that they were not interested in managerial responsibility. The HR director boasted that he browbeat the managers into submission, and through training, the women candidates became more confident and excited about managerial work. He felt that, with the example of these women, male managerial resistance would fade.

Like other initiatives to increase female managerial representation, the Pixisa case relies explicitly and implicitly on the logic that getting women into managerial positions will expand social consciousness about women's motivations and capabilities.[61] Indeed, absent this logic, top-down initiatives to increase women's managerial authority make little sense as a broader tool to mitigate gender inequality. Managerial positions represent less than 2 percent of all jobs in the Japanese economy.[62] Thus, even if Japan achieved complete gender parity in management, only a tiny number of women would reap the direct benefits. Efforts to achieve gender equality by placing women in management thus presuppose that managerial women transform the work environment for all women, at least in part by subverting and transforming gender stereotypes.

Although beliefs about long work hours and women's absence in management are logical, their social scientific foundation is not ironclad. Scholarship in both the United States and Japan often associates negative beliefs about women's motivation and potential with overwork culture,[63] yet no research assesses whether attitudes toward women are, in fact, more positive in organizational environments in which long work hours are not the norm. Similarly, vanishingly few studies investigate the relationship between women's representation in management and attitudes toward women. Some studies in this field examine only organizations in which management is male-dominated and thus can only speculate that attitudes toward women would be more positive if more female managers were present.[64] Many studies explore the relationship between female managerial representation and downstream outcomes, such as the gender pay gap or gender desegregation in nonmanagerial jobs. These studies do not consistently find positive effects of women's managerial representation, and where the results are positive, the size of the impact is very small.[65] Only one study has explored the relationship between women's share of management and attitudes directly.[66] Although it found a positive relationship, it is a shaky foundation for the widespread faith in the power of women executives to transform gender attitudes. Thus, as Leonard Schoppa has detailed in regard to fertility policy, government efforts to reduce gender bias and by extension gender inequality rely more on "hope and logic" than on evidence.[67]

The heavy focus on the long work hour culture, and on women's representation in management, also elides other potentially important organizational determinants of attitudes toward women in the workplace. In Kanter's groundbreaking study, she notes that many of the negative stereotypes about women, such as emotionalism, irrationality, and inability to think in broad, strategic terms, were not so much stereotypes *of women* as they were stereotypes *of secretaries* and of behaviors typical of people in dead-end, monotonous jobs. Ogasawara, in her examination of a similar organization in which all the assistants were women, noted that stereotypes focused on women's pettiness and laziness. Like Kanter, Ogasawara describes these as natural responses to unfulfilling jobs with no advancement potion.[68] Status construction theory, too, points out that stereotypical beliefs emerge and are reinforced in interaction. Inevitably, there are many more people at the bottom of the organizational hierarchy than at the top. This means that most employees inevitably interact more frequently with assistants and secretaries than with senior managers. In combination, these insights suggest that women's overrepresentation in low-level subordinate positions may do as much, if not more, to shape views of women in the workplace as women's presence or absence at the top.

As discussed, managers' tendency to assign women less responsible work, even within the management track, is an important manifestation of bias. All of these organizational features—including long work hours and the related concern that women will be unable to meet them; women's absence in management and the associated belief that women are not capable of high-level leadership; women's overrepresentation in low-status assistant or temporary jobs and the related assumption that women are best suited to such support work—potentially induce managers to assign women less responsible tasks or otherwise treat them

unfairly. Although past research identifies these potential organizational mechanisms as driving bias and reinforcing gender inequality, it does not explore the
relative importance of these different factors.

In this arena, the current study, in its inclusion of twelve different firms,
offers a unique opportunity to investigate how outcomes and experiences for
women vary depending not just on individual behaviors but also on organizational characteristics that are assumed to produce gender biases. After accounting for individual work habits, is gender inequality higher in firms in which
typical work hours are longer? Is it higher in firms in which fewer women hold
positions in management? Is it higher in companies in which women hold a
larger share of subordinate positions? Answering these questions is critical for
grasping the underlying causes of gender inequality, where conventional explanations based on individual work habits or gendered job segregation fail.

Firm Characteristics

Table 3.3 details how average work hours among management-track workers,
women's share of managerial jobs, and women's share of subordinate jobs vary
across the twelve firms in the sample. Because irregular and clerical-track
employees almost by definition work fewer hours that management-track workers, I calculate average work hours based on management-track employees alone.

TABLE 3.3. Work hours, women's share of management, and women's share
of subordinate jobs by firm

COMPANY	AVERAGE WORK HOURS (MANAGEMENT TRACK)	WOMEN'S REPRESENTATION IN MANAGEMENT JOBS (%)	WOMEN'S REPRESENTATION SUBORDINATE JOBS (%)
Upstore	45.1	11.1	60.0
Asahi	49.6	0.0	42.9
FuturaCorp	44.4	25.0	75.0
Kaneda	47.1	17.6	45.5
Hamabe	40.5	0.0	33.3
Takematsu	47.2	9.1	72.4
Dazan	43.6	33.3	80.0
Cyatec	40.4	22.2	30.0
Henderson	38.6	17.6	17.4
Maruyama	48.7	0.0	25.0
Pixisa	46.8	0.0	20.0
Green Elm	45.0	14.3	0.0

Women's share of management positions is calculated from the sample, among managers with six or more subordinates. All but one firm in the sample reports women's share of management to the government database created as part of Abe's womenomics initiatives. The figures in the public database correlate closely with those calculated from the sample.

Women's share of subordinate jobs is calculated by dividing the number of women in irregular or clerical-track positions in the firms' samples from the total number of irregular and clerical-track positions.

The figures on women's managerial representation illustrate why many of these firms have been poster children for government gender equality initiatives. Nationwide, the ratio of women managers in medium and large firms is typically miniscule, averaging between 4.2 percent and 5.4 percent for firms with more than three hundred employees.[69] In 80 to 90 percent of large firms, women's share of management is less than 10 percent.[70] In contrast, in seven out of twelve sample firms, women's share of management equals or exceeds 10 percent.

Four firms, however—Asahi, Hamabe, Maruyama, and Pixisa—do not include any female managers in their samples. This is not surprising given that the publicly available figures reveal that women's share of managers in each of these firms is less than 5 percent. Three of these firms are manufacturing firms, for which women's managerial representation falls well below the cross-industry average.[71] Thus, these firms are, if not gender equality leaders in their field, at least representative of the industry more broadly.

The first question of interest regarding these characteristics is whether firms adopt practices thought to be "woman friendly" or "woman unfriendly" as a bundle. Recalling the models referenced in chapter 1, Asahi, Kaneda, Hamabe, Maruyama, and Takematsu all adhere somewhat more closely to the classical long-term employment model. More employees in these firms believe coworkers view job change censoriously, and most employees entered these firms in their twenties. The general assumption in the literature is that, because ideal worker norms are so closely associated with the logic of long-term employment, these firms will be less friendly to women.

The data, however, show more contradictory results. Consistent with arguments about woman unfriendly practices in firms that prioritize long-term employment, in four out of five of these companies, work hours for management-track employees are lengthy. Hamabe, however, has some of the shortest work hours in the sample. In favor of the woman unfriendly characterization, these firms also have few women in management; counter to this characterization, however, with the exception of Takematsu, subordinate jobs in these firms are male dominated or gender balanced.

The remaining firms have adopted more flexible career models, as evidenced by the higher shares of employees who join at midcareer. But according to the metrics in table 3.3, this does not necessarily indicate other women friendly practices. Work hours, although shorter than in the firms that value long-term employment the most, are still somewhat long in Upstore, Green Elm, and Pixisa. Some of the firms, notably Dazan, FuturaCorp, and Cyatec, have particularly high shares of women in management, but Pixisa's share remains low, despite its initiatives to promote women. FuturaCorp and Dazan also have female-dominated subordinate jobs.

This variation shows that it is not simply a question of some firms being woman friendly, while others are not. The practices most thought to generate bias cluster somewhat in the case of work hours and women in management, but not at all in the case of either of these and women's overrepresentation at the bottom the organizational pyramid. This points to the importance of investigating the relationship between each separate organizational practice and attitudes toward, and treatment of, women.

The Gender Pay Gap and Organizational Determinants of Gender Bias

The current study, like previous research that investigates the impact of managerial women on organizational climate, does not measure gender attitudes directly. We can test whether these practices are associated with different treatment of women, and by extension, whether they are associated with greater gender bias in several alternative ways.

First, I examine whether this gender inequality in wages, net of individual job category and work habits, is greater in firms with higher and lower work hours, shares of women in management, and shares of women among subordinate job holders. On the basis of these findings, I then look at women's and men's subjective experience of feeling valued as a proxy for bias.

All models include the same adjustment variables as model 3. The coefficients for the adjustment variables are omitted from the table. In addition, I interact binary terms for firm-level long work hours (forty-six hours or more), high shares of women in management (15 percent and higher), and high shares of women in subordinate jobs (60 percent and higher) with the female indicator variable. If bias and treatment of women vary based on these organizational features, we would expect to find variation in the gender pay gap associated with these firm characteristics.

TABLE 3.4.   Regression of firm characteristics on annual earnings

	MODEL 4			MODEL 5			MODEL 6		
	BETA		SE	BETA		SE	BETA		SE
Women	−1.3	***	0.3	−1.7	***	0.4	−0.8	*	0.3
Long work hours	1.2		1.0						
Long work hours*women	−0.6		0.5						
High female representation in management				0.0		1.0			
High female managerial representation* women				0.3		0.5			
High female representation in subordinate jobs							1.6		1.0
High female representation in subordinate jobs*women							−2.1	***	0.5
Constant	−6.2	*	2.7	−5.7	*	2.7	−6.6	*	2.6
Model information									
Human capital controls[a]	Yes			Yes			Yes		
Work habits and job category controls[b]	Yes			Yes			Yes		
Observations	530			530			530		
Number of firms	12			12			12		

*** $p < 0.001$, ** $p < 0.01$, * $p < 0.05$
Note: All models are from hierarchical linear modeling (HLM) with random effects for firms.
[a]Education level, age, age squared, tenure, tenure squared.
[b]Weekly work hours, monthly socializing, job category.

Table 3.4 investigates whether the gender wage gap varies significantly by organizational characteristics. In model 4, the interaction term between firm-level long work hours and women's earnings is negative, indicating that women earn less, relative to men, in firms where work hours are longer, compared with those where work hours are shorter. Specifically, the gender wage gap is predicted at 1.3 million yen (17 percent) in firms with shorter work hours and at 1.9 million yen (22 percent) in firms with longer work hours. This effect is not statistically significant, however, meaning that the model might produce this same result even if gender inequality is not, in fact, greater in firms with long work hours. In sum, model 4 is consistent with theoretical predictions that bias and inequality are greater in firms with longer work hours, but this model does not offer strong evidence for the phenomenon.

Model 5 shows that firms with high female managerial representation are predicted to have a smaller gender gap—that is, 1.4 million yen (18 percent) compared with 1.7 million yen (21 percent). This is a modest difference. Moreover, the model does not adjust for women's individual managerial status, meaning that the smaller wage gap in firms with more women is driven at least partially by the fact that individual women working as managers earn more than nonmanagers. In a separate model (not shown), if individual managerial status is included as an adjustment variable, the difference in gender wage gap between firms with high and low shares of women in management shrinks to near zero. In sum, evidence does not suggest that women's managerial presence either reduces gender biases or improves conditions for nonmanagerial women.

In contrast to models 4 and 5, model 6 shows a large, statistically significant result. The gender wage gap is predicted at 0.8 million yen (11 percent) in firms with gender-balanced or male-dominated clerical tracks, and 3.2 million yen (32 percent) in firms where women make up 60 percent or more of the irregular or clerical-track jobs. Because the model adjusts for individual track status, this represents the difference in earnings within tracks.

Because these data are cross-sectional and the number of firms relatively small, they cannot conclusively demonstrate that women's overrepresentation at the bottom causes more biased gender beliefs and greater gender inequality. Nonetheless, the large, statistically significant findings are consistent with the argument that women's overrepresentation at the bottom of organizational hierarchy shapes the perception of women and their treatment. No such evidence is found in support of claims that work hours or women's managerial representation influence attitudes toward women.

Subjective Assessments of Feeling Valued

If women's lower pay in firms where subordinate jobs are female dominated arises from managers' and coworkers' biases about women's capabilities, it is likely that managers perceive women's day-to-day contributions as less valuable and important, and act accordingly toward them. To explore this possibility, I compare men's and women's subjective experiences of how their supervisors value them. If symbolic boundaries between women and men are more sharply drawn in firms in which subordinate jobs are female dominated, then we would expect a larger gender gap in feeling valued in these firms.

The survey asked employees to respond to the prompt, "My supervisors _____ value my contributions on the job," with options of "never," "rarely," "sometimes," "often," or "always."

Table 3.5 shows the responses to this question by gender, job type, and composition of subordinate jobs. Although women are less likely than men to say their supervisors "often" or "always" value their contributions in both types of firms, the difference with male peers is far more pronounced in firms in

TABLE 3.5. Likelihood of feeling valued by firm characteristics, job category, and gender

FIRM-LEVEL COMPOSITION OF SUBORDINATE JOBS	GENDER AND JOB CATEGORY	EMPLOYEES WHO ALWAYS OR OFTEN FEEL VALUED (%)	N
Female dominated	Men on the management track	42.6	204
	Women on the management track	38.4	78
	Men in subordinate jobs	42.3	52
	Women in subordinate jobs	36.3	22
Not female dominated	Men on the management track	47.7	88
	Women on the management track	28.5	28
	Men in subordinate jobs	53.3	15
	Women in subordinate jobs	25.6	43

Source: Reproduced with modifications from Holbrow (2022).

which subordinate jobs are female dominated. Women on the management track are 19 percent less likely to feel valued, and women in subordinate jobs are 27 percent less likely to feel valued, compared with just 5 and 6 percent for women in the other firms.[72] In sum, when subordinate jobs are female dominated, gender gaps in "feeling valued" are indeed wider. This finding, too, is consistent with the argument that a concentration of women in low-status, subordinate jobs leads coworkers to value all women less highly.

Japan's shrinking labor force has made it untenable for firms to exclude women. Faced with a smaller and smaller talent pool, the costs to firms of relegating women to short-term, dead-end jobs grow ever greater. In concert with these economic pressures, the government has outlawed many of the exclusionary practices of the past, such as marriage and pregnancy bars, and has enacted a generous parental leave law that allows women in regular employment to maintain long-term labor market attachment regardless of parental status. The companies in the sample have embraced these trends, and many are recognized as leaders in proactively encouraging women's careers.

Employment norms are also shifting to become more compatible with childrearing. Although barriers for women with family responsibilities remain—for example, both companies and workers expect employees to cede control over their careers to the firm—they are lower than in the past. Work hours are shorter; expectations for after-hours socialization are reduced.

Concurrently, women's orientation toward works has evolved as well; in the 1980s, few women in elite white-collar workplaces desired to fight the institutional barriers to their advancement; most saw their jobs as insignificant parentheses to their more important future careers as wives and mothers. As explicitly discriminatory practices have fallen away, more women enter elite firms in search of upward mobility. This tendency is especially marked in women from other Asian countries, who must invest considerably in language and cultural skills to land positions elite firms. And yet, gender inequality in pay remains vast for Japanese and Asian women alike.

Academics and employees account for this disparity by focusing on individual-level work habits, such as women's reluctance or inability to take on long work hours, accept distant job transfers, and maintain continuous employment. Tracking into irregular or clerical-track jobs is a second frequently cited reason for women's disadvantage. As I have shown, these arguments elide the large overlap in men's and women's work habits and job placements in these elite firms. Only 16 percent of women in the sample have children, and of women over age 40, only 30 percent do. Women without children, however, do not come close to obtaining gender parity in wages: The wage gap for women without children is still 18.8 percent, net of work commitment and job category controls. Of the thirty-four women over age 40 who do not have children, only four (12 percent) are managers. In contrast, of 171 men over age 40, 44 percent are managers. Large wage gaps in these firms persist *in spite of* many women's decisions to remain childless and invest in their careers, in spite of demographic pressures, and in spite of companies' investments in women's empowerment. In sum, the consensus narrative fails to explain the yawning gender gaps in promotion and in pay in elite firms.

This failure of the consensus narrative points to the importance of managers' discretionary decisions in work assignments, evaluation, and promotion. After all, upper management may be sensitive to broader labor market and government pressure to improve conditions for working women, but managers are relatively insulated from these macroeconomic and demographic forces. This insulation enables managers, and indeed all rank-and-file employees, to continue to think and act in ways that disadvantage women workers.

Work assignment is a particularly critical stage in the perpetuation of gender inequality. Although evaluation, job rotation, promotion are also important, managers and HR make these decisions based on employees' contributions to the tasks and projects the managers *have already allotted them*. I argue that, in this context of high managerial discretion, gender gaps in work assignments are a far weightier contributor to the gender pay gap in elite firms than the literature acknowledges.

In turn, the managerial discretion in work assignments highlights the importance of symbolic boundaries and stereotypical beliefs about men and women. As national surveys make clear, women frequently encounter beliefs that men are more capable of "high-value" tasks, including leadership and negotiation, whereas women's "emotional" or "irrational" tendencies disqualify them from responsible positions, regardless of parental status. These beliefs have a direct link to managers' decisions to assign women routine work and to exclude them from the most prestigious projects and teams.

Where do these stereotypes come from? Scholars have posited that a culture of long work hours as well as women's relative absence from the top of organizational pyramids contribute to these negative assessments of women's potential and capabilities. For example, Nemoto argues that "changing men's consciousness [about women's potential] . . . requires changing firms' sex-segregated customs such as extremely long hours."[73] She also argues: "To address [strong gender stereotypes], the number of women in leadership and authority positions does need to increase; if the population of women workers becomes far more diverse, workers and managers will realize that their imposition of monolithic traits and essentialist images on women does not reflect the reality of women workers."[74]

Several of the firms in this current study have met these criteria. In five firms, typical work hours are less than forty-five hours a week; there are also five firms in which female managerial representation exceeds "token" levels of 15 percent. Moreover, most of the women the firms employ work on the managerial track. The "diversity" of women employees that Nemoto predicts will transform gender attitudes is already present in many of the sample firms. Neither work hours nor women's managerial representation, however, is associated with significantly lower gender inequality.

Of course, this does not prove that such initiatives never change gender attitudes or mitigate gender inequality. No single study, including this one, can definitively settle this question. The findings do, however, cast doubt on the government's reliance on these initiatives as the bedrock of its gender equity policy. As described earlier, the evidentiary basis for these claims is already slim. The firms in this study fail to confirm them.

The study firms do suggest an overlooked driver of symbolic boundaries between men and women—that is, women's overrepresentation in low-status irregular and clerical jobs. There are many reasons to believe that women's predominance at the bottom of the organizational pyramid shapes the perception of women. Many of the negative stereotypes about women are, in effect, stereotypes about secretaries or other menial workers. Furthermore, in everyday office interactions, employees are more likely to work closely with assistants than with managers. Where all, or nearly all, assistants are women, employees may apply the "assistant lens" to all women, regardless of their individual positions, capabilities, or interests. In turn, managers in these firms may be more likely to assign tedious grunt work to managerial-track women as well as cleri-cal track or irregular women employees, impeding advancement and salary growth for most women, even as a small number move into management.

Consistent with this perspective, gender pay gaps are considerably larger, and women are less likely to feel that their supervisors value them, in firms in which irregular or clerical-track jobs are dominated by women. This includes several firms, notably Dazan and FuturaCorp, that have sizable numbers of women in management and in which work hours are moderate. These findings imply that the people employees see when they "look down" the corporate hierarchy to these undervalued positions may be a more critical determinant of symbolic boundaries and inequality than the people employees see when they "look up."

These findings also shed further light onto the causes of persistent gender inequality. In Japan, and indeed globally, women have increasingly entered historically male-dominated professional and managerial jobs. Historically female-typed support jobs, such as secretaries, shop assistants, or nurses, remain highly female dominated. If women's overrepresentation in these roles rein-forces beliefs that women are less capable and worthy than men, women's work-place attainment will suffer.

Managerial discretion exacerbates this disadvantage in elite firms. Although upper-level management, which may be more sensitive to the long-term strategic consequences of population decline and the optics of low managerial representa-tion for women, may intervene to encourage HR to hire more women on the management track, or to assign women developmental job rotations in strategic units of the business, managers are insulated from macroeconomic forces as they make the day-to-day decisions that shape women's and men's careers. In cases in which organizations "teach" managers that women are assistants by maintain-ing a female-dominated support staff, managers will treat them as such, denying them the full benefits demographic decline might otherwise bring.

4

WORKING IN "THE JAPANESE WAY"

The Limits of Acculturation

"My coworkers in HR [human resources] think that foreign workers don't understand the way that things are done. They are very concerned about identifying gaps in their understanding, and 'educating' them in the correct way to do things," Liling told me. Liling's words struck a chord: I, too, encountered the (not necessarily inaccurate) assumption that foreign workers are ignorant of appropriate workplace behavior. On my first day at the Canon Institute for Global Studies (CIGS), a member of the office staff presented me with a handbook of rules for staff and researchers and reviewed it carefully with me. Many of the regulations focused on safety. All affiliates had electronic badges which we scanned to unlock the office door. These were not to be shared with others under any circumstances. Upon arrival, we were to hang up a name badge on the attendance board, so the staff could see at a glance who was present. The office personnel used the board primarily to determine whether they should transfer phone calls or take messages. It could also serve as a basis for a headcount in the event of an evacuation, an eventuality that weighed heavily on my coworkers' minds three years after the massive 3.11 earthquake, tsunami, and nuclear disaster.

Beyond these safety policies, the handbook was particularly expansive on the topic of proper attire. Jeans and miniskirts were verboten. Women were permitted to wear boots while commuting, but had to change into heels or flats upon arrival at the office. To ward off quibbling about the distinction between mini- and regular skirts or between boots and shoes, the handbook included illustrations of inappropriate clothing choices in the style of no-smoking signs.

112

Flip-flops and board shorts were also out. Somewhat apologetically, the staff member told me that these items had been added because, "in the past, sometimes the foreign researchers came in dressed that way on the weekends." Later, I wondered how the guilty party had been apprehended: On the rare occasions I stopped by the office on a weekend, it was dark and deserted. Had a building security guard spotted the hapless foreign researcher on closed-circuit television footage and reported him? Chastened, I was always meticulous in my dress in the area around Tokyo station, even when I had no plans to drop by the office.

The perception (and reality) that foreigners are ill-equipped to follow the practices and norms of elite workplaces is a recurring theme in scholarly and popular discussion of immigrants' workplace integration in Japan. Japanese firms notoriously expect a high degree of Japanese language competency from foreign employees, compliance with explicit rules such as those laid out in the CIGS employee handbook, and adherence to unspoken rules and implicit communication styles, to the extent that they can conduct their work entirely in "the Japanese way." These beliefs about foreigners' ignorance of the "the Japanese way" of doing things can be seen as a symbolic boundary Japanese draw between themselves and others.

The International Organization for Migration (IOM) defines acculturation as "the progressive adoption of elements of a foreign culture (ideas, words, values, norms, behavior, institutions)."[1] I use this term to refer to immigrants' knowledge of and ability to adhere to the expectations of the Japanese workplace. Following common usage in scholarship on Japan, I use the term *assimilation* to describe acculturation so complete that immigrants' behavior is indistinguishable from that of natives.[2]

Scholars sometimes cite strong assimilative pressure as evidence of Japan's uniquely intense xenophobia and a corresponding proclivity to discriminate against or entirely exclude non-Japanese.[3] At the same time, both scholars and foreign workers believe that foreign workers can overcome disadvantage associated with their foreign background, if only partially, by internalizing and adhering to the norms of the Japanese workplace.[4] Just as women's concentration in irregular or clerical-track work and their outsize share of household labor are thought to explain gender inequality, so too is foreign workers' inability to meet firms' high standards seen as the primary driver of immigrants' disadvantage in white-collar workplaces, and hence, of their ability to reap the benefits of population decline.[5] Thus, the dominant perspective on foreign workers in white-collar firms is that the most salient symbolic boundary is not nationality or ethnicity per se, but rather one's (in)ability to do things in "the

Japanese way." This boundary is permeable in theory, but only through immigrant workers' total or near-total assimilation. Because this is so difficult to achieve, parity between foreign workers and Japanese is seen as unlikely.[6]

The assumed primacy of acculturation to immigrant workers' success also exerts a powerful influence on policy. Due in part to this narrative, policymakers have privileged the most acculturated migrants for admittance and permanent residency, under the presumption that this will "solve" the challenges of immigrant integration, not just in the workplace but in society more broadly.

At the same time, there are also reasons to doubt the narrative about the primacy of acculturation to white-collar immigrants' success. In comparison to the huge gender gap women face, the penalties associated with Asian foreign background alone are modest. Indeed, both Asian men and women achieve parity or near parity with same-sex Japanese counterparts, albeit through educational and linguistic overachievement. If acculturation or assimilation are as central to upward mobility in elite firms as is usually assumed, it is surprising that Asian men would be better positioned to close wage gaps with Japanese men than Japanese women.

In this chapter, I explore the acculturative pressure immigrants face, as recounted through the voices of immigrants and their Japanese coworkers. As shown in chapter 2, only Asian foreign workers experience disadvantage in earnings relative to Japanese (net of skills). Furthermore, Asians are held to an even higher standard of acculturation than are Westerners.[7] This suggests that the payoffs for acculturation, or the penalties of imperfect acculturation, will be most significant among Asians.

Consistent with prior research, I show that Asian men and women in the sample firms feel pushed to do things in "the Japanese way." They see acculturation as a necessary, if not sufficient, condition for their upward mobility.

I then examine the relationship between acculturation and three workplace outcomes: Asian employees' assessed performance, their ability to build strong social networks in the firm, and their pay. There is a noisy but positive relationship between acculturation, on one hand, and performance and networks, on the other. Counterintuitively, however, the most acculturated Asian workers experience the largest wage gaps with Japanese peers; in fact, it is the least acculturated Asian workers who attain equality.

I argue that this unexpected relationship occurs not because acculturation does not improve Asian immigrants' perceived workplace performance, but because acculturation occurs *in parallel to* discrimination. The longer Asians are employed in Japanese firms, the more they acculturate, but the greater their exposure to small acts of discrimination. Over time, the costs of facing this discrimination are greater than the payoffs for acculturation. The results highlight how an immigration policy focused on selecting the most accultur-ated immigrants does not eliminate inequalities.

At the same time, these results undercut claims that intense assimilative pressure is indicative of equally intense discrimination against foreigners. Although assimilative pressure in interpersonal interactions alienates foreign workers, when it comes to employment decisions, managers also look beyond acculturation in their valuation of foreign workers' skills and contributions. I argue that Japan's ethnonationalist discourse provides an explicit, assimila-tive vocabulary for expressing discomfort with ethnoracial others. Other coun-tries, such as the United States, may lack this vocabulary, but that lack does not indicate the absence of bias or discrimination. Conversely, Japan's assimilative discourse should not be read as evidence for unusually virulent xenophobia or racism, nor as a proclivity to discriminate with unusual harshness against imperfectly acculturated immigrants. Asian immigrants do experience dis-crimination, but the frequency and severity of that discrimination do not match the strong assimilative pressure.

Past Research on Acculturation in Japanese Firms

Across national contexts, employers prefer white-collar workers who can com-petently navigate the linguistic, social, and cultural waters. Scholars often describe Japanese firms' expectations for acculturation as unusually rigid and high, however.[8] Sociologist Helena Hof, for example, castigates "Japanese lan-guage-only working culture" for discouraging long-term migration of Europe-ans to Japan, and criticizes the "conservative business mentality" of employers who do not want to do business with non-Japanese employees through an interpreter.[9] Business scholars Harald Conrad and Hendrik Meyer-Ohle simi-larly decry the "considerable and constant assimilative pressure" that denies foreign workers the opportunity to bring their authentic selves to work.[10] Soci-ologist Yen-Fen Tseng laments that foreign workers "are expected to under-stand hidden rules as much as natives do" and describes firms as having an "overemphasis on cultural skills."[11]

The implicit comparisons in many of these criticisms are the citizens and firms of North American and Europe, which are presumed to be more flexible or realistic in their expectations for immigrant workers and to be more willing to reward culturally foreign modes of work.

Scholars highlight two implications of the intense assimilative pressure: First, it alienates foreign workers, making them more likely to abandon careers in Japan.[12] Second, foreign workers cannot advance in their careers unless they fully "conform to [the] inflexible work culture" and achieve unaccented fluency in Japanese.[13] Such scholarship implies that, because of this very high bar, the majority of foreign workers are inevitably relegated to second-class citizenship in elite firms.

Acculturation in Japan's Migration Policy

This belief that Japanese language and cultural skills are critical for foreign workers' or immigrants' success and smooth integration is deeply embedded in Japan's border control policy toward white-collar workers.

One way in which Japan's border control policy demonstrates this emphasis on acculturation is its reliance on what Gracia Liu-Farrer has called "educationally channeled migration."[14] Japan heavily prioritizes migration of students, establishing targets for numbers of international students in Japan for the first time in 1983, and increasing the target to three hundred thousand in 2008, and again to four hundred thousand in 2023.[15] From the beginning, these plans aimed to have students put down roots and settle in Japan, after transforming them into the acculturated workforce businesses seek.[16]

Student visas are available not just for those who enroll in accredited higher education institutions but also for those who enter less regulated private Japanese language schools. Many Asian students first attend Japanese language schools while working part time, matriculate at university, and then seek jobs in white-collar companies. This pathway ensures that, by the time they obtain full-time professional jobs and white-collar work visas, they have already spent a considerable amount of time developing a familiarity with Japanese language and culture.[17]

Beginning in the 2000s, government publications began to refer to foreign students as "embryonic global talent."[18] Highlighting the importance of college students and the cultivation of acculturated human resources to Japan's migration strategy, in early 2022, Prime Minister Kishida went a step farther, naming foreign students a "national treasure" as he announced plans to prioritize their entry over other travelers, amid Japan's continued pandemic control measures that limited daily arrivals.[19]

A second example of the high value placed on acculturation is the point system for highly skilled professional (HSP) migrants working in academia and business, promulgated in 2012. Unlike standard white-collar work visa holders, who must reside in Japan for at least ten years before applying for permanent residency, migrants with the requisite number of points in the HSP system can obtain permanent residency in one to five years, depending on the number of points.[20] The single-largest contributor to points is the applicant's income. Both advanced Japanese language skills and a Japanese university degree contribute a smaller number of points. In other words, even among high-earning white-collar professionals, the government fast-tracks the most acculturated to permanent residency.

In line with this logic, some politicians have called linguistic and cultural adaptation the most critical criteria for determining whether potential migrants should be admitted.[21] The broader public also values acculturation as a criterion for whether immigrants deserve citizenship.[22]

Underlying these policies and preferences is a faith that highly acculturated migrants are less "troublesome."[23] Government officials believe acculturated migrants are more likely to follow spoken and unspoken rules of Japanese culture at work and in their communities.[24] And, in part because acculturated migrants follow the rules, they are more likely to be successful in their jobs or careers. Furthermore, many trust that economically successful migrants are less likely to drain state coffers with demands on the welfare system and also are less likely to commit crimes.[25] Consequently, government officials and members of the public often see acculturation as part of a win-win virtuous cycle that benefits migrants individually, and spares Japanese society the economic burdens or sociocultural friction associated with accepting immigrants in other national contexts.[26]

Acculturation Demands in the Sample Firms

The firms in this sample are no exception to the typical Japanese employers described in prior research. Famously, a handful of Japanese companies, such as e-commerce giant Rakuten, have made English the common company language. Most firms list Japanese language ability as the most important skill they seek when they hire foreign college graduates, however, and cite unfamiliarity with Japanese language and culture as the number one issue they face in managing them.[27] The sample firms followed this more typical model, and preferred a high level of fluency in Japanese. As an HR manager told me,

> When you're working with a client, you need to make a proposal together with them based on deep knowledge of their sales and business. But to gather that information, you have to be able to have a nuanced conversation. Clients sometimes tell us, "We can't have in-depth conversations with this [foreign account executive], could you

please turn our account over to a Japanese person?" This happens even for foreign employees with quite a high level of Japanese. So that's a problem we're currently grappling with.

The result of these preferences and concerns is that most foreign employees, particularly Asians, speak Japanese at a very high level. I conducted most of the interviews with Asian immigrant workers in Japanese, and respondents were not just competent but eloquent in what was their second or third language. Among all Asian survey respondents, around four-fifths of both women and men rated their Japanese language skills as advanced or higher on a scale ranging from beginner to fluent native speaker.

To obtain a more granular sense of Japanese proficiency, I asked respondents to rate the ease or difficulty with which they could complete various tasks in Japanese. These skills included opening a bank account, writing a business letter, reading the newspaper, debating politics and economics with friends, understanding jokes on television, conducting business negotiations, and reading a novel. I classify respondents as highly acculturated when they report that they can do all these tasks very easily or with moderate ease.[28] Although this measure relies on linguistic acculturation alone, and does not explicitly capture cultural assimilation, I assume that those with stronger linguistic skills are also more culturally competent.

In this more demanding assessment of language ability, 51 percent of Asian women and 61 percent of Asian men fall into the "highly acculturated" category, indicating they can complete even rather difficult tasks in Japanese. Acculturation is much lower among Western respondents, of whom only 31 percent, including both men and women, are highly acculturated. Table 4.1 displays Asian respondents' self-ranking of Japanese language ability, and the acculturation measure derived from the ease or difficulty with which the respondents could complete the various Japanese-language tasks.

At the same time, although most Asian employees are highly skilled in Japanese, this is not universal. As table 4.1 shows, around one-fifth of Asian respondents describe their language skills as intermediate or below. A small minority (8 percent) of Asian respondents say that even opening a bank account

TABLE 4.1. Asian respondents' acculturation

	ASIAN MEN (N = 33)	ASIAN WOMEN (N = 41)
	%	%
Advanced or higher Japanese language (overall self-rating)	78.8	85.4
Highly acculturated (easy/difficulty scale)	60.6	51.2

would be at least a little difficult. Around a quarter (24 percent) report they find it challenging to read the newspaper, and nearly half (47 percent) say they would struggle with a business negotiation, which was rated the most difficult of any of the tasks. In sum, fluent Japanese language ability, while preferred, is not an absolute condition of employment. Moreover, for around half of Asian respondents, their Japanese language skills still pose barriers in some important workplace domains.

Notably, however, when Japanese interviewees criticized or complained about foreign workers' language skills, it was not usually about foreign workers' ability or inability to communicate substantively, but rather about their ability to adhere to culturally correct styles of communication or ways of working. For one thing, foreign employees tend to have a weaker grasp of polite linguistic forms, referred to collectively as *keigo*.[29] *Keigo* relies on a different vocabulary than does language used in informal settings. Speakers must use appropriately humble words when referring to themselves or their in-group, and appropriately honorific words for superiors and clients. Before entering the workplace, many young Japanese also lack full competency in *keigo*. For non-native speakers, particularly those most familiar with Mandarin or English, which lack equivalent linguistic markers of respect and relative status, becoming proficient in this linguistic form is more challenging.

Asked about his experiences working with non-Japanese, Hideki praised his foreign colleagues' cultural adaptation at length, contrasting it favorably with the parochialism of his Japanese peers. He concluded: "Their work is high quality. But, sometimes I can't help feeling . . . there's something a little bit *risky* about working with people from a different cultural background." Pressed further, Hideki answered, "Using *keigo* incorrectly . . . there's situations where that's just not acceptable."

Beyond language and vocabulary, interviewees also highlighted other points of friction over communication styles. Scholars describe Japanese firms as relying on unspoken understandings and implicit communication to a greater degree than firms in other national contexts.[30] This theme also emerged in the survey.

Masato, a manager in his forties, described how this expectation for implicit communication creates conflict. He said:

> My coworkers try to manage foreign employees the same way they do Japanese. But, that [management style] doesn't fit the foreign workers' way of thinking, and that leads to frustration at times. The managers give ambiguous instructions, and they rely on implicit understanding [*aun no kokyuu*]. Managers are not explicit in what they want, and then, when they don't get what they want, their attitude is, "Your [foreign workers'] way of doing it is wrong."

Non-Japanese respondents, even those who were quite fluent, reported their experiences with the same struggle. Chaoxiang, a Chinese man in his late twenties, attended university entirely in Japan. He reported that although he could conduct all the Japanese language tasks with ease, this did not eliminate all barriers to communication:

> I am Asian, just like [my Japanese coworkers]. So, there's a lot of culture we hold in common. But sometimes I don't get the nuances. I don't know whether they're angry or not because I did something a certain way. Japanese people don't necessarily say things directly, and it takes some time to understand that. So, I might not be able to tell whether someone is angry, or what their opinions are. A Japanese person would understand [their attitude] just fine, of course. But as a foreigner, I'm in the dark.

Xinyan, also from China, had ten years of work experience at her company. She felt she could effectively navigate the expectations for implicit communication, but that other, less experienced Chinese workers could not:

> There are other Chinese employees at my firm, and from what I hear, they often tell me they have trouble communicating with Japanese coworkers. For example, a Japanese employee will say, "Let's discuss 'that,' or let's discuss 'that issue,' right?" WHAT issue? Because of the cultural element, mutual comprehension is really difficult for a lot of people. But for my part, maybe because I've been here a long time and am used to it, I'll know, "Oh yeah, THAT issue."

Implicit communication is important in work-related social contexts as well as on the job. Hideki, for example, complained that foreign workers make certain social situations uncomfortable. In after-hours drinking parties, he explained, conversation might be flowing freely, but a foreign coworker would suddenly interrupt with a completely different topic, to the consternation of the Japanese present. He cited this as a failure to properly "read the air," that is to say, to intuit the social dynamics and react appropriately.

Although foreign workers encounter challenges in understanding and fulfilling unspoken expectations in both formal and informal work settings, in other cases, foreign workers bump up against an opposite problem: expectations for *more* detailed, *more* explicit communication than some foreign workers feel is appropriate or necessary. Derek, a white American man, complained bitterly that even though he did not receive clear instructions from his bosses, he was expected to keep his superiors closely informed about his day-to-day progress in his work. He grumbled that "the Japanese [business style] is just naturally micromanaged," and spoke wistfully of perhaps moving to a foreign company where he might have greater independence and be subject to less irritating oversight.

What Derek called micromanagement is related to a culture in which quality, accuracy, and attention to detail are valued for their own sake.[31] Wei, a Taiwanese man who spoke almost no Japanese, also complained: "As you know, most of the Japanese are 'perfect workers.' I would say, they don't release work until it's perfect. I don't like that. I think what we want is to create a reliable product *in a sustainable time.*"

In some cases, Japanese coworkers may value Wei's attitude toward efficiency, but more often, Japanese coworkers see this attitude as simply sloppy. For example, Emi complained: "You know, it's typical to have a discussion of whether a report is ready to submit to a client. But the standard for initiating that conversation is different for people from other countries. . . . The minimum baseline for Japanese is higher. Foreigners are ready to just go and drop something [half-baked] in the clients' lap. Whereas we [Japanese] say, 'That is NOT going to fly and there's no way it's ready.'" Although the immigrant employees in Emi's firm included people from both Western and Asian countries, the foreigners on her team were all from Asian countries, so we can presume these remarks refer to Asians.

Not all foreign workers resent this culture, however. Xinyan, who was optimistic about her chances for promotion, had internalized these standards. She described herself as building a successful network in the firm, and having good relationships with her boss, her boss's superiors, and even the company CEO. When asked how she had managed this feat, she said, "Fundamentally, the number one thing is to do your work perfectly."

As these examples illustrate, full acculturation to the business environment entails not only mastery of Japanese language to the extent that foreign employees can accurately communicate the content or substance of their work in Japanese but also adhering to culturally correct styles of communication, learning to understand unspoken rules and implicit communication, and navigating asymmetries between expectations for how junior employees communicate with senior employees as compared with how senior employees communicate with their subordinates—all the while being held to a very high standard for quality work.

Acculturation and Career Success

Most respondents felt that their chances for advancement hinged on their ability to meet these expectations for acculturation fully. Derek, an American man, griped: "Oh, sure. Getting promoted as a foreigner is no problem. So long as you can do everything exactly like a Japanese person."

Yuanyuan, who was one of the less acculturated Asian interviewees, spoke to me in English. She also felt her imperfect acculturation held her back and said: "I'm a foreigner so I have several disadvantages [as far as promotion is concerned] in terms of the language and the culture. Even though I try, still there is some gap. I would say the gap is smaller compared to two or three years ago when I started working here. But still I feel there is some disadvantage."

According to the interviewees, acculturation is important to their careers for three main reasons. First, because many workers feel that employers' expectations are ambiguous, acculturation would better allow them to understand those expectations, and hence fulfill them, as with Xinyan's remarks about coworkers' tendency to refer to "this issue" or "that issue" without specifying which project they mean.

Second, acculturation helps them meet expectations (once they understand what they are). As Yuanyuan said: "We [foreigners] definitely make more mistakes than Japanese because we don't know Japanese culture. Making the boss unhappy." Dawen, who is fluent in Japanese, said: "You have to follow the Japanese rules. If you don't, you're not likely to get a good evaluation." I asked Chaoxiang if he thought that, as a foreigner, he had an opportunity to push back against cultural norms that irked him. "Absolutely not," he replied, "to the contrary, my coworkers' position is, 'this is the Japanese way of doing things—please conform to it.'"

Finally, foreign workers see acculturation as critical for building social networks within their company. Xinyan, who worked "perfectly" and felt confident in her strong and supportive network of colleagues and supervisors, described acculturation—which originated in her youthful obsession with Japanese dramas and crush on the boyband idol and actor Kimura Takuya and then was nurtured through long study as a student and as an employee—as critical to her success. She said of her path: "Of course, language skills are important [for success in the firm]. But when I say language, I don't mean just speaking good Japanese. Just studying your hardest isn't all of it. You have to know the culture. You have to understand how Japanese people think, how they interact. . . . Finally, it comes down to love. Loving Japan and Japanese culture. . . . You need that and you need the language both."

Chaoxiang, who like Xinyan is highly acculturated, emphasized that having a strong network within the firm is critical for long-term success, but he lamented the challenges of building one as non-Japanese. He said: "If you set your mind to it, you can build the same social networks as a Japanese person. It's just, as a foreigner, it takes an order of magnitude more effort," both because of the language barrier and also because of implicit cultural assumptions about appropriate behavior.

Notably, I could not discern any gender differences in the pressure to acculturate. Less acculturated migrants of both genders, like Yuanyuan and Wei, sometimes struggle with basic communication. More acculturated migrants like Liling, Xinyan, Dawen, and Chaoxiang confront challenges about communication styles, expectations for perfection, and building networks within the firm. Both men and women feel that firms expect them to "conform to the Japanese way of doing things," and that career success is contingent on meeting those expectations. Although Xinyan thought this was possible, other acculturated migrants, as described in chapter 2, view acculturation as a necessary, but not necessarily sufficient, precondition for career success.

Overstating Acculturation's Benefits to Immigrants?

A large body of research from traditional countries of immigration, such as the United States and Australia; from countries that have more recently expanded immigration, such as Germany and Sweden; and from Japan, shows that on average immigrants who have lived and worked longer in the host country, and who have strong host country language skills, are more successful in the labor market than their less acculturated counterparts.[32] Beyond a shadow of a doubt, this research shows that, across a wide range of national contexts, acculturation predicts better outcomes for immigrants.

On the surface, this overwhelming evidence seems to validate both the emphasis on acculturation in Japanese border control, and the survey respondents' endorsement of the narrative that what holds them back in their Japanese places of employment is primarily, if not exclusively, their imperfect acculturation.

It does not follow from these studies, however, that more acculturation leads to better outcomes for immigrants in every setting. The evidence for the benefits of acculturation comes from analysis of highly heterogenous samples of immigrants, who arrive through different legal channels, such as asylum, family reunification, or employment, and land in different occupations, ranging from farm laborers and cleaners to doctors. Even if initial and subsequent levels of acculturation help immigrants land better jobs in high-paying firms or occupations, acculturation does not necessarily act as a fine sorter of workers within similar occupations and workplaces. Despite the hegemonic narrative around acculturation, other immigrant characteristics or skills may be more predictive of outcomes among workers in similar employment settings.

There are further reasons to scrutinize the narrative as well. First, for all the pressure foreign workers feel to assimilate, not all Japanese employees or managers see full assimilation as necessary or even desirable for immigrant workers. Many companies assert that the technical and intercultural skills foreign workers bring outweigh the disadvantages of their imperfect acculturation. As one HR officer told me:

> We had a Chinese employee who was the son of [a high ranking government official in China]. But, over there, someone who's number 25 today might be purged tomorrow, so [such elite connections] are not something we can count on. But what he could do is tell us "this is how Chinese people think about this issue." And that is very helpful. We are very grateful for that type of cultural interpretation. The main thing we are looking for is not interpretation of the language; it's interpretation of a way of thinking.

This suggests a way of evaluating foreign workers that rewards other knowledge and abilities beyond assimilation to Japanese culture.

Another HR manager described to me many of the same areas of conflict highlighted in the employee interviewees. He explained that his office takes a flexible approach to these issues, in some cases working with managers to change their behavior, rather than forcing foreign workers to change theirs. Masato, as quoted previously, also endorsed this model. When asked about conflict or friction associated with foreign workers' employment, he criticized his fellow managers rather than foreign workers. Managers, he felt, were all too willing to place blame entirely on foreign subordinates for any misunderstandings or miscommunications, when in fact, managers' unreasonable expectations set immigrant workers up for failure.

Although these examples do not negate the considerable assimilative pressure that Asians face in elite Japanese firms, they show that not all managers equate assimilation with excellence, and that acculturation is not the sole metric by which managers assess foreign workers. Unsurprisingly, pressure to assimilate is more salient to immigrant workers. Perhaps unnoticed by immigrants, however, at least some managers also make adjustments to accommodate immigrant workers and look beyond their level of acculturation in their assessments of Asian workers, even if they also encourage assimilation.

Second, foreign workers' views of their outcomes and prospects at Japanese firms may be inaccurate. As we saw in chapter 2, Asian women overestimate their opportunities. Xinyan is a case in point. Her income falls at the ninety-fifth percentile of all women respondents. She is thus rightly confident in her upwardly mobile trajectory. At the same time, however, her optimism does not tell the full story: She is also slightly underpaid relative to men of similar age at her firm. When I initially interviewed her in 2015, she was in her late thirties, and did not feel it was her "turn" to be promoted yet. Eight years later, I looked her up in her company directory. Now in her mid-forties, and past the typical age of first promotion, she remains in the same position as when I first spoke with her. At the very least, then, we should not uncritically accept imperfect acculturation as the primary barrier to foreign workers' advancement based on immigrants' incomplete knowledge of their workplace conditions.

Third, as we saw in chapter 3, hegemonic narratives about the reasons for women's disadvantage do not hold up well to scrutiny. Although women's lower ambitions are frequently cited as a source of women's workplace disadvantage, Asian women's outcomes are roughly similar to those of Japanese women, despite their much higher levels of ambition. Similarly, although observers place the blame for inequality between women and men on women's disproportionate share of household and parenting responsibilities, single and childless women fare little better than women with children. The hegemonic narrative on acculturation is worthy of similar investigation.

More and Less Acculturated Asian Workers

To assess the relationship between acculturation and Asian workers' ability to achieve in the workplace I examine how more and less acculturated Asians compare with Japanese coworkers in terms of their job performance and workplace networks. In these analyses, I use a binary measure of acculturation based on language skill. As before, I consider Asians highly acculturated if they report that they can complete all the Japanese-language tasks with ease or moderate ease. If the acculturation narrative is correct, we would expect the lowest performance and weakest networks among less acculturated Asians, followed by more acculturated Asians, followed by Japanese.

Next, I model whether Asians who are more acculturated are more successful at obtaining parity in pay with Japanese, net of human capital and other background characteristics. As in prior chapters, these models use hierarchical linear models with random effects for firms. In these analyses, I use the binary measure of higher and lower acculturation described previously, as well as a continuous measure of Asians' years of work experience in Japan. Although these two estimates of acculturation do not fully capture all its nuances—a

TABLE 4.2. Characteristics of Asian employees by level of acculturation

	HIGHLY ACCULTURATED ASIANS (N = 41)		LESS ACCULTURATED ASIANS (N = 33)	
	MEAN OR %	SD	MEAN OR %	SD
Women	51.2		60.6	
Education above BA	43.9		45.5	
East Asian	90.2		72.7	
Age	33.9	8.1	30.4	5.0
Tenure	6.2	7.8	3.2	3.4
Years in Japan	13.7	11.2	5.0	3.9
Years of work in Japan	9.1	7.4	5.4	3.9
Job category				
Management track	80.5		72.7	
Clerical track	12.2		15.2	
Irregular job	7.3		12.1	
Engineering or IT job	17.1		21.2	

worker may speak excellent Japanese and have worked in Japan a long time but may still be unwilling to "do things in the Japanese way"—they are commonly used in the literature because they proxy foreign workers' potential to adhere to sociocultural expectations. I use Japanese work experience rather than total years in Japan, or, alternatively, years in Japanese education, because many of the expectations placed on foreign workers are specific to the white-collar work environment and are not taught in school.

Table 4.2 shows descriptive statistics of Asian employees by level of acculturation. These statistics underscore the dynamic nature of acculturation. More acculturated Asians are older, have lived in Japan longer, have more Japanese work experience, and have longer tenure in their firms. Unsurprisingly, because acculturation occurs over time, it is those who have lived and worked in Japan the longest who have the strongest language skills.

Other than this distinction, the two groups are quite similar. The share with advanced degrees is essentially equivalent. Although highly acculturated Asians are more likely to hail from China, South Korea, and Taiwan, East Asians represent a sizable majority of both groups. Highly acculturated Asians are slightly more likely to be in promotional management-track jobs, but the difference is relatively modest. Moreover, in both groups, the great majority of respondents work in nontechnical jobs, rather than in engineering or IT. In other words, the two groups are largely comparable, except for acculturation and variables associated directly with acculturation, such as time in Japan.

(Assessed) Performance and Acculturation

Like many large firms, the firms in this sample calculate bonuses as a number of months' salary equivalent.[33] Individual performance, as assessed by the employer and expressed in a performance grade or score, is the single-largest determinant of the salary equivalent employees receive as bonus.[34] This makes bonus, transformed to months' salary equivalent, a useful if rough yardstick of employees' assessed performance—with an emphasis, of course, on rough. As we saw in chapter 1, the process of assessment exerts centripetal pressure on performance scores, and by extension on bonuses, with a tendency to adjust scores downward for the highest performers and upward for the lowest performers. Moreover, other factors, particularly age, affect how bonuses are calculated net of performance scores.

Figure 4.1 plots a smoothed relationship between bonus in months' salary equivalent and age for Japanese men and women in the sample. As this plot shows, Japanese women typically receive lower bonuses than same-age male peers, suggesting systematically lower performance rankings.

Comparing bonus amounts for more and less acculturated Asian employees against these two lines provides a useful, if noisy, measure of whether employers perceive more acculturated Asian employees as higher performers, and

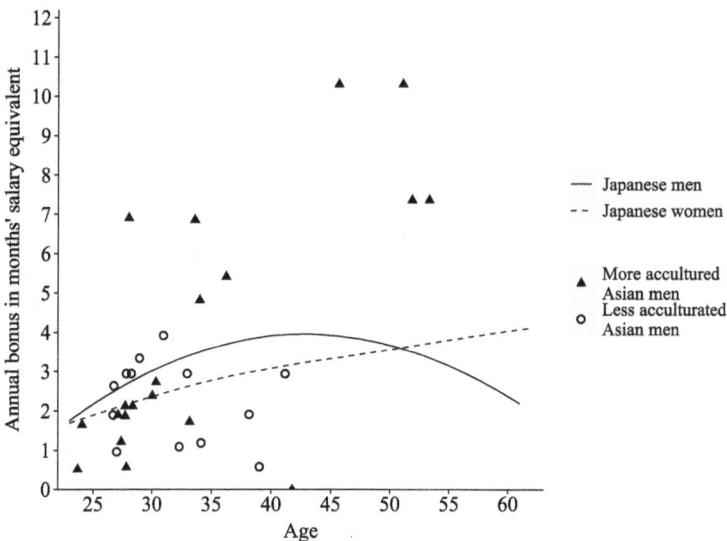

FIGURE 4.1.   Annual bonus by age for Asian men, compared with Japanese men and women. Calculated from author's survey data.

whether assessed performance of more acculturated Asians is closer to that of Japanese peers.

According to this estimation, the highest performers among Asian men are all highly acculturated. They are also older, implying greater experience in Japanese workplaces. This strongly suggests that, as Asian men suspect, acculturation is helpful for positive evaluation in these elite firms. These acculturated Asian men, however, do not simply obtain parity with Japanese in terms of evaluation. Their bonuses suggest that they are evaluated even more highly than a typical Japanese male employee of the same age. This supports the view of Asians, particularly acculturated Asians, as overachieving relative to Japanese employees on average, even though their overall earnings are on par, or slightly lower than, those of Japanese men.

At the same time, acculturation is not a perfect determinant of favorable evaluation. A few less acculturated Asian men earn higher-than-expected bonuses. In addition, some highly acculturated Asian men earn lower-than-expected bonuses, suggesting poorer evaluation. This pattern is particularly striking among younger Asian employees. Even with very strong language skills, they appear to suffer in evaluation compared with same-age peers.

For Asian women, the picture is similar, as shown in figure 4.2. The highest performers are all in their late thirties and older and all are highly acculturated.

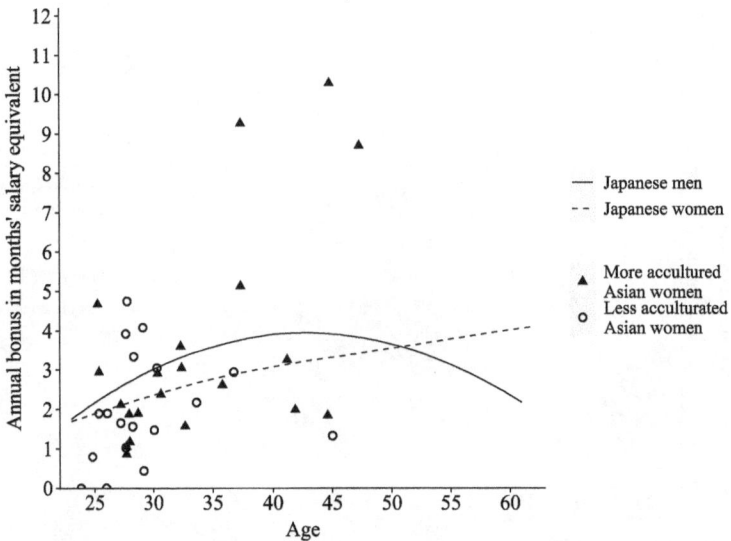

FIGURE 4.2. Annual bonus by age for Asian women, compared with Japanese men and women. Calculated from author's survey data.

There is also some suggestion that acculturation does not benefit Asian women as much as Asian men. Four highly acculturated Asian women in their mid-thirties and older earn bonuses close to or less than those of Japanese female peers, whereas highly acculturated Asian men in the same age-group are all evaluated highly relative to Japanese men. As with Asian men, being highly acculturated is no guarantee of positive evaluation relative to Japanese peers.

In regard to overachievement, these results for Asian women also suggest that they must do more only to attain less. Fourteen Asian women in the sample receive bonuses that are close to or higher than those of same-age Japanese peers. Despite this highly assessed performance, Asian women's overall earnings are far below those of Japanese men, as we saw in chapter 2.

In sum, these results are consistent with arguments that Asians who are highly acculturated are better able to meet or exceed employers' expectations. The Asian men and women with the highest (assessed) performance are all highly acculturated. Acculturation offers no guarantees, however: Many acculturated Asians, particularly women and younger employees, have an assessed performance that is lower than typical for Japanese peers. Conversely, some less acculturated Asians also have above-average (assessed) performance. Acculturation is positively, but weakly, associated with higher assessed performance.

At the same time, these findings are somewhat surprising from the perspective of the prior literature, which suggests that *no matter what*, foreign employees will be found wanting by dint of imperfect acculturation. Older, more acculturated Asian men, and to a lesser extent, older, acculturated Asian women, are often evaluated *more* highly than their Japanese peers. This finding suggests that, despite the tremendous pressure to acculturate and do things in "the Japanese way," managers and employers do not exclusively rely on foreign workers' adherence to or deviance from "the Japanese way" of doing things to evaluate their performance. Although acculturative pressure is undeniable, it does not preclude foreign workers being recognized and rewarded for their distinct contributions as foreigners.

Professional Networks and Acculturation

As described in the interviews, respondents also believe that their ability to forge professional networks within their firms is a key factor to advancement and success, and this ability is contingent on their level of acculturation. To examine the relationship between acculturation and these critical networks within the firm, figures 4.3 and 4.4 plot the number of managers Asian men

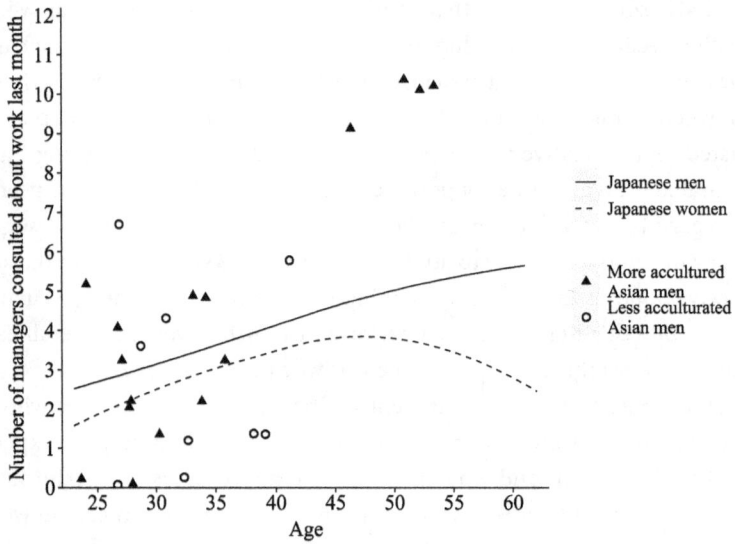

FIGURE 4.3. Asian men's contact with managers by age, compared with Japanese men and women. Calculated from author's survey data.

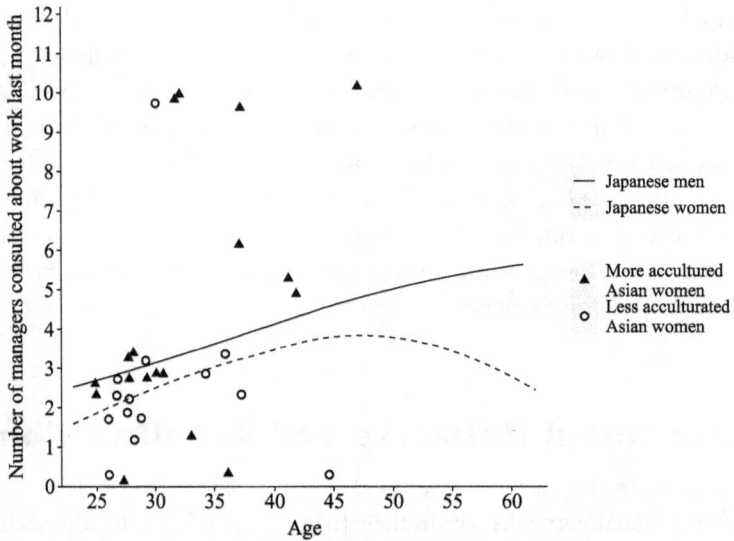

FIGURE 4.4. Asian women's contact with managers by age, compared with Japanese men and women. Calculated from author's survey data.

and women spoke to about work in the past month, against the smoothed average for Japanese, over age.

The patterns are similar to those for bonuses. Among Japanese, women's levels of contact with managers are considerably lower, and this disadvantage persists across age-groups. Contrary to narratives of isolation, however, highly acculturated Asian men and women typically have levels of contact that exceed the average for Japanese peers. Among men, however, even less acculturated Asians sometimes have relatively high levels of contact. Among women, high levels of contact are rare among the less acculturated respondents.

These results support the argument that acculturation is important to Asian workers' careers. Consistent with Asian workers' accounts, the tendency is for more acculturated Asians to have both higher assessed performance and broader contacts with managers. Notably, for both metrics, in many cases, acculturated Asians' outcomes not only match but even exceed those of Japanese.

Acculturation and Earnings

These results support Asian workers' intuition that acculturation benefits their ability to please their managers and helps them build networks in their firms. The question remains whether acculturation also allows them to close the pay gap with Japanese.

To test for this possibility, I model earnings, adjusted for age and tenure, and compare the earnings of both more and less acculturated Asians with those of Japanese. Because of the small sample size, I group all Asians together, and use a dummy variable to account for the large gender gap in pay. As in prior chapters, I use hierarchical linear modeling with random effects to account for firms' differing levels of pay.

As model 1 shows, net of age and tenure, neither highly acculturated nor unacculturated Asians experience a significant wage disadvantage compared with Japanese. Results, however, offer no evidence that the more acculturated fare better than the less acculturated. Indeed, if anything, the larger coefficient for the less acculturated group suggests that they may have more favorable outcomes.

From the perspective of the literature and from Asians' perceptions of the importance of acculturation, this is a surprising finding. One possible explanation is that "foreign human capital"—that is to say, high levels of educational attainment and ability to work in non-Japanese languages and cultures—is more highly valued than foreign workers' (imperfect) ability to approximate native Japanese working habits. It is plausible that less acculturated immigrant workers are more likely to have these rarer skills.[35]

To test for this possibility, model 2 adds the same adjustments for human capital used in chapter 2—that is, education level and number of languages spoken at an advanced level. In this model, however, acculturated Asian workers are predicted to earn significantly less than comparable Japanese workers. The coefficient for the less acculturated workers is also negative, although smaller in magnitude and nonsignificant. This too runs counter to the prevailing narrative about the source of foreign workers' workplace disadvantage.

It is possible that unacculturated Asians, by virtue of foreign education and work experience, have in-demand technical or managerial skills. As such, they may be more likely to work in technical and managerial jobs with higher rates of pay. In contrast, acculturated Asians may be less likely to fill these positions because their work and educational backgrounds are more similar to those of their Japanese counterparts. To determine if this explains why the more acculturated are paradoxically at a greater disadvantage relative to Japanese, model 3 adjusts for number of employees the respondents supervises and whether the respondent is in a technical job. These results show, however, that acculturated Asians are still at a relatively greater disadvantage than Japanese after adjustments for age, tenure, human capital, and managerial and technical job categories.

This is a puzzling result. As discussed previously, acculturation is generally assumed to be a critical predictor of immigrant outcomes across national contexts, but particularly so in Japan and in Japanese elite firms, because of their high standards for acculturation or assimilation. Why, then, do acculturated Asian immigrants fare worse?

One possibility is that this measure of acculturation, based on language ability, fails to capture important aspects of familiarity with Japanese business culture. As we have seen, expectations for acculturation go far beyond language and also encompass Asian workers' ability to accomplish tasks in "the Japanese way." I therefore assess whether acculturation is associated with greater earnings parity using a second proxy measure for acculturation—that is, the number of years respondents have worked in Japan.

A second possible reason why acculturated workers fare worse is the presence of prejudice or discrimination against Asians, regardless of level of acculturation. The fact that levels of acculturation, as measured by Japanese language skill, do not explain why, net of other skills, Asians experience pay gaps with same-sex Japanese peers suggests that Asians face prejudice and discrimination

TABLE 4.3. Regression of level of acculturation on annual earnings

	MODEL 1			MODEL 2			MODEL 3		
	BETA		SE	BETA		SE	BETA		SE
Women	−2.0	***	0.3	−1.9	***	0.3	−1.8	***	0.3
Region of origin and level of acculturation[a]									
More acculturated Asians	0.2		0.5	−1.1	*	0.6	−1.2	*	0.5
Less acculturated Asians	0.8		0.6	−0.4		0.6	−0.5		0.6
Westerners	2.6	***	0.7	1.5	*	0.7	0.8		0.7
Age	0.1		0.1	0.2		0.1	0.3	*	0.1
Age*age	0.0		0.0	0.0		0.0	−0.0		0.0
Tenure	0.3	***	0.1	0.3	***	0.1	0.2	***	0.1
Tenure*tenure	−0.0	***	0.0	−0.0	***	0.0	−0.0	***	0.0
Education[b]									
BA/BS				1.7	***	0.5	1.5	**	0.5
MA/MS				1.9	***	0.6	1.6	**	0.6
MBA/JD/PhD				2.9	***	0.7	2.6	***	0.7
Advanced language skills[c]									
Two advanced languages				1.0	***	0.3	1.0	***	0.3
Three or more advanced languages				1.9	***	0.5	2.0	***	0.5
Number of employees supervised							0.1	***	0.0
Technical job							−0.7	*	0.3
Constant	−0.7		2.5	−4.6		2.6	−4.4		2.5
Model information									
Observations	528			528			528		
Number of firms	12			12			12		

*** $p < 0.001$, ** $p < 0.01$, * $p < 0.05$
Note: All models are from hierarchical linear modeling (HLM) with random effects for firms.
[a]Reference category is Japanese.
[b]Reference category is below BA/BS.
[c]Reference category is one advanced language.

based on their ethnoracial backgrounds or national origins. The significance of race or national origin is also consistent with the divergent experiences of Asians and of Western men. At the same time, Asians' ability to achieve parity with same-sex peers *before* accounting for skills suggests that prejudice and discrimination against Asian-origin immigrants is unlikely to be as widespread or severe as gender bias in this context.

Nevertheless, even small or infrequent acts of discrimination could accumulate over the course of Asians' careers in Japanese firms to produce disadvantage. In this case, we would expect relative equality among Asians and

TABLE 4.4. Regression of years' work in Japan on annual earnings

	MODEL 4			MODEL 5		
	BETA		SE	BETA		SE
Women	−1.7	***	0.3	−1.7	***	0.3
Region of origin[a]						
Asians	0.0		0.6			
Westerners	−2.3		1.2			
Years of work in Japan	−0.1		0.0	−0.1		0.0
Years of work in Japan*Asian	−0.1	*	0.1			
Years of work in Japan*Westerner	0.3	**	0.1			
Region of origin and level of acculturation[a]						
More acculturated Asians				−0.2		0.8
Less acculturated Asians				0.4		0.9
Westerners				−2.3		1.2
Years of work in Japan*more acculturated Asian				−0.1		0.1
Years of work in Japan*less acculturated Asian				−0.2		0.1
Years of work in Japan*Westerner				0.3	**	0.1
Model information						
Observations	528			528		
Number of firms	12			12		

*** $p < 0.001$, ** $p < 0.01$, * $p < 0.05$
Note: All models are from hierarchical linear modeling (HLM) with random effects for firms.
Adjustment variables identical to model 3.
[a]Reference category is Japanese.

Japanese when they enter the Japanese labor market, with gaps emerging over time. This stands in contrast to gender inequality, which, as we saw in chapter 1, emerges at the very earliest career stage and continues to widen.

For Asians, then, the risk of facing impactful discrimination at some point may increase the longer they work in Japan. Even as longer stays expose Asians to greater discrimination, they also give them the opportunity to acculturate. Thus, even if acculturation is valuable in and of itself, more acculturated Asians may be more likely to experience wage inequality with Japanese workers simply because they have been working longer in Japan and thus have a longer exposure to discrimination. This could explain why acculturated Asians appear to experience a larger earnings disadvantage than less acculturated Asians, even though analysis of bonuses and managerial contact suggests that acculturation improves Asians' ability to perform on the job.

Examining the relationship between years of Japanese work experience and the wage gap for Asians thus also allows us to adjudicate between two possible scenarios. On one hand, if Asians who have worked in Japan longer come closer to parity with Japanese, this would support the standard narrative that imperfect acculturation is to blame for wage gaps between Asians and Japanese. On the other hand, if wage gaps widen with greater work experience in Japan, this implies a cumulative process of disadvantage, driven by bias and discrimination.

To test for this possibility, model 4, using the same adjustment variables as model 3, interacts years of work in Japan with region of origin.[36] To increase statistical power, all Asians, regardless of level of acculturation, are grouped together. Model 5 examines the trends separately for more and less acculturated Asians. Although small sample size in each group makes it less likely to detect statistical significance, this model allows us to examine whether the trend is similar for both groups, as we would expect if ethnoracial discrimination is at fault; or whether the trend works in opposite directions, suggesting that the career paths of the less acculturated Asians are simply different from those of the more acculturated Asians from the start.

The findings from models 4 and 5 are highly suggestive of ethnoracial or national-origin discrimination against Asians. The coefficient for Asian regional origin is zero, indicating that Asians with zero years of experience in Japan have earnings equal to Japanese, net of skills. The coefficient for years of work in Japan is nonsignificant, indicating that there is no detectable advantage or disadvantage for Japanese based on whether they have ever worked abroad or have worked exclusively in Japan, net of skills. The interaction effect between years of work in Japan and Asian regional origin is negative and significant. In sum, Asians who have worked longer in Japan earn less than comparable Japanese, whereas those with shorter Japanese work experience do not. The estimated Asian disadvantage relative to Japanese by years of Japanese work experience is plotted in figure 4.5.

An alternative explanation is that what companies value about foreign workers is their foreign skills and that these foreign skills deteriorate the longer they spend in Japan. This explanation, however, does not fit the data. First, model 4 shows that Western men experience growing advantage relative to Japanese counterparts the longer they work in Japan. If Asians' increasing disadvantage were an effect of losing "foreign skills," we would expect a similar relationship between work in Japan and earnings for Western men. Second, total length of time in Japan, including periods in school or as a child rather than as a member of the workforce are not significantly associated with earnings for Asians (models not shown). This too indicates that it is a workplace-specific process that produces disadvantage, rather than a loss of "foreign human capital."

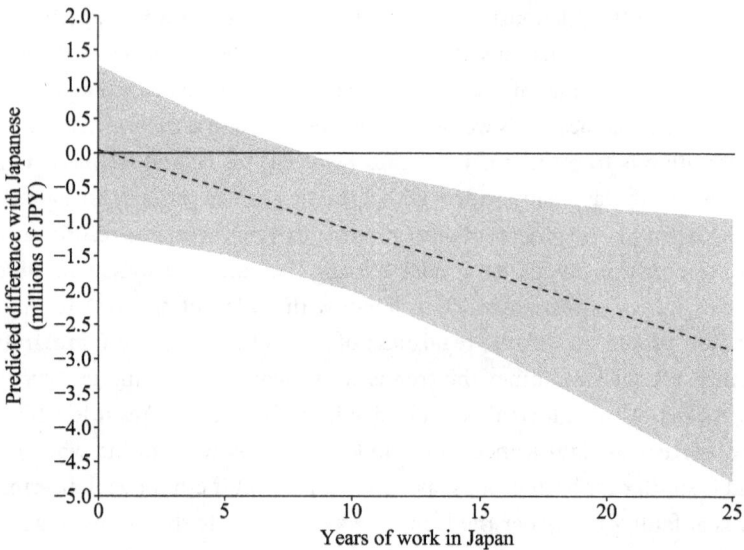

FIGURE 4.5. Asian employees' predicted annual earnings by years of work in Japan, compared with Japanese employees' predicted earnings. Calculated from author's survey data.

In turn, this strongly points to gradually accretive effects of workplace bias and discrimination as drivers of Asians' disadvantage.

Model 5, which separates more and less acculturated Asians, also supports this finding. Although neither coefficient is statistically significant, years of work in Japan is negatively associated with earnings for both groups. If these trajectories were very different, we might interpret this as evidence for two different career paths for acculturated and unacculturated Asians. We would expect ethnoracial or region-of-origin-based bias and discrimination to affect both groups.

Many Asian immigrant workers in these elite firms do everything in their power to acculturate and work in "the Japanese way." Without such efforts, they believe, they have little chance of advancement and success. Their belief in the power of acculturation echoes the claims of previous scholarship that unless foreign workers meet firms' high expectations for acculturation, they are certain to remain second-class workers in elite firms, and even with extensive acculturation, they may never overcome their disadvantage as foreigners. Counterintuitively, however, it is *less* acculturated Asians who come closer to obtaining parity with Japanese men and women in the elite firms in this sample.

Although discrimination is not directly visible in these data, this observed relationship is consistent with parallel processes of acculturation on the part of Asian employees and of discrimination on the part of firms. Asian employees become more acculturated over time; but coterminous, cumulative discrimination means that improving their skills allows them, at best, to keep up with otherwise less skilled and lower-performing same-sex Japanese peers. Compared with Japanese with similar skills, they fall behind. This suggests that perhaps we can best see acculturation as a *by-product of* Asians' attempts to get ahead, rather than as a critical determinant of their assessed performance or rewards.

Indeed, the results strongly suggest that deviance from idealized "Japanese work styles" are not the primary driver of Asian immigrants' disadvantage in this setting. First, the counterintuitive negative relationship between acculturation and earnings is unlikely if the sample firms awarded compensation on the basis of foreign workers' levels of acculturation. Second, qualitative comments from managers about Asians' distinct skills as foreigners hint that the sample firms do not reflexively reward Asians less because of their inability to fully conform to these norms, even if they are criticized for violating them.[37] Finally, if acculturation was the primary axis on which elite firms evaluate foreign workers, we would expect to see a similar positive relationship between years of work in Japan and earnings for both Asians and Westerners, given that acculturation improves with time for both groups. In fact, Western men earn more the longer they have worked in Japan, whereas Asian men and women earn less relative to same-sex peers. This varying relationship implies that, for foreign workers, symbolic boundaries related specifically to ethnoracial background or region of origin drive patterns of advantage and disadvantage, rather than individual variation in workers' level of acculturation.[38] These other forms of symbolic boundaries are explored for Asians in chapter 5 and for Westerners in chapter 6.

These analyses demonstrate the limits of the strategy of privileging acculturation as a way to "solve" perceived problems of immigrant integration in the workplace and in society more broadly.

First, at the level of the company, hiring only the most acculturated foreign employees and then pushing them to assimilate still further does not ensure equality. Companies' failure to offer equal treatment, even and especially when Asian workers acculturate as fully as possible, violates basic principles of fairness. In addition, it harms the financial interests of Japanese companies. Particularly under the conditions of Japan's ongoing labor shortage, companies can benefit from the contributions not only of migrants whose abilities and motivation outstrip those of Japanese workers but also of those who "merely" match them. Moreover, foreign workers are key to consolidating or expanding firms' reach into foreign markets. In cases in which foreign workers must outperform Japanese workers to receive the same treatment, Japanese companies may both overlook qualified immigrant job candidates and lose the immigrants they do hire to attrition. Thus, in failing to treat these workers equally, companies sabotage themselves. Firms can and must take greater responsibility for ensuring fair treatment, both in the interests of equity, and in the interests of economic competitiveness.

Second, the results highlight flaws and contradictions in the high-skilled professional visa program and its preferential fast-track to permanent residency for the most acculturated foreign workers. Although on a macrolevel, foreign workers who are acculturated will likely be more successful at landing jobs in elite firms, these analyses highlight how it makes little sense to differentiate between professional workers in elite firms who attended a Japanese university or speak Japanese at a higher level from otherwise similarly employed workers who speak poorer Japanese and attended universities abroad. By excluding somewhat less acculturated but otherwise successful professionals from easier access to permanent residency, the system of allocating lower points to those with less advanced Japanese language skills or foreign degrees may discourage the settlement of these workers, who, given time, would inevitably acculturate further.

These results also offer an opportunity to reflect on the government's and firms' treatment of foreign workers in comparative perspective. Some scholars portray the Japanese government's decision to privilege acculturated, professional foreign workers for admittance, and the social pressure within firms to acculturate, as an outgrowth of uniquely intense Japanese xenophobia or racism.[39]

The narrative of Japanese exceptionalism looks problematic in light of two facts: First, on average, Asian men and women obtain parity or near parity with same-sex Japanese peers, albeit through overachievement; and, second, relative to Japanese peers, less acculturated Asians fare better. Although this appears to be because cumulative effects of small acts of discrimination have not yet taken their toll, it undermines the argument that foreign workers' success in the workplace is *contingent on* acculturation. It also shows the value that firms place on other skills that Asian foreign workers possess, even as they also discriminate on the basis of region or nation of origin, irrespective of acculturation.

Beyond the findings of the current study, there are further reasons to question the narrative of Japanese exceptionalism in attitudes toward, and workplace treatment of, white-collar foreign workers. Citizens of many wealthy countries share a preference for acculturated migrants of high occupational status over less acculturated migrants in lower-paid occupations.[40] What is unusual, then, is not that Japanese prefer these migrants, but that border control policy has reflected these preferences, instead of employers' demands for inexpensive labor at the bottom end of the labor market.[41]

Companies in other contexts also assess immigrants by their degree of assimilation. Studies of hiring in elite US consulting and technology firms, for example, show that hiring committees are sensitive to signals of foreignness, including accented English or interaction styles deemed "too passive" or "too aggressive," and count these qualities against immigrant applicants.[42] In hiring at elite US consulting firms, interviewers reject international student applicants for accented English or minor linguistic slip-ups, on the grounds that these missteps break the "flow, ease, or rapport that characterize good interviews."[43] At the very least, these examples illustrate that unspoken cultural rules, and penalties for breaking them, are not specific to Japanese companies.

The puzzle of the Japanese case is not, therefore, why attitudes toward foreign workers are so different from those in other national contexts, but how and why strong assimilative pressure coexists *alongside* relatively modest wage gaps between Asian workers and their same-sex Japanese peers.

One piece of the puzzle may be that elite Japanese firms differ less in their underlying degree of ethnoracial prejudice or tendency to discriminate against Asians in employment decisions than they do in their expression of prejudice. Japan's ethnonationalist discourse, which equates full political and social membership in the nation with Japanese blood as well as linguistic and cultural fluency, provides a framework for Japanese people to interpret their discomfort toward ethnoracial others, a vocabulary to express that discomfort, and a plan of action to address it, namely demanding a high level of assimilation.[44] As we have seen, this plan of action does not eliminate inequalities: even when Asians adhere to it, they still face discounts to their skills and experience in the workplace. The persistence of inequality, even for immigrants who do everything "right," implies that cultural difference and imperfect acculturation are, at least in part, mere scapegoats for underlying prejudices of other types, which are explored in greater depth in chapters 5 and 6.[45] The existence of this vocabulary and plan of action, however, do not necessarily indicate that the prejudice that underpins them is more intense than in other contexts, or that discrimination in employment is greater.

The prototypical Silicon Valley "tech bro" is a white native-born man, and the many Indian and Chinese engineers who work in Silicon valley are penalized for ethnoracial and cultural difference.[46] Nevertheless, the US national narrative of immigrant acceptance is antithetical to the explicitly assimilative stance many Japanese managers and firms adopt, even as immigrant workers in the United States face judgment for failing to adhere to the cultural norms of their workplaces.

Liu-Farrer writes that "an obstinate corporate Japan still tries to turn global talents into Japanese salarymen."[47] If US tech managers do not invest as much effort into turning immigrant workers into American tech bros, this is perhaps because they have fewer or different cultural tools for openly expressing ethnoracial bias or cultural chauvinism in interpersonal interactions. This less intense assimilative pressure is not necessarily because underlying attitudes are more favorable toward ethnoracial others or immigrants, nor is it because expectations that immigrants behave in culturally "correct" ways are lower. Instead, US managers may be less likely to directly express these sentiments. Indeed, this lack of assimilative pressure, although more comfortable for immigrants in their day-to-day work lives, may in fact leave them with greater ignorance of cultural expectations for their behavior, impeding their careers above and beyond the barriers they face as ethnoracial others.

In Japanese firms, by contrast, even if the standard for acculturation is a moving or unreachable target, at the level of discourse, the Asian foreign workers' primary deficiencies are not unchangeable or fundamental to their natures. Unlike supposed gender differences in capabilities, imperfect acculturation is seen as a problem to be solved through immigrants' own efforts and through firms' efforts to educate foreign workers in appropriate workplace behavior. The resulting acculturative pressures lend the boundary between foreigners and Japanese hypervisibility and lead to alienation among foreign employees. And yet, they coexist with, rather than preclude, opportunities for Asian men's upward mobility in elite firms.

CRIMINALS AND SUPERSTARS

Anti-Asian Biases and Asians' Workplace Representation

The most visible symbolic boundary between immigrants and Japanese is quite different from those that divide women and men. Unlike the supposed deficiencies of women, Japanese workers often see immigrant employees' imperfect acculturation to the Japanese white-collar workplace as rooted in their lack of appropriate training. At least at the level of discourse, coworkers can "correct" immigrants' cultural differences through education. Thus, Japanese coworkers do not usually describe imperfect acculturation as an *immutable* cultural predisposition, nor as an indelible biological difference.

Nonetheless, ideas about "stickier" biological or cultural inferiorities of Asians are by no means absent in Japanese society, as vividly illustrated in a casual encounter with a Japanese homestay sister of an American friend. I knew Hanako, as I will call her, exclusively from awkward high school photos in my friend's albums: half hidden behind her hair, smiling in a way that did not reach her lips. The poised and fashionable young woman eagerly flagging us down from the café table disarmed me. Hanako chatted happily about her distant hometown, her Tokyo apartment, and her Tokyo boyfriend. I asked about her job. Giggling, she asked me if I wanted to see her "work face." Before I could even answer, her smile slid off her face like butter off a hot knife. Whipping a police badge on a lanyard out from the neck of her blouse, she commanded me curtly and authoritatively, "Stop what you're doing. I need to ask you some questions." Her stern face and tone froze me in my seat. Seeing this, she burst out laughing, the young woman about town once again replacing the police officer.

Talking about her job as a Tokyo Metropolitan police officer, Hanako's "work face" supplanted her casual, friendly "street face" from time to time, but never more so when she brought up the subject of her interactions with Chinese residents. "I hate Chinese people," she practically spat. "They only come to Japan to commit crimes."

As a junior, female officer, Hanako was by no means tasked with high-profile investigations. To the contrary, she laughingly admitted that she worked mostly in traffic enforcement and parking violations, during which she had encountered so-called Chinese criminals, who were sometimes found to have overstayed their visas, in addition to having parked illegally.

Racism of this variety is not uncommon among the police. Although crime rates among noncitizens are no higher than those for Japanese, the National Police Agency singles out "foreigner crime" as a topic of special attention.[1] A flier distributed by two police branch offices in Tokyo instructed residents to "Call the police if you see a Chinese. . . . Call the police if you see a person speaking in Chinese in your apartment building."[2] Contemporary media reporting, statements by right-wing politicians, and anonymous online hate speech further propagate this discourse of Asian criminality.

Unlike the general narrative about foreign workers' unfamiliarity with Japanese business culture, the criminality discourse presupposes a *fixed* criminal orientation, conceived of as biological, cultural, or both. As such, the criminality discourse represents a harder delineation between Asian immigrants and Japanese than generalized complaints about immigrants' imperfect acculturation. Because Asian criminality is seen as deeply rooted in either upbringing or biology, those who hold these prejudicial beliefs do not see the boundary as surmountable through education or effort. Former Tokyo Governor Shintaro Ishihara exemplified this perspective in a 2001 front-page op-ed in the conservative *Sankei Shimbun*, in which he referred to the "criminal DNA" of Chinese people as a reason to curtail Chinese migration to Japan.[3]

To what extent and how do these harder boundaries between Asians and Japanese manifest themselves in elite white-collar workplaces? How is the criminality discourse—the rhetorical association between non-Japanese background and criminal predisposition—affecting Asian foreign workers' advancement prospects as their numbers grow? Is there a way to reconcile the ubiquity of the discourse in the broader culture with Asian workers' relatively successful outcomes in these firms?

In this chapter, I explore the contours of the moral boundaries Japanese draw between themselves and other Asians. This exploration is important for two reasons. First, it offers a deeper look at the factors that prevent Asians from obtaining parity net of skills, beyond the consensus narrative about imperfect acculturation. Second, it illuminates how male Asian immigrants in Japan overcome the worst effects of bias to reap the fruits of demographic decline. I argue that, despite its ubiquity in the broader culture, structural features of the workplace and of the immigration system create an environment in which Asians can overturn the tropes of the criminality discourse. Although other negative stereotypes of more recent origin nonetheless emerge, interactions in the workplace (and outside of it) tend to undermine stereotypes. This stands in contrast to the experiences of women, whose concentration in low-status jobs reinforces negatives stereotypes in the course of daily interactions.

Criminality Discourse in Contemporary Japanese Society

In contemporary Japanese society, discourses of Asian criminality are a bed of warm coals that can be fanned to light in service of any number of political and personal agendas. Furthermore, even among those who do not explicitly subscribe to such beliefs, their haze nonetheless distorts interpretations of foreigners' actions, particularly Koreans and Chinese, but also other Asians, and in some cases foreigners from beyond Asia.[4]

Examples of how these discourses of criminality are deployed in contemporary Japan abound. In the early 2000s, Tokyo Governor Ishihara Shintaro notoriously called on Japan's Self-Defense Forces to protect the capital from rioting "third-country nationals" (a term for Chinese, Koreans, and Taiwanese during Japan's colonial era, now widely perceived as derogatory) in the event of a national emergency.[5] The governor also accused Chinese of having "criminal DNA" in a front-page opinion column in the *Sankei Shimbun*.[6] These statements were widely but not universally condemned; yet these condemnations served to keep the discourse in the public eye, and Ishihara is far from the only politician to espouse such views.[7]

After major disasters, rumors have appeared on social media, claiming falsely that Chinese and Koreans were committing crimes. For example, in 2016, in the wake of an earthquake in Kyushu, one Twitter user wrote, "I hear that Koreans are going around poisoning wells!!! Citizens of Kumamoto, protect yourselves by forming self-defense brigades!!! You can recognize Koreans by making them say 'Ga Gi Gu Ge Go'!!!"[8]

Apart from times of disaster, the Japanese internet is a hotbed of racist diatribe against Chinese and Koreans, including X (formerly Twitter), the popular message board 5channeru (formerly 2channeru), and the comments sections of online news sites, such as Yahoo! News.[9] An analysis of Twitter found that 10 percent of tweets referencing Koreans and 6 percent of tweets referencing China contained words such as "heinous," "crime," "theft," and "rape."[10]

The discourse also has widespread emotional resonance among the broader population. Some 40 percent of Japanese agree that "immigrants are more to blame for crime than other groups," compared with 19 percent in the United States.[11] The ubiquity of this discourse makes it possible for individuals and groups to "explain" the behavior of foreigners, particularly Asians, in a wide variety of contexts. For example, in interviews with men in the queer bar district of Shinjuku Nichome in Tokyo, Baudinette found that Japanese men characterize Korean men in the bar scenes as "thieves" who "steal" white men from the Japanese, and Chinese as destructive "hooligans."[12]

Foreigners, particularly Chinese, may come to internalize the criminality discourse and resort to distancing themselves from their Chinese identity to avoid being pigeonholed into these stereotypes.[13]

Moral Boundaries in the Elite White-Collar Workplace

In contrast to its pervasiveness in the broader culture, I observed little overt expression of the criminality discourse in white-collar firms. Perhaps the only example of this discourse came from a human resources (HR) officer, who described going on an overseas business trip with a Chinese coworker. The HR officer passed quickly through passport control at their destination, he told me, but his People's Republic of China (PRC) passport-holding colleague was pulled aside for lengthy questioning. The HR officer treated this difference in their reception as a matter of course, saying, "Japanese people don't do bad things, that's why our passports are so powerful." It was not that he saw his Chinese coworker as a criminal per se, but that he considered it natural for the coworker (and not himself) to fall under suspicion.

To allow them to speak more freely about these sensitive topics, my Japanese research assistant conducted all of the formal interviews with Japanese survey respondents. Even so, most interviewees went out of their way to praise their Asian coworkers. When asked about his experiences with "foreign coworkers," Hideki began with compliments: "My number one impression is that foreign employees demonstrate a high standard of excellence. For myself, it never occurred to me to get a job abroad. So, the first thing is, they have a lot of guts. The second thing is, this company is pursuing a global strategy. But none of us speak English. But the foreign workers, they actually *have* those global skills [emphasis in original]." Although Hideki did not specify *Asian* foreign workers, it was clear from the context that this is who he meant. Asian coworkers were impressive for having *learned* English, unlike Japanese coworkers who had not.

The concept of "excellence" or "superiority" (*yuushuu*) of foreign employees in general, and Asian employees in particular, came up repeatedly in the interviews. HR officers whom I spoke with in the earliest stages of the project, in 2013, told me that foreign workers "exceeded expectations" and contrasted them favorably to "complacent" Japanese coworkers for their ambition and drive.

Yuichi, a manager in the sample firms, explained:

> Foreign employees have learned Japanese. They speak two or even three languages. And, they have smarts. They have high potential. But I'm not saying that's because they are foreigners. No. It's because they've burnished their skills in a [high-pressure] environment. And, because the foreign employees have been to language school, they tend to be a little older than their Japanese colleagues hired at the same time. So, for all those reasons, their skills and their smarts are superior.

Although, like Hideki, Yuichi did not specify the nationality of the foreign workers in question, this insight can only refer to Asians, because foreign workers from Western countries do not typically attend language school.

As much as HR officers, and to a lesser extent, coworkers, lauded the "hungry spirit" of their Asian immigrant coworkers, a few drew moral boundaries and interpreted these attributes as inappropriately self-interested.[14] One HR officer reflected that managers had to use care in dealing with Asian coworkers, as they could be "touchy" and "proud," in contrast to more self-effacing Japanese. Takeshi elaborated the most fully:

> To put it plainly, the stereotype of Chinese people is, they are loud and self-centered. I want to think that's just a stereotype. But, the person who I happened to work with fits that stereotype to a T. I really want to think that's just a coincidence . . . but I just could not get along with him. We had a fundamentally different approach to work. It wasn't about "How should we approach this as a team? He was more like, "Check out how much *I've* done and recognize *my* contributions. I'm pretty great, right?" [emphasis in original] That more or less applies to my current boss [who is Korean] as well. . . . I was shocked. It's a moat that can't be bridged.

The metaphor of a "moat that cannot be bridged" is telling, indicating a fundamentally different, and to Takeshi, less virtuous, work orientation of his Asian coworkers. This virtue did not preclude acknowledgment of his coworkers' talents, however. Despite his resentment, Takeshi too used the term "excellence" to describe his Korean boss. His boss, he said, reached a managerial rank usually only obtainable by those 50 years old or older at the young age of 37, something he begrudgingly accepted as justified based on his boss's performance.

Critically, when drawing this boundary around "prideful" or "self-seeking" work attitudes, respondents explicitly referenced "Chinese" and "Korean" coworkers. In contrast, when discussing "perfectible" deficiencies of acculturation discussed in chapter 3, interviewees exclusively used nonethnic terms, such as "foreign workers," as they did when offering praise. The ethnoracial connotation of this symbolic boundary is thus far stronger than that of Japanese/non-Japanese distinctions based on linguistic competency or culturally correct styles of communication.

The gendered implications of these symbolic boundaries around careerism and self-seeking are also noteworthy. Because the Japanese language does not require speakers to specify gendered pronouns, Japanese interviewees' general statements about "foreign workers" or "Asians" could be taken to refer to men, to women, or to immigrant coworkers of both genders. When speaking about specific coworkers, however, Japanese interlocutors did in many cases make the gender clear. Mentions of Asians' "excellence" occasionally applied to women as well as men, but complaints about Asian coworkers' careerism focused solely on men. This gave the strong impression that, to the predominantly male Japanese interviewees, the default "Asian foreign worker" is male, even though more than half of the Asian employees at the firms are women. Moreover, this use suggests a marginal position for Asian women, *as women*, to the extent that ethnoracial boundaries in regard to Asian women are largely irrelevant to Japanese male interlocutors.

Overall, however, most Japanese respondents did not describe "unbridgeable" divides between Asians and Japanese. The few who did always leavened these with some mitigating factors. Takeshi went on to say that foreign workers, by being "loud," had helped create a more positive culture that was less obsequious and blindly obedient to the misguided dictates of upper-level managers. Emi, who railed against her foreign coworkers' sloppiness and low standards, noted that they did not necessarily place work at the center of their lives, which, she grudgingly conceded, could be a positive thing, even if she did not personally like their way of doing things. Thus, despite the prevalence of racist and racialist discourse in the broader society, such discourse was rare and muted—although not absent—among my interlocutors. Furthermore, even as a few Japanese respondents drew moral boundaries about "the dark side" of Asian's excellence, particularly men's excellence, they forewent the culturally pervasive criminality discourse.

Social Desirability or Limited Prejudice?

There are two possible ways of looking at this apparent absence of the criminality discourse, as well as respondents' careful qualification of negative evaluations of the "dark side of excellence" with at least semipositive mitigating factors. On one hand, despite their deep historical roots, symbolic boundaries focused on criminality and moral worth may in fact be absent or at least fading in elite firms. On the other hand, respondents may simply be motivated to hide socially unacceptable views.

Studies comparing Japanese citizens' willingness to express anti-immigrant or anti-Asian immigrant sentiment openly or covertly reveal that most people with anti-immigrant sentiments are willing to express those sentiments openly.[15] The firms in the sample, however, because of their explicit emphasis on increasing workforce diversity and proactive measures to hire foreign workers, may be exceptions to this general rule.

Pixisa, for example, proclaims on its HR page that "We respect all [our company's] people's differences—race, religion, culture." At the time of the study, such a direct statement on race or national origin was rare in firms' public relations material, but many HR officers whom I talked to stressed the importance of "nationality-blind" HR management, insisting that they seek to employ and reward "the best people" regardless of citizenship (or gender). Although I did my best to mitigate the pressures of social desirability bias by conducting interviews outside the workplace and by hiring a Japanese research assistant to conduct the interviews with Japanese interlocuters, this climate might have discouraged respondents from expressing bias against their Asian coworkers, even if they held these views.

At the same time, it is also possible that workplace dynamics erode the moral boundaries Japanese draw between themselves and other Asians. Contact theory holds that sustained, cooperative, equal-status contact reduces prejudicial attitudes and discriminatory behavior toward members of minoritized groups.[16] Japanese firms' efforts to build team spirit and foster personal connections among employees may facilitate exactly the type of contact that is most effective in mitigating bias and discrimination.[17] Moreover, ethnic and racial prejudice are most salient in the absence of "individuating information"—as those around the minoritized individual get to know him or her as a person, they are less likely to see that person through the lens of stereotypes.[18] Thus, racial and ethnic discrimination are thought to be more severe in contexts such as police encounters or hiring, when interlocutors know relatively little about the minoritized person.[19] In sum, long-term contact with other Asians in the workplace may wear down conscious and unconscious associations of Asians with criminality among Japanese employees or may make them less likely to apply those stereotypes to their Asian coworkers and act on the basis of that ethnoracial prejudice.

Survey Experimental Examination of Bias

To assess whether symbolic boundaries related to Asians' deservingness and moral worth, including those associated with the criminality discourse, are widespread but hidden, or whether they are indeed relatively rare, I use a set of survey experimental vignettes, summarized in table 5.1. Respondents viewed four short narratives about hypothetical employees and were asked to recommend a reward, in the case of laudable employee behavior, or a penalty, in the case of employee malfeasance. At the level of the respondent, the name of the hypothetical employee varied randomly to indicate region of origin, with names that represent Japanese ethnicity (Tanaka, Suzuki, Takahashi, Ikeda), Korean ethnicity (Pak, Kim), Chinese ethnicity (Li, Wang), and Anglo ethnicity (Smith, Brown).[20] If respondents draw boundaries related to morality and deservingness, we would expect less systematically less favorable treatment for Asian-named employees.[21]

The survey experimental method has several advantages for measuring these types of prejudices. In an environment where leaders advocate for

TABLE 5.1. Summary of vignettes

VIGNETTE	PORTRAYAL OF EMPLOYEE BEHAVIOR	SUMMARY	POSSIBLE LONG-TERM CONSEQUENCE
Records falsification	Negative	An employee falsifies records to exaggerate own sales figures.	Firing or demotion
Tardiness	Negative	An employee has been tardy and absent without an explanation.	Firing or demotion
Cost saving	Positive	An employee negotiates a cost-saving contract with vendors.	Promotion
Coworker assistance	Positive	An employee helps out a coworker who is swamped with work.	Promotion

inclusivity, people who hold negative views of the outgroup may prefer to avoid disclosing their beliefs. Although explicit attitudinal measures, such as questions about endorsement of a stereotype, might not yield meaningful results because of social desirability bias, the vignette methodology is more unobtrusive.[22] Respondents view one version of each vignette, so participants are not made aware that bias is being measured.[23] Further, because bias is measured at the aggregate level by comparing responses between individuals who viewed different versions of the vignette, no *individual* can be "outed" as biased, and respondents are less likely to censor themselves even if they are aware of the researcher's intent to assess levels of prejudice.

Two vignettes describe an employee who has done something blameworthy—falsified records, and been absent and tardy without explanation—and two vignettes describe an employee who has done something praiseworthy—negotiated a cost-saving contract with vendors, and helped a coworker swamped with work.

In the case of the negative vignettes, respondents could recommend one of several courses of action, including doing nothing, a warning, a one-time salary deduction, an unpaid suspension from work, demotion, or firing. Because both demotion and firing have serious long-term consequences, I analyze the likelihood that respondents recommended either option.

In the case of the positive vignettes, respondents could recommend multiple reactions from the hypothetical employee's supervisor, including doing nothing, praising the employee in private, praising the employee to teammates, praising the employee to managers and HR, recommending the employee for a higher-than-usual bonus, and recommending the employee for a promotion. Because promotion has the most significant career consequences, I focus the analysis on promotion recommendations alone.

I exclude Asians' responses to the vignettes from the analysis. Further, because the Japanese (and non-Asian immigrant workers) may not be able to distinguish between Chinese and Korean names, and because, in practice, the pattern of the results was quite similar for Chinese- and Korean-named hypothetical employees, I combine responses to both.

The records falsification vignette is the most likely to detect criminality-associated biases, through a more widespread selection of the harshest penalty for hypothetical employees with Asian names. This is because the criminality discourse may lead respondents to interpret Asians' records falsification as lawbreaking, as opposed to merely negligent or selfish for Japanese.

The cost-saving and coworker assistance vignettes, in contrast, are the most likely to trigger biases relating to the "dark side of excellence." If Asians are thought to be hyperfocused on their careers, high performance described in

TABLE 5.2. Penalties and rewards recommended for Japanese-named and Chinese/Korean-named employees

	JAPANESE-NAMED EMPLOYEE		CHINESE/KOREAN-NAMED EMPLOYEE	
	DEMOTION/FIRING RECOMMENDED (%)	TOTAL N	DEMOTION/FIRING RECOMMENDED (%)	TOTAL N
Records falsification vignette	30.8	253	37.5 *	120
Tardiness vignette	1.6	245	0.8	131
	Promotion recommended (%)	Total N	Promotion recommended (%)	Total N
Cost-saving vignette	17.4	265	16.0	131
Coworker assistance vignette	16.9	248	13.8	138

* Statistically significantly different from recommendation for Japanese at the 0.05 level.
Note: Based on responses from non-Asian employees only.

the cost-saving event, and prosocial behavior described in the coworker assistance event, will be viewed with more skepticism, leading to lower recommended rewards.

The tardiness vignette does not speak directly to either the criminality discourse or to the dark side of excellence, but rather to a tendency associated with the narrative of imperfect acculturation that foreigners' flouting of standard employment norms is more damning than when Japanese do the same.

The full text of the vignettes appears in appendix A, and results of the vignettes appear in table 5.2.

Intriguingly, the starkest disadvantage for Asians appears in the records falsification vignette, in which the harshest penalties are recommended for Asians in 37.5 percent of cases, compared with 30.8 percent for Japanese. This result indicates that, although none of the interviewees expressed it openly, the criminality discourse may lead respondents to interpret Asian coworkers' workplace malfeasance as more damning than the same malfeasance committed by Japanese employees. At the same time, however, the gap in recommendations for the Japanese-named employees compared with the Asian-named employees is not vast. So, although the records falsification vignette implies that the criminality discourse is not absent in the elite white-collar employment environment, it does not suggest that it is widespread.

The tardiness vignette does not show any evidence of stereotypes or bias against Asians. Respondents do not respond harshly to tardiness: The vast majority indicate that no formal penalty is necessary and responses to Japanese-named employees and Asian-named employees are essentially identical.

For the positive vignettes, differences in recommendations are slight and do not reach statistical significance, although in both cases, respondents recommend promotion marginally less often for Asians. In sum, although Japanese interviewees' comments demonstrate the emergence of negative stereotypes related to the dark side of Asians' excellence in the workplace, the vignettes do not demonstrate any effects of such biases on employee responses to Asians' positive workplace contributions.

Bias and Representation

Nearly all Japanese are exposed to the criminality discourse in some form—either directly through internet diatribes on message boards and comment sections, the statements of politicians and bureaucrats, and avid coverage in the mainstream media of the (fairly rare) cases in which foreign residents or visitors are actually arrested; or indirectly through media articles criticizing hate speech rallies, and debunking and pushing back against the criminality discourse.[24] The survey experimental data suggest that negative stereotypes associated with the criminality discourse are present, but not widespread, among the non-Asian respondents in the sample. What does this bode for the future of Asians' integration into elite firms and their access to the most remunerative opportunities?

Theory on intergroup relations suggests two possible trajectories. Contact theory posits that increased interaction between members of the minoritized group (Asians) and the dominant group (Japanese) will lead to a reduction in prejudice.[25] This phenomenon has been documented widely in correlational data in many national contexts. People who have more contact with ethnoracial others report more favorable attitudes toward individuals, toward the target group as a whole, and toward policies that benefit out-group members.[26] There is no evidence that Japan is an exception. Because of limited data, explorations of contact theory in Japan rely on proximal measures of contact, including frequency of seeing foreigners in one's neighborhood, and English-language ability. These measures, however, are positively associated with more favorable attitudes toward immigration, suggesting lower prejudice.[27]

Given the considerable discretion managers exercise in how they evaluate, mentor, and recommend employees for promotion, the contact mechanism strongly implies that Asians' careers will benefit from reductions in managerial prejudice. Although biased managers may, consciously or unconsciously, treat Asian employees disadvantageously in evaluation or in recommendation from promotion, the less prejudiced are managers' views, the more similar managers' treatment of Asians is likely to be in comparison with that of Japanese subordinates. Thus, contact theory suggests that Asians' increased presence in the white-collar workplace will erode, if not eliminate, Asian ethnic or national origin as a source of economic disadvantage in the workplace.

The literature, however, also suggests a second possible way in which Asians' increased workplace presence may shape ethnic biases: At large scales of aggregation, such as the municipal or prefectural level, larger (or growing) numbers of foreigners are associated with decreased support for immigration among Japanese residents, indicating greater prejudice.[28] Scholars have found similar patterns in other national contexts as well and argue that, as immigration increases, natives may see immigrants as a threat, either to their economic security, to their culture, or both.[29] The threat principle may well operate within the white-collar workplace. Even as population decline makes it easier for Asians to find employment in Japanese firms, posthire Asians and Japanese remain in competition for a limited number of managerial posts. This feeling of threat could potentially reinvigorate the criminality discourse, or heighten other forms of prejudice, including those beliefs about Asians' self-seeking, careerist orientations. If Asians' presence triggers this sense of threat, managers' unfavorable treatment of Asians relative to Japanese might intensify over time, exacerbating the economic penalties associated with Asian origin in the white-collar workplace.

Whether Asians' growing presence erodes symbolic boundaries or heightens them, Asian men are likely to see the largest effects of these changes. As we have seen in previous chapters, Asian women remain caught in the same "gender trap" as Japanese women: Yawning gender pay gaps for both groups of women dwarf the comparatively smaller penalty associated with Asian origin. Consequently, because erosions of ethnic boundaries are unlikely to change the gender hierarchy, Asian women stand to benefit relatively little from this potential change. Conversely, Asian women's opportunities are unlikely to fall much further even if ethnic prejudice intensifies, because as we have seen, Japanese coworkers see the prototypical "Asian employee" as a man.

To explore the relationship between attitudes toward Asians and Asians' presence in the workplace, I calculate bias scores at the firm level from the records falsification vignette (estimating the pervasiveness of the criminality discourse), the cost-savings vignette, and the coworker assistance vignette (estimating the dark side of excellence narratives). In the case of the records falsification vignette, I subtract the proportion of (non-Asian) respondents at each firm who recommend demotion or firing for Japanese-named employees from the proportion of those at the same firm who recommend the harshest penalties for Chinese- or Korean-named employees. This produces a measure with a theoretical maximum of 1 and a minimum of −1, in which 0 indicates no difference in treatment recommendations for Japanese-named and Asian-named employees. Negative numbers indicate that the harshest penalties are recommended more often for Asian-named employees, compared with Japanese employees, suggesting that the criminality discourse is more widespread within the firm.

I create similar bias measures based on the cost-saving and coworker assistance vignettes. In the case of the positive vignettes, I subtract the proportion of (non-Asian) respondents who recommend promotion for Chinese or Korean-named employees from the proportion of those who recommend promotion for Japanese-named employees. In this case, because the target outcome is positive, the order of subtraction is reversed. Thus, for all three bias measures, negative numbers indicate that Asians are disfavored, meaning they are penalized more often in the negative vignette or are rewarded less often in the positive vignettes.[30]

These attitude scores are necessarily subject to measurement error, which is large because the sample size within each firm is small. They offer, however, perhaps the only feasible tool for uncovering attitudes and beliefs that respondents prefer to keep hidden. Although measurement error means we cannot be certain that the criminality discourse is indeed significantly more widespread among respondents at Upstore (−0.20 on the records falsification vignette, indicating respondents recommended the harshest penalty 20 percent more often for Asian-named employees) and FuturaCorp (−0.17), I assume that, as a general tendency, negative numbers, particularly at, or below −0.1, indicate more negative attitudes toward Asians among the respondents in a given firm.

I then examine the relationship between the attitude scores and Asians' share of the sample. If bias is exacerbated by Asians' presence, we would expect more negative bias scores in firms with a larger share of Asian respondents; if Asians' presence reduces bias, we would expect to see more positive scores in firms with high shares of Asian respondents.

The three bias scores, as well as Asians' share of each firms' sample appear in table 5.3. Firm-level correlations between the three bias scores and the share of Asian respondents in each firm appear in table 5.4.

Turning first to the three firm-level bias scores, the strongest effects appear in the records falsification vignette, with eight of twelve firms showing some disfavor toward Asian-named employees, including five firms with bias scores of −0.1 or less. For the cost-saving and coworker assistance vignettes, most firms fall quite close to 0, indicating equal treatment. In the coworker assistance vignette, the trend is slightly more negative than in the cost-saving vignette, but many firms cluster quite close to 0. In sum, when we disaggregate the vignette results by firm, we see that the overall vignette results do not hide surprising variability among the firms. The cost-saving and coworkers

TABLE 5.3.   Attitudes toward Asians by firm

COMPANY	PERCENT ASIAN	RECORDS FALSIFICATION ATTITUDE SCORE	COST- SAVINGS ATTITUDE SCORE	COWORKER ASSISTANT ATTITUDE SCORE
Upstore	15.6	−0.20	−0.04	−0.25
Asahi	27.9	0.32	0.04	−0.03
FuturaCorp	8.6	−0.17	−0.05	0.19
Kaneda	16.0	−0.20	−0.15	−0.02
Hamabe	13.3	0.09	0.00	−0.08
Takematsu	16.0	−0.10	−0.09	0.09
Dazan	7.4	−0.05	0.00	−0.06
Cyatec	24.3	0.07	0.03	−0.26
Henderson	4.9	−0.05	−0.02	−0.09
Maruyama	34.8	0.18	0.15	0.03
Pixisa	3.4	−0.23	0.26	−0.01
Green Elm	20.0	−0.08	0.00	0.50

assistance vignettes showed only very small and nonsignificant gaps between recommendations for Japanese-named versus Asian-named employees overall, and indeed most firms cluster near 0. Similarly, the moderate disfavor for Asians detected in the overall results of the records falsification vignette is widespread, although not universal, among firms.

Table 5.4 shows the relationship among the three bias scores and Asians' share of the sample from each firm, using Pearson's r, which ranges between −1 (perfect negative correlation) and 1 (perfect positive correlation). In the social sciences, correlation coefficients greater in magnitude than 0.5 (whether positive or negative) are generally considered to be strong, and those smaller than 0.3 are generally considered weak.

Table 5.4 reveals three important patterns. First, the three firm-level bias measures are not strongly correlated with each other, indicating that the three

TABLE 5.4.   Correlations between firm-level bias measures and Asians' representation in the sample

	RECORDS FALSIFICATION	COST SAVING	COWORKER ASSISTANCE	PERCENT ASIAN
Records falsification vignette	1.00			
Cost-saving vignette	0.21	1.00		
Coworker assistance vignette	−0.13	−0.03	1.00	
Percent Asian	0.71 *	0.08	0.03	1.00

* Statistically significant at 0.05 level.
Note: Firm-level bias scores based on responses by non-Asians only.

vignettes pick up on different facets of coworkers' attitudes toward Asians. A firm climate in which the criminality discourse is more widespread, as indicated by the bias score from the records falsification vignette, is not necessarily one in which coworkers are less willing to reward Asian employees for helping coworkers or saving costs.

Second, to the extent that lower willingness to reward Asian employees reflects narratives on the dark side of Asians' excellence, table 5.4 shows no evidence that these attitudes are either more or less prevalent based on Asians' workplace presence. Correlations between the results of both positive vignettes and Asians' share of respondents at the firm are weak.

Finally, and most intriguingly, the results show a strong positive correlation between the records falsification results and Asians' representation. Because negative scores indicate less favorable attitudes, the positive correlation indicates that attitudes toward Asians more favorable when Asians' representation is higher. This correlation is also statistically significant.

Figure 5.1 plots this relationship, with each point representing a firm. In firms in which Asians' share of the sample is larger, attitudes (as captured by

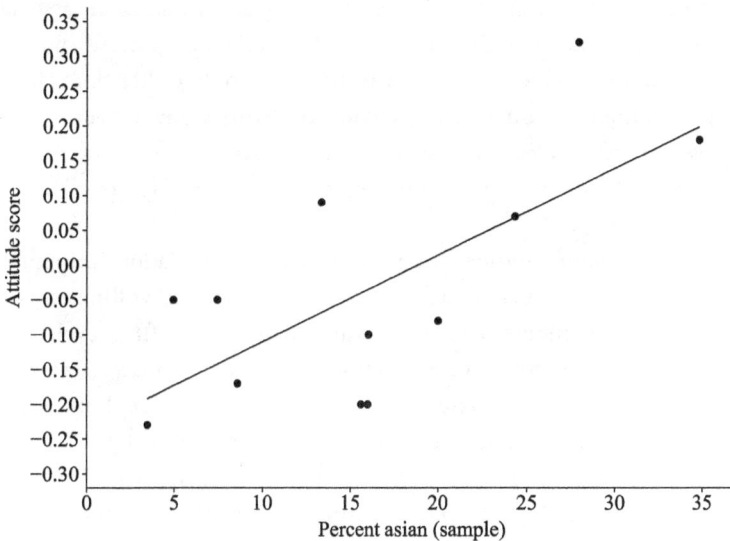

FIGURE 5.1. Relationship between firm-level attitude scores and share of Asian employees. Calculated from author's survey data. Attitude scores are derived from responses to the records falsification vignette at each firm. Attitude scores below zero indicate that Japanese and Western respondents at that firm were more likely to recommend the harshest penalties (demotion or firing) for Asian-named employees than for Japanese-named employees.

the records falsification vignette) are more positive. This suggests that in the firms with more Asian employees, the criminality discourse is less widespread, and indeed, potentially absent.

As Asians' vignette responses are excluded from the firm-level bias score calculation, this relationship is not a result of Asians' positive attitudes toward their in-group, but rather of more favorable attitudes among Japanese (and Western) respondents.

Causality in the Relationship Between Bias and Representation

Contact theory posits that sustained interpersonal interactions between members of different ethnic groups can improve majority group members' attitudes toward the out-group. In other words, it argues for a causal relationship between the two. These findings show a correlation: The criminality discourse is less widespread in firms in which Asians are a larger relative presence. Is a causal relationship plausible?

Psychologists have criticized correlational investigations of the relationship between contact and prejudice. Even if such studies show an association between contact and prejudice, it is possible that less prejudiced individuals are more likely to seek out contact with the out-group, rather than that contact changes their attitudes.[31] In the context of this study, however, respondents are not freely selecting their contact with Asian coworkers. As we saw in chapter 1, HR departments assign employees to teams, irrespective of their preferences.

Second, we should consider the possibility that the relationship represents Asians' selection into less biased firms, or less biased firms' willingness to hire Asians in greater numbers. This, too, is improbable. At the firm level, the rates at which Asians are represented are uniformly low: In all cases, Asian employees make up a miniscule share of the workforce—less than 1 percent. The higher shares of Asians in the samples of some firms represent greater concentration on particular teams, rather than higher representation in the firm overall. Thus, Asians' higher concentration (and coworkers' attitudes) can best be seen as a local, team phenomenon.

A third possibility is that HR departments deliberately assign Asian employees to teams in cases in which they believe the environment will be more positive. This is also unlikely, however. Universally, HR managers described to me team assignment practices that were focused on developing foreign (and Japanese) employees' skills and exposure to different business areas, not providing a "comfortable" working environment. In addition, all the firms in the sample reported that they assign non-Japanese employees throughout the company, and do not consciously concentrate them on particular teams. Thus, in this case, selection onto teams (or firms) is unlikely to explain why the criminality discourse is more prevalent in cases in which there are fewer Asian respondents.

Hence, although we cannot definitively rule out noncausal explanations for the relationship between the criminality discourse and Asians' presence using cross-sectional data, the observed relationship supports the contact hypothesis, and the possibility that the criminality discourse is weakened through extensive contact with many Asian coworkers.

Two interviewees in low-bias firms also made remarks consistent with the possibility that working alongside a more diverse group of Asian employees might topple negative stereotypes. Masato said:

> About a third [of our recent hires] are from China, but other than that, there are people from more than 20 countries. Everyone tries to make them work "in the Japanese way," but that doesn't fit their way of thinking, so of course that leads to friction. But, you know, [their way of thinking] isn't determined by the country of origin. I mean, every country's culture is different. And, just looking among Chinese employees, they are all different from each other. My impression is that, maybe friction is less about cultural differences than Japanese managers' inability to explain their expectations.

This perspective, which acknowledges diversity among the foreign employees in general, and among Chinese employees in particular, stands in stark contrast to the essentialist thinking inherent in stereotypes, including both the criminality discourse and the narrative about Asian employees as self-seeking and egocentric.

It also implies that contact, as it is usually conceptualized in the literature, is not always enough to erode stereotypes. Although the literature operationalizes contact in different ways, many studies examine contact between a member of the majority and one out-group member—for example, a randomly assigned conversation partner or roommate.[32] As we saw in the example of Hideki's experiences with foreign coworkers, his sustained, daily contact with just two out-group members served only to confirm his stereotypes of Chinese and Koreans. In contrast, interactions with a diversity of foreigners led Masato to the conclusion that not only was the foreigner/Japanese dichotomy too simplistic but also that even members of a particular national origin group could have variegated personalities and work orientations.

Yuichi, also in a low-bias firm with a relatively high share of non-Japanese workers, described in some detail how the presence of foreign worker had led him to rethink the foreigner/Japanese dichotomy:

> One big change [with the arrival of more foreign workers] is in personnel evaluation. Between Japanese people, the way we've done it is to say, "this is your score, let's move on." But with foreigners, you have to explain how you arrived at that score, with a thorough and logical account of why the evaluation is below or above average. *Ultimately, this isn't a question of foreigners versus Japanese* [emphasis added]. It's the responsibility of the manager to explain. The fact is, Japanese managers have neglected that responsibility. Foreigners will ask why they got a certain score. But managers' lack of explanation is a problem *with managers* [emphasis in original], not a problem with the foreigners making the request.

Like Masato, Yuichi's perspective shows a rejection of the idea that something is "wrong" with the foreign employees' ways of doing things. Although foreigners' "demands" for a clear explanation of their performance scores could be interpreted as an example of self-seeking, careerist behavior, in a work environment with a relatively high share of Asian workers, Yuichi interpreted it as a push for Japanese managers to do what they should have been doing all along— providing a clear explanation and justification of the performance score.

Hideki and Emi, both in high-bias firms, offered some positive assessment of their Asian coworkers. But in their cases, these positive statements leavened more passionate, essentialized criticisms. Yuichi and Masato, in low-bias firms with higher shares of Asian coworkers, were both more positively inclined and less essentialist in their thinking, which is consistent with the positive contact mechanism. Although the survey experiment shows only that Asians' greater presence in the workplace is associated with lower prevalence of the criminality discourse, these interview responses suggest that Asians' presence may erode other prejudices as well.

Although the association of criminality with Asian ethnic origin is ubiquitous in Japanese society, its presence is not obvious in the sample firms. In these elite white-collar environments, Japanese employees rarely openly express this form of bias. Despite this lack of open expression, the survey experimental investigation reveals that the criminality discourse is not entirely absent, as reflected in respondents' greater willingness to recommend harsh penalties for Chinese- and Korean-named employees who engage in workplace malfeasance. Moreover, the interviews also reveal new forms of bias lacking the deep historical roots of the criminality discourse in respondents' aspersions cast on Asians' achievement and ambition as inappropriate and self-seeking.

These subtle but persistent stereotypes of Asian employees likely contribute to the inequalities (net of skills) described in chapter 4, which emerge and grow over the course of Asians' careers in Japan. Over the course of a worker's career, managers (and coworkers) make hundreds of small decisions that potentially affect workers' outcomes, ranging from everyday decisions about how to allocate work; how to encourage, train, and mentor employees; and how to assign credit when things go well or to assign blame when things go poorly. More infrequently, managers and HR personnel also determine performance scores, job placement, raises and bonuses, and promotion. Biases potentially influence what information is recalled or deemed pertinent at the point of decision, and how that information is acted on in every one of these hundreds of instances. Even if treatment is equal in the great majority of decisions, a small percentage of differential decisions may result in outcomes that become more unequal by ethnicity over the course of workers' careers. Managers who see Asians as potential criminals, or who see their excellence as inappropriately self-seeking, are less likely to give them the full-throated support they would need to obtain full equality, net of skills, with Japanese men.

Yet these findings also offer grounds for optimism, at least for Asian men's future trajectories: Despite deep historical roots and contemporary visibility, on teams in which Asians make up a higher share of immediate coworkers, there is little evidence that the criminality discourse persists. Although the current study does not conclusively demonstrate a causal relationship between Asians' presence and the absence of bias, it is nonetheless plausible that Asians' presence reduces prejudice both *across* and *within* individuals. As firms hire Asian employees in higher numbers, a larger number non-Asian employees have the opportunity for sustained, cooperative interactions with at least one Asian coworker, which according to contact theory should erode biases. In addition (or alternately), in cases in which contact is with just one or two Asian employees, other workers may perceive stereotype-disconfirming interactions and individuals as exceptional. But when Japanese employees have opportunities to work closely with a more diverse group of Asian coworkers, this may inculcate a stronger tendency to see Asians as individuals rather than as stereotypical representatives of their group, or as exceptions to the racial rule. In turn, this blurring of symbolic boundaries around criminality likely reduces the discrimination Asians face in white-collar workplaces.

Indeed, prejudice and discrimination that decrease with contact are consistent with the general pattern of Asian earnings disadvantage described in chapter 4. In contrast to gender inequality in pay, which emerges in the very earliest stages of workers' careers, inequality associated with Asian origin materializes gradually over the course of workers' careers in Japan. Moreover, Asians are not systematically disadvantaged relative to same-sex peers in evaluation (as estimated by bonuses) but only in overall pay-setting processes. One plausible interpretation is that bias reductions occur mostly among immediate coworkers and supervisors—those who have the closest contact with Asian employees. As a result of this contact, supervisors may even-handedly evaluate and assign work regardless of Asian origin. Bias that persists among those who have less contact with Asians, such as HR and senior managers, means that Asians still face hurdles to advancement, even as their immediate managers recognize and reward their accomplishments.

These findings raise a question: How is it possible that these ethnoracial stereotypes are apparently so readily overturned in the context of elite firms? By their numbers, Japanese women's presence is far larger than that of Asian immigrants. Why are the ethnoracial stereotypes more subject to disruption, whereas gender stereotypes are more tenacious?

Although the data for the current study do not allow for a test of this question, it is plausible that Asians' low representation in low-status jobs, both in firms and in Japanese society more broadly, make stereotypes of Asians more vulnerable to disruption than stereotypes of women.

As we have seen, women are "the face" of low-status positions in many (if not all) of the sample firms. Although the majority of both Japanese and Asian women work on the managerial track, in firms where all or nearly all assistants are women, coworkers continue to perceive even managerial women through an assistant lens. This leads to disadvantage both in how immediate supervisors treat women in task assignment and evaluation and in how more distant managers weigh in on their advancement and promotion. Within firms, however, no corresponding structural mechanism reinforces the symbolic boundaries between Asians and Japanese. Indeed, Asians' presumed lack of cultural competence means they are perceived to be *less* well suited than Japanese women for positions for which culturally specific performances of deference and subordination are required.

Furthermore, arguably the most indelible symbolic boundary between Japanese and other Asians has been that of other Asians' supposed criminality. These stereotypes flowered in Japan's colonial era, fostered by leaders who portrayed East and Southeast Asians' resistance to colonial rule as lawlessness and pointed to these neighboring countries' relatively low levels of development as evidence of cultural and moral inferiority. Japanese colonizers' contact with Asians could easily have "confirmed" these beliefs, whether this contact occurred with the often impoverished colonial-era migrants to Japan or with colonial peoples in Korea, Manchuria, Taiwan, and further afield.[33]

From 1952 until 1990, however, government policy sharply restricted all new migration to Japan. Policy reforms of 1990 permitted some forms of migration and long-term settlement but established stringent restrictions on migration for the purpose of low-paid agricultural, blue-collar, or service work. As a result, postwar migration policy has precluded the settlement of large numbers of migrants working in low-status jobs, and overall migration to Japan has remained low in international comparison. Thus, even today, the majority of Japanese report that they rarely or never encounter foreigners in their daily lives.[34]

Poverty is often viewed as "evidence" of poor moral character of individuals and groups.[35] The near absence of visible communities of impoverished East and Southeast Asians in Japan, therefore, limits opportunities for Japanese to "confirm" negative stereotypes of other Asians in interpersonal encounters, even as media, internet discourse, or statements of politicians continue to propagate the criminality discourse.

These broader structural conditions mean that, for most of my informants, the workplace is the only site where they have meaningful encounters with other Asians. In the absence of confirmatory encounters, this type of equal-status workplace contact may be particularly likely to blur the moral boundaries implied by the criminality discourse and to destabilize Japanese employees' biases.

This possibility presents an ironic twist on the dynamics of xenophobia and racism in Japan. Japan's restrictions on so-called low-skilled immigration are often touted as evidence of unique xenophobia. As discussed in chapter 4, however, a preference for well-educated, highly paid migrants is common across postindustrial countries. What makes Japan unusual is that policy aligns with these citizen preferences. But perhaps even more counterintuitively, the very restrictions cited as evidence of xenophobia may make moral boundaries for disfavored groups more permeable in the context of white-collar employment than they are in countries with more open immigration policies.

Indeed, qualitative research on Asians living in Japan shows a shared belief that they can overcome Japanese prejudice through achievement. Liu-Farrer writes, "My Chinese respondents often stated that the only way to win Japanese people's respect was to show that you, as an individual, were more capable than them."[36] This is consistent with the quantitative findings from the current study that Asians do, on average, attain equity with same-sex peers, although wage gaps emerge for the migrants who have worked in Japan the longest. This ability to attain equity in spite of bias and discrimination, however, may be contingent on restrictive immigration policy that creates the structural conditions for contact to destabilize biases most effectively.

This is not to say that Japan's restrictions are, in some universal sense, necessarily better for white-collar migrants than more open policies in other countries. A more open policy could enable, for example, the formation of larger coethnic communities that could enhance immigrants' sense of belonging and create greater opportunities to mobilize and advocate for rights. In a narrower sense, Japan's restrictions may benefit white-collar immigrants by reducing the barriers to upward mobility in white-collar firms that such moral boundaries present.

In contrast, contact with high-achieving women in the workplace, including Asian women, does not have the same effects on gender biases, because devaluative beliefs about women are also constantly reinforced through women's role as "the face" of low-status positions in the firms.

Barring sweeping migration reform that brings in much larger numbers of low-wage workers from Asian countries, Asian men's prospects for attaining parity with Japanese men are not only good but also improving. Even stereotypes about supposedly "sticky" biological or cultural inferiorities appear to be vulnerable to disruption through contact in the white-collar workplace. Increasing demand for their cross-national skills will result in larger and larger workplace presence, which may reduce essentialized, racialized perceptions and, by extension, position white-collar Asian men to reap the benefits of population decline even more fully.

BANKING ON THE *GAIJIN* CARD

Pro-Western Biases and the Western Male Pay Advantage

> **Whiteness functions in Japan as the transparent and free-floating signifier of upward mobility and assimilation in "world culture"; it is the primary sign of the modern, the universal subject, the "citizen of the world."**
>
> —Karen Kelsky, *Women on the Verge*

> **Looking at hitherto flawed analysis on Japan. . . . reveals . . . insights on a newfound discriminated group in Japan, the Visible Minorities, are treated, and how racialization processes are normalized to the point of hegemony within Japanese identity, to the point where one must "look Japanese" in order to be treated as one.**
>
> —Debito Arudou, "Japan's Under-Researched Visible Minorities"

In 2014, Japan rolled out a new visa program, the HSP, or high-skilled professional, visa. The program offers people who meet income, age, educational, and occupational requirements a fast-track to permanent residency as well as other benefits. Some of the benefits exceed even those available to Japanese citizens, such as the right to sponsor a visa for a domestic employee.

Promotional material for the HSP program references intersecting narratives of foreigners, Caucasians, and Westerners in Japan. One flyer depicts nine adult figures standing on a map of Japan, their faces smiling and attentive. Although Westerners account for a small minority of all foreigners on the HSP visa—just 13 percent in 2020, and about 9 percent of Japan's foreign population overall, seven of the nine adult figures on the flyer appear to be Caucasian.[1] The image thus plays off ideas of Caucasians as "the other"—to be a foreigner is to be white and to be white is to be alien. It also invokes the many positive associations with white foreignness: The people standing on the map clearly represent aspirational values of professionalism and cosmopolitanism, and they have important contributions to make to Japan.

Of course, the leaflet does not encapsulate the complex reality of Westerners working in Japan. Although most Japanese assume North Americans or

Europeans are white by default, Westerners in Japan hail from a variety of racial and ethnic backgrounds.[2] In addition, Westerners living in Japan are not necessarily "aliens": Westerns can and do naturalize as Japanese citizens, and children with at least one Western parent are born and raised in integrated Japanese environments. Nor are Westerners exclusively employed as professionals in prestigious fields like management, finance, and higher education.[3]

Nonetheless, the flyer epitomizes two types of symbolic boundaries—perhaps unduly positive assessments of Westerners' skills and contributions but also their indelible alienness—that play conflicting roles in the lives of Western migrants to Japan. On one hand, Westerners' (perceived) abilities and knowledge have been used to rationalize unusually high pay or levels of responsibility. On the other hand, a discourse of alienness has also been deployed to justify exclusion. In recent years, scholarship has tended to emphasize this exclusion and suggest an "end of privilege." In this chapter, I offer a corrective to this developing narrative, showing how positive stereotypes associated with Western origin and Caucasian race continue to benefit Western men in elite firms in Japan.

Contemporary Attitudes Toward Westerners

In contrast to East or Southeast Asians, who face stereotypes such as "cunning" and "unclean," large shares of Japanese people associate positive terms, such as "kind and friendly" with Americans and Australians (although they rate them as somewhat less hard-working or intelligent as the Japanese).[4] Other Western groups (Germans, British) are seen as equal to the Japanese in both friendliness and intelligence.[5]

The racial connotations of the concept of the West mean that such positive attitudes apply most strongly, although not exclusively, to Caucasians.[6] Although Western migrants of African or Asian descent report greater hostility or suspicion, particularly from strangers, than do migrants of European descent, they also highlight how proactively identifying themselves by nation of origin—for example as Americans—leads to more respectful treatment.[7] Thus, the positive valence of Western origin in contemporary Japan is a potential resource to Westerners of various ethnoracial backgrounds, even if its racial overtones privilege migrants of European descent above others.[8]

Scholars have associated these positive attitudes with what Milos Debnár calls "small benefits," including showers of praise and attention for Western students or tourists; white, Western men's popularity in the dating and marriage markets; and Western foreigners' ability to flout minor rules without consequence, a practice known as "playing the *gaijin* card."[9]

At the same time, however, symbolic boundaries between Japanese and Westerners of various racial backgrounds have also cast Westerners as indelible aliens.[10] Edwin O. Reischauer recounts how, in his childhood in 1930s Japan, he sometimes heard terms like *ijin* (strange people) and *keto* (hairy barbarian) to refer to whites.[11] Anthropologist Hiroshi Wagatsuma's study of racial attitudes in the 1960s revealed similar discourses of alienation, including, "When I think of actual Caucasians walking along the street, I feel that they are basically different beings from us. Certainly, they are humans but I don't feel they are the same creatures as we are. There is, in my mind, a definite discontinuity between us [Japanese] and the Caucasians."[12] Enduring stereotypes that Caucasians and other Westerners without East Asian heritage cannot learn Japanese, use chopsticks, or eat sushi continue to underscore the narrative of (most) Western people as indelibly other. Indeed, some of the "small benefits" Debnár cites, such as the ability to play the *gaijin* card, also reflect a degree of othering—Westerners may be permitted to flout the rules precisely because they *are* outsiders, albeit outsiders who are usually accorded both respect and friendliness.[13]

"Internationalization" as Lucrative Employment Niche

Beyond attitudes toward Western people, the concept of "the West" itself looms large in the Japanese imagination. Calls to adopt Western practices or adapt Western institutions to the Japanese context are a recurrent strategy for dealing with any number of social, cultural, or economic ills, and come from both within and outside the country. Faced with Japan's trade surplus with the United States in the 1980s, US commentators hotly criticized Japan for its alleged failures to integrate itself within "global" (really, Anglo-American) economic and political frameworks.[14] These criticisms resonated with many Japanese politicians and bureaucrats concerned with raising Japan's perceived status among peer countries, who responded with various initiatives to "internationalize" Japan by improving English-language education and encouraging young Japanese to study in and travel to Western countries.[15]

The end of rapid economic growth in the early 1990s and the so-called lost decades prompted a renewed wave of calls urging the adoption of Western practices, this time with a focus on private firms.[16] Practices such as long-term employment, which both US and Japanese commentators had praised as the grounding of Japan's phenomenal economic growth, came under fire as responsible for Japan's economic stagnation.[17] To enhance Japan's international competitiveness and to make Japan more hospitable to foreign investment, the government proposed reforms to align Japanese firms' practices more closely with those of US firms, particularly in the realms of human resource management and corporate governance.[18]

Well before efforts to hire and retain "global talent" went mainstream in the 2010s, various projects to enhance Japanese firms' "internationalization" or "globalization" generated lucrative employment niches for Westerners. Beginning in the 1970s and 1980s, large, elite firms hired a small number of Western employees (almost always men), often explicitly to advise on internationalization. Being from a Western country, speaking English, and having a college degree were considered qualifying in and of themselves, and firms did not screen prospective hires assiduously. Based on research conducted in the 1980s, business scholar Robert March notes that "Western foreigners were interviewed fewer times, for shorter periods, and little or no background checking with referees were done," even though many became regular employees with the same job security as Japanese. Hires in these jobs received what they termed "ludicrously high salaries," making them "grossly overpaid" relative to Japanese coworkers.[19]

Research documents that this niche persisted at least through the mid-1990s. Anthropologist Eric Clemons, who did fieldwork in 1995–1996, observed that elite firms continued to hire Westerners "as 'special' workers whose primary specialized skill is their foreignness."[20] Respondents in his study, including Black as well as white informants, reported they earned more than their Japanese counterparts and "revealed that they occasionally received special or unusual treatment such as being assigned to larger company apartments, granted extended vacation time, and allowed to reject or delay transfers," options that were not available to Japanese and Asian employees.[21]

Western men in these roles were thus hired and rewarded based on the *presumption* of capability to contribute to internationalization, rather than rigorous screening or quantitative assessments of the results they delivered for their firms. At the same time, these highly paid positions were also, both explicitly and implicitly, linked to their status as "outsiders" with an understanding of international business that was assumed to be inherent to their identities.

The End of Privilege?

More recent scholarship argues, however, that this niche has eroded. Whereas in the 1970s, 1980s, and even the 1990s, Westerners in elite firms benefited from assumptions of competence and capability, and received high rewards for their perceived ability to contribute to internationalization or globalization, a new generation of scholarship argues that whiteness or Western cultural background has become a "passive" form of capital that no longer generates "tangible advantages," such as higher earnings or easier access to managerial jobs for Western employees in mainstream white-collar jobs.[22] Rather, Western employees, like other foreign employees, are held to the same standards as Japanese employees, even if such standards are difficult for foreign employees of any national background to reach.[23]

If the "tangible advantages" of whiteness or a Western background persist at all, these scholars suggest, they do so only for upper-level executives and transferees with lucrative expatriate contracts, and Westerners in explicitly racialized occupations such as English teacher or wedding officiant.[24] In these cases, and others in which Westerners are temporary "guests," they may benefit from inflated earnings and various other forms of favorable treatment, at least for a time. Now that white-collar foreign employment has gone mainstream, however, Westerners are usually hired through standard channels. In these cases, they are disadvantaged for being non-Japanese, rather than advantaged as whites or Westerners.[25]

Other contemporary observers argue that Westerners experience systematic exclusion in the economic sphere, above and beyond that resulting from a lack of acculturation, which they associate with stereotypes of Caucasians and other Westerners without East Asian background as indelible others.[26] Media, activists, and scholars report instances in which Westerners have been denied employment under indefinite contracts and refused promotion to upper levels of management in Japanese firms.[27] Systematic research supports these more anecdotal claims of workplace exclusion to a degree. For example, one study of HR professionals found they perceived Americans as less hirable than Japanese, net of qualifications.[28] Similarly, a Ministry of Justice study of foreign residents in Japan found that approximately 10 percent of respondents from Western countries (the United States, the United Kingdom, and Russia) had been turned down for a job because of their non-Japanese background.[29] At the same time, these studies reveal that discrimination against Westerners is both less frequent and less severe than discrimination against other immigrant groups. HR managers perceive Brazilians, Koreans, and Chinese as considerably less employable than Americans, and Asian foreign residents are three times as likely as Westerners to report being denied a job on the basis of their foreign background.[30]

In sum, the contemporary literature on Westerners in Japan highlights economic disadvantage and exclusion of Westerners. Much of this research focuses explicitly on Caucasians and does not address economic outcomes for

Western men or women of African, Asian, or other non-European descent, although the global history of white supremacy, as well as local anti-Black and anti-Asian biases imply that other ethnoracial groups (with the possible exception of ethnic Japanese) would experience greater disadvantage still. The scholarship does indicate, however, that Caucasian women face gender barriers in addition to marginalization as foreigners.[31] Although the literature acknowledges "small benefits" that accrue to white men in the social realm, it denies that this social cachet translates to economic advantage in white-collar workplaces.[32]

Western Men in the Sample

In this study, I define Westerners as anyone who speaks a European language, including English, as their native language. Because only three Western women are in the sample, I do not analyze their experiences, and I focus on Western men alone.

As in Japan's overall foreign population, Western men are a minority among my survey respondents, representing just 19.4 percent of the non-Japanese sample for a total of nineteen respondents. They are overrepresented, however, relative to Western men's share of all foreign residents in Japan (4.2 percent), reflecting Western men's relative concentration in the large elite firms, compared with foreigners of other backgrounds.[33] This is admittedly a small subsample of Western men, meaning that the results should be interpreted with caution. This subsample, however, nonetheless offers a rare opportunity to consider outcomes and experiences of Western men in the context of native Japanese coworkers as well as coworkers from Asian countries.

Of the nineteen Western male respondents, sixteen are from English-speaking countries (the United States, the United Kingdom, Canada, and Australia). Two are from non-English-speaking countries in Western Europe; one was born in Japan. Because racial and ethnic categories are socially constructed, and relevant categories vary across national contexts, I did not ask survey respondents to self-identify race or ethnicity. Reflecting the ethnoracial composition of their birth countries, the Western male sample is likely to be predominantly white, although it is unlikely it is exclusively so.[34]

Compared with other immigrants, the average age of Western men in the sample is older, with a mean age of 40.6 years. Eight Western men are in their twenties and thirties, and the rest are in their forties and fifties. Although they are older, on average, than immigrants from Asian countries, most (twelve out of nineteen, or 74 percent) began their careers in Japan after the year 2000, missing the heady years of the 1980s and early 1990s when Western men were sometimes hired at high salaries and with little scrutiny. Moreover, the Western men can hardly be termed elite expatriate managers. Twelve of the nineteen have three or fewer years of work experience outside Japan. More than half hold either permanent residency visas or spousal visas. Only two of the nineteen report that they intend to leave Japan forever. In sum, the Western men in the sample are building Japan-based careers in domestic Japanese organizations, and thus are precisely those individuals scholars have suggested no longer enjoy the "tangible" benefits associated with Western background or Caucasian race. [35]

Western men in the sample are far more likely than Japanese men to have advanced degrees, with slightly more than half holding a master's degree or higher. In this regard, they are similar to Asian immigrant workers, particularly women, who also include very high shares of advanced degree holders.

Compared with Asian respondents, however, Western men tend to have poorer Japanese language skills. As described in chapter 4, respondents were asked the ease or difficulty with which they could complete a list of seven tasks in Japanese.[36] The task proficiency questions can also be used to calculate an overall proficiency score between 0 and 35, with a score of 35 indicating that the respondents can do all the tasks with ease. Koreans, Taiwanese, Mainland Chinese, Singaporeans, and Vietnamese have some advantage in learning Japanese because their languages share vocabulary with roots in written Chinese. Respondents from these countries scored 28 on average. Asians from other countries scored 22 on average. The two Latin American respondents both scored 19. Western men's average score was last, at 18.

These statistics offer a somewhat ambiguous portrait of Western men's position in their firms. On one hand, they are overqualified relative to Japanese coworkers in terms of their educational attainment. On the other, they are underqualified in their Japanese language skills, relative both to Japanese coworkers and immigrants from Asia. These patterns are consistent with a degree of disadvantage for Western men at the hiring stage, but they also suggest that Western men are "given a pass" and held to lower standards with regard to language ability, which implies a degree of privilege.

The interviewees in the study firms included two Western men: Derek from the United States, and Hugo from Scotland.[37] Derek had originally come to Japan on the Japan Exchange and Teaching (JET) program, where he met his future wife, a Japanese citizen. He had never worked outside Japan. He scored as highly acculturated on the task proficiency metric of Japanese language ability. Hugo had almost a decade of work experience in Europe. He studied Japanese in college, and finding himself between jobs in his mid-thirties, decided to enroll in an English-language MBA program in Japan with the aim of experiencing "a totally different culture." Following his MBA graduation, he began work at his current company. He had a serious girlfriend, a Japanese citizen, and planned to get married and stay in Japan. He was less skilled in Japanese than Derek, and he reported some difficulty with both written and spoken Japanese language tasks. Both men are white.

I supplement these interviews with two others I conducted as part of the preliminary data collection for this project in 2013, which offer a richer perspective on the diversity of Western men's experiences in elite firms. In addition to interviews, I use quantitative earnings data and survey experimental results to illuminate Western men's experiences.

Positive Stereotypes in Contemporary Workplaces

As in the broader society, positive stereotypes of Westerners are also evident in elite white-collar firms. I spoke with a new employee of a large financial Japanese financial firm as part of the preliminary research for this project. He described how this affected his experience as an entry-level trainee: "My name is [Robert]. Which sounds awesome to every Japanese person that I meet. And so there's different classes we'll be in the first two months. Every time they saw the list, they were like, aw man, [Robert] is in my class, so awesome. They haven't even met me yet. They see the name and are like, that's a cool guy."

Shouichiro, a Japanese employee in one of the sample firms, echoed these positive preconceptions about Western people. He told my Japanese research assistant that he saw Americans as "motivated" and "open-minded." Shouichiro, however, was unique in commenting specifically about Western immigrant workers from any country: Japanese respondents usually referred to "foreigners" generically, although often this clearly meant Asians specifically, or they referred to "Asian people" both collectively and by nationality.

Not all Westerners embrace the positive stereotypes they encounter. Robert, just quoted, found his colleagues' positive attention made him feel welcomed and included, but the literature reports many Westerners' frustration at being perceived through the lens of stereotypes, even positive ones.[38]

The presence of positive stereotypes does not preclude hostile treatment. Stanley, a white man from New Zealand, had come to Japan in the mid-1990s. Like Derek, he married a Japanese woman he met as a JET participant and moved to corporate employment. (He was, however, one of the preliminary interviewees and did not work at the sample firms.) He noted that "when foreigners were taken on, departments weren't necessarily asked so much as given the person. Just thrown in a department that's not asked for a foreigner." Of his first day in the job at this firm, he said: "I walked in there and the first thing that was said to me from one of the secretaries was, 'Why are you here? We don't need you. We don't want a foreigner.'"

Nonetheless, the positive assumptions stand in potent contrast to the stereotypical views some Japanese respondents expressed about Chinese or Koreans as "loud" and "self-centered." Derek, another white American man at one of the sample firms, acknowledged this fact when he told me: "It's so much easier for us [white Americans]. There're all these stereotypes about Asians."[39]

Region of Origin and Pressure to Acculturate

The recent literature on Caucasians and Westerners in white-collar workplaces has focused on what it portrays as a shared experience of immigrants from both Asian and Western countries: strong assimilative pressure and a resulting sense of alienation.[40] I argue that, contrary to this portrayal, pro-Western and pro-white attitudes result in significant differences in Western men's experience of assimilative pressure in workplace, compared with those of Asian immigrants.

I asked Hugo, introduced earlier, if the company treated him fairly compared with Japanese male employees. He said, "Well, yes, but I don't think they even treat their own people fairly. They get one week of holiday a year. That *isn't human* [emphasis in original]. Sometimes you want to play the *gaijin* card." Hugo insisted on taking two weeks of vacation to visit Scotland, despite the unwritten rule that vacations could be no longer than a week. He was successful in doing so.[41]

Hugo also mentioned a second instance in which he played the *gaijin* card. Hugo's supervisor came to him and said, "So, about overtime." Hugo told me, "I stopped him right there. I knew what he was going to say. If I have to stay till 4 a.m., I will. If I have to come in on a national holiday, I will. I have done those things. But when there's no work, staying till my boss leaves while spending two or three hours on Facebook, that's not going to happen."

Liling, a Chinese woman at the same firm, who likewise held an MBA from a top private school in Japan, reported no such flexibility in work hours or vacation time, nor did Asian employees at other firms. As quoted in chapter 4, Dawen remarked: "You have to follow the Japanese rules. If you don't, you're not likely to get a good evaluation." When I interviewed Chaoxiang, Hugo's successful pushback was fresh on my mind, particularly as he lamented the pressure to work long hours and to avoid vacation. But when I asked Chaoxiang if he could push back against these same expectations, he said: "Absolutely not. To the contrary, my coworkers' position is, 'this is the Japanese way of doing things, please conform to it.'" Asian workers in my sample were not able to "play the *gaijin* card" and were pressured to follow the spoken and unspoken rules without exception.

Of course, neither is the *gaijin* card all-powerful, nor are Western men exempt from the acculturative pressures described in chapter 4. Derek felt he was unlikely to be promoted unless he worked "exactly like a Japanese person." At the same time, he described his coworkers as responding "flexibly" to his proposals for doing things in a new way. "If you have an opinion [about the way things should be done], people are willing to listen to it," he said. Rather than unidirectional assimilative pressure, Derek's experience was one of (some) mutual accommodation and adaptation.

Hugo, too, experienced this mutual adaption. Of his ability to play the *gaijin* card to get longer vacations and reduce overtime, Hugo told me: "You have to pick your battles. You have to build your bank account balance [by following the Japanese rules]. Then when the time comes, you can say, 'no, I'm not doing this shit.'" His occasional use of the *gaijin* card was contingent on conformity for much of the time.

Both older and newer scholarship recounts a similar dynamic, in which Western workers' can sometimes deploy the *gaijin* card in the workplace, whereas employees from Asian countries cannot. The more recent scholarship, however, discounts this differential access as superficial and economically irrelevant.[42]

I argue that this perspective trivializes both the psychological and economic advantages of being able to (occasionally) play the *gaijin* card in the workplace. I asked Hugo if, as a foreigner, he found it difficult to build positive work relationships with his coworkers. Somewhat surprised at the question, he dismissed the possibility that he faced any special struggles in that regard:

> There are stereotypes of foreigners, you know, the American Roppongi[43] guy with a Japanese girlfriend who goes with him everywhere and is always translating for him. About Scotland,[44] people just think, ah, bagpipes, kilts. And if you speak Japanese, are on time, do what you say you will do, and if you are not dancing the flying Scotsman with your bagpipes in front of them, you overcome that perception and they say, oh, this guy is ok.

Although Hugo's invocation of bagpipes and kilts was joking, it illustrates that he had to tone down his expression of culture rather than eradicate it. Complete and total assimilation that would make him indistinguishable behaviorally from his Japanese coworkers was not necessary for them to see him as "an ok guy."

For Asian immigrants, positive relationships with coworkers require a higher degree of acculturation and more consistent conformity to "the Japanese way" of being at work. As described in chapter 4, Xinyan underscored "*loving Japan and Japanese culture*" [emphasis added] as a baseline condition both for career advancement and for building strong relationships with coworkers. Chaoxiang, too, emphasized that integrating fully into what he called the "delicate human relations" of the Japanese business world—for example, by golfing with his boss on weekends and departing the office only after his boss— as critical to building a strong network. Unlike the white Western men, their carefully constructed networks could not withstand selective flouting of the ordinary rules and expectations.

Playing the *gaijin* card did not notably damage Hugo's career prospects. He told me that, although there was an "unwritten rule" about the age at which someone could be promoted to manager, "I am a bit of an exception. I was hired as an assistant manager [at age 36], and I was promoted to manager in fifteen months."

As I argue in chapter 4, social pressure to assimilate fully can be seen as an expression of ethnic prejudice and discomfort with ethnoracial others. Asians, to a far greater degree than Caucasians, face many negative stereotypes in the broader society. The pressure for Asians to assimilate is thus not solely a project to Japanize them but rather to stamp out their supposedly undesirable cultural attributes. In contrast, many (if not all) of the most widespread stereotypes about Western foreigners are positive. These positive stereotypes curb assimilative pressures on Western men. Even if they cannot do things in "the Japanese way," they are *assumed* to be "cool," "openminded," and capable, and thus they require less assimilative correction. Coworkers' and managers' acceptance of the *gaijin* card is thus a form of grace extended in part because of these underlying positive assumptions about Westerners, which grants Western immigrant men greater, if only partial, leeway to live according to their values and priorities. Moreover, Hugo's case suggests that avenues for upward mobility are opened more readily for Western men in the absence of perfect acculturation.

Western Men's Earnings Advantage

In addition to these points, and contrary to claims in the recent literature, Western men in the current sample are *not* on average disadvantaged in earnings relative to same-age Japanese men. Although Asian men earn less than

Japanese men net of skills and training, their Western counterparts earn considerably more than either group. Model 1 (identical to model 2 in chapter 2), a hierarchical linear model with random effects for firms to account for their varying levels of pay, illustrates this advantage. With adjustments for age, tenure, education levels, and language skills, this model estimates Western men's pay advantage to be about 1.8 million yen ($18,000). The sizable pay advantage does not mean that every Westerner earns more than is typical for Japanese men of the same age; however, as illustrated in figure 2.5 in chapter 2, the majority do earn more, and the size of that earnings advantage is considerable, comparable in magnitude to or even greater than women's disadvantage.[45]

What accounts for this earnings advantage? Since collecting the earnings data in 2015, I have presented these results to many different audiences of students, scholars, and businesspeople, and audiences are often eager to offer an "objective" explanation for Western men's earnings advantage. The most common is the "special skills" argument. Surely, commentators say, this pay advantage is a rational market response to specific skills and qualifications, such as English-language ability or an MBA degree, both of which are rare in the overall Japanese labor market. A second tack is Westerners' bargaining position. Audience members have contended that the Western men in my sample must be intercompany transfers coming from North America, Europe, or Oceania, where wages are higher; or, if they were hired locally, they have worked abroad or in foreign firms in Japan, giving them leverage to demand higher salaries. A final argument focuses on trade-offs. Western men, several interlocutors have suggested, may have negotiated higher-paid contract-based jobs in exchange for waiving the job security Japanese men enjoy as regular employees.

None of these counterarguments are consistent with the data. To begin with the "special skills" argument, English skills are by no means exclusive to Western men in the sample. Because these are elite firms with global presence, they can select highly skilled employees of all national backgrounds. A quarter (26 percent) of Japanese men in the sample speak English at an advanced level, as do one-third (34 percent) of the Japanese women. More than half of Asian respondents speak English at an advanced level, and a quarter of them are fluent. Thus, Western men's English proficiency is not particularly remarkable in the context of their workplaces. Modeling earnings as a function of English skills, as well as age, tenure, and educational qualifications in model 2, likewise fails to explain their advantage.

Turning next to claims about Western men's advanced degrees: Only three of the Western men in the sample hold MBAs. As a percentage, the share of Asian women who hold MBAs is equivalent.[46] And yet, Asian women earn far

TABLE 6.1. Regression of human capital on annual earnings

	MODEL 1			MODEL 2		
	BETA		SE	BETA		SE
Region of origin and gender[a]						
Japanese women	−2.1	***	0.3	−2.1	***	0.3
Asian men	−1.3	*	0.6	−0.8		0.5
Asian women	−2.4	***	0.6	−1.7	***	0.5
Western men	1.8	*	0.8	1.7	*	0.8
Age	0.2		0.1	0.2		0.1
Age*age	0.0		0.0	0.0		0.0
Tenure	0.3	***	0.1	0.3	***	0.1
Tenure*tenure	−0.0	***	0.0	−0.0	***	0.0
Education[b]						
BA/BS	1.7	***	0.5	1.8	***	0.5
MA/MS	1.9	**	0.6	1.9	***	0.6
MBA/JD/PhD	2.9	***	0.8	3.0	***	0.8
Advanced language skills[c]						
Two advanced languages	1.1	***	0.3			
Three or more advanced languages	1.9	***	0.5			
Advanced English language				1.1	***	0.3
Constant	−3.2		2.6	−3.2		2.6
Model information						
Observations	525			525		
Number of firms	12			12		

*** $p <0.001$, ** $p <0.01$, * $p <0.05$
Note: All models are from hierarchical linear modeling (HLM) with random effects for firms.
[a]Reference category is Japanese men.
[b]Reference category is below BA/BS.
[c]Reference category is one advanced language.

less than Japanese men. Moreover, model 1 in table 6.1 shows Western men's predicted earnings advantage when the relationship between MBAs and other advanced degrees and pay is modeled. Model 3 also demonstrates that Western men's advanced degrees do not account for their high earnings. This model includes only respondents who hold a terminal bachelor's degree. The coefficient for Western men is still significant and positive. The Western male earnings advantage applies also to those who do not hold advanced degrees.

Certainly, Western men likely do have other skills that are not captured by these variables. However, there is no reason to assume that Western men are *unique* among all the sample respondents in having such valuable, unobserved skills.

TABLE 6.2. Regression of human capital on annual earnings, with exclusions

	MODEL 3 (TERMINAL BA HOLDERS ONLY)		MODEL 4 (NO FOREIGN WORK EXPERIENCE)		MODEL 5 (REGULAR EMPLOYEES ONLY)	
	BETA	SE	BETA	SE	BETA	SE
Region of origin and gender[a]						
Japanese women	−2.0 ***	0.4	−1.9 ***	0.3	−1.6 ***	0.4
Asian men	−1.4	0.8	−2.3 **	0.9	−0.7	0.6
Asian women	−3.3 ***	0.8	−3.0 ***	0.7	−1.4 *	0.6
Western men	2.4 *	1.1	2.4 *	1.1	2.1 *	0.8
Model information						
Human capital controls[b]	Yes		Yes		Yes	
Observations	359		371		392	
Number of firms	12		12		12	

*** p <0.001, ** p <0.01, * p <0.05
Note: All models are from hierarchical linear modeling (HLM) with random effects for firms.
[a]Reference category is Japanese men.
[b]Includes age, age squared, tenure, tenure squared, education, and number of languages spoken at an advanced level.

Turning next to arguments about bargaining power, as discussed earlier, the Western men in the sample are overwhelmingly local hires, not intercompany transferees from foreign offices where prevailing wages are higher. Moreover, foreign work experience does not explain these men's advantage. In model 3 in table 6.2, I remove all respondents with any foreign work experience. If foreign experience explained Western men's earnings advantage, whether because they are intercompany transferees, or because they previously earned high salaries abroad, excluding these respondents should reduce or eliminate Western men's earnings advantage. To the contrary, they are still predicted to earn more than Japanese men, and the magnitude of the coefficient actually increases.

It is also unlikely that work experience in foreign firms explains Western men's advantage. Foreign firms in Japan are desirable employers precisely because of their high wages, but they represent a tiny sliver of the labor market.[47] Most foreign workers I spoke to, including the Western men whose experiences I discussed previously, as well as many of the Asian respondents, aspired to work for Western companies in Japan but had never done so. Derek had worked in Japan for nine years without receiving an offer from a foreign company. Six years later, after fifteen years of work in Japan, he had switched jobs again, to another Japanese company. Stanley had been in Japan for almost twenty years and had not realized this ambition. Not only is it difficult to secure a job at a foreign firm, but the high pay these firms offer also means that people who do secure these jobs only seldom move back into Japanese firms. Although this does not preclude the possibility that some Western men in the sample have done so, it suggests that this path is rare and cannot plausibly account for the fact that the majority of Western men earn more than their Japanese colleagues.

To test the merits of the argument that Western men make a trade-off between job security and earnings, model 5 excludes all nonregular employees. As the positive coefficient for Western men shows, Western men's wage advantage is also present only among regular employees.

Models 1 through 5 do not include various metrics of on-the-job behavior, such as work hours and frequency of socializing after work. The results, however, do not change substantively when these variables are included. In sum, although the small sample size of Western men indicates the need for caution in generalizing these results, within these limitations, the data offer no evidence to support counterarguments that Western men's advantage in the sample firms has an "objective" explanation based on skills, bargaining, or trade-offs.

Western Men's Deservingness and Visibility

As discussed in chapter 2, Western men are more likely to be managers than any of the other groups. About half of the Western men over age 35 are managers, compared with a third of Japanese men. When number of subordinates is added to the baseline of model 1, their predicted earnings advantage shrinks to 0.9 million yen and is no longer statistically significant (model not shown). This result indicates that at least some part of Western men's pay premium is related to their overrepresentation in managerial roles. This raises the secondary question of why Western men are more likely than others to land management roles, resulting in an earnings advantage.

I argue that, contrary to claims that whiteness or Western background have become a form of passive capital that yield no advantage in mainstream white-collar employment, positive stereotypes, likely about deservingness, capability, and ability to contribute to internationalization and globalization, continue to benefit Western men, particularly by increasing their access to managerial jobs.

The survey experiment offers some evidence for this interpretation. As described in chapter 5, the survey included an experimental section with a

TABLE 6.3.   Penalties and rewards recommended for Japanese-named and Anglo-named employees

	JAPANESE-NAMED EMPLOYEE		ENGLISH-NAMED EMPLOYEE	
	DEMOTION/FIRING RECOMMENDED (%)	TOTAL N	DEMOTION/FIRING RECOMMENDED (%)	TOTAL N
Records falsification vignette	29.1	289	25.0	64
Tardiness vignette	1.4	277	2.7	74
	Promotion recommended (%)	Total N	Promotion recommended (%)	Total N
Cost-saving vignette	17.5	291	30.6 *	72
Coworker assistance vignette	17.4	281	15.3	72

*Statistically significantly different from recommendation for Japanese at the 0.05 level.
Note: Based on responses from non-Western employees only.

series of four vignettes. Two vignettes describe an employee who has engaged in praiseworthy behavior (assisted a busy coworker, negotiated a cost-saving contract with vendors). Two describe blameworthy behavior (being absent and tardy without explanation, falsifying sales records). Respondents were asked to recommend a reward for the praiseworthy behavior and a penalty in the case of the blameworthy behavior.

Names of the hypothetical employees in question randomly varied, such that respondents viewed either a Japanese name, a Chinese or Korean name, or an English name for each vignette. If positive stereotypes about Westerners and whites contribute to high earnings through their influence on employment decisions, we would expect more favorable treatment recommendations for English-named employees compared with Japanese-named employees.

Table 6.3 compares the penalties and rewards recommended by Japanese and other Asian respondents for Japanese and English-named subjects in all four vignettes. In the negative vignettes, respondents recommended the harshest penalties—demotion or firing—for English-named subjects at about the same rate as for Japanese.

In the cost-saving vignette, however, respondents recommended English-named subjects for promotion 30.6 percent of the time, compared with only 17.5 percent for Japanese. In sum, a Western man is seen as more deserving of promotion when he has done *the exact same thing as a Japanese man*. Thus, even if we accept the dubious premise that Western men have unobserved "special skills," this vignette shows that *in the absence of specific information about special or unique skills*, the Western employee is assumed to merit promotion more readily.

Interestingly, the vignettes also imply that this sense of greater deserving-ness may be triggered more in some situations than in others: Proposed rewards for Westerners are very similar to those proposed for Japanese in the coworker assistance vignette. As prior research on Westerners has argued, this result indicates that Western privilege does not operate universally in all times and places. Nonetheless, the favorable treatment for Westerners in the cost-saving vignette is remarkably consistent across firms. In all but one firm, Anglo-named employees in the cost-saving vignette are more likely to be recommended for promotion than Japanese-named employees.

The cost-saving vignette describes a mainstream sales job that is usually dominated by Japanese employees. Thus, it offers evidence that favorable treatment for Westerners is not limited to those occupations, such as English teaching, for which Western culture, Western languages, or white racial capital are especially salient. It also demonstrates one pathway through which positive stereotypes about Westerners can produce material benefits for Western men in mainstream employment.[48]

While the cost-saving vignette shows that, all else being equal, Western men may be treated more favorably than Japanese men, interpersonal dynamics in real workplaces may even further enhance Western men's advantage.

As George, a Latin American man of Japanese descent, observed, in his firm, "Western-looking" foreigners had special access to managers. George noted, "Without them [Caucasians] even trying, the people at the executive level will grab them." The quantitative survey data illustrate that this is no aberration. Survey respondents reported how many different managers they had spoken to about work in the past month. For nonmanagerial Western men, the average was six, compared with four for nonmanagerial Japanese men, and three for Asian men. For managerial Western men, the average was eleven, compared with seven for Japanese men and eight for Asian men.

Heightened visibility, positive stereotypes, and greater access to managers likely set in motion positive feedback loops for Western men. If managers "grab them," Western men may be more likely to be assigned to important, visible projects that further elevate their profile in the firm. Thus, Western men are not only more likely than Japanese men to be promoted, all else being equal, but also more likely to work on projects that enhance promotability and more likely to be recognized by managers for their contributions. Although Western men also face hurdles related to imperfect acculturation, as well as occasional exclusion related to ethnoracial background and citizenship, these feedback loops potentially provide a significant counterweight, particularly after they have secured employment within an elite firm.

Interactions of Exclusion and Advantage

At the same time, discrimination against Westerners and whites may simultaneously influence Western men's career patterns. Compared both with Japanese men and Asian immigrant men, Western men's job histories are distinctive. As illustrated in figure 6.1, Western men in their thirties, forties, and fifties typically have had three or more employers (including the current employer). This far exceeds the typical number of jobs Japanese men in the same age-groups have held.[49] In some cases, this is because, like Hugo, the men worked in their home countries for a few years before coming to Japan. Eight of the nineteen Western men in the sample have never worked outside Japan, however, and of these, six have had four or more employers.

One possible reason for this distinctive pattern is the interplay between symbolic boundaries asserting Westerners' otherness, on one hand, and positive stereotypes about Westerners, on the other. As Stanley's experience of being told "We don't want a foreigner" illustrates, not every office or every person is welcoming to Western men. Experiences of rejection or exclusion within the workplace are a push factor that can lead Western men to seek new employment. At the same time, the prospect of favorable treatment related to

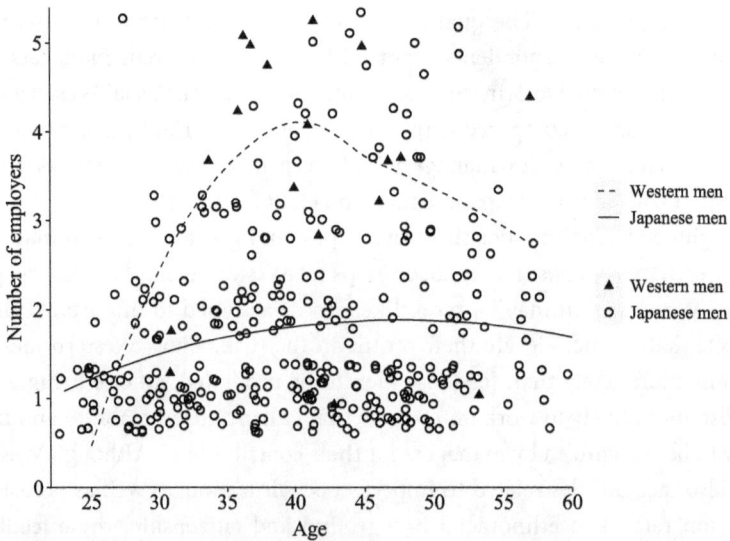

FIGURE 6.1.   Western and Japanese men's number of employers by age. Calculated from author's survey data.

pro-Western attitudes at other workplaces is also a pull factor. Thus, Western men's career paths may be forged by *both* hostility and excessively generous treatment in some (but not all) workplaces.

Unreliable Narrators of Privilege and Skill

What accounts for the dissonance between these findings and the claims from recent studies that "tangible" benefits of Western or white privilege are limited to workers in specific racialized occupations and lucrative expatriate positions?

One possibility is that past research may rely too heavily on Western immigrant men's self-reports to conclude that workplace privilege is a thing of the past. Western men in this sample, like those in past qualitative studies, deny any economic advantage. This is apparent in Western men's ratings of their compensation relative to their contributions, their peers at their current firm, and their peers at other firms. As table 6.4 illustrates, nearly all Western men believe their compensation to be low or equal relative to their contributions and relative to the salaries of peers. Across all metrics, Western men are *less* likely than Japanese men to report their compensation as high.

Western men in this sample *feel* they are treated no more generously than Japanese employees. But the compensation data tell a different story. Earnings are indisputably higher among Western men than in any other group. Were we to take the self-reports about compensation fairness at face value, we might erroneously conclude that Western men in the sample firms are not

TABLE 6.4. Perceptions of compensation fairness among Japanese and Western men

	COMPENSATION, GIVEN CONTRIBUTIONS				
	LOW (%)	APPROPRIATE (%)	HIGH (%)	DON'T KNOW (%)	N
Japanese men	41.6	42.3	16.1	NA	305
Western men	43.8	50.0	5.6	NA	18
	Compensation, compared with peers at current firm				
	Low (%)	Equal (%)	High (%)	Don't know (%)	N
Japanese men	31.7	44.8	12.1	11.4	306
Western men	26.3	36.8	10.5	26.3	19
	Compensation, compared with peers at other firms				
	Low (%)	Equal (%)	High (%)	Don't know (%)	N
Japanese men	42.7	20.5	26.7	10.1	307
Western men	36.8	31.6	10.5	21.1	19

particularly advantaged in terms of their earnings. The earnings data and the comparison with Japanese and Asian immigrant workers, however, demonstrate that these subjective perceptions are not a reliable guide to Western men's place within the stratification order.

Western men's perception that their (unusually high) compensation is no more, or perhaps even less, than their due, is likely related to the praise and attention heaped on Western men in social situations. Past research dismisses this praise as irrelevant for economic outcomes, in part because it is far more likely to occur outside the workplace than inside it. Praise in social situations, however, may inflate Western men's assessments of their own skills and worth.

A tendency to overestimate their skills is apparent in Western men's reports of their Japanese language ability. Respondents were asked to qualitatively rate their Japanese skill overall, on a scale from "beginner" to "fluent native."[50] In addition, respondents who chose one of the intermediate scale points were asked to rate the ease or difficulty with which they could complete various task in Japanese. If they could complete all seven tasks with ease (or rated themselves as native speakers), their task proficiency score is 35. If they could complete none of the tasks (or rated themselves as beginners), their proficiency score is 0.

As figure 6.2 illustrates, most Asians who rated themselves as "fluent" could easily complete all the tasks, scoring 35 on the more rigorous measurement of language ability. Of the six Western men who rated themselves as fluent, however, only one could easily complete all the tasks. Western men also demonstrate a lower skill bar for rating themselves as advanced or very advanced, compared with Asians. Even if Westerners do not receive effusive praise for their language skills in the workplace, the recognition and attention they get for their language skills elsewhere likely contributes to these inflated assessments. In turn, an overassessment of their skills, perhaps not limited to Japanese language skill, may make Western men perceive their objectively outsize rewards as only natural.

Recent research has asserted that Western men in mainstream, white-collar employment can no longer capitalize on the lucrative internationalization employment niche, or on positive attitudes toward Westerners and whites. This body of research argues that, although positive attitudes toward Westerners and whites might bestow some "small benefits" outside the workplace, as well as access to racialized jobs such as English teaching, Western background offers no "tangible" economic rewards, such as higher wages or access to managerial jobs, in standard white-collar work.[51]

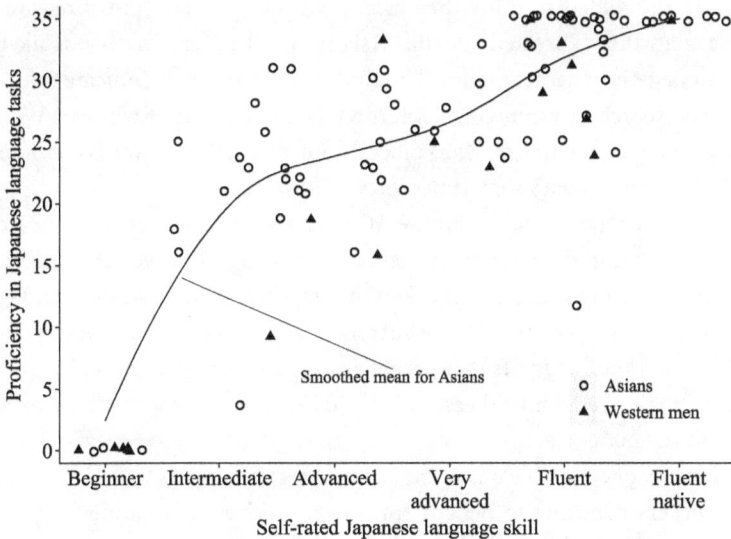

FIGURE 6.2. Relationship between task proficiency and self-rated Japanese language skill for Asians and Western men. Calculated from author's survey data.

The data in the current study offer reason to doubt these claims. They suggest that not only are positive stereotypes about Westerners present in elite white-collar workplaces but also that they continue to offer a source of economic advantage. Of course, the small sample size of Western men raises the risk of statistically aberrant results. This is not a reason to dismiss the findings, however; small though the sample size is, these data offer, to my knowledge, the *only* available comparison of Western men and Japanese men's earnings within the same firms, and as such, they improve on previous studies that speculate on Western men's disadvantage without drawing on any comparative data. Thus, although the small sample size precludes settling once and for all the question of Western men's advantage or disadvantage, the data do provide new evidence hinting that conclusions about the "end of privilege" may be premature.

In contemporary Japan, many Western men's expectations for the workplace are likely conditioned by the "celebrity" treatment they receive in some casual social interactions, as well as by longstanding narratives of Westerners as saviors who will modernize Japan and elevate its institutions to match global standards.[52] Furthermore, white Western men's sense of dislocation as they move from being the invisible ethnoracial "default" in their societies to being highly visible ethnoracial "others" in Japan can throw into sharp relief the assimilative pressures and added scrutiny they face, even though those pressures are less intense than those directed at other Asians, and the scrutiny is less likely to focus on negative characteristics. The findings of this study indicate that what previous research has sometimes interpreted as the limits of white or Western privilege may reflect, in part, workplaces' failure to deliver rewards commensurate with Western men's sometimes lofty self-image.

The recent studies that examine Westerners' experiences in white-collar workplaces have highlighted in particular that *young* white workers experience little advantage and conclude, based on this experience, that Western and white privilege is thing of the past.[53] The current study, which includes both younger and older workers, suggests that perhaps advantage accrues gradually over the course of male Western workers' careers, just as disadvantage accrues over the course of Asians' careers.

Of course, one possible objection to this interpretation is that older Western male workers continue to benefit from overly generous treatment in earlier decades and that the careers of younger workers will not follow the same trajectory. Several pieces of evidence, however, undercut this interpretation. First among these are the results of the survey experiment, which show that respondents in contemporary workplaces are more likely to recommend promotion for Anglo-named employees than for Japanese employees, all else being equal. Second, both Western and non-Western employees observe that white Western employees enjoy a special visibility in these elite firms. Self-reports of contact with managers also demonstrate that Western men have more extensive managerial networks than all other groups, whether or not they hold managerial roles. This indicates that symbolic boundaries privileging whites or Westerners are persistent. Western men in the sample, on average, earn more than Japanese male peers, and they are more likely to be in managerial roles, not because they are hired from abroad as "expat managers" but because they have worked their way up from within Japanese organizations.

This is not to say, however, that Western men never experience disadvantage in the Japanese workplace. A labor market emphasizing new graduate hiring poses barriers to anyone not educated in the Japanese university system, such as people who come to Japan for English teaching or seeking to change careers. Poorer Japanese skills can handicap Western men in hiring, even though they are held to a lower standard than Asian immigrants. Finally, symbolic boundaries casting Westerners as indelible others are also sometimes a basis for outright exclusion and hostility.[54] For all these reasons, not every Western man is able to capitalize on pro-white and pro-Western attitudes. Moreover, the sheer magnitude of Western men's advantage in these elite firms cannot be simplistically extrapolated to the rest of the economy—at a nationwide level, some combination of structural barriers to foreigners' labor market entry, Western-ers' relatively low levels of acculturation, and exclusion or other discrimination could result in a net disadvantage for Western men. The current study, how-ever, indicates that, for those who obtain jobs at large elite firms, positive beliefs about Western men's capabilities and deservingness carry greater weight for workers' attainment than do the symbolic boundaries about otherness.

Under conditions of population decline, exclusion, whether on the basis of language and cultural skills, or on the basis of region of origin or race, becomes more costly to firms. Moreover, as population declines and international mar-kets grow in importance to Japanese corporations, Western men's status as emblems of global cosmopolitanism and global business is likely to increase their appeal to Japanese employers. Consequently, the balance between exclu-sionary pressures and positive attitudes may shift in ways that benefit Western men still more. As in the past, then, we can predict that pro-Western and pro-white attitudes will continue to serve as a potent resource to Western men working in elite firms in Japan and will amplify their ability to take advantage of the structural conditions of a shrinking population.

CONCLUSION

The media frequently, if inaccurately, depict Japan as a country "closed" to immigration, and policy decisions of the COVID-19 era initially seemed to confirm this view.[1] During the early months of the pandemic, the government ceased issuing new visas to foreigners; from April 2020 to September 2020, it barred even permanent residents who had traveled abroad from reentry to Japan.[2] New visas and entry for those with existing, nonpermanent visas remained severely restricted until March 2022.[3] International observers characterized these policies as a recapitulation of the *sakoku* (closed country) strategy of the Tokugawa era, and accused Japan of "taking a sledgehammer to immigration policy" as a trial run for a no-immigration future.[4]

In fact, it is the pandemic-era border controls that are the aberration. Since I began this research in 2013, the population of technical and humanities specialist visa holders has more than doubled; indeed, although the pandemic entry restrictions severely disrupted the lives of many visa applicants and visa holders in the process of moving to Japan, they barely stemmed the broader influx of foreign workers. By June 2022, a mere three months after visa restrictions were loosened, the number of technical and humanities specialist visa holders registered in Japan hit an all-time high, exceeding three hundred thousand for the first time.

Businesses' decisions to incorporate larger numbers of foreigners as white-collar workers is not a symptom of blindly following a fleeting trend. In addition to changing norms and economic pressures to expand into overseas markets, structural labor market shortages driven by population aging and decline give businesses little choice but to seek talent more widely than ever before. Even though the government has not significantly reformed the white-collar migration system since the 1990s, and even though it put in place draconian restrictions during the pandemic, migration for professional work has grown dramatically.[5] As population decline intensifies, it will accelerate still further, even in the absence of further changes to border control laws.

Japanese women's presence in elite firms is growing even more rapidly. Between 2013 and 2022, the female workforce employed in regular, full-time jobs increased by 2.2 million workers.[6] Long criticized for its low rates of female labor force participation, Japan now exceeds the United States and France in this, and its rate is similar to Germany and the United Kingdom.[7]

In contrast to the continuity of white-collar immigration policy, policies on women's workplace inclusion and advancement have evolved significantly. Innovations include the 2013 establishment of targets for women to hold 30 percent of leadership and management roles by 2020 (later extended to 2030); a 2014 increase in wage replacement for parental leave from 50 percent to 67 percent; the 2016 launch of a public database reporting firms' progress toward gender equality, such as women's share of managerial roles or the ratio of female-to-male wages at the firm; a massive expansion of the public daycare system that has nearly cut waitlists for care by 90 percent since 2017; a 2019 cap on overtime work hours, with fines for companies that violate the law; and a 2023 commitment by the Kishida government to increase Japan's per capita spending on children to match Sweden's.[8]

The backdrop for the policy changes and increases in women's labor force participation is population decline. Before 2010, former Prime Minister Abe, who later became a vocal proponent of increasing women's managerial representation, idealized and advocated for a male-breadwinner/female-caregiver family model. Without the spur of population decline, his conversion into a champion of women's workplace advancement is inconceivable.[9] The closely intertwined normative and economic forces generated by both the changing legal environment and the shrinking size of the workforce have motivated firms to employ women in positions from which they have historically excluded them.

By generating pressure to employ women and immigrants in greater numbers, population decline creates conditions in which Japanese women and immigrants have far greater opportunities than in the past to achieve parity with Japanese men in elite workplaces and throughout the broader economy. But do they? How will stratification in elite firms change as the numbers of Japanese women and immigrants of both genders working in elite firms continue to grow?

As I have shown throughout this book, elite Japanese business is still a salaryman's world. Despite the spur of population decline, gender remains an exceedingly powerful predictor of earnings and managerial authority. The persistent "gender trap" in elite firms ensnares not only Japanese women but also Asian immigrant women. Asian immigrant women are more highly educated than either Japanese men or women; they work longer hours and are more ambitious. Their pay, however, is little better than that of Japanese women. Even when they forego marriage and childrearing and "work like men," Asian and Japanese women continue to experience tremendous workplace disadvantage.

Although elite business remains a salaryman's world, the *ethnoracial* boundaries of the salaryman category are weakening. All but absent from the echelons of Japanese business in the past, immigrant men, whether from Asia or the West, can now become successful salarymen and obtain parity or better with Japanese men. At the same time, however, ethnoracial background and region of origin also matter for immigrant men's access to and experience in "the center of the circle." Asian men achieve parity with same-age Japanese peers through overachievement; Western men earn even more than Japanese men both in absolute terms and relative to their measurable skills. Ironically, given both the government and private firms' intensive attention to issues of women's workplace inclusion and advancement, and the popular conception of Japan as distinctly xenophobic, proportional to their smaller presence in the workplace, immigrant men reap an outsized share of the material benefits of population decline in elite firms.

Much past research on gender inequality in corporate Japan has focused on women's violations of ideal worker norms—that is, expectations that employees work long hours, socialize extensively afterhours, work continuously without breaks for childrearing, stay with one employer, and accept transfers to far-flung job postings.[10] For immigrants, scholarship emphasizes firms' expectations that foreign employees conform fully to Japanese business culture.[11] In both cases, the literature blames firms' culture and organizational practices for creating an environment in which women and foreign workers cannot compete on an equal footing with Japanese men. At the same time, however, the literature implies that a minority of women who "work like men" and immigrants who "work like Japanese" can narrow gaps in pay and promotion.

This study empirically undercuts several aspects of these dominant narratives in the case of elite firms. First, close investigation of the organizational environments of the study firms shows that the purportedly most consequential barriers to women's and immigrants' advancement—ideal worker norms and insistence on total assimilation to the Japanese business environment—are less monolithic than they are usually portrayed. Work hours have moderated significantly since the high growth era, after-hours socializing has decreased, and job change is more widely accepted. Similarly, although it is all but inconceivable that someone with almost no English ability would be hired for a white-collar job in the United States, elite Japanese firms hire foreign workers who in some cases barely speak Japanese; managers value the distinct perspectives and skills that immigrants bring, and in some cases, they make mutual accommodations that absolve foreign workers from adhering to the same expectations as Japanese employees. This challenges narratives casting these features as the most decisive determinants of women's and immigrants' disadvantage at work.

Second, individual-level analysis of earnings does not bear out the predictions that women who "work like men" or immigrants who "work like Japanese" come significantly closer to achieving parity with Japanese men. For Asian immigrants, wage gaps are larger for the most, rather than the least, acculturated; furthermore, Western men, who are far less acculturated than Asians on average, earn more than both Asian and Japanese men. For women, individual-level violations of ideal worker norms explain only a small portion of the wage gap with men. These findings push us to look beyond conventional explanations of gender and ethnic inequalities in elite firms.

The conventional arguments assume a fundamentally rules-based decision-making process in firms, in which employers and managers judge and reward individuals on the basis of their adherence to or deviance from the objective standards of ideal worker norms and assimilative expectations. In this account, group-level inequality emerges because, on average, women and immigrants are less successful at adhering to the rules than are Japanese men. Both employees' accounts of managers' decision-making processes and their earnings outcomes, however, belie this model. Employees report considerable idiosyncrasy in how managers evaluate employees. In other words, managers are *not* uniformly applying consistent rules in their employee evaluations, despite the widespread diffusion of quantitative "results-based" performance evaluation systems. Moreover, managers enjoy considerable discretion in how they assign work and whom they recommend for promotion. Managerial decisions in these realms are even less formalized and rule-based than are performance evaluations. Although in theory, idiosyncrasies in managers' standards might wash out in aggregation, individual and group outcomes do not support the contention that workers' conformity to the "rules" of ideal worker norms or assimilative expectations is the most important driver of gender or ethnic inequalities in the workplace.

I argue that, particularly in this environment of high managerial discretion, beliefs about the values and capabilities of different groups—what Michèle

Lamont calls "symbolic boundaries"—are central to the production of inequalities.[12] Symbolic boundaries that cast a certain group as less capable or worthy mean that members of that group are likely to suffer in work assignment, evaluation, and promotion *regardless* of what objective standards managers attempt to use to assess employees. Previous investigations of the Japanese workplace place too great an importance on the rules and too little on beliefs that undervalue or overvalue groups independent of the rules.

Before the 1990s, firms engaged in rules-based exclusion of women from positions of responsibility and of immigrants from nearly all white-collar employment. In this context, individual managers' beliefs about immigrants and women were largely irrelevant. But population decline, labor shortages, and a changing legal landscape have made blanket exclusions untenable. Women and immigrants increasingly work in management-track jobs in elite firms. Now that immigrants and women are, in theory, in the running for advancement in elite firms, coworkers' beliefs and attitudes take on a far more significant role in their outcomes.

It is not just the fact of symbolic boundaries—beliefs that groups are in some way different—but also the content that matters for workers' outcomes. Symbolic boundaries between men and women highlight women's supposedly lesser capabilities and lower ambitions. Symbolic boundaries between Japanese and foreigners emphasize foreigners' supposed ignorance of Japanese language and culture; and they paint other Asians as morally degenerate, even criminal, and Westerners as friendly, intelligent agents of globalization.

For women, regardless of nationality, assumptions about their capabilities and ambitions lead managers to assign them less highly valued tasks, which holds them back from the earliest stages of their careers. Without a track record of success in highly valued work, women are less likely to receive strong evaluations and are less likely to achieve rapid promotion. Asian men do not suffer in task assignment, but they are nonetheless rewarded less highly for their accomplishments, earning less than Japanese men with similar skills and experience. In contrast, narratives of difference do not consistently work against Western men. Compared with Japanese jobseekers, it is more difficult for immigrant workers to find employment in Japanese firms, regardless of region of origin. Once Western men are employed in an elite firm, however, symbolic boundaries that cast them as skilled and deserving reduce assimilative pressure and increase recognition and rewards for their accomplishments.

As organizational scholars have long noted, people assume that access to power and resources is earned, and consequently, we attribute greater capability, value, and moral worth to members of powerful and well-resourced groups than to those of less powerful, less resourced groups.[13] This means that social structure and macrohistorical trends profoundly shape the content of symbolic boundaries. For example, Japanese colonialism in Asia, like Japanese encounters with Western military and economic might dating back to the era of Perry's "black ships," continue to influence perceptions of Asians and Westerners. These boundaries are not fixed, however. Everyday interaction and experience, as well as macrohistorical trends, can soften or strengthen symbolic boundaries.

In elucidating the dynamics of symbolic boundaries in the workplace, empirical scholarship has focused almost exclusively on the demographic composition of management and top leadership. Because women and members of marginalized ethnoracial groups are absent from the top of organizational hierarchies, or are present only in token numbers, the argument goes, skepticism about their capacities and suitability for leadership persists, reinforced by everyday work routines.[14] This view ignores the other side of the status coin: those in poorly paid, low-level, subordinate positions.

The case of the elite Japanese workplace calls into question the primacy of managerial representation in the construction and reinforcement of symbolic boundaries. Certainly, Japanese women remain a minority in leadership positions in elite firms. Compared with immigrant men of any background, their numbers are far greater; however, if presence in management were enough to destabilize biases, Japanese women would face less severe bias than immigrant men, and they would come closer to obtaining parity with Japanese men with similar educational backgrounds and work behaviors. In fact, however, managers are less willing to assign Japanese women important and valuable work; and Japanese women experience far larger wage gaps, net of job category, qualifications, and skill, than do immigrant men.

It is not that biases against women were simply more severe, or more counter to ideal worker characteristics, from the get-go. There is a long history of vitriolic hate speech against Asian residents of Japan, castigating them as unintelligent, incapable, and criminal; and until lawsuits forced their hands, companies explicitly refused to hire employees with Asian immigrant backgrounds. In the contemporary workplace, however, coworkers describe Asian immigrant workers as ambitious superstars; Asian men achieve parity or near-parity with Japanese men, albeit through overachievement. Why are biases against Asians subject to disruption? Why are Asian men obtaining parity despite a long history of bias and outright exclusion?

I argue that Asian men have achieved parity because negative and devaluative attitudes toward women receive persistent reinforcement through women's overrepresentation in subordinate jobs. Whereas previous scholarship focuses on women's absence from the top, I propose that when women are predominantly responsible for mundane tasks, this predominance also reifies the view that women's strengths lie in routine work. In turn, this view affects the perception and treatment of all women, native and immigrant alike, regardless of individual capacity and ambition, even as more women enter management and management-track jobs.

There is simply no corollary reinforcing ethnoracial boundaries between Asians and Japanese, or between Westerners and Japanese. Neither region of origin group is ever "the face" of low-status, devalued jobs within elite firms. Indeed, the exacting expectations for fluency in Japanese cultural norms in low-status customer-facing roles within firms makes Japanese natives preferred for these roles and further insulates foreign workers of any background from becoming overrepresented there.

Testing the relationship between Asian over- and underrepresentation in low-status jobs and attitudes toward Asians is outside the scope of this study. Indeed, because there are few, if any, elite organizations in Japan in which subordinate jobs are Asian dominated, an empirical test of this hypothesis may well be impossible. Observations of how women's role as the face of low-status positions perpetuates gender bias, however, imply that Asians' near-absence from these roles is likely to be a source of relative advantage.

Moreover, because of Japan's restrictive stance toward immigration for low-paid work, interpersonal experiences that would buttress negative stereotypes of Asians or Westerners outside the workplace are uncommon. If Japan admitted large numbers of Asian immigrants to work as cleaners, trash collectors, dishwashers, or farmworkers, the presence of immigrant communities of concentrated poverty would likely reinvigorate negative stereotypes about the moral worth and intellectual capacity of Asians. In the absence of mass immigration for low-paid work, Japanese coworkers are unlikely to encounter Asians other than those employed as white-collar workers in their own places of employment.

We can thus speculate that Asians' near absence *from the bottom* of organizational and societal hierarchies sets the stage for the erosion of symbolic boundaries between Asians and Japanese. In the context of this absence, small numbers of white-collar Asian workers chip away at long-standing negative stereotypes, and Asian men obtain parity with Japanese men through overachievement; held back by gender biases, Japanese and Asian women do not.

To what extent do these stratification patterns reflect those in the broader economy? Certainly, the conclusion that gender pay gaps outstrip ethnoracial inequalities does not apply to manufacturing, agricultural, or construction enterprises in which most foreign workers are employed through de facto guest worker initiatives such as the Technical Intern Training Program (TITP) and the Specified Skilled Worker (SSW) visa. Average pay for workers in these categories, whose labor mobility and length of stay are tightly controlled, fall far below averages for Japanese men and women as well as for immigrants on white-collar visas.[15] Nor does it apply in the case of foreign workers whose visa status restricts them to part-time employment, such as students.

It is reasonable to hypothesize, however, that these patterns are consistent with those in other white-collar places of employment, including in small and midsize firms, albeit with a few qualifications. In general, because the salary ceiling is far lower in small firms, pay gaps tend to be smaller. As government data highlights, women's earnings disadvantage is far more modest in smaller firms, largely because men earn so much less than they do in large firms.[16] There is far less data about nation or region of origin and earnings, but recent analyses of data drawn from the entire economy in the Basic Survey on Wage Structure estimate that, net of human capital, tenure, and prevailing regional and firm-level wages, immigrant men on white-collar working visas earn about 6 percent less than Japanese men, and immigrant women on white-collar working visas earn about 12 percent less.[17] This fairly modest wage gap for immigrant men (not disaggregated by region of origin) suggests that they fare moderately well at small and midsize firms. The far larger disadvantage between immigrant women and Japanese men, by contrast, highlights the significance of gender as a predictor of workplace outcomes.

More speculatively, symbolic boundaries in smaller firms may operate somewhat differently, resulting in slightly less favorable treatment for immigrant men than we observe in elite firms. Because most firms still hire few non-Japanese, the chance of being the *only* foreigner in one's place of employment remains high outside large firms. As such, negative stereotypes about Asians may be somewhat more persistent among coworkers in small and midsize firms, as they are less likely to interact with a many different Asian foreign workers. Additionally, symbolic boundaries casting Western men as valuable agents of globalization may not be as compelling and relevant in small and midsize firms, which are less likely to do business in Western countries. This may reduce their economic advantage in this context.

The study results, and their applicability to other white-collar workplaces, offer a new perspective on race and ethnicity in Japanese society more broadly. The popular understanding of Japanese identity both inside and outside Japan is that it entails the complete correspondence of race, culture, and citizenship.[18] To be fully Japanese under what Gracia Liu-Farrer terms an "ethnonationalist" framework, one must be born to two racially Japanese parents, fully assimilated to Japanese culture, and hold Japanese citizenship.[19] Journalistic accounts take the dominant ethnonationalist conceptualization of Japanese identity to reveal uniquely extreme xenophobia and racism.[20] Moreover, scholars argue that ethnonationalism (and the xenophobia or racism it is thought to represent) results in exclusionary immigration policies and discrimination against non-Japanese living in Japan.[21] These narratives imply that to be non-Japanese, whether by virtue of bloodline, culture, or citizenship, is to occupy a categorically inferior place in Japanese society.

This implication has rarely been tested, however. Scholars have documented "hierarchies of foreigners," pointing to inequities among non-Japanese associated with visa and legal status, occupation, race, and gender.[22] It remains rare, however, to consider how these hierarchies of foreigners intersect with outcomes and experiences of those considered to be "full Japanese" by virtue of race, cultural fluency, and citizenship.[23]

The dearth of comparative studies is due in no small part to ethnonationalist discourses, which have shaped, and impoverished, social scientific data collection on ethnoracial stratification in Japan. Under the assumption that Japan is a homogeneous society in which non-Japanese are a negligible presence, the Stratification and Social Mobility Survey (SSM), Japan's most comprehensive and accessible dataset on inequality and stratification, has, since its inception in 1955, excluded noncitizens from its sampling frame and omitted any questions on place of birth, race, or ethnicity that might be used to identify naturalized Japanese or native-born minorities.[24] Government administrative data, including the national census and, since 2019, the Basic Survey on Wage Structure, include and identify noncitizens, but these surveys fail to ask about ethnoracial heritage of citizens, because citizens are presumed to be ethnoracially Japanese. Their rather sparse collection of ancillary information about noncitizens also makes it difficult to disaggregate heterogeneous experiences of noncitizens. Scholars in both Japan and in Western countries who research various categories of non-Japanese almost always consider non-Japanese in isolation.[25] As a result, the contours of ethnoracial inequalities between Japanese and different categories of "non-Japanese" remain largely uncharted. The assumption of disadvantage for *all* non-Japanese, also born of ethnonationalist discourse, fills this informational vacuum.

The present study disrupts this assumption. If ethnonationalist discourse corresponded neatly to discrimination in employment, we would expect non-Japanese background to correlate strongly with disadvantage in earnings. It does not. Rather, the relationship between non-Japaneseness and earnings can be negative, neutral, or positive, depending on region of origin and gender.

Although ethnonationalist discourse precludes immigrants from being recognized as Japanese, it does not block immigrants employed in elite firms from obtaining parity (or better) with same-sex Japanese peers, something that immigrant and ethnic minority workers do not necessarily obtain in elite firms in supposedly more "open" societies, including the United States.[26]

This finding highlights a broader insight about ethnoracial relations in contemporary Japan. Ironically, the more relevant and telling aspect of ethnoracial relations in ethnonationalist Japan is the wide variation in legal treatment and social reception of non-Japanese by social identity categories *other than their non-Japaneseness*, including but not limited to gender, visa status, country of origin, and phenotype or ethnoracial background.[27] As the case of workers in elite firms underscores, what stands out about ethnoracial relations in Japan is not extreme xenophobia, racism, or unfavorable attitudes toward or treatment of those who do not fit a restrictive definition of Japaneseness.[28] Rather, it is the *contingency, inconsistency,* and *variety* in the ways that being non-Japanese affects individuals, in ways that are positive as well as negative.

There are many examples of this phenomenon beyond the current study. Indeed, visa and border control reflect this contingency of attitudes and treatment far more closely than they reflect straightforward xenophobia or racism. This is apparent in the generous legal rights afforded to white-collar migrants, which sometimes even exceed those of Japanese nationals. Noncitizens on white-collar work visas can sponsor dependent visas for spouses and children; they can renew their visas indefinitely; they are permitted to change employers at will; and they are eligible for permanent residency and citizenship. In the case of white-collar workers on the High-Skilled Professional (HSP) visa, residency requirements for a permanent visa are as short as one year. Furthermore, although Japan does not recognize same-sex marriage, the Ministry of Justice issues visas for white-collar migrants' same-sex spouses if they are legally married in their home country. HSP visa holders may also sponsor a visa for a domestic worker, another right not afforded to Japanese nationals.

Visa policy toward categories of migrants deemed "undesirable" is far more restrictive and or even punitive. Japan notoriously approves only a tiny fraction of refugee applications; those seeking refugee status can face indefinite detention as they go through the application and appeals process.[29] Migrants on the TITP (currently being revamped as the "Work Training System"), who work in low-paid jobs in construction, manufacturing, and agriculture, experience heavy constraints on their labor mobility; cannot sponsor family members; and have a long, treacherous, and narrow path to permanent residency and citizenship.[30]

If straightforward xenophobia and racism explained visa and border control policy, we would expect restrictiveness across the board, or restrictiveness that targets nonpreferred ethnoracial groups. To the contrary, however, visa policy is generous in international comparison to "desirable" white-collar migrants who are predominantly Asian; but this policy is constraining and repressive for migrants deemed undesirable, including those who are *also* predominantly Asian. Rather than reflecting particularly intense underlying racism or xenophobia, the dizzying variation in policy toward migrants in different circumstances illustrates and reinforces the contingency of non-Japaneseness and ethnoracial background as axes of hostility, exclusion, and discrimination.

Looking beyond policy to social reception of immigrants, other markers of difference often matter more than non-Japanese identity or ethnoracial background. We might expect coethnic return migrants—that is to say, descendants of Japanese emigrants to other countries—to have some advantages in an ethnonationalist society; they are often phenotypically indistinguishable from Japanese and are considered to be of the same race or "blood."[31] Japanese Americans (who tend to come as students or work in white-collar occupations) report largely warm, favorable receptions that share a good deal in common with those of white Americans, whereas Latin Americans of Japanese descent (who tend to work in blue-collar occupations) face considerable negative stereotypes and social hostility.[32] In this case, nation of origin and occupation override both race and non-Japaneseness as the most salient influences on reception.

In other cases, phenotypical aspects of race are one of the most significant determinants of treatment. This is particularly true of encounters with Japanese interlocutors who have no information about their non-Japanese counterparts other than their appearance or speech. Being stopped by the police on the street is a common and well-documented example of this type of interaction. Regardless of race, Japanese language ability, visa or citizenship status, non-Japanese report being stopped by the police at a high rate.[33] People of Latin American, Middle Eastern, and African descent are stopped most frequently. People of European descent are stopped at somewhat lower rates; but despite prejudice and criminality narratives about Asians, people of East or Southeast Asian descent, who can often visually pass as Japanese, are stopped at the lowest rates of all.[34] In these encounters, whites are at an advantage relative to other visible non-Japanese but are at a disadvantage relative to Japanese-passing Asians. Thus, even white Westerners are not immune to unfavorable treatment in certain circumstances, even if they experience an advantage in others, and other racial groups experience greater profiling risks.

In the 1940s, sociologist Everett Hughes coined the term "master status" to refer to an identity characteristic that affects all aspects of a person's life and tends to override other characteristics in how others evaluate or treat the person.[35] Hughes concluded that race (referring particularly to the Black/white divide) represents such a "master status" in the United States, superseding other aspects of identity. Ironically, however, Japan's ethnonationalist paradigm does *not* mean that either non-Japaneseness or more specific ethnoracial categories, such as "Chinese" or "Caucasian" necessarily compose a "master status" within a given social context or in Japanese society more broadly. In Japanese employment, gender is such a master status, whereas non-Japanese origin is not.

Rather than conceptualizing Japanese society as uniquely xenophobic or racist, we might productively think of it as a place where the possession of favored characteristics, such as high occupational standing, citizenship of a wealthy (Western) country, or Caucasian racial background, are unusually potent tools for *insulating* oneself from xenophobic or racist attitudes and treatment, even if such insulation is incomplete.

The findings of this study also offer new angles for thinking about gender inequality in Japan. Notoriously, Japan ranks near the bottom of the World Economic Forum's Gender Gap Index, scoring closer to Iran and Saudi Arabia than to the United States, France, or Germany.[36] The reason for Japan's abysmal placement is women's low representation in high-paid employment in private firms, and in national politics.[37] On one hand, this research supports the view, common in media and government reports on Japanese employment, that sexism and ideas about fixed gender roles hold women back in elite firms; but on the other, it also cautions against a simplistic understanding of sexism as unchanging and indelibly embedded in Japanese culture.

Sociologists describe sexism and gender bias as socially constructed, meaning they are perpetuated and reinforced by structural and institutional arrangements. One example of how such social construction operates is the set of ways in which women's concentration in low-status jobs shapes how women are perceived. Beyond this, however, this research prompts consideration of other ways in which institutional arrangements, including Japan's restrictions on migration for low-paid work, also contribute to gender inequality and gender bias.

Conventionally, scholars see immigration as facilitating highly educated, native-born women's advancement in the workplace, because it allows women in high-earning jobs to outsource domestic labor to immigrant women and increase the time they can devote to "greedy" jobs.[38] The current study, however, suggests that this logic might not hold in the case of Japan. Japanese women who work longer hours and have fewer household responsibilities do not fare notably better than women who violate "ideal worker norms" in the sample firms. Even if the female respondents to the study could (and wanted to) outsource more domestic labor, this would not necessarily benefit their careers.

There may be other mechanisms—beyond the opportunity to outsource household labor—by which low immigration affects native-born women's career trajectories in elite firms and beyond. In many countries, immigrants and native-born ethnoracial minorities are "the face" of low-status, undervalued jobs. In Japan, restrictions on low-paid migration preclude this. The absence of immigrants to fill low-paid jobs means that native-born women are more likely to hold low-paid positions that might go to immigrants in other national contexts, including irregular jobs across sectors, and clerical-track jobs within elite firms.

Although it is beyond the scope of the current study, it is possible that, by keeping native-born women as "the face" of low-paying, low-status roles in many organizational contexts, immigration restrictions indirectly reinforce gender biases. Native-born women's concentration in low-paying jobs contributes to beliefs that *all* women are best suited for routine work. Furthermore, even women who are privileged by nativity, race, education, or social class are more heavily associated with the devalued household sphere. Just as immigrant men in Japan can insulate themselves from ethnoracial biases by virtue of high-status occupations, so too in the United States can a subset of women shield themselves from gender bias by separating themselves from the domestic sphere through the employment of immigrant women caregivers and other household employees. That this option is largely unavailable in Japan likely sustains beliefs that (native-born, highly educated) women belong in the home.

In terms of education, language, and cultural skills, native-born Japanese women are ideally positioned to reap the benefits of population decline. That they benefit less, relative to their numbers, than do immigrant men may in part be an unintended consequence of Japan's restrictive stance toward immigration for low-paid work.

Indeed, we can speculate that Japan's immigration rules "trade off" ethnoracial inequality and bias on a national scale against greater gender inequality and gender bias. By keeping low-paid migration to a minimum, the government has, by design, prevented the emergence of large-scale poverty concentrated along ethnoracial lines.[39] At the same time, these policy decisions have inadvertently set Japan on a different track from many other wealthy countries, where the presence of low-paid migrants spurs well-educated, native-born women's career advancement. In sum, although this study locates the sources of white-collar gender inequality in gender bias within firms, this bias is rooted not only in the broader culture and in firms' gendered practices but also in other policy decisions in which sexism has played little part.

The decline in Japan's working-age population will deepen in future decades. In 2015, when I was a resident at the Canon Institute for Global Studies, Japan's working-age population had fallen by 11 percent since its peak in 1995. The government projects a deficit of nearly half that peak, or forty-two million people by 2070.[40] This loss exceeds the current population of the entire Tokyo metropolitan area, which, at thirty-seven million, is the world's largest megacity.

Some commentators argue that artificial intelligence and robots may fill the void population decline leaves in the labor market. To date, however, the ability of AI and robotics to substitute for human labor has fallen far short of labor demands; and it is doubtful that, even with further rapid advances, it could replace population loss at this scale. Elite firms, in particular, succeed and fail on the basis of their human resources. Although population decline is not the only factor to drive increases of women and immigrants in elite white-collar employment, it nonetheless provides a spur to elite firms to incorporate them in greater numbers than ever before and to reduce structural barriers to their advancement, which become more and more costly as population decline accelerates.

As structural barriers to women's and white-collar migrants' employment have fallen, individual attitudes, and hence symbolic boundaries, have come to matter more for these workers' workplace opportunities. How might symbolic boundaries evolve, and how might this affect stratification in elite firms as population decline intensifies? Although it is impossible to answer these questions with any certainty, I suspect that institutional dynamics lend themselves more to continuity than to change.

First, gender inequality is likely to persist, despite splashy government initiatives to overcome it. Since 2013, the Japanese government has promoted numerical targets to increase women's representation in management and on corporate boards. This is appealing for two main reasons. First, many people sincerely believe that women in management reduce gender bias and thus benefit all women.[41] More cynically, however, these initiatives are a relatively easy way of creating *the appearance* of social change.[42] It is easy because managers represent a small share of the total employment structure—fewer than 2 percent of all workers in Japan are managers.[43] Even attaining full gender parity in these roles thus involves occupational advancement for a vanishingly small number of women. It creates the appearance of change because women in management are highly visible. Women's managerial representation weighs heavily in the World Economic Forum's gender gap index, in which Japan fares so poorly. By increasing women's presence in management, Japan can dramatically improve its standing in the rankings, and hence its international reputation on gender issues, even if progress toward gender equality stagnates in other areas.

Even when they represent a sincere desire for change, however, "trickle down" gender equality initiatives are unlikely to revolutionize perceptions or treatment of the much larger number of women who never become managers.[44] Improving the terms and conditions of "bad" irregular and clerical-track jobs, such that holding one of these positions does not so strongly mark the job holder and members of her demographic group as being low in ability or ambition, would likely do far more to erode gender bias than initiatives narrowly focused at the sparsely populated pinnacle of the organizational pyramid.

To date, however, efforts to improve conditions at the bottom of the pyramid have been piecemeal. Although legislation prohibits "unreasonable" dissimilarities in employment terms for regular and irregular employees, courts have deemed many forms of disadvantageous treatment for irregular workers "reasonable," including lower job security and lower compensation.[45] Similarly, although management and clerical tracks offer unequal pay and promotion opportunities even among regular workers, as long as firms avoid calling them "men's" and "women's" tracks, the courts have determined that tracking complies with equal opportunity laws.[46] Although all societies have jobs with low prestige and pay, these legally legitimated inferior job categories throw into sharp relief the perceived lesser worth of clerical and irregular workers, and by extension, the types of people who hold them. This policy neglect implies that women's overrepresentation in low-status jobs, and the poor pay and advancement opportunities associated with such jobs, will likely persist. This persistent structural disadvantage, in turn, will slow women's ability to reap the full benefits of population decline, including both immigrant and Japanese women.

In contrast, for Asian men, structural conditions favor continued progress toward equality with Japanese men. Indeed, the Asian men in this sample already achieve parity on average, albeit through overachievement in education and language ability. Overachievement may be increasingly unnecessary in the future. Longstanding stereotypes about Asians' criminality are already weak in elite firms, and weaker still on teams with larger shares of Asian employees. This weakness implies that Asians' growing presence is eroding symbolic boundaries that have held back Asian men in the past. As population decline advances, firms are likely to increase their employment of white-collar Asian workers still further, particularly because recent growth in native-born women's labor force participation leaves fewer and fewer nonworking native-born women willing to be drawn into the labor market. Increased employment for Asian workers, in turn, may further destabilize biases and reduce the barriers to Asian men's advancement, obviating the need for overachievement to obtain parity.

At the same time, if the government revises border control policy to admit more Asians for low-paid work, this could breathe new life into old stereotypes about Asians and worsen both attitudes toward and treatment of Asian men employed in elite firms. Although such a radical revision to border control policy is possible, strong countervailing pressures work against this possibility.

First, the norm in the border control policymaking process is that any of the three government ministries tasked with overseeing migration—the Ministry of Justice; Ministry of Health, Labor and Welfare; and Ministry of Economy, Trade, and Industry—can kill proposed changes to visa and border control law. Second, the influential Abe faction within Japan's Liberal Democratic Party (LDP) have long opposed expansions that would bring more low-paid foreign workers to Japan. As a result, reforms that survive the consultative and legislative process have historically been small in scope.[47]

The SSW visa, launched in 2019, is a case in point. Media heralded SSW as a sea change in Japan's approach to migration, because it opens various low-paid occupations, such as eldercare, to foreign workers. In theory, at least, it also creates a path to permanent residency for certain foreign workers in manufacturing and services.[48] To date, however, the program's implementation is noteworthy primarily for its conservativism.

SSW visa applicants from abroad must demonstrate basic Japanese language skills, possess work experience in the relevant occupation, and pass an exam.[49] These burdensome requirements have kept the scale of the program small and heavily favor foreign workers *already present in Japan* at time of application, primarily workers on the TITP, who are exempted from testing requirements if they stay with the same employer.[50]

In addition, the incentives the SSW offers with the aim of attracting more low-paid workers are difficult to access in practice. Unlike the TITP, SSW permits workers to change jobs. It restricts job change to the same occupation and industry, and even within these restrictions, all job changes require Ministry of Justice approval. This comes with a heavy paperwork burden that puts workers at the mercy of unscrupulous employers and brokers, who can keep workers captive by refusing to provide the necessary documentation.[51]

After spending five years with SSW-1 status, workers become eligible to apply to SSW-2. SSW-2 visa holders gain family reunification rights to bring a spouse and minor children to Japan. After ten years on SSW-2, they become eligible to apply for permanent residency. But these are very long wait times. Because most SSW workers spend three years as TITP workers, it takes at least eight years' residence to earn family reunification rights, and eighteen years for permanent residency.[52] As of the end of 2022, only 8 out of about 131,000 SSW holders had upgraded to SSW-2 status.[53]

In sum, high barriers to obtaining SSW-1 status, tight controls on SSW workers' labor mobility, and logistical barriers to progression within the SSW visa hierarchy all raise doubts about the program's appeal to prospective migrants. Of course, policy in this area remains in flux. Demographic pressures may still lead to more dramatic migration reforms. Policies in place as of this writing, however, seem unlikely to transform the immigration landscape in the near term. This implies that Asian men's relative advantage in elite firms may solidify and expand.

As for Western men, the study shows enduring advantage: Coworkers see Western men as more deserving of promotion than Japanese men, and Western men in fact earn more and are more likely to be managers than are Japanese men. How persistent will this advantage be? On one hand, just as contact with a diversity of Asian coworkers seems to promote more balanced, less stereotypical views of Asians, it is possible that contact with Westerners in white-collar workplaces might promote a more balanced, and hence less positive, view of Western men. Illustrative of this, Shouichiro told my research assistant that he initially believed Americans to be unusually "motivated" and "open-minded," but he eventually concluded that his naïve views were overly rosy. "It turns out," he said, "there are some people who fit that image, and others who don't."

Shouichiro is unusual, however. His revelation stemmed not from working alongside Americans in Japan, but from an eight-year stint working in the United States. Most Japanese employees do not, and will not, experience the extensive contact with Westerners that gradually unraveled Shouichiro's original assumptions. Since the border control reforms of 1990, growth in the Asian immigrant population has dwarfed that in the Western population. Moreover, prospects for future growth are minimal. Because of Japan's already permissive legal stance toward white-collar migration, there is little room for further policy innovation to draw Western professional migrants in greater numbers. An influx of Westerners to work in low-paid jobs is also unlikely: Westerners willing to take low-paying service or manufacturing jobs, such as emigrants from Eastern Europe, usually have options closer to home. As a result, I expect pro-Western bias and Western men's attendant advantages to remain intact in the near and medium term.

Many other countries are following in Japan's demographic footsteps. Although the trend is not so advanced as it is in Japan, working-age populations are declining in South Korea, Taiwan, Germany, France, and Italy, among others.

The case of Japan is useful for thinking through the possible effects of population decline in these and many other countries where population decline is either already occurring or immediately in the offing.

Despite the catastrophizing accounts of population decline so prevalent in the media, it is a mathematical surety that if the population falls faster than a slowdown in economic growth, each person's proportional share of the economic pie expands. Furthermore, labor becomes scarcer in relation to capital. Workers' bargaining power can grow, leading to improvement in wages and work conditions for all, and new chances at advancement and equity for members of historically excluded groups. Of course, such equity gains are not inevitable: The resources freed by population decline could also be captured by existing powerholders. The case of Japanese elite firms demonstrates that the chance for greater equity is a real possibility, however. How might these dynamics play out elsewhere? Who is likely to benefit in elite employment in other countries as population declines? To understand changing dynamics of elite employment in other countries with declining populations, we might think of who is, or is not, the face of low-status work in organizations, and in society more broadly.

In terms of the demography of low-status jobholders, Japanese society and elite Japanese organizations are unusual compared with most wealthy, Western nations. Whether they have admitted immigrants primarily through family reunification, as in the United States; or as refugees and asylum seekers, as in Sweden; or as guest workers, as in Germany, wealthy countries in Western Europe and North America have much larger communities of immigrant and native-born ethnoracial minorities, who often are overrepresented in low-paid, low-status jobs. Like Japan, these countries have made inadvertent trade-offs between gender and ethnoracial inequality. Unlike Japan, however, their trade-offs favor women privileged by race, nativity, and social class, eroding somewhat the associations between white or native-born women and low-status work and making it easier to outsource household labor to immigrant women. As these countries' demographic declines deepen, highly educated, native-born, white women may narrow gaps with male counterparts relatively rapidly. By contrast, similarly highly educated, white-collar immigrant men, such as college-educated Hispanic men in the United States, or college-educated Middle Eastern men in Europe, might face relatively higher barriers to parity in white-collar places of employment.

Japan's neighbors in East Asia, South Korea, and Taiwan resemble it more closely in terms of their levels of migration. Noncitizens represent 3.4 percent of the population in both Taiwan and South Korea, slightly higher than Japan at 2.4 percent.[54] The composition of their migrant populations is very different, however. Taiwan permits temporary domestic worker migration, and Southeast Asian women working as domestic laborers account for a sizable share of its foreign population. (Taiwan is also far more gender equal than either Japan or South Korea.[55]) South Korea accepts coethnic workers from China to work in a variety of low-paid industries and occupations; it maintains a guestworker scheme for Southeast Asians in low-paid manufacturing jobs; and it is currently considering proposals to expand domestic worker migration from Southeast Asia.[56] Like Japan, both Taiwan and South Korea eagerly court foreign white-collar workers, but they have attracted these workers in much lower numbers. As a result, migration for low-paid work is a larger share of their (im)migrant populations, which is likely to grow more swiftly in both countries than in Japan. This growth implies that these countries may, to some extent, converge with those in Europe and North America, tolerating more prominent ethnoracial inequalities, while easing the path to parity for native-born women.

Population decline lends yet another meaning to the versatile 1970s catchphrase that "the future is female." Despite a longstanding preference for men in elite employment, as the population shrinks, private firms in wealthy countries have greater and greater incentives to hire and promote women into elite roles. Other developments, including women's educational gains and international migration of domestic workers, also spur women's integration into elite employment. In Japan, however, the future may be foreign, not female.

Acknowledgments

I am profoundly grateful to the people who have lent me the generous support that made this book possible.

My wonderful Boston University professors Sarah Frederick and Corky White laid the intellectual and academic groundwork for this project, as did many talented Japanese teachers, particularly Itoh-sensei at BU, the Kyoto Center for Japanese Studies teaching staff, and Otake-sensei at the Inter-University Center for Japanese Language Studies in Yokohama, where the graduate students in the class of 2008–2009 inspired me to apply for a doctoral program. I am particularly grateful to Yulia Frumer and Kate Goldfarb, whose successful book prospectuses provided models for my own.

As a sociology doctoral student at Cornell, Victor Nee, Kim Weeden, Paromita Sanyal, Filiz Garip, and Eli Friedman gave me a thorough grounding in sociology of immigration, gender, and work; provided thoughtful advice; and remained tactfully silent when I did not take it. Mary Brinton generously served as outside member and wise voice of Japan expertise on my committee. Although many people can say they had amazing graduate school classmates, I imagine I am alone in saying that two of them became, very suddenly, inadvertent midwives to my second child. What is more, they did a darn good job (reader, feel free to ask me about this over beers), and, perhaps even more astonishingly, had they not been there, there are several other Cornellians whom I trust would have done the same, including not just my fellow doctoral students but also Sue Meyer in the sociology office.

I feel overwhelmed with gratitude considering the "cast of thousands" who provided material assistance of all kinds during my research as I worked on the preliminary stages of the project from 2013 onward and especially during my stay in Tokyo from 2014–2015.

Thanks to an introduction by Shinju Fujihira, Jun Kurihara graciously hosted me at the Canon Institute for Global Studies (CIGS) as an international research fellow from 2014 to 2015, and has continued to welcome me back for short visits in the intervening years. Without the Canon affiliation, Kurihara-san's can-do, "move fast and break things" attitude, and the sponsorship of CIGS board member Akinari Horii, I would never have been able to gain access to the firms that participated in this study, and I remain deeply humbled by their confidence and support.

During (and after) my time in Tokyo, CIGS sponsored several events for business audiences at which I presented my work. In organizing these events, and in their day-to-day tasks, the office staff at CIGS blew me away with their competence, friendliness, and professionalism. I am especially grateful to Yasuko Nagatsuka, Taro Okabe, and Yukihiro Watanabe for thorough and repeated native checks of documents that I produced in Japanese, as well as for testing the survey. They and others shared stories about their work and family lives, taught me the ins and outs of the Marunochi area, and brought tears to my eyes with the adorable gown they bought as a gift for my son born during my time in Tokyo.

Hirohisa Takenoshita also welcomed me as a visiting scholar at Sophia University, where I joined his weekly seminar. Takenoshita-sensei's kindness and commitment to fostering young scholars is legendary. His seminar was a convivial place to familiarize myself with recent sociological research on Japan written in Japanese, and seminar participants provided intelligent feedback at multiple stages as my project progressed.

Many people assisted with the translation of the employee survey. Professional translator Nanae Nohrdahl and sociology colleagues Namie Nagamatsu, Akihiro Takekawa, Hirohisa Takenoshita, and Fumiya Uchikoshi all worked to perfect the Japanese version. Professional translators Zuoxian Si and Winnie Chang, as well as sociology colleagues Shun Gong, Ningzi Li, Yuqi Lu, Jie (Jamie) Zhang, Shuo Zhang, Xueyan Zhao, and Cornell undergraduate research assistant Quichen Yang all contributed to the Mandarin version.

Kaori Blalock did native checks of introductory documents I prepared for preliminary research in 2013, and in 2014, Keiko Shibatani transformed my amateurish firm recruitment documents to something far more eloquent and impeccably formatted.

Staff at the Japan Association of Corporate Executives were critical to advancing the project. I am deeply grateful to Natsuko Kasahara and Kiyohiko Ito for responding positively to Akinari Horii's request for their assistance, for refining the firm recruitment strategy, and for reaching out to member firms on my behalf. I extend sincere thanks and appreciation to the CEOs who generously granted research access, to the human resource personnel who took time from their many other duties to put those commitments into action, and to the individual employees who responded to the survey with such care and thoughtfulness, and especially those who agree to be interviewed and shared their experiences in depth.

Fumiya Uchikoshi arranged and conducted the interviews with Japanese respondents, yielding a wealth of data I would not have been able to match on my own. I am also grateful for meticulous interview transcription by Christina Pankiw, Kazyura Koto Shima, Brie Williams, and Mizuki Yamakawa.

I extend special thanks to Hiroshi Ono for his sage advice, much-needed encouragement, and irreverent sense of humor, as well as for cowriting and administering the grants that supported later stages of this project. Others, including Jesper Edman, Yoshinori Fujikawa, Tristan Ivory, Gracia Liu-Farrer, Kikuko Nagayoshi, Gregory Noble, Glenda Roberts, Mitch Sato, Daiichi Shirai, and Sayaka Osanami Tőrngren, provided kind words, helpful suggestions, and practical assistance while in Tokyo.

After completing my doctorate at Cornell, I had the great good luck to land back at Harvard, where I had first worked as an assistant from 2009–2011 at the Program on US-Japan Relations (USJRP). In 2017–2018, I returned to the program as a postdoctoral fellow, and from 2018 to 2020, I worked as the associate director for undergraduate studies in the Sociology Department. Once again, it was a delight to be part of the vibrant Japan studies community at Harvard, including USJRP staffers Nina Li Coomes, Kendall Kelly, Bill Nehring, Amy Stockton, Jenny Ting, and Sophie Welch. Susan Pharr has been a stalwart mentor since my days as her assistant. She taught me by example the importance of telling compelling stories, and continues to pave the academic pathway before me with singularly incisive advice and a tireless commitment to my success. Mary Brinton offers an exemplary model of how to bridge Japanese studies and contemporary sociology, and Andrew Gordon offered a nuanced observation of Japanese employment. Dan Smith stepped in at a critical juncture with reassuring advice. The late Ezra Vogel was not only infallibly kind but also took me seriously as a student and scholar of Japan before I had many accomplishments to back it up. In sociology, Jason Beckfield was a fierce advocate for me. Jocelyn Viterna—supernova and warrior queen—and Laura Thomas rocked my world and saved my sanity in the dark days of the pandemic. I also benefited from participation in the intellectual community of the Weatherhead Research Cluster on Comparative Inequality and Inclusion under the leadership of Michèle Lamont, whose work on symbolic boundaries deeply influenced this project.

In December 2020, I moved from Harvard to Indiana University (IU), where I took a faculty position and began to write this book in earnest. It has been a great privilege to be part of a community of brilliant teachers and scholars of East Asian languages, humanities, and social sciences in the Department of East Asian Languages and Cultures (EALC), where my colleagues welcomed me warmly from even before day one. Wendy Leutert by Facetiming us through a house walk through with a real estate agent; Hannah Airriess for making sure the house didn't burn down; Ethan Michelson for single-handedly hauling in a truck-full of Ikea boxes; Scott O'Bryan and Adam Liff for getting me started on the right foot with practical teaching advice tailored to the pandemic era. Last but not least, many thanks to Lisa Aten, master of all she surveys.

I benefited tremendously from the book workshop that EALC funded in December 2021, where I received constructive feedback on an early version of this manuscript from Koji Chavez, Erin Chung, Jennifer Lee, Ethan Michelson, and Kiyoteru Tsutsui. Their comments gave me a needed push to tackle the unfamiliar and seemingly impossible task of transitioning from article writing to book writing.

In writing and revising this book, writing partners and other junior faculty working on books provided accountability and encouragement in converting inchoate thoughts to words on the page, including Hannah Airriess, Vanessa Baker, Ben Bartlett, Russell Burge, Elisheva Cohen, Amy Hackenberg, Hiroko Kumaki, Mary McCarthy, Anna Skarpelis, and Kristin Vekasi, as well as participants in the IU Faculty Writing Groups.

Jesse Gonzales, Lillian Klem, Chaewon Lee, Yun-Kiu Lo, Riko Maeda, Amy Martin, Sarah Mick, Adam Noffsinger, Aika Noguchi, and Lorenzo Panozzo-Reid provided late-stage research assistance. If this book is at all fun to read, it is thanks to their push for me to make it so. If it is not, the fault lies with me for not implementing their good advice. I am particularly grateful to Chaewon Lee's clearsighted (and warm-hearted) comments on successive drafts, and Lillian Klem's painstaking work on the bibliographic entries. Chris Lehrich and Maureen O'Driscoll's thorough copyediting and Rachel Lyon's indexing were also invaluable.

Some of the findings of chapter 3 were previously published in a 2022 article titled "When All Assistants Are Women, Are All Women Assistants" in *RSF: The Russell Sage Foundation Journal of the Social Sciences*. I received insightful comments on this article from Hazel Markus and Cecelia Ridgeway, whose work on status has been a powerful source of inspiration, and from the other authors in the RSF double issue on status. Many thanks to the RSF for permission to reprint portions of the article.

I also wish to thank Vitas Bhargava and Fabiola Castro, personal trainers at IU Rec Sports. Little did I know when I reluctantly signed up for personal training in 2023 that they would eliminate the back pain that doctors had told me was a lost cause, and, in Vi's case, become my kids' favorite ever babysitter. The endorphin hits from their workouts pushed this book over the finish line. They deserve full credit for my now looking and feeling like Linda Hamilton from *Terminator II*, at least if she were a mild-mannered assistant professor.

I gratefully acknowledge the extensive financial support from many different institutions that have, over the years, made this book possible. The Blakemore-Freeman Fellowship funded my year at the IUC, which gave me the language skills to conduct research in Japan. A Graduate Research Fellowship from the Fulbright Commission brought me to Japan to collect the survey and interview data, and a postdoctoral fellowship at the USJRP at Harvard, two Grants-in-Aid for Scientific Research from the Japan Society for the Promotion of Science, and a Fellowship for Advanced Social Science Research on Japan from the National Endowment for the Humanities supported me in developing this project and ultimately in transforming it into a book. Programs organized by the Maureen and Mike Mansfield Foundation, including the US-Japan Network for the Future, the Bridging the Divide Program, and the Maureen Mansfield Women's Empowerment Initiative, and the connections these programs have fostered with fellow participants, have been intellectually inspiring and spiritually invigorating. Finally, I thank the Japan Foundation for providing the seed funding for my position at IU, and the Japan Politics and Society Initiative for fostering a dynamic research environment in contemporary Japanese studies at IU.

Working with Jim Lance and the rest of the editorial staff at Cornell University Press has been terrific. Thank you for shepherding this project through the circuitous first book publishing process, with time for entertaining asides about college women's basketball. The anonymous book reviewers offered detailed, thoughtful comments that strengthened this book further.

I am blessed in my family, including in my husband Gabriel; my children Martin and Francis; my siblings Charles, Giles, and Felicity; my late grandfather Charles Holbrow; my grandmother, eternal optimist Mary Holbrow; and my embarrassment of riches of aunts, uncles, and cousins, who have been known to show up to my Zoom talks under false names so as not to people the audience with an unseemly percentage of Holbrows; and in ride-or-die friends from so many different periods in my life, especially Julia Coym and Elisabeth Mevissen. I thank my parents, Gwen and Mark Holbrow, for raising me to be someone who (in the words of my husband) "does whatever she wants," including letting me go utterly unsupervised to Japan when I was 16 years old. And, in Japan, the Ikeda family, the Kosugi family, the Teramura family, and the Nogami family have made me feel like an adopted family member and welcomed, educated, and fed me in innumerable ways.

Finally, I would like thank the person who wrote to me: "Incidentally, I thought I would find this book utterly boring . . . but it's actually fascinating." I hope a few other readers may share some part of the second half of the sentiment.

VIGNETTE METHODOLOGY

Respondents viewed the two positive and the two negative vignettes in succession. The order of the vignettes within and between the positive/positive set and the negative/negative set was random: Approximately half of respondents saw the two negative vignettes first, and approximately half saw the two positive vignettes first; within the positive set, approximately half saw the Cost-Saving Vignette first, and within the negative set, approximately half saw the Records Falsification Vignette first. The randomizer presented respondents with a maximum of two vignettes (one positive and one negative) with non-Japanese names. For the individual vignettes, the likelihood of viewing a Japanese name was four in seven, and the likelihood of viewing a foreign name was three in seven. The likelihood of viewing a Chinese/Korean name was two in seven, and the likelihood of viewing an English name was one in seven.

Negative Vignettes

Tardiness

Names: Suzuki (Japanese), Pak (Korean), Li (Chinese), Brown (English)[1]

_____-san is an employee with 5 years of seniority. Recently, he did not come to work for two days, without requesting permission or informing anyone in advance. Now he is back at work. He apologized, but has not explained why he was absent. Since returning to work, he has been late to several departmental meetings, and to one meeting with clients.

Records Falsification

Names: Takahashi (Japanese), Pak (Korean), Li (Chinese), Brown (English)

Sato-san and _____-san are responsible for entering the sales records of employees in their department into a computer database. Supervisors use the information in the database when they evaluate employees. One day, Sato-san needs to look up information that _____-san entered the week before. He finds that _____-san's entries do not match records kept elsewhere. Sato-san decides to check some of _____-san's other work. He finds that, in fact, all _____-san's entries for the past 8 weeks, and possibly even longer, are false. It appears that _____-san exaggerated his own sales records and those of his friend. Sato-san tells his supervisor what he has discovered.

Follow-up Questions to Negative Vignette

Q1. How should the supervisor respond?

Check what the supervisor should do. You may check more than 1 item.

The supervisor should not do anything.

The supervisor should have a discussion with _____-san about his behavior.

The supervisor should have a discussion with other employees in his section about _____-san's behavior.

The supervisor should have a discussion with other managers or HR about _____-san's behavior.

Q2. Should the supervisor or HR issue a formal warning or punishment for _____-san?

No

Yes

[Viewed by respondents who chose "Yes" for Q2]

Q3. What type of formal warning or punishment would be the most appropriate for _____-san?

Warning

One-time salary reduction

Unpaid suspension from work

Demotion

Firing

Other, please specify:

[Viewed by respondents who chose "One-time salary reduction" for Q3]

Q4. By what percent should _____-san's base salary be reduced, when he receives the one-time salary reduction?

Write the percentage below.

[Viewed by respondents who chose "Unpaid suspension from work" for Q3]

Q5. How many weeks unpaid suspension from work should _____-san receive as punishment?

Write the number of weeks below.

Positive Vignettes

Cost Saving

Names: Tanaka (Japanese), Kim (Korean), Wang (Chinese), Smith (English)

_____-san has been assigned to negotiations with vendors that his company uses for business services. Recently, business costs have been rising, and his supervisor tells _____-san that he should do his utmost to control the costs, even if it means breaking off relationships with long-term vendors and finding new ones. However, _____-san successfully negotiates with his company's two largest existing vendors to lower their prices by 5%, while keeping the level of services the same. This keeps overall costs in control and means that employees at _____-san's firm can continue working with the familiar vendors.

Coworker Assistance

Names: Ikeda (Japanese), Kim (Korean), Wang (Chinese), Smith (English)

It is the busiest season in the human resources department. Everyone is desperately trying to complete their work. However, _____-san notices that Fujiwara-san, the newest member of their group, is really struggling. _____-san offers to help Fujiwara-san, even though he is very busy himself. At first, Fujiwara-san tries to decline _____-san's help, because he doesn't want to be a burden. Nonetheless _____-san insists, and eventually, Fujiwara-san gratefully accepts his help.

Once the busy season is over, his supervisor congratulates Fujiwara-san on how well he did. Fujiwara-san explains that although he worked hard, it is really thanks to _____-san that he was able to complete his job.

Follow-up Questions to Positive Vignettes

Q1. How should the supervisor respond?

Check what the supervisor should do. You may check more than 1 item.

The supervisor should not do anything.

The supervisor should privately tell _____-san he did a good job.

The supervisor should praise _____-san to other members of the section.

The supervisor should praise _____-san to managers in other departments or to HR.

The supervisor should recommend _____-san for a higher-than-usual bonus.

The supervisor should recommend _____-san for a promotion.

[Viewed by respondents who chose "The supervisor should recommend _____-san for a higher-than-usual bonus." for Q1]

Q2. By what percentage should _____-san's bonus be increased? Write the percentage below.

Notes

INTRODUCTION

1. Dorinne Kondo, *Crafting Selves: Power, Gender, and Discourse of Identity in a Japanese Workplace* (University of Chicago Press, 1990), 51; Chie Nakane, *Japanese Society* (University of California Press, 1970), 109.

2. MyNavi Career Research Lab, "2022nensotsu daigakusei shuushoku ishiki chousa," [Opinion survey of 2022 college graduates on job hunting], MyNavi, updated April 26, 2021, https://career-research.mynavi.jp/reserch/20210426_8553.

3. Rodney Clark, *The Japanese Company* (Charles E. Tuttle, 1979), 216.

4. Ross E. Mouer and Hirosuke Kawanishi, *A Sociology of Work in Japan* (Cambridge University Press, 2005), 99.

5. Ministry of Health, Labor and Welfare, "Reiwa 2nen chingin kouzou kihon toukei chousa no gaikyou" [Overview of the 2020 basic survey on wage structure], updated May 13, 2021, https://www.mhlw.go.jp/toukei/itiran/roudou/chingin/kouzou/z2020/dl/04.pdf. Although my interviewees rarely mentioned it, pay, job stability, and work conditions are all better at large firms.

6. For example, see Thomas P. Rohlen, *For Harmony and Strength: Japanese White-Collar Organization in Anthropological Perspective* (University of California Press, 1974); Yuko Ogasawara, *Office Ladies and Salaried Men: Power, Gender, and Work in Japanese Companies* (University of California Press, 1998).

7. Ogasawara, *Office Ladies and Salaried Men*, 10.

8. Clark, *Japanese Company*, 216; Ogasawara, *Office Ladies and Salaried Men*.

9. Mary C. Brinton, *Women and the Economic Miracle: Gender and Work in Postwar Japan* (University of California Press, 1993); Ogasawara, *Office Ladies and Salaried Men*.

10. Ogasawara, *Office Ladies and Salaried Men*, 58; Rohlen, *For Harmony and Strength*, 78–79.

11. Clark, *Japanese Company*.

12. Gender Equality Bureau, "Kigyou ni okeru josei no sankaku" [Women's participation in private firms], updated 2016, https://www.gender.go.jp/about_danjo/whitepaper/h28/zentai/html/honpen/b1_s02_02.html.

13. John Lie, *Multiethnic Japan* (Harvard University Press, 2001), 107.

14. Bumsoo Kim, "Changes in the Socio-economic Position of Zainichi Koreans: A Historical Overview," *Social Science Japan Journal* 14, no. 2 (Summer 2011): 233–45. In 1974, only 6.5 percent of the employed Zainichi community worked in professional, technical, or managerial jobs.

15. Bumsoo Kim, "Blatant Discrimination Disappears, But . . . : The Politics of Everyday Exclusion in Contemporary Japan," *Asian Perspective* 35, no. 2 (2011): 287–308.

16. Yoon Shin Kim, "Recent Demographic Developments of the Korean Population in Japan," *Japanese Journal of Health and Human Ecology* 43, no. 3–4 (1977): 91–102.

17. Ministry of Health, Labor and Welfare, "Zuhyou 1-1-7: shusshousuu, goukei tokushu shusshouritsu no suii" [Chart 1-1-7: Changes in the number of births and total fertility rate], updated 2018, https://www.mhlw.go.jp/stf/wp/hakusyo/kousei/19/backdata/01-01-01-07.html.

18. Ministry of Internal Affairs and Communications, "Nenrei (5sai kaikyuu oyobi 3kubun), danjo betsu jinkou (kakunen 10gatsu 1tachi genzai)—soujinkou 2000nen-2020nen" [Total population by age-group (5-year and 3-category) and sex (as of October 1 annually), 2000–2020], updated June 28, 2022, https://www.e-stat.go.jp/stat-search/fil es?layout=datalist&cycle=0&toukei=00200524&tstat=000000090001&tclass1=000000 090004&tclass2=000001051180&tclass3val=0&stat_infid=000013168603; Ministry of Internal Affairs and Communications, "Nenrei (5sai kaikyuu oyobi 3kubun), danjo betsu jinkou (kakunen 10gatsu 1tachi genzai)—soujinkou taishou 9nen—heisei 12nen" [Total population by age-group (5-year and 3-category) and sex (as of October 1 annu-ally), 1920–2000], updated January 30, 2018, https://www.e-stat.go.jp/stat-search/files?p age=1&layout=datalist&cycle=0&toukei=00200524&tstat=000000090001&tclass1=00 0000090004&tclass2=000000090005&cycle_facet=tclass1%3Atclass2&tclass3val=0&s tat_infid=000000090263; National Institute of Population and Social Security Research, "Nihon no shourai suikei jinkou (Reiwa 5nen suikei)" [Japan's future esti-mated population (2023 estimate)], updated March 7, 2023, https://www.ipss.go.jp /pp-zenkoku/j/zenkoku2023/db_zenkoku2023/db_zenkoku2023syosaikekka.html.

19. David Coleman and Robert Rowthorn, "Who's Afraid of Population Decline? A Critical Examination of Its Consequences," *Population and Development Review* 37 (2011): 217–48.

20. CAES: Research Center for Aged Economy and Society, "Web Clock of Counting Children's Population in Japan," updated 2022, https://sites.google.com/view/caestop /JCCC?authuser=0.

21. For the "looming crisis," see Steven L. Myers et al., "China's Looming Crisis: A Shrinking Population," *New York Times,* January 17, 2020. For "a new population bomb," see Kazuo Yanase et al., "The New Population Bomb: For the First Time, Humanity Is on the Verge of Long-Term Decline," *Nikkei Asia,* September 22, 2021. For a "death cross," see Jessie Yeung and Gawaon Bae, "South Korea Reports Population Drop, with More Deaths Than Births for First Time," *CNN,* January 4, 2021.

22. Francisco Toro, "Japan Is a Trumpian Paradise of Low Immigration Rates. It's Also a Dying Country," *Washington Post,* August 29, 2019.

23. Coleman and Rowthorn, "Who's Afraid of Population Decline?"

24. Richard Alba, *Blurring the Color Line: The New Chance for a More Integrated America* (Harvard University Press, 2009).

25. Small and Medium Enterprise Agency, "Koyou no doukou" [Employment trends], updated June 22, 2021, https://www.chusho.meti.go.jp/pamflet/hakusyo/2021 /shokibo/b1_1_3.html.

26. Small and Medium Enterprise Agency, "Koyou no doukou."

27. Gary S. Becker, *The Economics of Discrimination* (University of Chicago Press, 1957).

28. This corresponds with the concept of labor queues articulated in Barbara F. Reskin and Patricia A. Roos, *Job Queues, Gender Queues* (Temple University Press, 1995).

29. Alba, *Blurring the Color Line,* 145.

30. Kim, "Blatant Discrimination Disappears, But . . ."

31. Erin A. Chung, *Immigration and Citizenship in Japan* (Cambridge University Press, 2010).

32. Stephanie Assmann, "Gender Equality in Japan: The Equal Employment Oppor-tunity Law Revisited," *Asia-Pacific Journal: Japan Focus* 12, no. 45 (November 2014): 1-23.

33. Eunmi Mun, "Negative Compliance as an Organizational Response to Legal Pressures: The Case of Japanese Equal Employment Opportunity Law," *Social Forces* 94, no. 4 (June 2016): 1409–37.

34. Kristina T. Geraghty, "Taming the Paper Tiger: A Comparative Approach to Reforming Japanese Gender Equality Laws," *Cornell International Law Journal* 41, no. 2 (Summer 2008): 503–43.

35. See, for example, Takeyuki Tsuda, "Reluctant Hosts: The Future of Japan as a Country of Immigration," U.C. Davis Research and Seminars, accessed August 20, 2024, https://migration.ucdavis.edu/rs/more.php?id=39; Leonard Schoppa, *Race for the Exits: The Unraveling of Japan's System of Social Protection* (Cornell University Press, 2006); Leonard Schoppa, "The Policy Response to Declining Fertility Rates in Japan: Relying on Logic and Hope over Evidence," *Social Science Japan Journal* 23, no. 1 (2020): 3–21.

36. Michèle Lamont and Virág Molnár, "The Study of Boundaries in the Social Sciences," *Annual Review of Sociology* 28 (2002): 167–95.

37. Also see Hilary J. Holbrow, "Detangling Capital from Context: A Critical Investigation of Human Capital Explanations for Immigrant Wage Inequality," *Journal of Ethnic and Migration Studies* 46, no. 19 (2020): 4043–65.

38. Hilary J. Holbrow, "When All Assistants Are Women, Are All Women Assistants? Gender Inequality and the Gender Composition of Support Roles," *Russell Sage Foundation Journal of the Social Sciences* 8, no. 7 (2022): 28–49.

39. Ulrike Schaede, *The Business Reinvention of Japan: How to Make Sense of the New Japan and Why It Matters* (Stanford Business, 2020).

40. See Ministry of Health, Labor and Welfare, "Sangyou jigyousho kibo sei shuugyoukeitai betsu roudousha wariai" [Percentage of workers by industry, establishment size, sex, and employment type], updated 2014, https://www.mhlw.go.jp/toukei/youran/roudou-nenpou2014/xls/039.xls; Ministry of Health, Labor and Welfare, "'Gaikokujin koyou joukyou' no todokede joukyou matome (Reiwa 2nen 10gatsumatsu genzai)" [Compilation of employer reports on foreigners' employment (as of the end of October 2020)], updated January 29, 2021, https://www.mhlw.go.jp/stf/newpage_16279.html. The government does not publish the distribution of foreign workers by firm size, but rather by establishment size. Establishments are an economic unit that produces goods and services, usually in one physical location. A large firm may include both many smaller and larger establishments, but small firms usually include only one small establishment. Some 32 percent of all employees in Japan work in establishments with at least one hundred employees, compared with 42 percent of foreign workers.

41. Gender Equality Bureau, "Todoufukenbetsu juugyousha kibobetsu kigyousuu" [Number of firms by prefecture and number of employees], updated 2018, https://www.gender.go.jp/kaigi/senmon/kihon/kihon_eikyou/pdf/02_2_chosakai_todoufuken.pdf.

42. Ministry of Internal Affairs and Communications, "Juugyousha kibobetsu hinouringyou koyou shasuu" [Number of nonagricultural and forestry employees by firm size], updated 2022, https://www.stat.go.jp/data/roudou/longtime/zuhyou/lt04-02.xlsx.

43. Paul J. DiMaggio and Walter W. Powell, "The Iron Cage Revisited: Institutional Isomorphism and Collective Rationality in Organizational Fields," *American Sociological Review* 48, no. 2 (April 1983): 147–60.

44. James N. Baron and William T. Bielby, "Bringing the Firms Back in: Stratification, Segmentation, and the Organization of Work," *American Sociological Review* 45, no. 5 (1980): 737–65.

45. HR selection of the teams was nonrandom; other than requesting that HR select teams with at least two foreign workers, I did not provide instructions about how to select the teams. I operate, however, under the assumption that the nonrandom team selection does not bias the results and that the selected teams are unusual only in their

overrepresentation of foreign workers. There are two bases for this assumption. First, because workers are regularly transferred throughout the firm, nonrandom selection of teams should not, in theory, bias the analyses. Second, all but one of the firms post their company-level share of women managers on a government-sponsored website as part of their compliance with gender equity legislation, offering an opportunity to compare a firm-level characteristic with the characteristics of the sample teams. The firm-level measure of women's share of management jobs is highly correlated (Pearson's $r = 0.77$) with women's share of management jobs on the sample teams. This provides some assurance that the sample teams are microcosms of their firms.

46. Survey Research Center, "Guidelines for Best Practice in Cross-Cultural Surveys," Institute for Social Research, University of Michigan, updated 2016, http://ccsg .isr.umich.edu.

47. Gracia Liu-Farrer, *Immigrant Japan* (Cornell University Press, 2020); Harumi Befu, *Hegemony of Homogeneity: An Anthropological Analysis of Nihonjinron* (Trans Pacific, 2001).

48. Pascale Hatcher and Aya Murakami, "The Politics of Exclusion: Embedded Racism and Japan's Pilot Refugee Resettlement Programme," *Race and Class* 62, no. 1 (2020): 60–77; Liang Morita, "Some Manifestations of Japanese Exclusionism," *SAGE Open* 5, no. 3 (2015): 1–6.

49. Brinton, *Women and the Economic Miracle*; Ogasawara, *Office Ladies and Salaried Men*; Kumiko Nemoto, *Too Few Women at the Top: The Persistence of Inequality in Japan* (Cornell University Press, 2016).

50. Philip N. Cohen and Matt L. Huffman, "Working for the Woman? Female Managers and the Gender Wage Gap," *American Sociological Review* 72, no. 5 (2007), 700; Matt L. Huffman, Philip N. Cohen, and Jessica Pearlman, "Engendering Change: Organizational Dynamics and Workplace Gender Desegregation, 1975–2005," *Administrative Science Quarterly* 55, no. 2 (2010), 273; Nemoto, *Too Few Women at the Top*; Andrea S. Kramer and Alton B. Harris, *It's Not You, It's the Workplace: Women's Conflict at Work and the Bias That Built It* (Nicholas Brealy, 2019); Safi Shams and Donald Tomaskovic-Devey, "Racial and Gender Trends and Trajectories in Access to Managerial Jobs," *Social Science Research* 80 (2019): 15–29.

51. Calculated from United Nations, "Total Population (Both Sexes Combined) by Broad Age Group, Region, Subregion and Country, 1950–2100 (Thousands)," updated August 27, 2019, https://population.un.org/wpp2019/Download/Files/1_Indicators%20 (Standard)/EXCEL_FILES/1_Population/WPP2019_POP_F08_1_TOTAL _POPULATION_BY_BROAD_AGE_GROUP_BOTH_SEXES.xlsx.

52. Calculated from United Nations, "Total Population."

53. Calculated from United Nations, "Total Population."

54. PRB.org, "Population of Older Adults Increasing Globally Partly Because of Declining Fertility Rates," *PRB*, July 10, 2020, https://www.prb.org/news/population -of-older-adults-increasing-globally.

1. INSIDE THE CIRCLE

1. John Van Maanen, "Rediscovering Japan: Some Thoughts on Change and Continuity in Traditional Japanese Careers," *Career Development International* 11, no. 4 (June 2006): 280–92.

2. Robert E. Cole, *Work, Mobility, and Participation* (University of California Press, 1979), 11; Hiroshi Ono, "Lifetime Employment in Japan: Concepts and Measurements," *Journal of the Japanese and International Economies* 24, no. 1 (March 2010): 1–27.

3. Chiaki Moriguchi and Hiroshi Ono, "Japanese Lifetime Employment: A Century's Perspective," in Institutional Change in Japan, ed. Magnus Blomström and Sumner La Croix (Routledge, 2006), 152–76.

4. Ulrike Schaede, *The Business Reinvention of Japan: How to Make Sense of the New Japan and Why It Matters* (Stanford Business Books, 2020), 55.

5. Thomas P. Rohlen, *For Harmony and Strength: Japanese White-Collar Organization in Anthropological Perspective* (University of California Press, 1974), 74.

6. Rohlen, *For Harmony and Strength*, 158.

7. Rodney Clark, *The Japanese Company* (Charles E. Tuttle, 1979), 114; Harald Conrad, "From Seniority to Performance Principle: The Evolution of Pay Practices in Japanese Firms since the 1990s," *Social Science Japan Journal* 13, no. 1 (2009): 115–35.

8. Rohlen, *For Harmony and Strength*, 138–142; Clark, *Japanese Company*, 116.

9. For example, Chie Nakane, *Japanese Society* (University of California Press, 1970), 29; Kazuo Noda, "Big Business Organization," in *Modern Japanese Organization and Decision-Making*, ed. Ezra F. Vogel (University of California Press, 1975), 136.

10. Rohlen, *For Harmony and Strength*, 137–42.

11. Noda, "Big Business Organization," 142–44.

12. Rohlen, *For Harmony and Strength*, 110–11; Clark, *Japanese Company*, 201–2.

13. Rohlen, *For Harmony and Strength*, 74.

14. Clark, *Japanese Company*, 185.

15. Hilary J. Holbrow, "How Conformity to Labor Market Norms Increases Access to Job Search Assistance: A Case Study from Japan," *Work and Occupations* 42, no. 2 (2015): 135–73.

16. Moriguchi and Ono, "Japanese Lifetime Employment"; Andrew Gordon, *The Evolution of Labor Relations in Japan: Heavy Industry 1853–1955* (Harvard University Press, 1985).

17. Mary C. Brinton, *Women and the Economic Miracle: Gender and Work in Postwar Japan* (University of California Press, 1993).

18. Clark, *Japanese Company*, 168–170, 212.

19. Ono, "Lifetime Employment in Japan."

20. Cole, *Work, Mobility, and Participation*, 44.

21. Anne Allison, *Precarious Japan* (Duke University Press, 2013); Nana Okura Gagné, *Reworking Japan: Changing Men at Work and Play Under Neoliberalism* (Cornell University Press, 2021); Christina L. Ahmadjian and Patricia Robinson, "Safety in Numbers: Downsizing and the Deinstitutionalization of Permanent Employment in Japan," *Administrative Science Quarterly* 46, no. 4 (2001): 622–54.

22. Conrad, "From Seniority to Performance Principle."

23. Ahmadjian and Robison, "Safety in Numbers."

24. Machiko Osawa and Jeff Kingston, "Risk and Consequences: The Changing Japanese Employment Paradigm," in *Japan: The Precarious Future*, ed. Frank Baldwin and Anne Allison (New York University Press, 2015), 58–86.

25. Rohlen, *For Harmony and Strength*, 144–145; Conrad, "From Seniority to Performance Principle," 4.

26. Gagné, *Reworking Japan*, 76.

27. Gagné, *Reworking Japan*.

28. Gagné, *Reworking Japan*, 62.

29. Gagné, *Reworking Japan*, 76–77.

30. Chizuko Ueno, "Why Do Japanese Women Suffer from the Low Status? The Impact of Neo-Liberalist Reform on Gender," *Japanese Political Economy* 47, no. 1 (2021): 9–26.

31. Allison, *Precarious Japan*, 27.

32. Anne Allison, "From Lifelong to Liquid Japan," in *Japan: The Precarious Future*, ed. Frank Baldwin and Anne Allison (Duke University Press, 2013), 21–43; Gagné, *Reworking Japan*, 88.

33. Hiroshi Ono, "Why Do the Japanese Work Long Hours?," *Japan Labor Issues* 2, no. 5 (2018): 35–49; Gracia Liu-Farrer and Helena Hof, "Ōtebyō: The Problems of Japanese Firms and the Problematic Elite Aspirations," *Journal of Asia-Pacific Studies* 34 (2018): 65–84.

34. Glenda S. Roberts, "Leaning Out for the Long Span: What Holds Women Back from Promotion in Japan?," *Japan Forum* 32, no. 4 (2020): 555–76; Kazuya Ogura, "Working Hours and Japanese Employment Practices," *Japan Labor Review* 4, no. 4 (2007): 139–60.

35. Eunmi Mun, "Negative Compliance as an Organizational Response to Legal Pressures: The Case of Japanese Equal Employment Opportunity Law," *Social Forces* 94, no. 4 (2016): 1409–37.

36. Cabinet Secretariat, "Josei katsuyaku danjo kyoudou sankaku no juuten houshin 2022" [Major policies on gender equality and women's empowerment 2022], updated June 3, 2022, https://www.gender.go.jp/policy/sokushin/pdf/sokushin/jyuten2022_honbun.pdf.

37. For hiring women into irregular jobs and establishing a clerical track, see Mun, "Negative Compliance as an Organizational Response"; for allowing women to remain in the workforce after having children, see Roberts, "Leaning Out for the Long Span" and Mary C. Brinton and Eunmi Mun, "Between State and Family: Managers' Implementation and Evaluation of Parental Leave Policies in Japan," *Socio-Economic Review* 14, no. 2 (2016): 257–81; and for relegating women to the sidelines, see Eunmi Mun and Jiwook Jung, "Policy Generosity, Employer Heterogeneity, and Women's Employment Opportunities: The Welfare State Paradox Reexamined," *American Sociological Review* 83, no. 3 (2018): 508–35.

38. Some Japanese men in the study are in irregular jobs, mostly as contract employees. A smaller number work in regular jobs on the clerical track (see table 2.5 for details). The analyses of men's earnings and promotion in this chapter focus on regular, management-track workers alone. Neoclassical models predict such workers would continue to benefit from age-wage increases and job security, whereas neoliberal models suggest that such benefits have faded, even for this relatively privileged group.

39. Ministry of Health, Labor and Welfare, "Chingin no bunpu" [Wage distribution], updated 2015, https://www.mhlw.go.jp/toukei/itiran/roudou/chingin/kouzou/z2015/dl/07.pdf.

40. Ministry of Health, Labor and Welfare, "Chingin no bunpu."

41. Rohlen, *For Harmony and Strength*, 110.

42. Rohlen, *For Harmony and Strength*, 111; Clark, *Japanese Company*, 202.

43. Most nonmanagerial white-collar workers in Japan are eligible to receive overtime pay when they work more than forty hours per week. Some firms seek to circumvent their legal obligation to pay overtime by pressuring workers not to report overtime hours on their timecards. It is unlikely, however, that survey respondents underreported work hours on the survey, because their employers could not see their responses, and the survey specifically requested that respondents report actual rather than contractual work hours.

44. During repeated waves of COVID-19 in 2020–2021, local governments requested eating and drinking establishment restrict their hours and discouraged large gatherings. At elite firms in Tokyo, formal *nomikai* (drinking parties) all but halted during this period. Although participation workplace *nomikai* has risen since the restrictions

were lifted, it has still not recovered to prepandemic levels, implying that pandemic-era practices may have accelerated the decline in coworker *nomikai* as a central element of business culture.

45. Emilio J. Castilla, "Bringing Managers Back In: Managerial Influences on Workplace Inequality," *American Sociological Review* 76, no. 5 (2011): 667–94.

46. Emilio J. Castilla, "Gender, Race, and Meritocracy in Organizational Careers," *American Journal of Sociology* 113, no. 6 (May 2008): 1479–526.

47. During the same period, the number of prime working-age men in regular employment fell from 18.7 million to 17.6 million, a decrease of 6 percent. Nonetheless, because of population decline, the *share* of the prime working-age population in regular employment increased for both sexes, from 71 percent to 73 percent for men, and from 25 percent to 38 percent for women. Data on population size by age-group comes from Ministry of Internal Affairs and Communications, "Nenrei (5sai kaikyuu oyobi 3kubun), danjo betsu jinkou (kakunen 10gatsu 1tachi genzai)—soujinkou 2000nen–2020nen" [Total population by age-group (5-year and 3-category) and sex (as of October 1 annually), 2000–2020], updated June 28, 2022, https://www.e-stat.go.jp/stat-search/files?layout=datalist&cycle=0&toukei=00200524&tstat=000000090001&tclass1=000000090004&tclass2=000001051180&tclass3val=0&stat_infid=000013168603; and Ministry of Internal Affairs and Communications, "Nenrei (5sai kaikyuu oyobi 3kubun), danjo betsu jinkou (kakunen 10gatsu 1tachi genzai)—soujinkou taishou 9nen—heisei 12nen" [Total population by age-group (5-year and 3-category) and sex (as of October 1 annually), 1920–2000], updated January 30, 2018, https://www.e-stat.go.jp/stat-search/files?page=1&layout=datalist&cycle=0&toukei=00200524&tstat=000000090001&tclass1=000000090004&tclass2=000000090005&cycle_facet=tclass1%3Atclass2&tclass3val=0&stat_infid=000000090263. Data on number of regular and irregular workers by age and gender come from the Japan Institute for Labor Policy and Training, "Kaku nenrei kaikyuu no seiki, hiseiki betsu koyoushasuu" [Number of regular and irregular employees by age-group], updated March 3, 2023, https://www.jil.go.jp/kokunai/statistics/timeseries/html/g0209.html.

48. Ministry of Health, Labor and Welfare, "Reiwa 4nen koyou doukou chousa kekka no gaikyou" [Overview of the 2022 employment trends survey], updated August 22, 2023, https://www.mhlw.go.jp/toukei/itiran/roudou/koyou/doukou/23-2/dl/gaikyou.pdf.

49. Ministry of Health, Labor and Welfare, "Reiwa 2nen chingin kouzou kihon toukei chousa no gaikyou."

50. Ministry of Internal Affairs and Communications, "Zouka keikou ga tsuzuku tenshokusha no joukyou 2019 nen no tenshoku shasuu wa kako saidai" [Continued increase in job changers; the number of job changers in 2019 is the highest ever], updated February 21, 2020, https://www.stat.go.jp/data/roudou/topics/topi1230.html.

51. Transtructure, "Sou roudou jikan no suii" [Trends in total working hours], updated January 17, 2024, https://www.transtructure.com/hr-data-analysys/search/hr-analysis-report/p7281.

52. Ministry of Health, Labor and Welfare. "Jinkou kouzou, roudou jikan nado ni tsuite" [On population structure and work hours], updated January 19, 2024, https://www.mhlw.go.jp/content/11201250/001194507.pdf, 26.

53. Ministry of Health, Labor and Welfare, "Reiwa 2nen chingin kouzou kihon toukei chousa no gaikyou."

54. Although workplace flexibility has increased and job stability has held relatively constant, real wages for workers have remained flat or even declined in recent decades. Japan Federation of Labor Unions, "Rengou chingin repooto 2023" [JFLU wage report 2023], updated December 2023, https://www.jtuc-rengo.or.jp/activity/roudou/shuntou

/2024/wage_report/wage_report.pdf, 29–31. It remains to be seen whether increasing political and demographic pressure on firms will lead to increases in real wages going forward.

2. (IN)VISIBLE INEQUALITIES

1. Allan Bird and May Mukuda, "Expatriates in Their Own Home: A New Twist in the Human Resource Management Strategies of Japanese MNCs," *Human Resource Management* 28, no. 4 (1989): 437–53; Scott M. Fuess, "Immigration Policy and Highly Skilled Workers: The Case of Japan," *Contemporary Economic Policy* 21, no. 2 (2003): 243–57.

2. DISCO, "Gaikokujin ryuugakusei koudo gaikoku jinzai no saiyou ni kansuru chousa," [Survey on foreign student and highly-skilled foreign professional hiring], updated December 2019, https://www.disc.co.jp/wp/wp-content/uploads/2020/01/2019kigyou-global-report.pdf; DISCO, "'Gaikokujin ryuugakusei no saiyou' ni kansuru chousa" [Results of the 'survey on foreign student hiring'], updated August 2010, https://www.disc.co.jp/wp/wp-content/uploads/2012/01/10kigyou-oversea-report8.pdf.

3. Gracia Liu-Farrer, "'I Am the Only Woman in Suits': Chinese Immigrants and Gendered Careers in Corporate Japan," *Journal of Asia-Pacific Studies* 13 (2009): 37–48.

4. For insider cultures, see Ulrike Schaede, *The Business Reinvention of Japan: How to Make Sense of the New Japan and Why It Matters* (Stanford Business Books, 2020). For racial and cultural homogeneity, Eric Clemons, "Transcending National Identity: Foreign Employees and Organizational Management in Corporate Japan" (PhD diss., Columbia University, 1999).

5. Sayaka Osanami Törngren and Hilary J. Holbrow, "Comparing the Experiences of Highly Skilled Labor Migrants in Sweden and Japan: Barriers and Doors to Long-Term Settlement," *International Journal of Japanese Sociology* 26, no. 1 (2017): 67–82.

6. Immigration Services Agency, "Zairyuu shikaku ichiranpyou" [Status of residence list], accessed July 21, 2022, https://www.moj.go.jp/isa/applications/guide/qaq5.html. See also Ministry of Justice, "Shutsunyuukoku zairyuu kanri wo meguru kinnen no joukyou" [Recent circumstances of border control and residence management], updated November 28, 2022, https://www.moj.go.jp/isa/content/001385111.pdf. Other visas for more narrowly defined occupations, such as professors, lawyers, or accountants, are available but far less common.

7. The forms and materials required for application are described in Immigration Services Agency, "Zairyuu shikaku 'gijutsu jinbun chishiki kokusai gyoumu'" ["Technical, specialist in humanities, and international services" residence status], accessed March 26, 2023, https://www.moj.go.jp/isa/applications/status/gijinkoku.html.

8. Gracia Liu-Farrer, "Educationally Channeled International Labor Mobility: Contemporary Student Migration from China to Japan," *International Migration Review* 43, no. 1 (2009): 178–204.

9. Fuess, "Immigration Policy and Highly Skilled Workers."

10. Erin A. Chung, *Immigration and Citizenship in Japan in Japan* (Cambridge University Press, 2010).

11. Gracia Liu-Farrer, *Immigrant Japan* (Cornell University Press, 2020), 68.

12. Ministry of Justice, "Shutsunyuukoku zairyuu kanri wo meguru kinnen no joukyou," 30. In comparison, there are about ten thousand applications for naturalization approved every year. See Ministry of Justice, "Kika kyoka shinsei shasuu, kika kyoka shasuu oyobi kika fukyoka shasuu no suii" [Trends in applications for naturalization, approvals, and denials], accessed August 19, 2024, https://www.moj.go.jp/content/001414946.pdf.

13. In 2021, there were more than eight hundred thousand permanent residents, excluding special permanent residents (i.e., descendants of colonial-era migrants from Asia). The total size of the of the white-collar foreign worker population is therefore likely two to three times larger than is suggested by the number of white-collar work visa holders. Ministry of Justice, "Shutsunyuukoku zairyuu kanri wo meguru kinnen no joukyou," 26.

14. Glenda S. Roberts, "An Immigration Policy by Any Other Name: Semantics of Immigration to Japan," *Social Science Japan Journal* 21, no. 1 (2018): 89–102; Gracia Liu-Farrer, *Labour Migration from China to Japan: International Students, Transnational Migrants* (New York: Routledge, 2011), 12–13.

15. This classification system makes comparisons in outcomes between Japanese and foreigners more conservative. Simply, if any native minorities, including Zainichi Koreans, appear in the sample, they are counted as "Japanese," and any disadvantage they face reduces the average outcomes for the Japanese comparison group.

16. I collected data on respondents' native languages and countries of birth. In cases in which these are incongruent (e.g., native Japanese speaker born in the United States, or a native Chinese speaker born in Japan), native language takes precedence over country of birth in classifying respondents as Japanese or non-Japanese.

17. Many of the Southeast Asians in the sample are from Vietnam, Singapore, or Malaysia, and speak advanced Chinese, suggesting ethnic Chinese ancestry. As such, their coworkers may perceive them more as Chinese than as Southeast Asian. In addition, Southeast Asians share with East Asians the experience of colonial exploitation and its justification in discourses of their inferiority to Japanese; see John Lie, *Multiethnic Japan* (Harvard University Press, 2001). As such, we can theoretically expect some overlap in their treatment and outcomes. As for other Asians, those who hail from various countries in South and Central Asia, they arguably face different attitudes and treatments than East and Southeast Asians based on phenotypic differences and the absence of a colonial history. Their placement in the pan-Asian category is pragmatic, based on their small numbers.

I also analyze all Westerners together regardless of national origin. This reflects a common-sense understanding of background in Japan, which does not make strong distinctions among white Western Europeans, North Americans, and Australians; see Kikuko Nagayoshi, "Imin no tougou wo kangaeru" [Thoughts on immigrant integration], in *Nihon no imin tougou: Zenkoku chousa kara miru genjou to shouheki*, ed. Kikuko Nagayoshi (Akashi Shoten, 2021), 25. Unfortunately, it elides racial or ethnic differences among Westerners. Collecting meaningful racial information in the survey was impossible, however; because racial classification systems vary around the globe, no survey question or set of questions on race would be legible to diverse survey respondents with roots in twenty-one countries spread across four continents. Hence, other than the two Western respondents I interviewed, both of whom identify as white, I have no knowledge of Western respondents' race. Because whiteness is highly valued in global ethnoracial hierarchies and in Japan, if the sample of Westerners includes people of color as well as whites, the results will likely understate disadvantages for people of color from Western countries and overstate it for white Westerners. See Harumi Befu, *Hegemony of Homogeneity: An Anthropological Analysis of Nihonjinron* (Trans Pacific, 2001); Eiji Oguma, *A Genealogy of Japanese Self-Images* (Trans Pacific Press, 2002).

18. I exclude Latin Americans from the quantitative analyses, because with only two respondents, it is not possible to draw firm conclusions about their experiences.

19. Gracia Liu-Farrer, "Educationally Channeled International Labor Mobility."

20. For a description of the recruitment process, see Yen-Fen Tseng, "Becoming Global Talent? Taiwanese White-Collar Migrants in Japan," *Journal of Ethnic and Migration Studies* 47, no. 10 (2021): 2288–304.

21. With the exception of the two intercompany transferees.

22. These far exceeded the number (15 percent) who expressed positive plans to return home or move on to a third country. The remainder are undecided.

23. Roberts, "An Immigration Policy by Any Other Name"; Liu-Farrer, *Labour Migration from China to Japan*, 12–13.

24. Kimberle Crenshaw, "Demarginalizing the Intersection of Race and Sex: A Black Feminist Critique of Antidiscrimination Doctrine, Feminist Theory, and Antiracist Politics," *University of Chicago Legal Forum* 1989, no. 1 (1989): 39–52; Kimberle Crenshaw, "Mapping the Margins: Intersectionality, Identity Politics, and Violence Against Women of Color," *Stanford Law Review* 43, no. 6 (1991): 1241–99; Joya Misra, Celeste Vaughan Curington, and Venus Mary Green, "Methods of Intersectional Research," *Sociological Spectrum* 41, no. 1 (2020): 1–20.

25. Young Asian and Western men reported even higher "hunger" for promotion, with 79 percent and 75 percent of those under 35 describing it as "absolutely critical" or "very important" to their job satisfaction, respectively.

26. On immigrants who apply for entry-level jobs, see Philip Oreopoulos, "Why Do Skilled Immigrants Struggle in the Labor Market? A Field Experiment with Thirteen Thousand Resumes," *American Economic Journal: Economic Policy* 3, no. 4 (2011): 148–71. On hiring after interviewing, see Koji Chavez, "Penalized for Personality: A Case Study of Asian-Origin Disadvantage at the Point of Hire," *Sociology of Race and Ethnicity* 7, no. 2 (2021): 226–246. On lower raises after adjusting for performance, see Emilio J. Castilla, "Gender, Race, and Meritocracy in Organizational Careers, *American Journal of Sociology* 113, no. 6 (May 2008): 1479–526."

27. Chavez, "Penalized for Personality"; Oreopoulos, "Why Do Skilled Immigrants Struggle in the Labor Market?"; Lauren A. Rivera, *Pedigree: How Elite Students Get Jobs* (Princeton University Press, 2015), 224–30.

28. For qualitative studies, see Liu-Farrer, *Labour Migration from China to Japan*; Liu-Farrer, *Immigrant Japan*; Miloš Debnár, *Migration, Whiteness, and Cosmopolitanism: Europeans in Japan* (Palgrave Macmillan, 2016); Helena Hof, "'Worklife Pathways' to Singapore and Japan: Gender and Racial Dynamics in Europeans' Mobility to Asia," *Social Science Japan Journal* 21, no. 1 (2017): 45–65; Tseng, "Becoming Global Talent?"; Helena Hof and Yen-Fen Tseng, "When 'Global Talents' Struggle to Become Local Workers: The New Face of Skilled Migration to Corporate Japan," *Asian and Pacific Migration Journal* 29, no. 4 (December 2020): 511–31; Yuko Tsukasaki, *Gaikokujin senmonshoku gijutsushoku no koyoumondai: Shokugyou kyaria no shiten kara* [Employment problems of professional and technical foreign workers: from the perspective of occupations and careers] (Akashi Shoten, 2008).

For quantitative studies using convenience samples, see Ayumi Takenaka, Kenji Ishida, and Makiko Nakamuro. "Negative Assimilation: How Immigrants Experience Economic Mobility in Japan," *International Migration Review* 50, no. 2 (2016): 506–33; Kenji Ishida, "Nihon ni okeru imin no chii tassei kouzou" [Structure of immigrants' status attainment in Japan], in *Jinkou mondai to imin*, ed. Hiroshi Komai and Yu Korekawa (Akashi Shoten, 2019), 92–113.

For quantitative studies using a systematic sampling strategy, see Hirohisa Takenoshita, "The Differential Incorporation into Japanese Labor Market: A Comparative Study of Japanese Brazilians and Professional Chinese Migrants," *Japanese Journal of Population* 4, no. 1 (2006): 56–77; Hilary J. Holbrow and Kikuko Nagayoshi, "Economic Integration of Skilled Migrants in Japan: The Role of Employment Practices,"

International Migration Review 52, no. 2 (2018): 458–86; Kikuko Nagayoshi, "Nihon ni okeru gaikokusekisha no kaizouteki chii" [Class position of foreign citizens in Japan], in *Jinkou mondai to imin*, ed. Hiroshi Komai and Yu Korekawa (Akashi Shoten, 2019), 114–33; Hilary J. Holbrow, "When All Assistants Are Women, Are All Women Assistants? Gender Inequality and the Gender Composition of Support Roles," *RSF: The Russell Sage Foundation Journal of the Social Sciences* 8, no. 7 (2022): 28–49.

For studies based on administrative and government data, see Yu Korekawa, *Imin ukeire to shakaiteki tougou no riariti* [The reality of immigration and social integration] (Keisou Shobou, 2019); Cabinet Office, "Kigyou no gaikokujin koyou ni kansuru bunseki" [Analysis of companies' employment of foreigners], updated September 2019, https://www5.cao.go.jp/keizai3/2019/09seisakukadai18-6.

29. Kikuko Nagayoshi, "Imin no kaizouteki chii tassei" [Immigrants' class attainment], in *Nihon no imin tougou: Zenkoku chousa kara miru genjou to shouheki*, ed. Kikuko Nagayoshi (Akashi Shoten, 2021), 70–3; Korekawa, *Imin ukeire to shakaiteki tougou no riariti*, 136.

30. See, for example, Clemons, "Transcending National Identity."

31. Holbrow and Nagayoshi, "Economic Integration of High-Skilled Migrants in Japan."

32. For example, Tseng, "Becoming Global Talent?"; Harald Conrad and Hendrik Meyer-Ohle, "Training Regimes and Diversity: Experiences of Young Foreign Employees in Japanese Headquarters," *Work, Employment and Society* 36, no. 2 (2020): 1–18.

33. Tseng, "Becoming Global Talent?," 2299–300; Hof and Tseng, "When 'Global Talents' Struggle to Become Local Workers."

34. Recruit, "Gaikokujin ryuugakusei no saiyou shuushoku ni kansuru deetashuu" [Collection of data on recruitment and employment of international students], *Shuushoku Mirai*, updated July 3, 2017, https://shushokumirai.recruit.co.jp/wp-content/uploads/2017/11/data_foreign201706.pdf.

35. Gracia Liu-Farrer and Helena Hof, "Ōtebyō: The Problems of Japanese Firms and the Problematic Elite Aspirations," *Journal of Asia-Pacific Studies* 34 (2018): 65–84; Tsukasaki, *Gaikokujin senmonshoku gijutsushoku no koyou mondai*; Nana Oishi, "The Limits of Immigration Policies: The Challenges of Highly Skilled Migration in Japan," *American Behavioral Scientist* 56, no. 8 (2012): 1080–100.

36. Oreopoulos, "Why Do Skilled Immigrants Struggle in the Labor Market?"

37. Center for Employment Equity, "Is Silicon Valley Tech Diversity Possible Now?," updated 2018, https://www.uMAedu/employmentequity/sites/default/files/CEE_Diversity%2Bin%2BSilicon%2BValley%2BTech.pdf; Kweilin Ellingrud et al., "Closing the Gender and Race Gaps in North American Financial Services," McKinsey and Company, updated October 21, 2021, https://www.mckinsey.com/industries/financial-services/our-insights/closing-the-gender-and-race-gaps-in-north-american-financial-services; Buck Gee and Janet Wong, "The Illusion of Asian Success: Scant Progress for Minorities in Cracking the Glass Ceiling from 2007–2015," Ascend, Pan-Asian Leaders, updated 2017, https://www.ascendleadershipfoundation.org/research/the-illusion-of-asian-success; Sharla Alegria, "Escalator or Step Stool? Gendered Labor and Token Processes in Tech Work," *Gender and Society* 33, no. 5 (2019): 722–45.

38. Center for Employment Equity, "Is Silicon Valley Tech Diversity Possible Now"; Ellingrud et al., "Closing the Gender and Race Gaps"; Gee and Wong, "The Illusion of Asian Success"; Alegria, "Escalator or Step Stool?"

39. Mary J. Lopez, "Skilled Immigrant Women in the US and the Double Earnings Penalty," *Feminist Economics* 18, no. 1 (2012): 99–134.

40. Liu-Farrer, "I Am the Only Woman in Suits"; Ruth Achenbach, "'Having It All'—At What Cost? Strategies of Chinese Highly Skilled Women in Japan to Combine

Career and Family," *Contemporary Japan* 26, no. 2 (2014): 223–43; Tseng, "Becoming Global Talent."

41. Career Connection, "Susumu 'shinsotsu gaikokujin saiyou' kahogona nihonjin yori 'hanguriina ajiajin'" ['Entry-level foreigner hiring' increases 'hungry Asians' over coddled Japanese], Career Connection, updated April 23, 2014, https://careerconnection.jp/biz /economics/content_1375.html; Saitou Takeshi, "Gaikokujin ryuugakusei ga shuukatsu no raibaru ni? Fueru nihon kigyou he no shuushoku" [Are foreign students becoming rivals in the job hunt? An increasing number find employment in Japanese firms], *Benesse*, updated August 31, 2015, https://benesse.jp/kyouiku/201508/20150831-1.html.

42. Liu-Farrer, "I Am the Only Woman in Suits," 42.

43. Holbrow and Nagayoshi, "Economic Integration of Skilled Migrants in Japan"; Kikuko Nagayoshi and Hirohisa Takenoshita, "Imin no kyouiku tassei to chingin" [Immigrants' educational attainment and earnings], in *Nihon no imin tougou: Zenkoku chousa kara miru genjou to shouheki*, ed. Kikuko Nagayoshi (Akashi Shoten, 2021), 88–110; Takenaka et al., "Negative Assimilation."

44. For a review, see Hilary J. Holbrow, "Detangling Capital from Context: A Critical Investigation of Human Capital Explanations for Immigrant Wage Inequality," *Journal of Ethnic and Migration Studies* 46, no. 19 (2020): 4043–65.

45. See, for example, Nagayoshi, "Imin no kaizouteki chii tassei," 74.

46. Adam Komisarof, *At Home Abroad: The Contemporary Western Experience in Japan* (Reitaku University Press, 2012); Robert M. March, *Working for a Japanese Company: Insights Into the Multicultural Workplace* (Kodansha, 1992), 112–13, 120–21, 132.

47. On special attention given to Westerners, see Clemons, "Transcending National Identity"; Liu-Farrer, *Immigrant Japan*, 99, 146. On converting special status into higher returns, see Helena Hof, "Intersections of Race and Skills in European Migration to Asia: Between White Cultural Capital and 'Passive Whiteness,'" *Ethnic and Racial Studies* 44, no. 11 (2020): 1–22; Miloš Debnár, *Migration, Whiteness, and Cosmopolitanism: Europeans in Japan* (Palgrave Macmillan, 2016).

48. Holbrow and Nagayoshi, "Economic Integration of Skilled Migrants in Japan"; Takenaka et al., "Negative Assimilation;" Nagayoshi and Takenoshita, "Imin no kyouiku tassei to chingin."

49. "Managers" are defined as those supervising at least six subordinates.

50. In large, heterogenous samples, it is common to analyze logged, rather than raw, income. Logging compresses the midrange of the data and draws high outliers toward the center. This approach makes sense in cases in which the variation of interest derives from the far right tail of a variable's distribution, or when high outliers would wield undue influence over the results. As shown in the scatterplots of Japanese men's income in chapter 1, compared with US firms, income inequality between the lowest and highest earners is modest. Consequently, high outliers do not exercise an outsize influence. Moreover, because most outsider employees are young, as a matter of course, their earnings tend to fall toward the middle and lower end of the overall distribution. Logging the data would therefore inappropriately compress the variation in which I am most interested.

51. A few respondents (six Japanese men and three Western men) drop out of the income analyses because they did not share information on their earnings.

52. I do not systematically analyze occupation, because occupation is relatively less important determinant of wages in the Japanese economy overall; see Dustin Avent-Holt et al., "Occupations, Workplaces or Jobs? An Exploration of Stratification Contexts Using Administrative Data," *Research in Social Stratification and Mobility* 70 (June 2020): 100456. This holds true in the current sample, in which occupation

explains only 5 percent of variation in wages after accounting for job category (management track, clerical track, and irregular).

53. Korekawa, *Imin ukeire to shakaiteki tougou no riariti*, 132.

54. Japanese women also report spending 6 percent of their time with managers.

55. Oguma, *A Genealogy of Japanese Self-Images*; Befu, *Hegemony of Homogeneity*.

56. Pascale Hatcher and Aya Murakami, "The Politics of Exclusion: Embedded Racism and Japan's Pilot Refugee Resettlement Programme," *Race and Class* 62, no. 1 (2020): 60–77; Liang Morita, "Some Manifestations of Japanese Exclusionism," *SAGE Open* 5, no. 3 (2015): 1–6.

57. Liu-Farrer and Hof, "Ōtebyō"; Oishi, "The Limits of Immigration Policies."

58. Asian women are placed beside Japanese women in table 2.8, rather than above them because their advantage in earnings compared with Japanese women does not reach statistical significance.

59. Liu-Farrer, "I Am the Only Woman in Suits"; Korekawa, *Imin ukeire to shakaiteki tougou no riariti*.

60. Peggy McIntosh, "White Privilege: Unpacking the Invisible Knapsack," *Peace and Freedom*, August (1989): 29–34; Kaidi Wu, "Invisibility of Social Privilege to Those Who Have It," *Academy of Management Proceedings* 2021, no. 1 (2021).

61. For example, Conrad and Meyer-Ohle, "Training Regimes and Diversity"; Oishi, "Limits of Immigration Policies"; Cabinet Office, "Kigyou no gaikokujin koyou ni kansuru bunseki."

3. THE LONG SHADOW OF THE SECRETARY

1. American Association of University Women, "The Motherhood Penalty," updated September 1, 2022, https://www.aauw.org/issues/equity/motherhood; Organization for Economic Co-operation and Development, "The Pursuit of Gender Equality: An Uphill Battle," updated July 18, 2018, https://www.oecd.org/japan/Gender2017-JPN-en.pdf.

2. Japan Institute for Labor Policy and Training, "'Ninshin nado o riyuu to suru furieki toriatsukai oyobi sekushuaruharasumento ni kansuru jittai chousa' kekka (gaiyou)" [Results of the "survey on disadvantageous treatment and sexual harassment due to pregnancy or related circumstances" (summary)], updated March 1, 2016, https://www.jil.go.jp/press/documents/20160301.pdf; Hatarakonetto, "800mei no josei ni kiita 'shokuba de no matahara/ikuhara no jittai" [We asked 800 women about "maternity- and childrearing-related harassment in the workplace"], updated October 15, 2015, https://www.hatarako.net/pr/2015/1015.

3. Japan Institute for Labor Policy and Training, "'Ninshin nado o riyuu to suru furieki toriatsukai"; Hilary J. Holbrow, "Tainted Leave: A Survey-Experimental Investigation of Flexibility Stigma in Japanese Workplaces," *Social Forces* (2025).

4. Kumiko Nemoto, *Too Few Women at the Top: The Persistence of Inequality in Japan* (Cornell University Press, 2016).

5. Linda C. Hasunuma, "Gender Gaiatsu: An Institutional Perspective on Womenomics," *U.S.-Japan Women's Journal* 48, no. 1 (2015): 79–114.

6. Nemoto, *Too Few Women at the Top*; Rosabeth M. Kanter, *Men and Women of the Corporation* (Basic Books, 1993); Matt L. Huffman et al., "Engendering Change Organizational Dynamics and Workplace Gender Desegregation, 1975–2005," *Administrative Science Quarterly* 55, no. 2 (2010): 255–77.

7. Leonard Schoppa, "The Policy Response to Declining Fertility Rates in Japan: Relying on Logic and Hope over Evidence," *Social Science Japan Journal* 23, no. 1 (2020): 3–21.

8. Organization for Economic Co-operation and Development, "Gender Wage Gap," updated 2023, https://data.oecd.org/earnwage/gender-wage-gap.htm.

9. World Economic Forum, *Global Gender Gap Report 2021*, updated March 30, 2021, https://www3.weforum.org/docs/WEF_GGGR_2021.pdf.

10. For international media, see Christine Levy, "Japanese Women Are Fighting Back Against Pervasive Sexism," *The Nation*, January 10, 2022, https://www.thenation.com/article/world/japan-womens-movement. For Japan's government, see Cabinet Secretariat, "Josei katsuyaku danjo kyoudou sankaku no juuten houshin 2022" [Major policies on gender equality and women's empowerment 2022], updated June 3, 2022, https://www.gender.go.jp/policy/sokushin/pdf/sokushin/jyuten2022_honbun.pdf. For longstanding issues, see Gill Steel, "Women's Work at Home and in the Workplace," in *Beyond the Gender Gap in Japan*, ed. Gill Steel (University of Michigan Press, 2019), 25–49.

11. Mary C. Brinton, *Women and the Economic Miracle: Gender and Work in Postwar Japan* (University of California Press, 1993); Nemoto, *Too Few Women at the Top*; Chizuko Ueno, "Why Do Japanese Women Suffer from the Low Status? The Impact of Neo-Liberalist Reform on Gender," *Japanese Political Economy* 47, no. 1 (2021): 9–26; Eunmi Mun and Mary C. Brinton, "Workplace Matters: The Use of Parental Leave Policy in Japan," *Work and Occupations* 42, no. 3 (March 2015): 355–69.

12. Eunmi Mun, "Negative Compliance as an Organizational Response to Legal Pressures: The Case of Japanese Equal Employment Opportunity Law," *Social Forces* 94, no. 4 (June 2016): 1409–37.

13. Brinton, *Women and the Economic Miracle*.

14. Holbrow, "Tainted Leave."

15. Holbrow, "Tainted Leave."

16. Mun and Brinton, "Workplace Matters"; Glenda S. Roberts, "Leaning Out for the Long Span: What Holds Women Back from Promotion in Japan?," *Japan Forum* 32, no. 4 (2020): 555–76.

17. Steel, "Women's Work at Home and in the Workplace"; Mary C. Brinton and Eunmi Mun, "Between State and Family: Managers' Implementation and Evaluation of Parental Leave Policies in Japan," *Socio-Economic Review* 14, no. 2 (2016): 257–81; Takao Kato et al., "Dynamics of the Gender Gap in the Workplace: An Econometric Case Study of a Large Japanese Firm," RIETI Discussion Paper Series 13-E-038, 2013.

18. Tomoko Hamada, "Japanese Company's Cultural Shift for Gender Equality at Work," *Global Economic Review* 47, no. 1 (2018): 63–87; Noriko Fujita, "Corporate Transfers for Dual-Career Couples: From Gendered Tenkin to Gender-Equal Negotiations?," *Social Science Japan Journal* 24, no. 1 (2021): 163–83.

19. Steel, "Women's Work at Home and in the Workplace."

20. Roberts, "Leaning Out for the Long Span"; Yuko Ogasawara, "Working Women's Husbands as Helpers or Partners," in *Beyond the Gender Gap in Japan*, ed. Gill Steel (University of Michigan Press, 2019), 83–103.

21. Nemoto, *Too Few Women at the Top*; Ulrike Schaede, *The Business Reinvention of Japan: How to Make Sense of the New Japan and Why It Matters* (Stanford Business Books, 2020), 41.

22. Steel, "Women's Work at Home and in the Workplace"; Nemoto, *Too Few Women at the Top*.

23. All my female interlocutors socialized with coworkers in the off hours. Although men can go golfing or drinking one-on-one with their bosses without comment, some women I spoke to avoided it out of concern that it would lead to unwanted romantic or sexual advances, or uncomfortable office rumors. Generally, women preferred to go in large groups, rather than one-on-one. But even in large groups, some had experienced

sexual harassment. Following multiple experiences like these, Yuanyuan took care when deciding whom she was willing to go out with after hours: Some groups were better than others, she said. And she adopted the "smart strategy" of going out to lunch with bosses, coworkers, and clients, rather than participating in the prolonged and open-ended barhopping that characterizes evening get-togethers.

24. On leaning out, see Roberts, "Leaning Out for the Long Span." On reducing time and effort, see Nemoto, *Too Few Women at the Top*; Takao Kato et al., "Working Hours, Promotion, and Gender Gaps in the Workplace," RIETI Discussion Paper Series 16-E-060, 2016.

25. Japan Institute for Labor Policy and Training, "Saiyou haichi shoushin to pojitibu akushon ni kansuru chousa kekka" [Survey results on hiring, placement, promotion, and affirmative action], updated May 15, 2015, https://www.jil.go.jp/institute/research/2014/132.html.

26. Ueno, "Why Do Japanese Women Suffer from the Low Status?"

27. Japan Institute for Labor Policy and Training, "Koyou keitaibetsu koyou shasuu" [Number of employees by employment type], updated March 30, 2023, https://www.jil.go.jp/kokunai/statistics/timeseries/html/g0208.html.

28. Mun, "Negative Compliance as an Organizational Response to Legal Pressures"; Kanai Kaoru, "'Tayou na seishain' shisaku to josei no hatarakikata he no eikyou" ['Diverse regular employee' policy and its influence on women's work], *Nihon roudou kenkyuu zasshi* 636 (July 2013): 63–76.

29. Ministry of Health, Labor, and Welfare, "Heisei 24 nendo koyou kintou kihon chousa no gaikyou" [Overview of the 2012 basic survey of equal employment], updated July 4, 2013, http://www.mhlw.go.jp/toukei/list/dl/71-24e.pdf.

30. Mun, "Negative Compliance as an Organizational Response to Legal Pressures."

31. Keidanren, "2013nen 6gatsudo teiki chingin chousa kekka" [Results of the June 2013 periodic survey of wages], updated April 28, 2014, https://www.keidanren.or.jp/policy/2014/040.pdf.

32. For example, Nemoto, *Too Few Women at the Top*, 100.

33. Kumiko Nemoto, "Why Women Won't Wed," in *Beyond the Gender Gap in Japan*, ed. Gill Steel (University of Michigan Press, 2019), 67–82.

34. On working shorter hours, see Gender Equality Bureau, "Nenkan sou jitsu roudou jikan no suii" [Trends in total annual working hours], updated 2015, https://www.gender.go.jp/about_danjo/whitepaper/h27/zentai/html/zuhyo/zuhyo01-03-02.html. On taking longer parental leave, see Ministry of Health, Labor and Welfare, "Ikuji kyuugyou kyuufu kankei" [Materials on parental leave payments], updated January 26, 2021, https://www.mhlw.go.jp/content/11601000/000728126.pdf. For an exception examining the relationship between parental leave and earnings, see Kato et al., "Dynamics of the Gender Gap in the Workplace."

35. For example, Kazuo Yamaguchi, *Gender Inequalities in the Japanese Workplace and Employment* (Springer Singapore, 2019); Kato et al., "Working Hours, Promotion, and Gender Gaps in the Workplace."

36. Holbrow, "Tainted Leave."

37. Some companies also employ "region-restricted" regular workers—that is to say, regular workers who are not eligible for or required to make distant job transfers. This sample does not contain region-restricted regular workers.

38. The gender difference in job transfers is more extreme for workers with longer tenures. Among workers with tenures of ten or more years, 35 percent of men reported distant transfers, compared with just 4 percent of women. This larger gaps highlights both that male employees' "risk" of transfer grows with tenure and that firms' inclusion of women in the pool of employees eligible for distant transfer is a relatively recent phenomenon.

39. For example, unobserved effort, or men's tendency to socialize later into the evenings with colleagues, even though the number of times per month is not so different.

40. Nemoto, *Too Few Women at the Top*, 100.

41. The models also omit occupation, because occupation is not typically an important determinant of earnings within Japanese firms. Consistent with this, including occupation does not substantively change the model results.

42. Irene Padavic et al., "Explaining the Persistence of Gender Inequality: The Work–Family Narrative as a Social Defense against the 24/7 Work Culture," *Administrative Science Quarterly* 65, no. 1 (2020): 61–111.

43. Hiroki Sato, "Expanding Work Opportunities for Women and Support for Work-Life Balance: The Roles of Managers," *Social Science Japan* 50 (March 2014): 23–28.

44. Schaede, *Business Reinvention of Japan*, 187.

45. 20 percent of management track men report "sales" as their primary function, compared with 12 percent of management track women; across the fourteen other categories of occupation/work content in the survey responses, differences between men and women on the management track are less than 5 percent, and usually with 1–2 percent.

46. Michèle Lamont and Virág Molnár, "The Study of Boundaries in the Social Sciences," *Annual Review of Sociology* 28 (2002): 167–95.

47. Andrew Gordon, "Managing the Japanese Household: The New Life Movement in Postwar Japan," in *Gendering Modern Japanese History*, ed. Barbara Molony and Kathleen Uno (Harvard University Asia Center, 2005), 423–62.

48. Cabinet Secretariat, "Josei katsuyaku danjo kyoudou sankaku no juuten houshin 2022."

49. Gender Equality Bureau, "Muishiki no omoikomi (ankonshasu baiasu): jirei shuu" [Case studies of unconscious bias], updated December 15, 2021, https://www.gender.go.jp/research/kenkyu/pdf/seibetsu_r03/04.pdf.

50. For qualitative descriptions of these stereotypes, see Nemoto, *Too Few Women at the Top*; Steel, "Women's Work at Home and in the Workplace."

51. Perry R. Hinton, *Stereotypes and the Construction of the Social World* (Routledge, 2019); Kanter, *Men and Women of the Corporation*.

52. Hiroko Takeda, "Between Reproduction and Production: Womenomics and the Japanese Government's Approach to Women and Gender Policies," *Journal of Gender Studies* 21 (2018): 49–70; Nemoto, *Too Few Women at the Top*.

53. For example, Nemoto, *Too Few Women at the Top*.

54. Prime Minister's Office of Japan, "Hatarakikata kaikaku jikkou keikaku" [Workstyle reform implementation plan], updated March 28, 2017, https://www.kantei.go.jp/jp/headline/pdf/20170328/01.pdf, 3.

55. Cecilia L. Ridgeway, *Status: Why Is It Everywhere? Why Does It Matter?* (Russell Sage Foundation, 2019); Cecilia L. Ridgeway and Hazel Rose Markus, "The Significance of Status: What It Is and How It Shapes Inequality," *RSF: The Russell Sage Foundation Journal of the Social Sciences* 8, no. 7 (2022): 1–25. We see this clearly in the case of Japanese firms, in which men are believed to be better at highly valued skills of negotiation, leadership, and logical thinking, whereas women excel in more undervalued areas, such as attention to detail, pleasant manners, and nurturing.

56. Philip N. Cohen and Matt L. Huffman, "Working for the Woman? Female Managers and the Gender Wage Gap," *American Sociological Review* 72, no. 5 (2007): 700; Huffman et al., "Engendering Change," 273; Nemoto, *Too Few Women at the Top*; Andrea S. Kramer and Alton B Harris, *It's Not You, It's the Workplace: Women's Conflict at Work and the Bias That Built It* (Nicholas Brealy, 2019); Safi Shams and Donald

Tomaskovic-Devey, "Racial and Gender Trends and Trajectories in Access to Managerial Jobs," *Social Science Research* 80 (2019): 15–29.

57. Nemoto, *Too Few Women at the Top*, 222.

58. Hiroko Takeda, "Between Reproduction and Production"; Linda C. Hasunuma, "Gender Gaiatsu: An Institutional Perspective on Womenomics," *U.S.-Japan Women's Journal* 48, no. 1 (2015): 79–114.

59. Reuters, "Japan to Delay 'Womenomics' Target for Female Leaders by up to a Decade," June 30, 2020, https://www.reuters.com/article/us-japan-politics-women-idUSKBN2410MA.

60. Emma Chanlett-Avery and Rebecca M. Nelson, *Womenomics in Japan: In Brief* (Congressional Research Service, 2014); Nobuko Nagase, "Has Abe's Womanomics Worked?," *Asian Economic Policy Review* 13, no. 1 (2018): 68–101.

61. Yagi Kaoru, "Josei katsuyaku o habamu ankonshasu baiasu 2: henken o norikoeru niwa" [Unconscious bias hindering women's empowerment 2: how to overcome prejudice], *Lightworks*, updated January 18, 2022, https://research.lightworks.co.jp/get-out-of-unconscious-bias#thosya_profile; Nemoto, *Too Few Women at the Top*.

62. Japan Institute for Labor Policy and Training, "Shokugyou betsu shuugyousha-suu" [Number of workers by occupation], updated May 16, 2023, https://www.jil.go.jp/kokunai/statistics/chart/html/g0006.html.

63. Ellen Ernst Kossek, Rong Su, and Lusi Wu, "'Opting Out' or 'Pushed Out'? Integrating Perspectives on Women's Career Equality for Gender Inclusion and Interventions," *Journal of Management* 43, no. 1 (2017): 228–54; Joan C. Williams et al., "Cultural Schemas, Social Class, and the Flexibility Stigma," *Journal of Social Issues* 69, no. 2 (2013): 209–34; Nemoto, *Too Few Women at the Top*.

64. Kanter, *Men and Women of the Corporation*; Nemoto, *Too Few Women at the Top*.

65. For a review, see Hilary J. Holbrow, "When All Assistants Are Women, Are All Women Assistants? Gender Inequality and the Gender Composition of Support Roles," *RSF: The Russell Sage Foundation Journal of the Social Sciences* 8, no. 7 (2022): 28–49.

66. Robin J. Ely, "The Power in Demography: Women's Social Constructions of Gender Identity at Work," *Academy of Management Journal* 38, no. 3 (1995): 589–634.

67. Schoppa, "The Policy Response to Declining Fertility Rates in Japan."

68. Yuko Ogasawara, *Office Ladies and Salaried Men: Power, Gender, and Work in Japanese Companies* (University of California Press, 1998), 162.

69. Ministry of Health, Labor, and Welfare, "Kigyou chousa kekka gaiyou" [Overview of company survey results], updated December 18, 2016, https://www.mhlw.go.jp/toukei/list/dl/71-27-02.pdf, 2023, 3.

70. Teikoku Databank, "Tokubetsu kikaku: Josei touyou ni taisuru kigyou no ishiki chousa (2018 nen)" [Special Project: Survey of companies' attitudes about promoting women, 2018], updated August 14, 2018, https://www.tdb.co.jp/report/watching/press/pdf/p180805.pdf, 2; Reuters, "Roitaa kigyou chousa: Josei kanrishoku 10-paasento miman ga 9wari mokuhyou 3wari touku" [Reuters survey: 90 percent of respondents have less than 10 percent female managers, far from the 30 percent target], updated September 13, 2018, https://jp.reuters.com/article/female-manager-idJPKCN1LT3HN.

71. Ministry of Health, Labor, and Welfare, "Kigyou chousa kekka gaiyou," 3.

72. These perceptions of feeling valued by supervisors are not simply proxies for dissatisfaction with pay. Men in subordinate jobs in the firms where such jobs are female-dominated report feeling valued at a high rate, even though their wages are low relative to management-track men.

73. Nemoto, *Too Few Women at the Top*, 189.

74. Nemoto, *Too Few Women at the Top*, 222.

4. "WORKING LIKE A JAPANESE"

1. David L. Sam, "Acculturation: Conceptual Background and Core Components," in *The Cambridge Handbook of Acculturation Psychology*, ed. David L. Sam and John W. Berry (Cambridge University Press, 2006), 11.

2. Helena Hof and Yen-Fen Tseng, "When 'Global Talents' Struggle to Become Local Workers: The New Face of Skilled Migration to Corporate Japan," *Asian and Pacific Migration Journal* 29, no. 4 (December 2020): 511-31; Stephen Nagy, "From Temporary Migrant to Integrated Resident: Local Government Approaches to Migrant Integration in the Tokyo Metropolis," *ASIEN* 124 (2012): 115-36. Note that this differs from the usage of the term in US-focused literature, in which "assimilation" refers to a process of mutual adaptation involving changes to the behavior and attitudes of both immigrants and natives; see, for example, Richard D. Alba and Victor Nee, *Remaking the American Mainstream: Assimilation and Contemporary Immigration* (Harvard University Press, 2003).

3. Liang Morita, "Some Manifestations of Japanese Exclusionism," *SAGE Open* 5, no. 3 (2015): 1-6; Hof and Tseng, "When 'Global Talents' Struggle to Become Local Workers."

4. Vesa Peltokorpi and Jinju Xie, "When Little Things Make a Big Difference: A Bourdieusian Perspective on Skilled Migrants' Linguistic, Social, and Economic Capital in Multinational Corporations," *Journal of International Business Studies* (2023); Hof and Tseng, "When 'Global Talents' Struggle to Become Local Workers"; Helena Hof, "'Worklife Pathways' to Singapore and Japan: Gender and Racial Dynamics in Europeans' Mobility to Asia," *Social Science Japan Journal* 21, no. 1 (2018): 45-65; Nana Oishi, "The Limits of Immigration Policies: The Challenges of Highly Skilled Migration in Japan," *American Behavioral Scientist* 56, no. 8 (2012): 1080-100; Yuko Tsukasaki, *Gaikokujin senmonshoku gijutsushoku no koyou mondai: shokugyou kyaria no shiten kara* [Employment problems of professional and technical foreign workers: from the perspective of occupations and careers] (Akashi Shoten, 2008).

5. Helena Hof, "Intersections of Race and Skills in European Migration to Asia: Between White Cultural Capital and 'Passive Whiteness,'" *Ethnic and Racial Studies* 44, no. 11 (2021): 2128; Miloš Debnár, *Migration, Whiteness, and Cosmopolitanism: Europeans in Japan* (Palgrave Macmillan New York, 2016), 157.

6. Peltokorpi and Xie, "When Little Things Make a Big Difference."

7. Hof and Tseng, "When 'Global Talents' Struggle to Become Local Workers," 525-26.

8. Moriya Takashi, "Nihon kigyou no ryuugakusei nado no gaikokujin saiyou he no kousatsu" [Investigation of international student recruitment at Japanese firms], *Journal of Japanese Labor Studies* 623 (2012): 29-36; Tsukasaki, *Gaikokujin senmonshoku gijutsushoku no koyou mondai*; Gracia Liu-Farrer and Helena Hof, "Ōtebyō: The Problems of Japanese Firms and the Problematic Elite Aspirations," *Journal of Asia-Pacific Studies* 34 (2018): 72.

9. Hof, "Worklife Pathways," 61.

10. Harald Conrad and Hendrik Meyer-Ohle, "Training Regimes and Diversity: Experiences of Young Foreign Employees in Japanese Headquarters," *Work, Employment and Society* 36, no. 2 (2020): 1-18.

11. Yen-Fen Tseng, "Becoming Global Talent? Taiwanese White-Collar Migrants in Japan," *Journal of Ethnic and Migration Studies* 47, no. 10 (2021): 2299.

12. Oishi, "The Limits of Immigration Policies"; Hof and Tseng, "When 'Global Talents' Struggle to Become Local Workers"; Conrad and Meyer-Ohle, "Training Regimes and Diversity"; Gracia Liu-Farrer, *Immigrant Japan* (Cornell University Press, 2020).

13. On conformity, see "Hof, "Intersections of Race and Skills," 2128. On unaccented fluency, see Peltokorpi and Xie, "When Little Things Make a Big Difference."

14. Garcia Liu-Farrer, "Educationally Channeled International Labor Mobility: Contemporary Student Migration from China to Japan," *International Migration Review* 43, no. 1 (2009): 178–204"; Garcia Liu-Farrer, *Labour Migration from China to Japan: International Students, Transnational Migrants* (Routledge, 2011).

15. For the 2008 target, see Reiko Nebashi, "Future Challenges Surrounding the 300,000 International Students Plan," Meiji.net, April 21, 2017, https://english-meiji .net/articles/273. For the 2023 target, see Chika Yamamoto, "Kishida Sets Goal of 400,000 International Students in 2033," *Asahi Shimbun*, April 2, 2023, https://www .asahi.com/ajw/articles/14873637.

16. Japan Institute for Labor Policy and Training, "Ryuugakusei no shuushoku katsudou: genjou to kadai" [Job hunting for foreign students: current situation and challenges], *JILPT Shiryou Shiriizu* no. 113, July 24, 2013, https://www.jil.go.jp/institute /siryo/2013/documents/0113.pdf, 1.

17. Liu-Farrer, "Educationally Channeled International Labor Mobility"; Liu-Farrer, *Labour Migration from China to Japan*.

18. Ministry of International Affairs and Communications, "Koudo gaikoku jinzai no ukeire ni kansuru seisaku hyoukasho" [Policy evaluation report on acceptance of highly skilled foreign professionals], updated June 21, 2019, https://www.soumu.go.jp /main_content/000627735.pdf, 60.

19. Kyouki no usagi, "Ryuugakusei ha Nihon no takara Kishida naikaku souri daijin kisha kaiken" [International students are Japan's national treasure, press conference by Prime Minister Kishida], press conference, March 3, 2022, YouTube, 1 hr., 40 min., https://youtu.be/96LqKl1uJf8.

20. Ministry of Justice, "Points-Based Preferential Immigration Treatment for Highly-Skilled Foreign Professionals," updated December 11, 2013, https://www .ro.emb-japan.go.jp/files/100500331.pdf.

21. Michael Strausz, *Help (Not) Wanted: Immigration Politics in Japan* (SUNY Press, 2019), 131–32.

22. Tetsuro Kobayashi et al., "Who Deserves Citizenship? An Experimental Study of Japanese Attitudes Toward Immigrant Workers," *Social Science Japan Journal* 18, no. 1 (2015): 3–22.

23. Kobayashi et al., "Who Deserves Citizenship?"

24. Immigration Services Agency, "Enkatsuna komyunikeeshon no tame no nihongo kyouiku nado no torikumi ni tsuite" [Japanese language education and other initiatives for smooth communication], updated March 19, 2021, https://www.moj .go.jp/isa/content/001344684.pdf.

25. Hidenori Sakanaka, *Japan as an Immigration Nation: Demographic Change, Economic Necessity, and the Human Community Concept*, trans. Robert D. Eldridge and Graham B. Leonard (Lexington, 2020), 125, 238.

26. Hilary J. Holbrow, "Detangling Capital from Context: A Critical Investigation of Human Capital Explanations for Immigrant Wage Inequality," *Journal of Ethnic and Migration Studies* 46, no. 19 (2020): 4043–65; Sakanaka, *Japan as an Immigration Nation*.

27. For Japanese language as the top qualification, see Japan Institute for Labor Policy and Training, "Ryuugakusei no shuushoku katsudou: genjou to kadai," 16, 18; Recruit, "Gaikokujin ryuugakusei no saiyou shuushoku ni kansuru deetashuu," [Collection of data on recruitment and employment of international students], *Shuushoku Mirai*, updated July 3, 2017, https://shushokumirai.recruit.co.jp/wp-content/uploads /2017/11/data_foreign201706.pdf 15. For unfamiliarity with Japanese language and

culture, see Recruit, "Gaikokujin ryuugakusei no saiyou shuushoku ni kansuru deetashuu," 15.

28. Respondents rated each of the tasks on an ease-difficulty scale ranging from 0 ("cannot do this") to 5 (can do it "very easily").

29. Moriya, "Nihon kigyou no ryuugakusei nado no gaikokujin saiyou he no kousatsu"; Recruit, "Gaikokujin ryuugakusei no saiyou shuushoku ni kansuru deetashuu," 15.

30. Moriya, "Nihon kigyou no ryuugakusei nado no gaikokujin saiyou he no kousatsu."

31. Liu-Farrer and Hof, "Ōtebyō"; Ulrike Schaede, *The Business Reinvention of Japan: How to Make Sense of the New Japan and Why It Matters* (Stanford Business Books, 2020), 172–73.

32. For the United States, see Andrés Villarreal and Christopher R. Tamborini, "Immigrants' Economic Assimilation: Evidence from Longitudinal Earnings Records," *American Sociological Review* 83, no. 4 (2018): 686–715. For Australia, see Barry R. Chiswick et al., "A Longitudinal Analysis of Immigrant Occupational Mobility: A Test of the Immigrant Assimilation Hypothesis," *International Migration Review* 39, no. 2 (2005): 332–53. For Germany, see Robert C. M. Beyer, "The Labor Market Performance of Immigrants in Germany," IMF Working Papers (2016): 1–39. For Sweden, see Pieter Bevelander and Nahikari Irastorza, "Catching Up: The Labor Market Integration of New Immigrants in Sweden," *Migration Policy Institute* (2014): 1–23. For Japan, see Brian C. Cadena et al., "The Labor Market Integration and Impacts of US Immigrants," in *Handbook of the Economics of International Migration*, ed. Barry R. Chiswick and Paul W. Miller (North-Holland, 2015), 1197–259.

33. Marcus Rebick, *The Japanese Employment System: Adapting to a New Economic Environment* (Oxford University Press, 2005), 44, 47.

34. Respondents to the current survey ranked various factors that influence the size of their bonus, and, across firms, the single-largest determinant of this value is individual performance, followed closely by firm performance. According to respondents' ratings of the various factors that influence bonus, individual and firm performance far outweigh other determinants, such as job title, age, tenure, or team performance.

35. Ayumi Takenaka et al., "Negative Assimilation: How Immigrants Experience Economic Mobility in Japan," *International Migration Review* 50, no. 2 (2016): 506–33.

36. It is possible to test this interactive effect because the survey also collected information on Japanese employees' work abroad. For Japanese who never worked outside Japan, years of total work experience and years of work in Japan are equal. For those who worked outside Japan, years of work in Japan is calculated by subtracting years spent working abroad from total work experience.

37. As described further in chapter 5, coworkers and managers also praise Asian employees' work ethic and abilities.

38. Holbrow, "Detangling Capital from Context."

39. Morita, "Some Manifestations of Japanese Exclusionism."

40. Nicholas A. Valentino et al., "Economic and Cultural Drivers of Immigrant Support Worldwide," *British Journal of Political Science* 49, no. 4 (2019): 1201–26.

41. On border control policy, see Kobayashi et al., "Who Deserves Citizenship?" On employers' demands for inexpensive labor, see Oh-Jung Kwon, "The Diverging Paths of Skilled Immigration in Singapore, Japan and Korea: Policy Priorities and External Labor Market for Skilled Foreign Workers," *Asia Pacific Journal of Human Resources* 57, no. 4 (2019): 418–44. This may be why Japan appears relatively positive on immigration relative to other G-20 countries: Jacob Poushter, "Methodology," *Pew Research Center*, uploaded December 7, 2018, https://www.pewresearch.org/wp-content/uploads/2018

/12/FT_18.12.10_MigrationViews_Topline2.pdf, 4; Global Migration Data Analysis Center, "How the World Views Migration," *International* Organization for Migration, updated December 22, 2015, https://publications.iom.int/system/files/pdf/how_the _world_gallup.pdf.

42. Koji Chavez, "Penalized for Personality: A Case Study of Asian-Origin Disadvantage at the Point of Hire," *Sociology of Race and Ethnicity* 7, no. 2 (2021): 226–46; Lauren A. Rivera, *Pedigree: How Elite Students Get Jobs* (Princeton University Press, 2015), 225–27.

43. Rivera, *Pedigree*, 227.

44. Liu-Farrer, *Immigrant Japan*.

45. That interpersonal assimilative pressure is more intense for other Asians than for white Westerners is also consistent with the idea that assimilative pressure is an expression of ethnoracial bias.

46. Chavez, "Penalized for Personality."

47. Liu-Farrer, *Immigrant Japan*, 9.

5. CRIMINALS AND SUPERSTARS

1. Damian J. Rivers, "Cultural Essentialism and Foreigner-as-Criminal Discourse," in *Cultural Essentialism in Intercultural Relations,* ed. Fred Dervin and Regis Machart (Palgrave Macmillan UK, 2015), 15–41.

2. Cited in Yuko Kawai, "Deracialised Race, Obscured Racism: Japaneseness, Western and Japanese Concepts of Race, and Modalities of Racism," *Japanese Studies* 35, no. 1 (2015): 25.

3. Shintaro Ishihara, "Nihon yo, uchinaru bouei wo" [Japan, defend yourself from internal threats], *Sankei Shimbun,* May 8, 2001.

4. For other Asians, see Nihon Keizai Shimbun, "Gaikokujin tekihatsu 11,000chou, betonamu, chuugoku de kahansuu" [Over 11,000 foreigners arrested, majority from Vietnam and China], *Nikkei Keizai Shimbun,* April 3, 2020. For foreigners from beyond Asia, see Ethel Volfzon Kosminsky, *An Ethnography of the Lives of Japanese and Japanese Brazilian Migrants: Childhood, Family, and Work* (Lexington, 2020), 199.

5. Ryoko Yamamoto, "Migrants as a Crime Problem: The Construction of Foreign Criminality Discourse in Contemporary Japan," *International Journal of Comparative and Applied Criminal Justice* 34, no. 2 (2010): 320.

6. Debito Arudou, *Embedded Racism: Japan's Visible Minorities and Racial Discrimination* (Lexington, 2015), 195–6.

7. Andrew Rankin, "Recent Trends in Organized Crime in Japan: Yakuza vs the Police, & Foreign Crime Gangs," *Asia-Pacific Journal Japan Focus* 10, no. 7 (2012): 1–21; Arudou, *Embedded Racism*.

8. Cited in Cho Kyongho, "Intaanetto-jou no saigai-ji 'gaikoku jin hanzai' no ryuugen ni kansuru kenkyuu" [A study on rumors of "foreign crime" on the internet during disasters], *Ouyou shakaigaku kenkyuu* 60 (2018): 83.
This is almost a word-for-word reproduction of the racist rumors that circulated about Koreans following the Great Kanto Earthquake of 1923. These 1923 rumors had deadly consequences for the hundreds of Koreans (and Japanese mistaken for Koreans) who were harassed, detained, and murdered by vigilantes under the unfounded supposition that Koreans used the post-earthquake chaos to exact revenge on Japanese for their colonization of Korean and subjugation of the Korean people. Jinhee Lee, "'Malcontent Koreans (Futei Senjin)': Towards a Genealogy of Colonial Representation of Koreans in the Japanese Empire," *Faculty Research and Creative Activity,* no. 36 (2013): 1–71; Michael Weiner, "Koreans in the Aftermath of the Kanto Earthquake of 1923," *Immigrants and Minorities* 2, no. 1 (1983): 5–32.

9. On X (formerly Twitter), see Fumiaki Taka, "Nihongo Twitter yuuzaa no korian ni tsuite no gensetsu no keiryou-teki bunseki" [A quantitative analysis of Japanese Twitter users' public opinions of Koreans], *Shinbun kenkyuu*, no. 183 (2014): 131–53; Fumiaki Taka, "Nihongo Twitter yuuzaa no chuugokujin ni tsuite no gensetsu no keiryou-teki bunseki: Korian ni tsuite no gensetsu to no hikaku" [A quantitative analysis of Japanese Twitter users' public opinions of Chinese people: A comparison with their opinions of Korean people], *Shinbungaku kenkyuu*, no. 53 (2015): 73–85.

On 5channeru, see Tomomi Yamaguchi, "Xenophobia in Action: Ultranationalism, Hate Speech, and the Internet in Japan," *Radical History Review*, no. 117 (2013): 98–118; Mark McLelland, " 'Race' on the Japanese Internet: Discussing Korea and Koreans On '2-Channeru,'" *New Media and Society* 10, no. 6 (2008): 811–29.

On Yahoo! News, see Satoru Ishido, "Nihon ni sukuu 'kenkan' no shutai" [The true nature of "anti-Korea" that nests in Japan], *Newsweek Japan*, October 10, 2019.

10. Taka, "Nihongo Twitter yuuzaa no chuugokujin ni tsuite no gensetsu," 80. This is an imprecise measure of how much the criminality discourse is promoted by Twitter users: Tweets arguing against the criminality discourse could also contain these words, and tweets that do not include the words (such as the example from after the Kumamoto quake) may also accuse Chinese and Koreans of crimes.

11. Ana Gonzalez-Barrera and Phillip Connor, "Around the World, More Say Immigrants Are a Strength Than a Burden," Pew Research Center, updated March 14, 2019, https://www.pewresearch.org/global-migration-and-demography/2019/03/14/around-the-world-more-say-immigrants-are-a-strength-than-a-burden/.

12. Thomas Baudinette, "Ethnosexual Frontiers in Queer Tokyo: The Production of Racialised Desire in Japan," *Japan Forum* 28, no. 4 (2016), 480–81.

13. Gracia Liu-Farrer, *Immigrant Japan* (Cornell University Press, 2020), 145–46.

14. Career Connection, "Susumu 'shinsotsu gaikokujin saiyou' kahogona nihonjin yori 'hanguriina ajiajin'" ["Entry-level foreigner hiring" increases; "hungry Asians" over coddled Japanese], updated on April 23, 2014, https://careerconnection.jp/biz/economics/content_1375.html."

15. Akira Igarashi and Kikuko Nagayoshi, "Norms to Be Prejudiced: List Experiments on Attitudes Towards Immigrants in Japan," *Social Science Research* 102 (2022): 102647.

16. Gordon W. Allport, *The Nature of Prejudice* (Addison-Wesley, 1954); Thomas F. Pettigrew and Linda R. Tropp, "A Meta-Analytic Test of Intergroup Contact Theory," *Journal of Personality and Social Psychology* 90, no. 5 (2006): 751–83; Elizabeth Levy Paluck et al., "The Contact Hypothesis Re-Evaluated," *Behavioural Public Policy* 3, no. 2 (2019): 129–58. For recent experimental tests of the contact hypothesis, see Alexandra Scacco and Shana S. Warren, "Can Social Contact Reduce Prejudice and Discrimination? Evidence from a Field Experiment in Nigeria," *American Political Science Review* 112, no. 3 (2018): 654–77.

17. Thomas P. Rohlen, *For Harmony and Strength: Japanese White-Collar Organization in Anthropological Perspective* (University of California Press, 1974); Hiroshi Ono, "Careers in Foreign-Owned Firms in Japan," *American Sociological Review* 72, no. 2 (2007): 267–90.

18. Joseph G. Altonji and Charles R. Pierret, "Employer Learning and Statistical Discrimination," *Quarterly Journal of Economics* 116, no. 1 (2001): 313–50; Rachel S. Rubinstein et al., "Reliance on Individuating Information and Stereotypes in Implicit and Explicit Person Perception," *Journal of Experimental Social Psychology* 75 (2018): 54–70.

19. The Tokyo University professor who tweeted that his private company would not consider applications from Chinese on the grounds that "their performance is poor" is

a case in point. This tweet was roundly criticized: Negishi Takuro and Tomoko Yamashita, "'Chuugokujin saiyou shinai' tsuiito no toudai tokunin jun kyouju ga shazai" [Specially appointed associate professor at the University of Tokyo apologizes for tweeting, "We don't employ Chinese people"], *Asahi Shimbun*, December 2, 2019.

20. Fewer names are used for non-Japanese, because respondents viewed a maximum of two vignettes with non-Japanese names, to avoid as much as possible priming respondents to the true purpose of the study. Non-Japanese names were rendered in katakana script in the Japanese-language version of the survey. The gender of the employees was not specified in the Japanese-language version of the survey. In keeping with workplace norms, the survey refers to hypothetical employees by their last name, followed by the gender-neutral suffix -*san*. In cases in which gendered pronouns were necessary in the English and Mandarin versions of the survey, I used male pronouns.

21. I review results for Anglo-named vignettes in chapter 6.

22. Lawrence D. Bobo et al., "The Real Record on Racial Attitudes," in *Social Trends in American Life: Findings from the General Social Survey*, ed. Peter V. Marsden (Princeton University Press, 2012), 38–83.; David O. Sears and P. J. Henry, "Over Thirty Years Later: A Contemporary Look at Symbolic Racism," *Advances in Experimental Social Psychology* 37 (2005): 95–150; Lincoln Quillian, "New Approaches to Understanding Racial Prejudice and Discrimination," *Annual Review of Sociology* 32 (2006): 299–328; Kerwin Kofi Charles and Jonathan Guryan, "Prejudice and Wages: An Empirical Assessment of Becker's *The Economics of Discrimination*," *Journal of Political Economy* 116, no. 5 (2008): 773–809.

23. Ariela Schachter, "From 'Different' to 'Similar': An Experimental Approach to Understanding Assimilation," *American Sociological Review* 81, no. 5 (2016): 981–1013; Cheryl S. Alexander and Henry J. Becker, "The Use of Vignettes in Survey Research," *Public Opinion Quarterly* 42, no. 1 (1978): 93–104.

24. Kanji Yana and Menju Toshihiro, "Maido, 'hannin wa gaikokujinda' to sakebu 'hoshu' no hitotachi ni konkyo wa aru no ka" [Do "conservatives" have grounds to frequently shout "foreigners are criminals"?], *President Online*, updated May 29, 2020, https://president.jp/articles/-/35337?page=2.

25. Allport, *Nature of Prejudice*; Thomas F. Pettigrew, "Advancing Intergroup Contact Theory: Comments on the Issue's Articles," *Journal of Social Issues* 77, no. 1 (2021): 258–73.

26. Pettigrew and Tropp, "Meta-Analytic Test of Intergroup Contact Theory."

27. James Laurence et al., "The Dynamics of Immigration and Anti-Immigrant Sentiment in Japan: How and Why Changes in Immigrant Share Affect Attitudes Toward Immigration in a Newly Diversifying Society," *Social Forces* 101, no. 1 (2022): 369–403.

28. Kikuko Nagayoshi, "Whose Size Counts? Multilevel Analysis of Japanese Anti-Immigrant Attitudes Based on JGSS-2006," *JGSS Research Series* 9, no. 6 (2009): 157–74; David Green and Yoshihiko Kadoya, "Contact and Threat: Factors Affecting Views on Increasing Immigration in Japan," *Politics and Policy* 43, no. 1 (2015): 59–93; Laurence et al., "Dynamics of Immigration and Anti-Immigrant Sentiment in Japan."

29. Laurence et al., "Dynamics of Immigration and Anti-Immigrant Sentiment in Japan."

30. I do not calculate bias scores based on the tardiness vignette, because there is so little variation in responses, with only eight respondents in the entire sample recommending a harsh penalty.

31. Paluck et al., "Contact Hypothesis Re-Evaluated"; Alexander W. O'Donnell et al., "Technological and Analytical Advancements in Intergroup Contact Research," *Journal of Social Issues* 77, no. 1 (2021): 171–96.

32. On conversation partners, see Marco Marinucci et al., "Intimate Intergroup Contact Across the Lifespan," *Journal of Social Issues* 77, no. 1 (2021): 64–85. On roommates, see for a review Paluck et al., "Contact Hypothesis Re-Evaluated."

33. Timothy Yun Hui Tsu, "Japan's 'Yellow Peril': The Chinese in Imperial Japan and Colonial Korea," *Japanese Studies* 30, no. 2 (2010): 161–183; Lee, "Malcontent Koreans."

34. See the supplementary material for Laurence et al., "Dynamics of Immigration and Anti-Immigrant Sentiment in Japan."

35. Michèle Lamont and Mario Luis Small, "How Culture Matters: Enriching Our Understanding of Poverty," in *The Colors of Poverty: Why Racial and Ethnic Disparities Persist*, ed. Ann Chih Lin and David R. Harris (Russell Sage Foundation, 2008), 76–102.

36. Liu-Farrer, *Immigrant Japan*, 145.

6. BANKING ON THE GAIJIN CARD

1. This estimate includes 160,000 registered citizens of European countries, the United States, Canada, Australia, and New Zealand as well as an estimated 100,000 US military personnel, contractors, and their dependents, who reside in Japan under the Status of US Forces Agreement (SOFA), and who are not included in foreigner registrations statistics.

2. Jane H. Yamashiro, *Redefining Japaneseness: Japanese Americans in the Ancestral Homeland* (Rutgers University Press, 2017), 51; Eric Clemons, "Transcending National Identity: Foreign Employees and Organizational Management in Corporate Japan" (PhD diss., Colombia University, 1999), 34.

3. See Miloš Debnár, *Migration, Whiteness, and Cosmopolitanism: Europeans in Japan* (Palgrave Macmillan New York, 2016) for a statistical portrait of Europeans in Japan. Westerners in Japan include poorly paid teachers at private chain English-learning academies, sex workers from Eastern Europe, and members of the US military stationed in Japan, among others.

4. Koji Murata, "Gaikokujin no imeeji no kouzou: Chousa deeta ni motodsuku kousatsu" [The structure of perceptions of foreigners: An inquiry based on survey data], *Hitotsubashi daigaku gakuin shakaigaku kenkyuuka sentan kadai kenkyuu sousho* 2 (2006): 202–33.

5. Kazuko Suzuki, *Divided Fates: The State, Race, and Korean Immigrants' Adaptation in Japan and the United States* (Lexington, 2016), 88–89.

6. Yamashiro, *Redefining Japaneseness*, 51; Clemons, "Transcending National Identity," 34.

7. For migrants of European descent, see Gracia Liu-Farrer, *Immigrant Japan* (Cornell University Press, 2020), 148–49. On identifying themselves by nation of origin, Yamashiro, *Redefining Japaneseness*, 50–57.

8. Debnár, *Migration, Whiteness, and Cosmopolitanism*; Various Authors, "Do Western Men Have It Bad Here in Japan?" *Japan Times*, April 8, 2015, https://www.japantimes.co.jp/community/2015/04/08/voices/western-men-bad-japan-readers-discuss/.

9. On small benefits, see Debnár, *Migration, Whiteness, and Cosmopolitanism*, 116. On praise and attention for Western students, see Helena Hof and Yen-Fen Tseng, "When 'Global Talents' Struggle to Become Local Workers: The New Face of Skilled Migration to Corporate Japan," *Asian and Pacific Migration Journal* 29, no. 4 (December 2020): 511–31. On playing the *gaijin* card, see Liu-Farrer, *Immigrant Japan*, 99; Debnár, *Migration, Whiteness, and Cosmopolitanism*, 117.

10. Debnár, *Migration, Whiteness, and Cosmopolitanism*, 147–51.

11. Edwin O. Reischauer, *The Japanese Today: Change and Continuity* (Belknap, 1988), 400.

12. Hiroshi Wagatsuma, "The Social Perception of Skin Color in Japan," *Daedalus* 96, no. 2 (1967): 421.

13. Debnár, *Migration, Whiteness, and Cosmopolitanism*, 153–54, 117.

14. David L. McConnell, *Importing Diversity: Inside Japan's JET Program* (University of California Press, 2000), 16–19.

15. McConnell, *Importing Diversity*, 21–24, 31–35; Toru Umakoshi, "Internationalization of Japanese Higher Education in the 1980's and Early 1990's," *Higher Education* 34 (1997): 265–66.

16. Ha-Joon Chang, "Globalization, Global Standards, and the Future of East Asia," *Global Economic Review* 34, no. 4 (2005): 363–78; Mitsuru Mizuno, "Institutional Investors, Corporate Governance and Firm Performance in Japan," *Pacific Economic Review* 15, no. 5 (2010): 653–65.

17. Steven K. Vogel, "Japan's Labor Regime in Transition: Rethinking Work for a Shrinking Nation," *Journal of Japanese Studies* 44, no. 2 (2018): 263.

18. Cabinet Office, "Seichouryoku kyouka ni mukete kigyou no sekkyokutekina koudou o unagasu shikumi" [Initiatives to encourage companies to proactively strengthen growth potential], updated 2016, https://www5.cao.go.jp/j-j/wp/wp-je16/h03-02.html.

19. Robert M. March, *Working for a Japanese Company* (Kodansha International, 1992), 112–13, 120–21, 132.

20. Clemons, "Transcending National Identity," 6.

21. Clemons, "Transcending National Identity," 186.

22. Helena Hof, "Intersections of Race and Skills in European Migration to Asia: Between White Cultural Capital and 'Passive Whiteness,'" *Ethnic and Racial Studies* 44, no. 11 (2021): 2128.

23. Hof and Tseng, "When 'Global Talents' Struggle to Become Local Workers," 526.

24. On lucrative expatriate contracts, see Hof, "Intersections of Race and Skills." On racialized occupations, see Debnár, *Migration, Whiteness, and Cosmopolitanism*, 120–26.

25. Debnár, *Migration, Whiteness, and Cosmopolitanism*, 160–63.

26. Doug Struck, "In Japan, U.S. Expat Fights the Yankee Way," *Washington Post*, July 5, 2003.

27. On employment under indefinite contracts, see Debito Arudou, *Embedded Racism: Japan's Visible Minorities and Racial Discrimination* (Lexington, 2015). On promotion to upper-level management, see Clemons, "Transcending National Identity," 66.

28. Akira Igarashi and Ryota Mugiyama, "Whose Tastes Matter? Discrimination Against Immigrants in the Japanese Labour Market," *Journal of Ethnic and Migration Studies* 49, no. 13 (2023): 3365–388.

29. Ministry of Justice, "Gaikokujin juumin chousa houkokusho" [Foreign resident survey report], updated June 1, 2017, https://www.moj.go.jp/content/001226182.pdf, 32.

30. Igarashi and Mugiyama, "Whose Tastes Matter?," 3365–388.

31. Helena Hof, "'Worklife Pathways' to Singapore and Japan: Gender and Racial Dynamics in Europeans' Mobility to Asia," *Social Science Japan Journal* 21, no. 1 (2018): 45–65; Debnár, *Migration, Whiteness, and Cosmopolitanism*, 127–34.

32. Hof and Tseng, "When 'Global Talents' Struggle to Become Local Workers," 526. Caucasian immigrants to Japan vary in their reaction to these "small benefits": although some relish feeling "special" and "important," for others the attention feels oppressive; see Liu-Farrer, *Immigrant Japan*, 148–49.

33. Ministry of Justice, "Kokuseki chiiki betsu zairyuu shikaku (zairyuumokuteki) betsu zairyuu gaikokujin" [Foreign residents by nationality/region, status of residence], updated December 11, 2020, https://www.e-stat.go.jp/stat-search/files?page=1&layout =datalist&toukei=00250012&tstat=000001018034&cycle=1&year=20200&month =12040606&tclass1=000001060399.

34. In addition to English fluency, three Western men also reported fluency in various Asian languages, suggesting possible Asian ethnoracial background.

35. Hof, "Intersections of Race and Skills," 2128.

36. The list of skills includes four listening and speaking tasks: opening a bank account, understanding the jokes in a television comedy show, conducting business negotiations, and debating politics or economics. It also includes three reading and writing tasks: writing a business letter, reading the newspaper, and reading a novel.

37. I have changed a few details of Hugo's biography to make him less identifiable.

38. Debnár, *Migration, Whiteness, and Cosmopolitanism*, 152–55.

39. Other scholars previously reported on this awareness of "specialness" among Western (especially white) migrants to Japan, although these reports have focused on social life rather than the workplace. See, for example, Debnár, *Migration, Whiteness, and Cosmopolitanism*, 116; Liu-Farrer, *Immigrant Japan*, 99.

40. Hof and Tseng, "When 'Global Talents' Struggle to Become Local Workers."

41. When workers move across borders, questions of what is "fair" can become complicated. For example, workers who come from Western countries may be unable to travel home to see their families without longer vacation periods (e.g., a week or two), whereas for Japanese employees or employees from nearby Asian countries, the norm of short vacations does not preclude seeing their families. Because Japanese firms are usually characterized as rigid in enforcing employment rules and norms, the special accommodations they offer Western men are noteworthy, whether or not they are "fair."

42. Hof and Tseng, "When 'Global Talents' Struggle to Become Local Workers," 526; Clemons, "Transcending National Identity."

43. Roppongi is a wealthy Tokyo neighborhood, home to both a notorious bar scene and many Western residents.

44. I have modified this quote to match the changes I have made to Hugo's biography, but the sense remains the same.

45. Three of the Western male respondents speak an Asian language fluently, suggesting they may have an Asian ethnic background. The magnitude of Western male advantages increases when these respondents are excluded from the analysis. This suggests that at least a portion of the Western advantage may be a white, or perhaps non-Asian, advantage.

46. Compare 16 percent of Western men with 15 percent of Asian women.

47. Hiroshi Ono, "Careers in Foreign-Owned Firms in Japan," *American Sociological Review* 72, no. 2 (April 1, 2007): 267–90.

48. It is possible to interpret the generous treatment for Western men in the cost-savings vignette as representing greater perceived deservingness, but an alternative is that Japanese (and other Asians) set the mental bar for Western men's success lower. This alternative interpretation is consistent with willingness to hire Western men even when their Japanese skills are relatively poor. The "lower bar" mentality, however, can still generate economic advantage for Western men in elite firms, even as it implies a less comfortable social reception.

49. Asian men fall in between, but on average, they are far more similar to Japanese men.

50. Respondents were instructed to choose fluent native only if they grew up speaking a language, and it is their strongest language for reading, writing, and speaking.

51. Hof, "Intersections of Race and Skills," 2128.

52. Špela Drnovšek Zorko and Miloš Debnár, "Comparing the Racialization of Central-East European Migrants in Japan and the UK," *Comparative Migration Studies* 9, no. 30 (2021); Adrijana Miladinović, "The Influence of Whiteness on Social and

Professional Integration: The Case of Highly Skilled Europeans in Japan," *Journal of Contemporary Eastern Asia* 19, no. 2 (2019): 84–103; Hof, "Intersections of Race and Skills."

53. Hof, "Intersections of Race and Skills"; Hof and Tseng, "When 'Global Talents' Struggle to Become Local Workers."

54. See Debnár, *Migration, Whiteness, and Cosmopolitanism*, 155–70, for an exploration of these factors. Naturalized Japanese citizen Debito Arudou, a white man originally from the United States, has directed particular attention to these issues of exclusion, drawing parallels between Caucasian (and other "visible minorities"') exclusion in Japan, Jim Crow in the United States, and apartheid in South Africa. These parallels are inapt for many reasons, including the history of foreign relations in Japan and the West, wherein Japan has struggled to be treated on equal terms with Western powers; the privileged economic position of many, although certainly not all, white and Western residents of Japan both historically and in the present; and, not least, the positive and aspirational attitudes toward Western and white men that these macrostructural conditions have fostered. For a discussion of the historical background of white supremacy in Japan, see Eiji Oguma, *A Genealogy of Japanese Self-Images* (Trans Pacific, 2002); W. Puck Brecher, *Honored and Dishonored Guests: Westerners in Wartime Japan* (Harvard University Asia Center, 2017); Tessa Morris-Suzuki, *Borderline Japan: Foreigners and Frontier Controls in the Postwar Era* (Cambridge University Press, 2010).

CONCLUSION

1. Emiko Jozuka and Junko Ogura, "Can Japan Survive Without Immigrants?," CNN.com, June 14, 2018; Chris Burgess, "Japan's 'No Immigration Principle' Looking as Solid as Ever," *Japan Times*, June 18, 2014.

2. Yu Korekawa, "Shingata korona pandemikku wa guroubaruna hito no idou no nagare wo kaeta no ka?" [Did the novel coronavirus pandemic change global flows of people?], IPSS Working Paper Series, no. 36 (January 2021).

3. Hounichi Rabo, "Nihon no 'kaikoku' he no ayumi wo jikeirei de furikaeru: Mizugiwa taisaku—ouhaba kanwa made" [A timeline of Japan's progress toward opening: From border control to large scale relaxation], *Hounichi Rabo*, updated December 29, 2022, https://honichi.com/news/2022/12/29/covidtimeline.

4. Eric Margolis, "Japan's Foreign Workers Face a New Post-COVID Landscape," *Japan Times*, updated September 5, 2022, https://www.japantimes.co.jp/news/2022/09/05/national/social-issues/foreign-workers-japan-covid19; Leo Lewis, "Japan's Immigration Experiment Under the Cover of COVID," *Financial Times*, updated January 29, 2022, https://www.ft.com/content/74bfd3fb-6987-4618-91a8-7e2c8f876fd6.

5. Erin Aeran Chung, "The Side Doors of Immigration: Multi-Tier Migration Regimes in Japan and South Korea," *Third World Quarterly* 43, no. 7 (2022): 1570–86.

6. Japan Institute for Labor Policy and Training, "Koyou keitai betsu koyoushasuu" [Number of employees by employment type], updated March 30, 2023, https://www.jil.go.jp/kokunai/statistics/timeseries/html/g0208.html. Women's participation in irregular work also increased, but at a slower pace; between 2013 and 2022, the irregular female labor force grew by 1.3 million.

7. World Bank, "Labor Force Participation Rate, Female (% of Female Population Ages 15–64)," updated April 25, 2023, https://data.worldbank.org/indicator/SL.TLF.ACTI.FE.ZS?locations=JP-US-DE-GB-FR-AU-KR.

8. On leadership and management roles, see UN News, "Japanese Leader Advocates 'Womenomics' in Address to UN General Assembly," United Nations, updated September 26, 2013, https://news.un.org/en/story/2013/09/450912. On wage replacement for

parental leave, see Ministry of Health, Labor and Welfare, "Ikuji kyuugyou kyuufu kankei" [Materials on parental leave payments], updated January 26, 2021, https://www.mhlw.go.jp/content/11601000/000728126.pdf 5. On the ratio of female-to-male wages, see Josei no katsuyou suishin kigyou deetabeesu, "Hon saito gaiyou" [Overview of this website], Ministry of Health, Labor and Welfare, updated 2023, https://positive-ryouritsu.mhlw.go.jp/positivedb/about.html. On the public daycare system, see Nippon.com, "Japan Sees 90 Percent Drop in Daycare Waiting Lists over the Last Five Years," updated September 14, 2022, https://www.nippon.com/en/japan-data/h01428. On a cap on overtime work hours, see Ministry of Health, Labor and Welfare, "Jikangai roudou no jougen kisei no tekiyou yuuyo jigyou gyoumu" [Businesses and occupations exempt from limits on overtime work], updated 2023, https://www.mhlw.go.jp/stf/seisakunitsuite/bunya/koyou_roudou/roudoukijun/gyosyu/topics/01.html. On per capita spending on children, Kyodo News, "Japan to Boost Child Care Spending to Match Sweden," updated June 1, 2023, https://english.kyodonews.net/news/2023/06/527c2e8ba284-japan-to-boost-child-care-spending-to-match-sweden.html.

9. Gill Steel, "Introduction: Changing Women's and Men's Lives in Japan," in *Beyond the Gender Gap in Japan*, ed. Gill Steel (University of Michigan Press, 2019), 8.

10. Mary C. Brinton, *Women and the Economic Miracle: Gender and Work in Postwar Japan.* University of California Press, 1993; Kumiko Nemoto, *Too Few Women at the Top: The Persistence of Inequality in Japan* (Cornell University Press, 2016); Chizuko Ueno, "Why Do Japanese Women Suffer from the Low Status? The Impact of Neo-Liberalist Reform on Gender," *Japanese Political Economy* 47, no. 1 (2021): 9–26; Eunmi Mun and Mary C. Brinton, "Workplace Matters: The Use of Parental Leave Policy in Japan," *Work and Occupations* 42, no. 3 (March 2015): 355–69.

11. Helena Hof, "Intersections of Race and Skills in European Migration to Asia: Between White Cultural Capital and 'Passive Whiteness,'" *Ethnic and Racial Studies* 44, no. 11 (2021): 2113–134, 2128; Miloš Debnár, *Migration, Whiteness, and Cosmopolitanism: Europeans in Japan* (Palgrave Macmillan New York, 2016), 157; Harald Conrad and Hendrik Meyer-Ohle, "Training Regimes and Diversity: Experiences of Young Foreign Employees in Japanese Headquarters," *Work, Employment and Society* 36, no. 2 (2020): 1–18; Yen-Fen Tseng, "Becoming Global Talent? Taiwanese White-Collar Migrants in Japan," *Journal of Ethnic and Migration Studies* 47, no. 10 (2021): 2299.

12. Michèle Lamont and Virág Molnár, "The Study of Boundaries in the Social Sciences," *Annual Review of Sociology* 28 (2002): 167–95.

13. Cecilia L. Ridgeway, *Status: Why Is It Everywhere? Why Does It Matter?* (Russell Sage Foundation, 2019); Cecilia L. Ridgeway and Hazel Rose Markus, "The Significance of Status: What It Is and How It Shapes Inequality," *RSF: The Russell Sage Foundation Journal of the Social Sciences* 8, no. 7 (2022): 1–25. We see this clearly in the case of Japanese firms, in which men are believed to be better at highly valued skills of negotiation, leadership, and logical thinking, whereas women excel in more undervalued areas, such as attention to detail, pleasant manners, and nurturing.

14. Philip N. Cohen and Matt L. Huffman, "Working for the Woman? Female Managers and the Gender Wage Gap," *American Sociological Review* 72, no. 5 (2007): 700; Matt L. Huffman et al., "Engendering Change: Organizational Dynamics and Workplace Gender Desegregation, 1975–2005," *Administrative Science Quarterly* 55, no. 2 (2010): 255–77, 273; Nemoto, *Too Few Women at the Top*; Andrea S. Kramer and Alton B Harris, *It's Not You, It's the Workplace: Women's Conflict at Work and the Bias That Built It* (Nicholas Brealy, 2019); Safi Shams and Donald Tomaskovic-Devey, "Racial and Gender Trends and Trajectories in Access to Managerial Jobs," *Social Science Research* 80 (2019): 15–29.

15. Yu Korekawa, "Determinants of Foreign Workers' Wages in Japan: An Analysis Focusing on Wage Gaps with Japanese," *IPSS Working Paper Series* 67 (2023).

16. Ministry of Health, Labor and Welfare, "Reiwa 2nen chingin kouzou kihon toukei chousa no gaikyou" [Overview of the 2020 basic survey on wage structure], updated May 13, 2021, https://www.mhlw.go.jp/toukei/itiran/roudou/chingin/kouzou/z2020/dl/04.pdf.

17. Korekawa, "Determinants of Foreign Workers' Wages in Japan," table 6, model 3.

18. Harumi Befu, *Hegemony of Homogeneity: An Anthropological Analysis of Nihonjinron* (Trans Pacific, 2001).

19. Gracia Liu-Farrer, *Immigrant Japan* (Cornell University Press, 2020).

20. Associated Press, "Tokyo Olympics Reignites Ugly 'Pure Japanese', Racial Identity Debate," Wide World of Sports, updated August 5, 2021, https://wwos.nine.com.au/olympics/tokyo-olympics-2021-reignites-ugly-pure-japanese-identity-debate/79d4d4ad-6866-456b-b632-90ffd6647a7b; Jake Adelstein, "Japan Needs 'Foreigner Blood' Like Naomi Osaka's," *Daily Beast*, updated September 17, 2018, https://www.thedailybeast.com/japan-needs-foreigner-blood-like-naomi-osakas.

21. Pascale Hatcher and Aya Murakami, "The Politics of Exclusion: Embedded Racism and Japan's Pilot Refugee Resettlement Programme," *Race and Class* 62, no. 1 (2020): 60–77; Liang Morita, "Some Manifestations of Japanese Exclusionism," *SAGE Open* 5, no. 3 (2015): 1–6.

22. Erin A. Chung, *Immigrant Incorporation in East Asian Democracies* (Cambridge University Press, 2020), 104–11; Apichai W. Shipper, *Fighting for Foreigners: Immigration and Its Impact on Japanese Democracy* (Cornell University Press, 2008), 25; Hilary J. Holbrow and Kikuko Nagayoshi, "Economic Integration of Skilled Migrants in Japan: The Role of Employment Practices," *International Migration Review* 52, no. 2 (2018): 458–86.

23. Some rare exceptions include Kenji Ishida, "Nihon ni okeru imin no chii tassei kouzou" [Structure of immigrants' status attainment in Japan], in *Jinkou mondai to imin*, ed. Hiroshi Komai and Yu Korekawa (Akashi Shoten, 2019), 92–113; Yu Korekawa, *Imin ukeire to shakaiteki tougou no riariti* [The reality of immigration and social integration] (Keisou Shobou, 2019); Kikuko Nagayoshi and Hirohisa Takenoshita, "Imin no kyouiku tassei to chingin" [Immigrants' educational attainment and earnings], in *Nihon no imin tougou: Zenkoku chousa kara miru genjou to shouheki*, ed. Kikuko Nagayoshi (Akashi Shoten, 2021), 88–110; Tristan Ivory et al., "Insider Out: Cross-National Differences in Foreign-Born Female Labor Force Participation in the United States, Sweden, and Japan," *International Migration Review* (2023): 1–30.

24. Kikuko Nagayoshi, "Imin no tougou wo kangaeru" [Thoughts on immigrant integration], in *Nihon no imin tougou: Zenkoku chousa kara miru genjou to shouheki*, ed. Kikuko Nagayoshi (Akashi Shoten, 2021), 6. This is slowly changing, however. See Korekawa, "Determinants of Foreign Workers' Wages in Japan," for a recent exception.

25. For example, Hirohisa Takenoshita, "The Differential Incorporation into Japanese Labor Market: A Comparative Study of Japanese Brazilians and Professional Chinese Migrants," *Japanese Journal of Population* 4, no. 1 (2006): 56–77; Yuko Tsukasaki, *Gaikokujin senmonshoku gijutsushoku no koyou mondai: shokugyou kyaria no shiten kara* [Employment problems of professional and technical foreign workers: from the perspective of occupations and careers] (Akashi Shoten, 2008); Liu-Farrer, *Immigrant Japan*; Chung, *Immigrant Incorporation*; Holbrow and Nagayoshi, "Economic Integration of Skilled Migrants in Japan."

26. Galen Gruman, "Tech Wages: Women, Minorities Still Paid Less in 2020," Computerworld, updated May 21, 2021, https://www.computerworld.com/article/3619891

/tech-wages-women-minorities-still-paid-less-in-2020.html; Emilio J. Castilla, "Gender, Race, and Meritocracy in Organizational Careers," *American Journal of Sociology* 113, no. 6 (May 2008): 1479–526.

27. Chung, *Immigrant Incorporation*, 104–11; Shipper, *Fighting for Foreigners*, 25.

28. John Lie, "The Persistence of Monoethnic Ideology in Multiethnic Japan," in *Globalization and Civil Society in East Asian Space*, ed. Khatharya Um and Chiharu Takenaka (Routledge, 2022), 102.

29. John W. Cheng and Nicholas Fraser, "Japanese Newspaper Portrayals of Refugees: A Frame Analysis from 1985 to 2017," *Journal of Refugee Studies* 35, no. 3 (September 2022), 1364–85.

30. Hilary J. Holbrow, "'Training' Foreign Workers, Cultivating Bias? TITP and Immigration to Japan," in *No Island is an Island: Perspectives on Immigration to Japan*, ed. Michael Strausz (University of Hawaii Press, 2025), 109–30; Hilary J. Holbrow and Qiaoyan Li Rosenberg, "Japan Has to Do More for Migrant Rights Than Drop 'Intern' Label," *Nikkei Asia*, March 1, 2024.

31. Yunchen Tian, "Workers by Any Other Name: Comparing Co-Ethnics and 'Interns' as Labour Migrants to Japan," *Journal of Ethnic and Migration Studies* 45, no. 9 (2019): 1496–514.

32. Jane H. Yamashiro, *Redefining Japaneseness: Japanese Americans in the Ancestral Homeland* (Rutgers University Press, 2017); Takeyuki Tsuda, "Racism Without Racial Difference? Co-Ethnic Racism and National Hierarchies Among Nikkeijin Ethnic Return Migrants in Japan," *Ethnic and Racial Studies* 45, no. 4 (2022): 595–615.

33. Tokyo Bengoshikai Gaikokujin no Kenri ni Kansuru Iinkai, "2021nendo gaikoku ni ruutsu wo motsu hito ni taisuru shokumu shitsumon (reisharu purofairingu) ni kansuru ankeeto chousa shaishuu houkokusho" [Final report on the 2021 survey on police questioning of persons with roots in foreign countries (racial profiling)], updated September 19, 2022, https://www.toben.or.jp/know/iinkai/foreigner/26a6af6c6f033511c ccf887e39fb794e_2.pdf, 14–19.

34. Tokyo Bengoshikai Gaikokujin no Kenri ni Kansuru Iinkai, "2021nendo gaikoku ni ruutsu wo motsu hito ni taisuru shokumu shitsumon (reisharu purofairingu) ni kansuru ankeeto chousa shaishuu houkokusho," 15.

35. Everett C. Hughes, *Dilemmas and Contradictions of Status* (Bobbs-Merrill, 1945).

36. World Economic Forum, *Global Gender Gap Report 2023*, updated July 11, 2023, https://www3.weforum.org/docs/WEF_GGGR_2021.pdf.

37. The fact that Japan has never had a woman prime minister, for example, weighs heavily against it in the rankings; in some of the submetrics of the Gender Gap Index, such as education and health, Japan scores very well in international comparison, but its ratings in politics and the economy sink its overall score.

38. Claudia Goldin, *Career and Family: Women's Century-Long Journey Toward Equity* (Princeton University Press, 2021), 9.

39. Michael Strausz, *Help (Not) Wanted: Immigration Politics in Japan* (SUNY Press, 2019).

40. Ministry of Internal Affairs and Communications, "Nenrei (5sai kaikyuu oyobi 3kubun), danjo betsu jinkou (kakunen 10gatsu 1tachi genzai)—soujinkou 2000nen-2020nen" [Total population by age-group (5-year and 3-category) and sex (as of October 1 annually), 2000–2020]. Updated June 28, 2022. https://www.e-stat.go.jp/stat-search /files?layout=datalist&cycle=0&toukei=00200524&tstat=000000090001&tclass1=0000 00090004&tclass2=000001051180&tclass3val=0&stat_infid=000013168603; Ministry of Internal Affairs and Communications, "Nenrei (5sai kaikyuu oyobi 3kubun), danjo betsu jinkou (kakunen 10gatsu 1tachi genzai)—soujinkou taishou 9nen—heisei 12nen"

[Total population by age-group (5-year and 3-category) and sex (as of October 1 annually), 1920–2000]. Updated January 30, 2018. https://www.e-stat.go.jp/stat-search/files?page=1&layout=datalist&cycle=0&toukei=00200524&tstat=000000090001&tclass1=000000090004&tclass2=000000090005&cycle_facet=tclass1%3Atclass2&tclass3val=0&stat_infid=000000090263; National Institute of Population and Social Security Research, "Nihon no shourai suikei jinkou (Reiwa 5nen suikei)" [Japan's future estimated population (2023 estimate)]. Updated March 7, 2023. https://www.ipss.go.jp/pp-zenkoku/j/zenkoku2023/db_zenkoku2023/db_zenkoku2023syosaikekka.html.

41. Nemoto, *Too Few Women at the Top.*

42. Eunmi Mun and Jiwook Jung, "Change Above the Glass Ceiling: Corporate Social Responsibility and Gender Diversity in Japanese Firms," *Administrative Science Quarterly* 63, no. 2 (June 2018): 409–40.

43. Japan Institute for Labor Policy and Training, "Shokugyou betsu shuugyousha-suu" [Number of workers by occupation]. Updated May 16, 2023. https://www.jil.go.jp/kokunai/statistics/chart/html/g0006.html.

44. Kevin T. Leicht, "Inequality and the Status Window: Inequality, Conflict, and the Salience of Status Differences in Conflicts over Resources," *RSF: The Russell Sage Foundation Journal of the Social Sciences* 8, no. 6 (2022): 103–21.

45. Ayaka Beniyama, "Barriers to 'Equal Pay for Work of Equal Value' for Women in Japan: Assessing the Potential for Change," *Journal of Industrial Relations* 62, no. 4 (2020): 630–50; Charles Weathers et al., "Litigating Equal Pay for Equal Work in Japan, 2012–2020," *Journal of Contemporary Asia* 54, no. 3 (2023): : 432–52.

46. Megan L. Starich, "The 2006 Revisions to Japan's Equal Opportunity Employment Law: A Narrow Approach to a Pervasive Problem," *Pacific Rim Law and Policy Journal* 16, no. 2 (2007): 551–78; Eunmi Mun, "Negative Compliance as an Organizational Response to Legal Pressures: The Case of Japanese Equal Employment Opportunity Law," *Social Forces* 94, no. 4 (June 2016): 1409–37.

47. Daisuke Wakisaka, "Unraveling Migration Policy-Making in the Land of 'No Immigrants': Japanese Bureaucracy and the Discursive Gap," *International Migration Review* 58, no. 3 (2023): 1507–31.

48. Martin Gelin, "Japan Radically Increased Immigration—and No One Protested," *Foreign Policy*, updated June 23, 2020, https://foreignpolicy.com/2020/06/23/japan-immigration-policy-xenophobia-migration.

49. Ministry of Foreign Affairs, "Procedures Required Before Working as an SSW," updated 2023, https://www.mofa.go.jp/mofaj/ca/fna/ssw/us/introduction; Qiaoyan Li Rosenberg, "A Semi-Skilled Guest Worker Regime: Specified Skilled Workers (SSW) in Japan" (panel presentation, American Sociological Association Annual Meeting, Philadelphia, PA, August 19, 2023).

50. Ministry of Justice, "Kokuseki chiiki betsu tokutei sangyou bunya betsu tokutei ginou 1gou zairyuu gaikokujinsuu" [Foreign residents on the SSW1 visa by nationality/region and designated industry], updated February 6, 2023, https://www.moj.go.jp/isa/content/001389886.xlsx; Ministry of Justice, "(Zenbunya) kokuseki chiiki shiken ruuto ginoujisshuu ruuto betsu tokutei ginou 1gou zairyuu gaikokujinsuu" [Foreign residents on the SSW1 visa by nationality/region and exam route/TITP entry route (all fields)], updated February 6, 2023, https://www.moj.go.jp/isa/content/001389889.xlsx.

51. Holbrow and Rosenberg, "Japan Has to Do More for Migrant Rights Than Drop 'Intern' Label."

52. Qiaoyan Li Rosenberg, "Labor-for-Citizenship Exchange in Japan: A Three-Step Pathway to Permanent Residence, and Precarious Labor for All" (unpublished manuscript, February 12, 2024).

53. Ministry of Justice, "Kokuseki chiiki betsu tokutei sangyou bunya betsu tokutei ginou 2gou zairyuu gaikokujinsuu," [Foreign residents on the SSW2 visa by nationality /region and designated industry], updated February 6, 2023. https://www.moj.go.jp /isa/content/001389892.xlsx.

54. For Taiwan and South Korea, see National Immigration Agency, "2023.1 Foreign Residents by Nationality," updated March 1, 2023, https://www.immigration.gov.tw/media /90897/20231foreign-residents-by-nationality.xls; Suk-yee Jung, "2022 Census Shows South Korea's Population Contracted for 2 Years Running," *Business Korea*, updated July 28, 2023, http://www.businesskorea.co.kr/news/articleView.html?idxno=119343. For Japan, see Mari Yamaguchi, "Japan Records Steepest Population Decline While Number of Foreign Residents Hits New High," *AP News*, updated July 26, 2023, https://apnews.com /article/japan-population-decline-foreign-low-births-d047ea6136a5c66ffc45508cb824d5f1.

55. Pei-Chia Lan, "Contested Skills and Constrained Mobilities: Migrant Carework Skill Regimes in Taiwan and Japan," *Comparative Migration Studies* 10, no. 1 (September 2022).

56. Seong Hyeon Choi, "South Korea Wants Southeast Asian Domestic Workers to Support Families. But Are They Welcome?," *South China Morning Post*, updated May 21, 2023,https://www.scmp.com/week-asia/people/article/3221195/south-korea-wants -southeast-asian-domestic-workers-support-families-are-they-welcome.

APPENDIX A: VIGNETTE METHODOLOGY

1. Because respondents viewed, at most, one negative and one positive vignette with a non-Japanese name, I used the same non-Japanese names across the tardiness and records falsification vignettes and used the same non-Japanese names across the helping and saving vignettes. To avoid the same name appearing twice for one respondent, I used different Japanese names in each of the four vignettes.

Bibliography

Achenbach, Ruth. "'Having It All'—At What Cost? Strategies of Chinese Highly Skilled Women in Japan to Combine Career and Family." *Contemporary Japan* 26, no. 2 (2014): 223–43. https://doi.org/10.1515/cj-2014-0011.

Adelstein, Jake. "Japan Needs 'Foreigner Blood' Like Naomi Osaka's." Daily Beast. Updated September 17, 2018. https://www.thedailybeast.com/japan-needs-foreigner-blood -like-naomi-osakas.

Ahmadjian, Christina L., and Patricia Robinson. "Safety in Numbers: Downsizing and the Deinstitutionalization of Permanent Employment in Japan." *Administrative Science Quarterly* 46, no. 4 (2001): 622–54. https://doi.org/10.2307/3094826.

Alba, Richard. *Blurring the Color Line: The New Chance for a More Integrated America.* Harvard University Press, 2009.

Alba, Richard, and Victor Nee. *Remaking the American Mainstream: Assimilation and Contemporary Immigration.* Harvard University Press, 2003.

Alegria, Sharla. "Escalator or Step Stool? Gendered Labor and Token Processes in Tech Work." *Gender and Society* 33, no. 5 (2019): 722–45. https://doi.org/10.1177 /0891243219835737.

Alexander, Cheryl S., and Henry J. Becker. "The Use of Vignettes in Survey Research." *Public Opinion Quarterly* 42, no. 1 (1978): 93–104. https://doi.org/10.1086/268432.

Allison, Anne. "From Lifelong to Liquid Japan." In *Japan: The Precarious Future,* edited by Frank Baldwin and Anne Allison, 21–42. Duke University Press, 2013. https:// doi.org/10.1515/9780822377245-003.

Allison, Anne. *Precarious Japan.* Duke University Press, 2013.

Allport, Gordon W. *The Nature of Prejudice.* Addison-Wesley, 1954.

Altonji, Joseph G., and Charles R. Pierret. "Employer Learning and Statistical Discrimination." *Quarterly Journal of Economics* 116, no. 1 (2001): 313–50. https://doi .org/10.1162/003355301556329.

American Association of University Women. "The Motherhood Penalty." Updated September 1, 2022. https://www.aauw.org/issues/equity/motherhood.

Arudou, Debito. *Embedded Racism: Japan's Visible Minorities and Racial Discrimination.* Lexington, 2015.

Arudou, Debito. "Japan's Under-Researched Visible Minorities: Applying Critical Race Theory to Racialization Dynamics in a Non-White Society." *Washington University Global Studies Law Review* 14, no. 4 (2015): 695–723. https://openscholarship .wustl.edu/cgi/viewcontent.cgi?article=1552&context=law_globalstudies.

Assmann, Stephanie. "Gender Equality in Japan: The Equal Employment Opportunity Law Revisited." *Asia-Pacific Journal: Japan Focus* 12, no. 45 (November 2014): 1–23. https://apjjf.org/2014/12/45/Stephanie-Assmann/4211.html.

Associated Press. "Tokyo Olympics Reignites Ugly 'Pure Japanese,' Racial Identity Debate." Wide World of Sports. Updated August 5, 2021. https://wwos.nine.com .au/olympics/tokyo-olympics-2021-reignites-ugly-pure-japanese-identity-debate /79d4d4ad-6866-456b-b632-90ffd6647a7b.

Avent-Holt, Dustin, Lasse Folke Henriksen, Anna Erika Hägglund, Jiwook Jung, Naomi Kodama, Silvia Maja Melzer, Eunmi Mun, Anthony Rainey, and Donald

Tomaskovic-Devey. "Occupations, Workplaces or Jobs? An Exploration of Stratification Contexts Using Administrative Data." *Research in Social Stratification
and Mobility* 70 (June 2020): 100456. https://doi.org/10.1016/j.rssm.2019.100456.

Baron, James N., and William T. Bielby. "Bringing the Firms Back In: Stratification,
Segmentation, and the Organization of Work." *American Sociological Review* 45,
no. 5 (1980): 737–65. https://doi.org/10.2307/2094893.

Baudinette, Thomas. "Ethnosexual Frontiers in Queer Tokyo: The Production of
Racialised Desire in Japan." *Japan Forum* 28, no. 4 (2016): 465–85. https://doi.org
/10.1080/09555803.2016.1165723.

Becker, Gary S. *The Economics of Discrimination*. University of Chicago Press, 1957.

Befu, Harumi. *Hegemony of Homogeneity: An Anthropological Analysis of Nihonjinron*.
Trans Pacific, 2001.

Beniyama, Ayaka. "Barriers to 'Equal Pay for Work of Equal Value' for Women in Japan:
Assessing the Potential for Change." *Journal of Industrial Relations* 62, no. 4
(2020): 630–50. https://doi.org/10.1177/0022185620927721.

Bevelander, Pieter, and Nahikari Irastorza. "Catching Up: The Labor Market Integration of New Immigrants in Sweden." *Migration Policy Institute* (2014): 1–23.
https://www.migrationpolicy.org/research/catching-labor-market-outcomes
-new-immigrants-sweden.

Beyer, Robert C. M. "The Labor Market Performance of Immigrants in Germany." IMF
Working Papers (2016): 1–39. https://doi.org/10.5089/9781498376112.001.

Bird, Allan, and May Mukuda. "Expatriates in Their Own Home: A New Twist in the
Human Resource Management Strategies of Japanese MNCs." *Human Resource
Management* 28, no. 4 (1989): 437–53. https://doi.org/10.1002/hrm.3930280402.

Bobo, Lawrence D., Camille Z. Charles, Maria Krysan, and Alicia Simmons. "The Real
Record on Racial Attitudes." In *Social Trends in American Life: Findings from the
General Social Survey*, edited by Peter V. Marsden, 38–83. Princeton University
Press, 2012.

Brecher, W. Puck, *Honored and Dishonored Guests: Westerners in Wartime Japan*. Harvard University Asia Center, 2017.

Brinton, Mary C. *Women and the Economic Miracle: Gender and Work in Postwar
Japan*. University of California Press, 1993.

Brinton, Mary C., and Eunmi Mun. "Between State and Family: Managers' Implementation and Evaluation of Parental Leave Policies in Japan." *Socio-Economic
Review* 14, no. 2 (2016): 257–81. https://doi.org/10.1093/ser/mwv021.

Burgess, Chris. "Japan's 'No Immigration Principle' Looking as Solid as Ever." *Japan
Times*. Updated June 18, 2014. https://www.japantimes.co.jp/community/2014/06
/18/voices/japans-immigration-principle-looking-solid-ever.

Cabinet Office. "Kigyou no gaikokujin koyou ni kansuru bunseki" [Analysis of companies' employment of foreigners]. Updated September 2019. https://www5.cao
.go.jp/keizai3/2019/09seisakukadai18-6.

Cabinet Office. "Seichouryoku kyouka ni mukete kigyou no sekkyokutekina koudou o
unagasu shikumi" [Initiatives to encourage companies to proactively strengthen
growth potential]. Updated 2016. https://www5.cao.go.jp/j-j/wp/wp-je16/h03
-02.html.

Cabinet Secretariat. "Josei katsuyaku danjo kyoudou sankaku no juuten houshin 2022"
[Major policies on gender equality and women's empowerment 2022]. Updated
June 3, 2022. https://www.gender.go.jp/policy/sokushin/pdf/sokushin/jyuten2022
_honbun.pdf.

Cadena, Brian C., Brian Duncan, and Stephen J. Trejo. "The Labor Market Integration
and Impacts of US Immigrants." In *Handbook of the Economics of International*

Migration, edited by Barry R. Chiswick and Paul W. Miller, 1197–259. North-Holland, 2015. https://doi.org/10.1016/B978-0-444-53768-3.00022-9.

CAES: Research Center for Aged Economy and Society. "Web Clock of Counting Children's Population in Japan." Updated 2022. https://sites.google.com/view/caestop/JCCC?authuser=0.

Career Connection. "Susumu 'shinsotsu gaikokujin saiyou' kahogona nihonjin yori 'hanguriina ajiajin'" ["Entry-level foreigner hiring" increases; "hungry Asians" over coddled Japanese]. Career Connection. Updated on April 23, 2014. https://careerconnection.jp/biz/economics/content_1375.html.

Castilla, Emilio J. "Bringing Managers Back In: Managerial Influences on Workplace Inequality." *American Sociological Review* 76, no. 5 (2011): 667–94. https://doi-org.proxyiub.uits.iu.edu/10.1177/0003122411420814.

Castilla, Emilio J. "Gender, Race, and Meritocracy in Organizational Careers." *American Journal of Sociology* 113, no. 6 (May 2008): 1479–526. https://doi-org.proxyiub.uits.iu.edu/10.1086/588738.

Center for Employment Equity. "Is Silicon Valley Tech Diversity Possible Now?" Center for Employment Equity. Updated 2018. https://www.uMAedu/employmentequity/sites/default/files/CEE_Diversity%2Bin%2BSilicon%2BValley%2BTech.pdf.

Chang, Ha-Joon. "Globalization, Global Standards, and the Future of East Asia." *Global Economic Review* 34, no. 4 (2005): 363–78. https://doi.org/10.1080/12265080500441354.

Chanlett-Avery, Emma, and Rebecca M. Nelson. *Womenomics in Japan: In Brief.* Congressional Research Service, 2014.

Charles, Kerwin Kofi, and Jonathan Guryan. "Prejudice and Wages: An Empirical Assessment of Becker's *The Economics of Discrimination.*" *Journal of Political Economy* 116, no. 5 (2008): 773–809. https://doi.org/10.1086/593073.

Chavez, Koji. "Penalized for Personality: A Case Study of Asian-Origin Disadvantage at the Point of Hire." *Sociology of Race and Ethnicity* 7, no. 2 (2021): 226–46. https://doi.org/10.1177/2332649220922270.

Cheng, John W., and Nicholas Fraser. "Japanese Newspaper Portrayals of Refugees: A Frame Analysis from 1985 to 2017." *Journal of Refugee Studies* 35, no. 3 (September 2022): 1364–85.

Chiswick, Barry R., Yew Liang Lee, and Paul W. Miller. "A Longitudinal Analysis of Immigrant Occupational Mobility: A Test of the Immigrant Assimilation Hypothesis." *International Migration Review* 39, no. 2 (2005): 332–53. https://doi.org/10.1111/j.1747-7379.2005.tb00269.x.

Cho, Kyongho. "Intaanetto-jou no saigai-ji 'gaikoku jin hanzai' no ryuugen ni kansuru kenkyuu" [A study on rumors of "foreign crime" on the internet during disasters]. *Ouyou shakaigaku kenkyuu* 60 (2018): 79–89. https://doi.org/10.14992/00016293.

Chung, Erin A. *Immigrant Incorporation in East Asian Democracies.* Cambridge University Press, 2020.

Chung, Erin A. *Immigration and Citizenship in Japan.* Cambridge University Press, 2010.

Chung, Erin A. "The Side Doors of Immigration: Multi-Tier Migration Regimes in Japan and South Korea." *Third World Quarterly* 43, no. 7 (2022): 1570–86. https://doi.org/10.1080/01436597.2021.1956893.

Clark, Rodney. *The Japanese Company.* Charles E. Tuttle, 1979. Distributed by Yale University Press.

Clemons, Eric. "Transcending National Identity: Foreign Employees and Organizational Management in Corporate Japan." PhD diss., Colombia University, 1999.

https://www.proquest.com/docview/304499302?pq-origsite=gscholar&fromope nview=true.

Cohen, Philip N., and Matt L. Huffman. "Working for the Woman? Female Managers and the Gender Wage Gap." *American Sociological Review* 72, no. 5 (2007): 681–704. https://doi.org/10.1177/000312240707200502.

Choi, Seong Hyeon. "South Korea Wants Southeast Asian Domestic Workers to Support Families. But Are They Welcome?" *South China Morning Post.* Updated May 21, 2023. https://www.scmp.com/week-asia/people/article/3221195/south-korea-wants-southeast-asian-domestic-workers-support-families-are-they-welcome.

Cole, Robert E. *Work, Mobility, and Participation.* University of California Press, 1979.

Coleman, David, and Robert Rowthorn. "Who's Afraid of Population Decline? A Critical Examination of Its Consequences." *Population and Development Review* 37 (2011): 217–48. https://www.jstor.org/stable/41762406.

Conrad, Harald. "From Seniority to Performance Principle: The Evolution of Pay Practices in Japanese Firms Since the 1990s." *Social Science Japan Journal* 13, no. 1 (2009): 115–35. https://doi.org/10.1093/ssjj/jyp040.

Conrad, Harald, and Hendrik Meyer-Ohle. "Training Regimes and Diversity: Experiences of Young Foreign Employees in Japanese Headquarters." *Work, Employment and Society* 36, no. 2 (2020): 1–18. https://doi.org/10.1177/0950017020966537.

Crenshaw, Kimberle. "Demarginalizing the Intersection of Race and Sex: A Black Feminist Critique of Antidiscrimination Doctrine, Feminist Theory, and Antiracist Politics." *University of Chicago Legal Forum* 1989, no. 1 (1989): 39–52. https://doi.org/10.4324/9780429499142-5.

Crenshaw, Kimberle. "Mapping the Margins: Intersectionality, Identity Politics, and Violence Against Women of Color." *Stanford Law Review* 43, no. 6 (1991): 1241–99. https://www.scopus.com/record/display.uri?eid=2-s2.0-84926443235&origin=inward&txGid=FE9082C8BF76CA5D0B9B1AAD235670AA.wsnAw8kcdt7IPYLO0V48gA:1.

Debnár, Miloš. *Migration, Whiteness, and Cosmopolitanism: Europeans in Japan.* Palgrave Macmillan New York, 2016.

DiMaggio, Paul J., and Walter W. Powell. "The Iron Cage Revisited: Institutional Isomorphism and Collective Rationality in Organizational Fields." *American Sociological Review* 48, no. 2 (April 1983): 147–160. https://doi-org.proxyiub.uits.iu.edu/10.2307/2095101.

DISCO. "Gaikokujin ryuugakusei koudo gaikoku jinzai no saiyou ni kansuru chousa" [Survey on foreign student and highly-skilled foreign professional hiring]. Updated December 2019. https://www.disc.co.jp/wp/wp-content/uploads/2020/01/2019kigyou-global-report.pdf.

DISCO. "'Gaikokujin ryuugakusei no saiyou ni kansuru chousa' ankeeto kekka" [Results of the "survey on foreign student hiring"]. Updated August 2010. https://www.disc.co.jp/wp/wp-content/uploads/2012/01/10kigyou-oversea-report8.pdf.

Ellingrud, Kweilin, Alex Krivkovich, Marie-Claude Nadeau, and Jill Zucker. "Closing the Gender and Race Gaps in North American Financial Services." McKinsey and Company. Updated October 21, 2021. https://www.mckinsey.com/industries/financial-services/our-insights/closing-the-gender-and-race-gaps-in-north-american-financial-services.

Ely, Robin J. "The Power in Demography: Women's Social Constructions of Gender Identity at Work." *Academy of Management Journal* 38, no. 3 (1995): 589–634.

Fuess, Scott M. "Immigration Policy and Highly Skilled Workers: The Case of Japan." *Contemporary Economic Policy* 21, no. 2 (2003): 243–57. https://doi.org/10.1093 /cep/byg008.

Fujita, Noriko. "Corporate Transfers for Dual-Career Couples: From Gendered Tenkin to Gender-Equal Negotiations?" *Social Science Japan Journal* 24, no. 1 (2021): 163–83.

Gagné, Nana Okura. *Reworking Japan: Changing Men at Work and Play under Neoliberalism.* Cornell University Press, 2021.

Gee, Buck, and Janet Wong. "The Illusion of Asian Success: Scant Progress for Minorities in Cracking the Glass Ceiling from 2007–2015." Ascend, Pan-Asian Leaders. Updated 2017. https://www.ascendleadershipfoundation.org/research/the-illusion -of-asian-success.

Gelin, Martin. "Japan Radically Increased Immigration—and No One Protested." *Foreign Policy.* Updated June 23, 2020. https://foreignpolicy.com/2020/06/23/japan -immigration-policy-xenophobia-migration.

Gender Equality Bureau. "Josei no nenrei kaikyuu betsu roudouryokuritsu no suii" [Changes in female labor force participation rate by age-group]. Updated December 2, 2022. https://www.gender.go.jp/about_danjo/whitepaper/r03/zentai/html /zuhyo/zuhyo01-02-04.html.

Gender Equality Bureau. "Kigyou ni okeru josei no sankaku" [Women's participation in private firms]. Updated 2016. https://www.gender.go.jp/about_danjo/whitepaper/h28 /zentai/html/honpen/b1_s02_02.html.

Gender Equality Bureau. "Muishiki no omoikomi (ankonshasu baiasu): jirei shuu" [Case studies of unconscious bias]. Updated December 15, 2021. https://www .gender.go.jp/research/kenkyu/pdf/seibetsu_r03/04.pdf.

Gender Equality Bureau. "Nenkan sou jitsu roudou jikan no suii" [Trends in total annual working hours]. Updated 2015. https://www.gender.go.jp/about_danjo /whitepaper/h27/zentai/html/zuhyo/zuhyo01-03-02.html.

Gender Equality Bureau. "Todoufukenbetsu juugyousha kibobetsu kigyousuu" [Number of firms by prefecture and number of employees]. Updated 2018. https:// www.gender.go.jp/kaigi/senmon/kihon/kihon_eikyou/pdf/02_2_chosakai _todoufuken.pdf.

Geraghty, Kristina T. "Taming the Paper Tiger: A Comparative Approach to Reforming Japanese Gender Equality Laws." *Cornell International Law Journal* 41, no. 2 (Summer 2008): 503–43. https://scholarship.law.cornell.edu/cilj/vol41 /iss2/6.

Global Migration Data Analysis Center. "How the World Views Migration." International Organization for Migration. Updated December 22, 2015. https:// publications.iom.int/system/files/pdf/how_the_world_gallup.pdf.

Goldin, Claudia. *Career and Family: Women's Century-Long Journey toward Equity.* Princeton University Press, 2021.

Gonzalez-Barrera, Ana and Phillip Connor. "Around the World, More Say Immigrants Are a Strength Than a Burden." Pew Research Center. Updated March 14, 2019. https://www.pewresearch.org/global-migration-and-demography/2019/03/14 /around-the-world-more-say-immigrants-are-a-strength-than-a-burden/.

Gordon, Andrew. *The Evolution of Labor Relations in Japan: Heavy Industry 1853–1955.* Harvard University Press, 1985.

Gordon, Andrew. "Managing the Japanese Household: The New Life Movement in Postwar Japan." In *Gendering Modern Japanese History,* edited by Barbara Molony and Kathleen Uno, 423–62. Harvard University Asia Center, 2005.

Green, David, and Yoshihiko Kadoya. "Contact and Threat: Factors Affecting Views on Increasing Immigration in Japan." *Politics and Policy* 43, no. 1 (2015): 59–93. https://doi.org/10.1111/polp.12109.

Gruman, Galen. "Tech Wages: Women, Minorities Still Paid Less in 2020." Computerworld. Updated May 21, 2021. https://www.computerworld.com/article/3619891/tech-wages-women-minorities-still-paid-less-in-2020.html.

Hamada, Tomoko. "Japanese Company's Cultural Shift for Gender Equality at Work." *Global Economic Review* 47, no. 1 (2018): 63–87. https://doi.org/10.1080/1226508X.2017.1393725.

Hasunuma, Linda C. "Gender Gaiatsu: An Institutional Perspective on Womenomics." *U.S.-Japan Women's Journal* 48, no. 1 (2015): 79–114. https://doi.org/10.1353/jwj.2015.0005.

Hatarakonetto. "800mei no josei ni kiita 'shokuba de no matahara/ikuhara no jittai'" [We asked 800 women about "maternity- and childrearing-related harassment in the workplace"]. Updated October 15, 2015. https://www.hatarako.net/pr/2015/1015.

Hatcher, Pascale, and Aya Murakami. "The Politics of Exclusion: Embedded Racism and Japan's Pilot Refugee Resettlement Programme." *Race and Class* 62, no. 1 (2020): 60–77. https://doi.org/10.1177/0306396820917068.

Hinton, Perry R. *Stereotypes and the Construction of the Social World.* Routledge, 2019.

Hof, Helena. "Intersections of Race and Skills in European Migration to Asia: Between White Cultural Capital and 'Passive Whiteness.'" *Ethnic and Racial Studies* 44, no. 11 (2021): 2113–134. https://doi.org/10.1080/01419870.2020.1822535.

Hof, Helena. "'Worklife Pathways' to Singapore and Japan: Gender and Racial Dynamics in Europeans' Mobility to Asia." *Social Science Japan Journal* 21, no. 1 (2018): 45–65. https://doi.org/10.1007/BF03053099.

Hof, Helena, and Yen-Fen Tseng. "When 'Global Talents' Struggle to Become Local Workers: The New Face of Skilled Migration to Corporate Japan." *Asian and Pacific Migration Journal* 29, no. 4 (December 2020): 511–31. https://doi.org/10.1177/0117196820984088.

Holbrow, Hilary J. "Detangling Capital from Context: A Critical Investigation of Human Capital Explanations for Immigrant Wage Inequality." *Journal of Ethnic and Migration Studies* 46, no. 19 (2020): 4043–65. https://doi.org/10.1080/1369183X.2018.1527682.

Holbrow, Hilary J. "How Conformity to Labor Market Norms Increases Access to Job Search Assistance: A Case Study from Japan." *Work and Occupations* 42, no. 2 (2015): 135–73. https://doi.org/10.1177/0730888415572377.

Holbrow, Hilary J. "Tainted Leave: A Survey-Experimental Investigation of Flexibility Stigma in Japanese Workplaces." *Social Forces* (2025). https://doi.org/10.1093/sf/soaf063.

Holbrow, Hilary J. "'Training' Foreign Workers, Cultivating Bias? TITP and Immigration to Japan." In *No Island Is an Island: Perspectives on Immigration to Japan*, edited by Michael Strausz, 109–130. University of Hawaii Press, 2025.

Holbrow, Hilary J. "When All Assistants Are Women, Are All Women Assistants? Gender Inequality and the Gender Composition of Support Roles." *RSF: The Russell Sage Foundation Journal of the Social Sciences* 8, no. 7 (2022): 28–49.

Holbrow, Hilary J., and Kikuko Nagayoshi. "Economic Integration of Skilled Migrants in Japan: The Role of Employment Practices." *International Migration Review* 52, no. 2 (2018): 458–86. https://doi.org/10.1111/imre.12295.

Holbrow, Hilary J., and Qiaoyan Li Rosenberg. "Japan Has to Do More for Migrant Rights Than Drop 'Intern' Label." *Nikkei Asia.* March 1, 2024. https://asia.nikkei.com/Opinion/Japan-has-to-do-more-for-migrant-rights-than-drop-intern-label.

Hounichi Rabo. "Nihon no 'kaikoku' he no ayumi wo jikeirei de furikaeru: Mizugiwa taisaku—ouhaba kanwa made" [A timeline of Japan's progress toward opening: from border control to large scale relaxation]. *Hounichi Rabo.* Updated December 29, 2022. https://honichi.com/news/2022/12/29/covidtimeline.

Huffman, Matt L., Philip N. Cohen, and Jessica Pearlman. "Engendering Change: Organizational Dynamics and Workplace Gender Desegregation, 1975–2005." *Administrative Science Quarterly* 55, no. 2 (2010): 255–77. https://doi.org/10.2189/asqu.2010.55.2.255.

Hughes, Everett C. *Dilemmas and Contradictions of Status.* Bobbs-Merrill, 1945.

Igarashi, Akira, and Kikuko Nagayoshi. "Norms to Be Prejudiced: List Experiments on Attitudes Towards Immigrants in Japan." *Social Science Research* 102 (2022): 102647. https://doi.org/10.1016/j.ssresearch.2021.102647.

Igarashi, Akira, and Ryota Mugiyama. "Whose Tastes Matter? Discrimination Against Immigrants in the Japanese Labour Market." *Journal of Ethnic and Migration Studies* 49, no. 13 (2023): 3365–88. https://doi.org/10.1080/1369183X.2022.2163230.

Immigration Services Agency. "Enkatsuna komyunikeeshon no tame no nihongo kyouiku nado no torikumi ni tsuite" [Japanese language education and other initiatives for smooth communication]. Updated March 19, 2021. https://www.moj.go.jp/isa/content/001344684.pdf.

Immigration Services Agency. "Zairyuu shikaku 'gijutsu jinbun chishiki kokusai gyoumu'" ["Technical, specialist in humanities, and international services" residence status]. Accessed March 26, 2023. https://www.moj.go.jp/isa/applications/status/gijinkoku.html.

Immigration Services Agency. "Zairyuu shikaku ichiranpyou" [Status of residence list]. Accessed July 21, 2022. https://www.moj.go.jp/isa/applications/guide/qaq5.html.

Ishida, Kenji. "Nihon ni okeru imin no chii tassei kouzou" [Structure of immigrants' status attainment in Japan]. In *Jinkou mondai to imin,* edited by Hiroshi Komai and Yu Korekawa, 92–113. Akashi Shoten, 2019.

Ishido, Satoru. "Nihon ni sukuu 'kenkan' no shutai" [The true nature of "anti-Korea" that nests in Japan]. *Newsweek Japan.* October 10, 2019. https://www.newsweekjapan.jp/stories/world/2019/10/post-13159.php.

Ishihara, Shintaro. "Nihon yo, uchinaru bouei wo" [Japan, defend yourself from internal threats]. *Sankei Shimbun,* May 8, 2001.

Ivory, Tristan, Guilherme Kenji Chilhaya, and Hirohisa Takenoshita. "Insider Out: Cross-National Differences in Foreign-Born Female Labor Force Participation in the United States, Sweden, and Japan." *International Migration Review* (2023): 1–30. https://doi.org/10.1177/01979183221133319.

Japan Federation of Labor Unions. "Rengou chingin repooto 2023" [JFLU wage report 2023]. Updated December 2023. https://www.jtuc-rengo.or.jp/activity/roudou/shuntou/2024/wage_report/wage_report.pdf.

Japan Institute for Labor Policy and Training. "Kaku nenrei kaikyuu no seiki, hiseiki betsu koyoushasuu" [Number of regular and irregular employees by age-group]. Updated March 3, 2023. https://www.jil.go.jp/kokunai/statistics/timeseries/html/g0209.html.

Japan Institute for Labor Policy and Training. "Koyou keitai betsu koyoushasuu" [Number of employees by employment type]. Updated March 30, 2023. https://www.jil.go.jp/kokunai/statistics/timeseries/html/g0208.html.

Japan Institute for Labor Policy and Training. "'Ninshin nado o riyuu to suru furieki toriatsukai oyobi sekushuaruharasumento ni kansuru jittai chousa' kekka (gaiyou)" [Results of the "survey on disadvantageous treatment and sexual harassment due to pregnancy or related circumstances" (summary)]. Updated on March 1, 2016. https://www.jil.go.jp/press/documents/20160301.pdf.

Japan Institute for Labor Policy and Training. "Ryuugakusei no shuushoku katsudou: genjou to kadai" [Job hunting for foreign students: current situation and challenges]. *JILPT Shiryou Shiriizu* no. 113. July 24, 2013. https://www.jil.go.jp/institute/siryo/2013/documents/0113.pdf.

Japan Institute for Labor Policy and Training. "Saiyou haichi shoushin to pojitibu akushon ni kansuru chousa kekka" [Survey results on hiring, placement, promotion, and affirmative action]. Updated May 15, 2015. https://www.jil.go.jp/institute/research/2014/132.html.

Japan Institute for Labor Policy and Training. "Shokugyou betsu shuugyoushasuu" [Number of workers by occupation]. Updated May 16, 2023. https://www.jil.go.jp/kokunai/statistics/chart/html/g0006.html.

Josei no katsuyou suishin kigyou deetabeesu. "Hon saito gaiyou" [Overview of this website]. Ministry of Health, Labor and Welfare. Updated 2023. https://positive-ryouritsu.mhlw.go.jp/positivedb/about.html.

Jozuka, Emiko, and Junko Ogura. "Can Japan Survive Without Immigrants?" *CNN.com*. Updated June 14, 2018. https://www.cnn.com/2017/08/01/asia/japan-migrants-immigration/index.html.

Jung, Suk-yee. "2022 Census Shows South Korea's Population Contracted for 2 Years Running." *Business Korea*. Updated July 28, 2023. http://www.businesskorea.co.kr/news/articleView.html?idxno=119343.

Kanai, Kaoru. "'Tayou na seishain' shisaku to josei no hatarakikata he no eikyou" ['Diverse regular employee' policy and its influence on women's work]. *Nihon roudou kenkyuu zasshi* 636 (July 2013): 63–76. https://www.jil.go.jp/institute/zassi/backnumber/2013/07/pdf/063-076.pdf.

Kanji, Yana, and Menju Toshihiro. "Maido, 'hannin wa gaikokujinda' to sakebu 'hoshu' no hitotachi ni konkyo wa aru no ka" [Do "conservatives" have grounds to frequently shout "foreigners are criminals"]. *President Online*. Updated May 29, 2020. https://president.jp/articles/-/35337?page=2.

Kanter, Rosabeth M. *Men and Women of the Corporation*. Basic Books, 1993.

Kato, Takao, Daiji Kawaguchi, and Hideo Owan. "Dynamics of the Gender Gap in the Workplace: An Econometric Case Study of a Large Japanese Firm." RIETI Discussion Paper Series 13-E-038, 2013. https://www.rieti.go.jp/jp/publications/dp/13e038.pdf.

Kato, Takao, Hiromasa Ogawa, and Hideo Owan. "Working Hours, Promotion, and Gender Gaps in the Workplace." RIETI Discussion Paper Series 16-E-060, 2016. https://www.rieti.go.jp/jp/publications/dp/16e060.pdf.

Kawai, Yuko. "Deracialised Race, Obscured Racism: Japaneseness, Western and Japanese Concepts of Race, and Modalities of Racism." *Japanese Studies* 35, no. 1 (2015): 23–47. https://doi.org/10.1080/10371397.2015.1006598.

Keidanren. "2013nen 6gatsudo teiki chingin chousa kekka" [Results of the June 2013 periodic survey of wages]. Updated April 28, 2014. https://www.keidanren.or.jp/policy/2014/040.pdf.

Kelsky, Karen. *Women on the Verge: Japanese Women, Western Dreams*. Duke University Press, 2001.

Kim, Bumsoo. "Blatant Discrimination Disappears, But . . .: The Politics of Everyday Exclusion in Contemporary Japan." *Asian Perspective* 35, no. 2 (2011): 287–308. https://doi.org/10.1353/apr.2011.0008.

Kim, Bumsoo. "Changes in the Socio-economic Position of Zainichi Koreans: A Historical Overview." *Social Science Japan Journal* 14, no. 2 (Summer 2011): 233–45. https://doi.org/10.1093/ssjj/jyq069.

Kim, Yoon Shin. "Recent Demographic Developments of the Korean Population in Japan." *Japanese Journal of Health and Human Ecology* 43, no. 3–4 (1977): 91–102. https://doi.org/10.3861/jshhe.43.3-4_91.

Kobayashi, Tetsuro, Christian Collet, Shanto Iyengar, and Kyu S. Hahn. "Who Deserves Citizenship? An Experimental Study of Japanese Attitudes Toward Immigrant Workers." *Social Science Japan Journal* 18, no. 1 (2015): 3–22. https://doi.org /10.1093/ssjj/jyu035.

Komisarof, Adam. *At Home Abroad: The Contemporary Western Experience in Japan.* Reitaku University Press, 2012.

Kondo, Dorinne. *Crafting Selves: Power, Gender, and Discourse of Identity in a Japanese Workplace.* University of Chicago Press, 1990.

Korekawa, Yu. "Determinants of Foreign Workers' Wages in Japan: An Analysis Focusing on Wage Gaps with Japanese." *IPSS Working Paper Series*, no. 67 (November 2023). https://doi.org/10.20955/r.85.67.

Korekawa, Yu. *Imin ukeire to shakaiteki tougou no riariti* [The reality of immigration and social integration]. Keisou Shobou, 2019.

Korekawa, Yu. "Shingata korona pandemikku wa guroubaruna hito no idou no nagare wo kaeta no ka?" [Did the novel coronavirus pandemic change global flows of people?] IPSS Working Paper Series, no. 36 (January 2021). https://doi.org /10.20955/r.85.67.

Kosminsky, Ethel Volfzon. *An Ethnography of the Lives of Japanese and Japanese Brazilian Migrants: Childhood, Family, and Work.* Lexington, 2020.

Kossek, Ellen Ernst, Rong Su, and Lusi Wu. "'Opting Out' or 'Pushed Out'? Integrating Perspectives on Women's Career Equality for Gender Inclusion and Interventions." *Journal of Management* 43, no. 1 (2017): 228–54. https://doi.org/10.1177 /0149206316671582.

Kramer, Andrea S., and Alton B Harris. *It's Not You, It's the Workplace: Women's Conflict at Work and the Bias That Built It.* Nicholas Brealy, 2019.

Kwon, Oh-Jung. "The Diverging Paths of Skilled Immigration in Singapore, Japan and Korea: Policy Priorities and External Labor Market for Skilled Foreign Workers." *Asia Pacific Journal of Human Resources* 57, no. 4 (2019): 418–44. https://doi .org/10.1111/1744-7941.12173.

Kyodo News. "Japan to Boost Child Care Spending to Match Sweden." Updated June 1, 2023. https://english.kyodonews.net/news/2023/06/527c2e8ba284-japan-to-boost -child-care-spending-to-match-sweden.html.

Kyouki no usagi. "Ryuugakusei wa Nihon no takara Kishida naikaku souri daijin kisha kaiken" [International students are Japan's national treasure, press conference by Prime Minister Kishida]. YouTube. March 3, 2022. Updated April 13, 2022. Press Conference, 1:40. https://youtu.be/96LqKl1uJf8.

Lamont, Michèle, and Mario Luis Small. "How Culture Matters: Enriching Our Understanding of Poverty." In *The Colors of Poverty: Why Racial and Ethnic Disparities Persist*, edited by Ann Chih Lin and David R. Harris, 76–102. Russell Sage Foundation, 2008.

Lamont, Michèle, and Virág Molnár. "The Study of Boundaries in the Social Sciences." *Annual Review of Sociology* 28 (2002): 167–95.

Lan, Pei-Chia. "Contested Skills and Constrained Mobilities: Migrant Carework Skill Regimes in Taiwan and Japan." *Comparative Migration Studies* 10, no. 1 (September 2022). https://doi.org/10.1186/s40878-022-00311-2.

Laurence, James, Akira Igarashi, and Kenji Ishida. "The Dynamics of Immigration and Anti-Immigrant Sentiment in Japan: How and Why Changes in Immigrant Share Affect Attitudes Toward Immigration in a Newly Diversifying Society." *Social Forces* 101, no. 1 (2022): 369–403. https://doi.org/10.1093/sf/soab136.

Lee, Jinhee. "'Malcontent Koreans (Futei Senjin)': Towards a Genealogy of Colonial Representation of Koreans in the Japanese Empire." *Faculty Research and Creative Activity*, no. 36 (2013): 1–71. https://thekeep.eiu.edu/history_fac/36.

Leicht, Kevin T. "Inequality and the Status Window: Inequality, Conflict, and the Salience of Status Differences in Conflicts over Resources." *RSF: The Russell Sage Foundation Journal of the Social Sciences* 8, no. 6 (2022): 103–21. https://doi.org/10.7758/RSF.2022.8.6.06.

Lewis, Leo. "Japan's Immigration Experiment Under the Cover of COVID." *Financial Times.* Updated January 29, 2022. https://www.ft.com/content/74bfd3fb-6987-4618-91a8-7e2c8f876fd6.

Levy, Christine. "Japanese Women Are Fighting Back Against Pervasive Sexism." *The Nation*, January 10, 2022. https://www.thenation.com/article/world/japan-womens-movement.

Lie, John. *Multiethnic Japan.* Harvard University Press, 2001.

Lie, John. "The Persistence of Monoethnic Ideology in Multiethnic Japan." In *Globalization and Civil Society in East Asian Space*, edited by Khatharya Um and Chiharu Takenaka, 97–111. Routledge, 2022. https://doi.org/10.4324/9781003079736-7.

Liu-Farrer, Gracia. "Educationally Channeled International Labor Mobility: Contemporary Student Migration from China to Japan." *International Migration Review* 43, no. 1 (2009): 178–204. https://doi.org/10.1111/j.1747-7379.2008.01152.x.

Liu-Farrer, Gracia. "'I Am the Only Woman in Suits': Chinese Immigrants and Gendered Careers in Corporate Japan." *Journal of Asia-Pacific Studies* 13 (2009): 37–48. https://core.ac.uk/download/pdf/144454665.pdf.

Liu-Farrer, Gracia. *Immigrant Japan.* Cornell University Press, 2020.

Liu-Farrer, Gracia. *Labour Migration from China to Japan: International Students, Transnational Migrants.* Routledge, 2011.

Liu-Farrer, Gracia, and Helena Hof. "Ōtebyō: The Problems of Japanese Firms and the Problematic Elite Aspirations." *Journal of Asia-Pacific Studies* 34 (2018): 65–84.

Lopez, Mary J. "Skilled Immigrant Women in the US and the Double Earnings Penalty." *Feminist Economics* 18, no. 1 (2012): 99–134. https://doi.org/10.1080/13545701.2012.658429.

Maanen, John Van. "Rediscovering Japan: Some Thoughts on Change and Continuity in Traditional Japanese Careers." *Career Development International* 11, no. 4 (June 2006): 280–92. https://doi.org/10.1108/13620430610672504.

March, Robert M. *Working for a Japanese Company: Insights into the Multicultural Workplace.* Kodansha International, 1992.

Margolis, Eric. "Japan's Foreign Workers Face a New Post-COVID Landscape." *Japan Times.* Updated September 5, 2022. https://www.japantimes.co.jp/news/2022/09/05/national/social-issues/foreign-workers-japan-covid19.

Marinucci, Marco, Rachel Maunder, Kiara Sanchez, Michael Thai, Shelley McKeown, Rhiannon N. Turner, and Clifford Stevenson. "Intimate Intergroup Contact Across the Lifespan." *Journal of Social Issues* 77, no. 1 (2021): 64–85. https://doi.org/10.1111/josi.12399.

McConnell, David L. *Importing Diversity: Inside Japan's JET Program.* University of California Press, 2000.

McIntosh, Peggy. "White Privilege: Unpacking the Invisible Knapsack." *Peace and Freedom*, August (1989): 29–34. www.nationalseedproject.oef.

McLelland, Mark. "'Race' on the Japanese Internet: Discussing Korea and Koreans On '2-Channeru.'" *New Media and Society* 10, no. 6 (2008): 811–29. https://doi.org/10.1177/1461444808096246.

Miladinović, Adrijana. "The Influence of Whiteness on Social and Professional Integration: The Case of Highly Skilled Europeans in Japan." *Journal of Contemporary Eastern Asia* 19, no. 2 (2019): 84–103. https://doi.org/10.17477/jcea.2020.19.2.084.

Ministry of Foreign Affairs. "Procedures Required Before Working as an SSW." Updated 2023. https://www.mofa.go.jp/mofaj/ca/fna/ssw/us/introduction.

Ministry of Health, Labor and Welfare. "Chingin no bunpu" [Wage distribution]. Updated 2015. https://www.mhlw.go.jp/toukei/itiran/roudou/chingin/kouzou/z2015/dl/07.pdf.

Ministry of Health, Labor and Welfare. "'Gaikokujin koyou joukyou' no todokede joukyou matome (Reiwa 2nen 10gatsumatsu genzai)" [Compilation of employer reports on foreigners' employment (as of the end of October 2020)]. Updated January 29, 2021. https://www.mhlw.go.jp/stf/newpage_16279.html.

Ministry of Health, Labor and Welfare. "Heisei 24 nendo koyou kintou kihon chousa no gaikyou" [Overview of the 2012 basic survey of equal employment]. Updated July 4, 2013. http://www.mhlw.go.jp/toukei/list/dl/71-24e.pdf.

Ministry of Health, Labor and Welfare. "Ikuji kyuugyou kyuufu kankei" [Materials on parental leave payments]. Updated January 26, 2021. https://www.mhlw.go.jp/content/11601000/000728126.pdf.

Ministry of Health, Labor and Welfare. "Jikangai roudou no jougen kisei no tekiyou yuuyo jigyou gyoumu" [Businesses and occupations exempt from limits on overtime work]. Updated 2023. https://www.mhlw.go.jp/stf/seisakunitsuite/bunya/koyou_roudou/roudoukijun/gyosyu/topics/01.html.

Ministry of Health, Labor and Welfare. "Jinkou kouzou, roudou jikan nado ni tsuite" [On population structure and work hours]. Updated January 19, 2024. https://www.mhlw.go.jp/content/11201250/001194507.pdf.

Ministry of Health, Labor and Welfare. "Kigyou chousa kekka gaiyou" [Overview of company survey results]. Updated December 18, 2016. https://www.mhlw.go.jp/toukei/list/dl/71-27-02.pdf.

Ministry of Health, Labor and Welfare. "Reiwa 2nen chingin kouzou kihon toukei chousa no gaikyou" [Overview of the 2020 basic survey on wage structure]. Updated May 13, 2021. https://www.mhlw.go.jp/toukei/itiran/roudou/chingin/kouzou/z2020/dl/04.pdf.

Ministry of Health, Labor and Welfare. "Reiwa 4nen koyou doukou chousa kekka no gaikyou" [Overview of the 2022 employment trends survey]. Updated August 22, 2023. https://www.mhlw.go.jp/toukei/itiran/roudou/koyou/doukou/23-2/dl/gaikyou.pdf.

Ministry of Health, Labor and Welfare. "Sangyou jigyousho kibo sei shuugyoukeitai betsu roudousha wariai" [Percentage of workers by industry, establishment size, sex, and employment type]. Updated 2014. https://www.mhlw.go.jp/toukei/youran/roudou-nenpou2014/xls/039.xls.

Ministry of Health, Labor and Welfare. "Zuhyou 1-1-7: shusshousuu, goukei tokushu shusshouritsu no suii" [Chart 1-1-7: Changes in the number of births and total fertility rate]. Updated 2018. https://www.mhlw.go.jp/stf/wp/hakusyo/kousei/19/backdata/01-01-01-07.html.

Ministry of Internal Affairs and Communications. "Jinkou suikei no kekka no gaiyou" [Summary of population estimation results]. Updated 2025. https://www.stat.go.jp/data/jinsui/2.html#annual.

Ministry of Internal Affairs and Communications. "Nenrei (5sai kaikyuu oyobi 3kubun), danjo betsu jinkou (kakunen 10gatsu 1tachi genzai)—soujinkou 2000nen-2020nen" [Total population by age-group (5-year and 3-category) and sex (as of

October 1 annually), 2000–2020]. Updated June 28, 2022. https://www.e-stat
.go.jp/stat-search/files?layout=datalist&cycle=0&toukei=00200524&tstat=00000
0090001&tclass1=000000090004&tclass2=000001051180&tclass3val=0&s
tat_infid=000013168603.

Ministry of Internal Affairs and Communications. "Nenrei (5sai kaikyuu oyobi
3kubun), danjo betsu jinkou (kakunen 10gatsu 1tachi genzai)—soujinkou taishou
9nen—heisei 12nen" [Total population by age-group (5-year and 3-category) and
sex (as of October 1 annually), 1920–2000]. Updated January 30, 2018. https://
www.e-stat.go.jp/stat-search/files?page=1&layout=datalist&cycle=0&toukei=00
200524&tstat=000000090001&tclass1=000000090004&tclass2=000000090005
&cycle_facet=tclass1%3Atclass2&tclass3val=0&stat_infid=000000090263.

Ministry of Internal Affairs and Communications. "Juugyousha kibobetsu hinouringyou koyou shasuu" [Number of nonagricultural and forestry employees by
firm size]. Updated 2022. https://www.stat.go.jp/data/roudou/longtime/zuhyou
/lt04-02.xlsx.

Ministry of Internal Affairs and Communications. "Koudo gaikoku jinzai no ukeire ni
kansuru seisaku hyoukasho" [Policy evaluation report on acceptance of highly
skilled foreign professionals]. Updated June 21, 2019. https://www.soumu.go.jp
/main_content/000627735.pdf.

Ministry of Internal Affairs and Communications. "Wagakuni ni okeru soujinkou no
choukiteki suii" [Our country's long-run population trends]. Updated February
7, 2024. https://www.soumu.go.jp/main_content/000273900.pdf.

Ministry of Internal Affairs and Communications. "Zouka keikou ga tsuzuku tenshokusha no joukyou 2019 nen no tenshoku shasuu wa kako saidai" [Continued
increase in job changers; the number of job changers in 2019 is the highest ever].
Updated February 21, 2020. https://www.stat.go.jp/data/roudou/topics/topi1230
.html.

Ministry of Justice. "Gaikokujin juumin chousa houkokusho" [Foreign resident survey
report]. Updated June 1, 2017. https://www.moj.go.jp/content/001226182.pdf.

Ministry of Justice. "Kika kyoka shinsei shasuu, kika kyoka shasuu oyobi kika fukyoka
shasuu no suii" [Trends in applications for naturalization, approvals, and denials].
https://www.moj.go.jp/content/001414946.pdf.

Ministry of Justice. "Kokuseki chiiki betsu tokutei sangyou bunya betsu tokutei ginou
1gou zairyuu gaikokujinsuu" [Foreign residents on the SSW1 visa by nationality
/region and designated industry]. Updated February 6, 2023. https://www.moj
.go.jp/isa/content/001389886.xlsx.

Ministry of Justice. "Kokuseki chiiki betsu tokutei sangyou bunya betsu tokutei ginou
2gou zairyuu gaikokujinsuu" [Foreign residents on the SSW2 visa by nationality
/region and designated industry]. Updated February 6, 2023. https://www.moj
.go.jp/isa/content/001389892.xlsx.

Ministry of Justice. "Kokuseki chiiki betsu zairyuu shikaku (zairyuu mokuteki) betsu
zairyuu gaikokujin" [Foreign residents by nationality/region, status of residence.]
Updated December 11, 2020. https://www.e-stat.go.jp/stat-search/files?page=1&l
ayout=datalist&toukei=00250012&tstat=000001018034&cycle=1&year=20200&
month=12040606&tclass1=000001060399.

Ministry of Justice. "Points-Based Preferential Immigration Treatment for Highly-
Skilled Foreign Professionals." Updated December 11, 2013. https://www.ro.emb
-japan.go.jp/files/100500331.pdf.

Ministry of Justice. "Shutsunyuukoku zairyuu kanri wo meguru kinnen no joukyou"
[Recent circumstances of border control and residence management]. Updated
November 28, 2022. https://www.moj.go.jp/isa/content/001385111.pdf.

Ministry of Justice. "Zairyuu gaikokujin toukei (kyuu touroku gaikokujin toukei) toukei-hyou" [Statistics on resident foreigners (formerly statistics on registered foreigners)]. https://www.moj.go.jp/isa/policies/statistics/toukei_ichiran_touroku.html.

Ministry of Justice. "(Zenbunya) kokuseki chiiki shiken ruuto ginoujisshuu ruuto betsu tokutei ginou 1gou zairyuu gaikokujinsuu" [Foreign residents on the SSW1 visa by nationality/region and exam route/TITP entry route (all fields)]. Updated February 6, 2023. https://www.moj.go.jp/isa/content/001389889.xlsx.

Misra, Joya, Celeste Vaughan Curington, and Venus Mary Green. "Methods of Intersectional Research." *Sociological Spectrum* 41, no. 1 (2020): 1–20. https://doi.org/10.1080/02732173.2020.1791772.

Mizuno, Mitsuru. "Institutional Investors, Corporate Governance and Firm Performance in Japan." *Pacific Economic Review* 15, no. 5 (2010): 653–65. https://doi.org/10.1111/j.1468-0106.2010.00521.x.

Moriguchi, Chiaki, and Hiroshi Ono. "Japanese Lifetime Employment: A Century's Perspective." In Institutional Change in Japan, edited by Magnus Blomström and Sumner La Croix, 152–76. Routledge, 2006.

Morita, Liang. "Some Manifestations of Japanese Exclusionism." *SAGE Open* 5, no. 3 (2015): 1–6. https://doi.org/10.1177/2158244015600036.

Moriya, Takashi. "Nihon kigyou no ryuugakusei nado no gaikokujin saiyou he no kousatsu" [An investigation of international student recruitment at Japanese firms]. *Journal of Japanese Labor Studies* 623 (2012): 29–36. https://www.jil.go.jp/institute/zassi/backnumber/2012/06/pdf/029-036.pdf.

Morris-Suzuki, Tessa. *Borderline Japan: Foreigners and Frontier Controls in the Postwar Era*. Cambridge University Press, 2010.

Mouer, Ross E., and Hirosuke Kawanishi. *A Sociology of Work in Japan*. Cambridge University Press, 2005.

Mun, Eunmi. "Negative Compliance as an Organizational Response to Legal Pressures: The Case of Japanese Equal Employment Opportunity Law." *Social Forces* 94, no. 4 (June 2016): 1409–37. https://doi.org/10.1093/sf/sov118.

Mun, Eunmi, and Mary C. Brinton. "Workplace Matters: The Use of Parental Leave Policy in Japan." *Work and Occupations* 42, no. 3 (March 2015): 355–69. https://doi.org/10.1177/0730888415574781.

Mun, Eunmi, and Jiwook Jung. "Change Above the Glass Ceiling: Corporate Social Responsibility and Gender Diversity in Japanese Firms." *Administrative Science Quarterly* 63, no. 2 (June 2018): 409–40.

Mun, Eunmi, and Jiwook Jung. "Policy Generosity, Employer Heterogeneity, and Women's Employment Opportunities: The Welfare State Paradox Reexamined." *American Sociological Review* 83, no. 3 (2018): 508–35. https://doi.org/10.1177/0003122418772857.

Murata, Koji. "Gaikokujin no imeeji no kouzou: Chousa deeta ni motodsuku kousatsu" [The structure of perceptions of foreigners: An inquiry based on survey data]. *Hitotsubashi daigaku gakuin shakaigaku kenkyuuka sentan kadai kenkyuu sousho* 2 (2006): 202–33. https://ci.nii.ac.jp/naid/120006928277.

Myers, Steven L., Jin Wu, and Claire Fu. "China's Looming Crisis: A Shrinking Population." *New York Times*, January 17, 2020. https://www.nytimes.com/interactive/2019/01/17/world/asia/china-population-crisis.html.

MyNavi Career Research Lab. "2022nensotsu daigakusei shuushoku ishiki chousa" [Opinion survey on job hunting for 2022 college graduates]. MyNavi. Updated April 26, 2021. https://career-research.mynavi.jp/reserch/20210426_8553.

Nagase, Nobuko. "Has Abe's Womanomics Worked?" *Asian Economic Policy Review* 13, no. 1 (2018): 68–101.

Nagayoshi, Kikuko. "Imin no tougou wo kangaeru" [Thoughts on immigrant integration]. In *Nihon no imin tougou: Zenkoku chousa kara miru genjou to shouheki*, edited by Kikuko Nagayoshi, 3–38. Akashi Shoten, 2021.

Nagayoshi, Kikuko. "Nihon ni okeru gaikokusekisha no kaizouteki chii" [Class position of foreign citizens in Japan]. In *Jinkou mondai to imin* [Immigration and the population problem], edited by Hiroshi Komai and Yu Korekawa, 114–133. Akashi Shoten, 2019.

Nagayoshi, Kikuko. "Imin no kaizouteki chii tassei" [Immigrants' class attainment]. In *Nihon no imin tougou: Zenkoku chousa kara miru genjou to shouheki* [Immigrant integration in Japan: Realities and barriers seen through a nationwide survey], edited by Kikuko Nagayoshi, 63–87. Akashi Shoten, 2021.

Nagayoshi, Kikuko. "Whose Size Counts? Multilevel Analysis of Japanese Anti-Immigrant Attitudes Based on JGSS-2006." *JGSS Research Series 9*, no. 6 (2009): 157–74. https://jgss.daishodai.ac.jp/research/monographs/jgssm9/jgssm9_10.pdf.

Nagayoshi, Kikuko, and Hirohisa Takenoshita. "Imin no kyouiku tassei to chingin" [Immigrants' educational attainment and earnings], in *Nihon no imin tougou: Zenkoku chousa kara miru genjou to shouheki* [Immigrant integration in Japan: Realities and barriers seen through a nationwide survey], edited by Kikuko Nagayoshi, 88–110. Akashi Shoten, 2021.

Nagy, Stephen. "From Temporary Migrant to Integrated Resident: Local Government Approaches to Migrant Integration in the Tokyo Metropolis." *ASIEN* 124 (2012): 115–136.

Nakane, Chie. *Japanese Society*. University of California Press, 1970.

National Institute of Population and Social Security Research. "Nihon no shourai suikei jinkou (Heisei 29nen suikei)" [Japan's future estimated population (2017 estimate)]. Updated in 2017. https://www.ipss.go.jp/pp-zenkoku/j/zenkoku2017/db_zenkoku2017/db_s_suikeikekka_1.html.

National Institute of Population and Social Security Research. "Nihon no shourai suikei jinkou (Reiwa 5nen suikei)" [Japan's future estimated population (2023 estimate)]. Updated March 7, 2023. https://www.ipss.go.jp/pp-zenkoku/j/zenkoku2023/db_zenkoku2023/db_zenkoku2023syosaikekka.html.

National Immigration Agency. "2023.1 Foreign Residents by Nationality." Updated March 1, 2023. https://www.immigration.gov.tw/media/90897/20231foreign-residents-by-nationality.xls.

Nebashi, Reiko. "Future Challenges Surrounding the 300,000 International Students Plan." Meiji.net. April 21, 2017. https://english-meiji.net/articles/273.

Negishi, Takuro, and Tomoko Yamashita. "'Chuugokujin saiyou shinai' tsuiito no toudai tokunin jun kyouju ga shazai" [Specially appointed associate professor at the University of Tokyo apologizes for tweeting, "We don't employ Chinese people."] *Asahi Shimbun*. December 2, 2019. https://www.asahi.com/articles/ASMD23CXJMD2UTIL00G.html.

Nemoto, Kumiko. *Too Few Women at the Top: The Persistence of Inequality in Japan*. Cornell University Press, 2016.

Nemoto, Kumiko. "Why Women Won't Wed." In *Beyond the Gender Gap in Japan*, edited by Gill Steel, 67–82. University of Michigan Press, 2019.

Nihon Keizai Shimbun. "Gaikokujin tekihatsu 11,000chou, betonamu, chuugoku de kahansuu" [Over 11,000 foreigners arrested, majority from Vietnam and China]. *Nikkei Keizai Shimbun*. April 3, 2020. https://www.nikkei.com/article/DGXMZO57608760T00C20A4CE0000.

Nippon.com. "Japan Sees 90% Drop in Daycare Waiting Lists over the Last Five Years." Updated September 14, 2022. https://www.nippon.com/en/japan-data/h01428.

Noda, Kazuo. "Big Business Organization." In *Modern Japanese Organization and Decision-Making*, edited by Ezra F. Vogel, 116–145. University of California Press, 1975.

O'Donnell, Alexander W., Maria Therese Friehs, Chloe Bracegirdle, Claudia Zúñiga, Susan Ellen Watt, and Fiona Kate Barlow. "Technological and Analytical Advancements in Intergroup Contact Research." *Journal of Social Issues* 77, no. 1 (2021): 171–96. https://doi.org/10.1111/josi.12424.

Ogasawara, Yuko. *Office Ladies and Salaried Men: Power, Gender, and Work in Japanese Companies.* University of California Press, 1998.

Ogasawara, Yuko. "Working Women's Husbands as Helpers or Partners." In *Beyond the Gender Gap in Japan*, edited by Gill Steel, 83–103. University of Michigan Press, 2019.

Oguma, Eiji. *A Genealogy of Japanese Self-Images.* Melbourne: Trans Pacific Press, 2002.

Ogura, Kazuya. "Working Hours and Japanese Employment Practices." *Japan Labor Review* 4, no. 4 (2007): 139–60.

Oishi, Nana. "The Limits of Immigration Policies: The Challenges of Highly Skilled Migration in Japan." *American Behavioral Scientist* 56, no. 8 (2012): 1080–100. https://doi.org/10.1177/0002764212441787.

Ono, Hiroshi. "Careers in Foreign-Owned Firms in Japan." *American Sociological Review* 72, no. 2 (April 1, 2007): 267–90. https://doi.org/10.1177/000312240707200207.

Ono, Hiroshi. "Lifetime Employment in Japan: Concepts and Measurements." *Journal of the Japanese and International Economies* 24, no. 1 (March 2010): 1–27. https://doi.org/10.1016/j.jjie.2009.11.003.

Ono, Hiroshi. "Why Do the Japanese Work Long Hours?" *Japan Labor Issues* 2, no. 5 (2018): 35–49.

Oreopoulos, Philip. "Why Do Skilled Immigrants Struggle in the Labor Market? A Field Experiment with Thirteen Thousand Resumes." *American Economic Journal: Economic Policy* 3, no. 4 (2011): 148–71.

Organization for Economic Co-operation and Development. "Gender Wage Gap." Updated 2023. https://data.oecd.org/earnwage/gender-wage-gap.htm.

Organization for Economic Co-operation and Development. "The Pursuit of Gender Equality: An Uphill Battle." Updated July 18, 2018. https://www.oecd.org/japan/Gender2017-JPN-en.pdf.

Osawa, Machiko, and Kingston, Jeff. "Risk and Consequences: The Changing Japanese Employment Paradigm." In *Japan: The Precarious Future*, edited by Frank Baldwin and Anne Allison, 58–86. New York University Press, 2015. https://doi.org/10.18574/nyu/9781479889389.003.0004

Padavic, Irene, Robin J. Ely, and Erin M. Reid. "Explaining the Persistence of Gender Inequality: The Work–Family Narrative as a Social Defense Against the 24/7 Work Culture." *Administrative Science Quarterly* 65, no. 1 (2020): 61–111. https://doi.org/10.1177/0001839219832310.

Paluck, Elizabeth Levy, Seth A. Green, and Donald P. Green. "The Contact Hypothesis Re-Evaluated." *Behavioural Public Policy* 3, no. 2 (2019): 129–58. https://doi.org/10.1017/bpp.2018.25.

Peltokorpi, Vesa, and Jinju Xie. "When Little Things Make a Big Difference: A Bourdieusian Perspective on Skilled Migrants' Linguistic, Social, and Economic Capital in Multinational Corporations." *Journal of International Business Studies* (2023). https://doi.org/10.1057/s41267-023-00598-y.

Pettigrew, Thomas F. "Advancing Intergroup Contact Theory: Comments on the Issue's Articles." *Journal of Social Issues* 77, no. 1 (2021): 258–73. https://doi.org/10.1111/josi.12423.

Pettigrew, Thomas F., and Linda R. Tropp. "A Meta-Analytic Test of Intergroup Contact Theory." *Journal of Personality and Social Psychology* 90, no. 5 (2006): 751–83. https://doi.org/10.1037/0022-3514.90.5.751.

Poushter, Jacob. "Methodology." *Pew Research Center*. Updated December 7, 2018. https://www.pewresearch.org/wp-content/uploads/2018/12/FT_18.12.10_MigrationViews_Topline2.pdf.

PRB.org. "Population of Older Adults Increasing Globally Partly Because of Declining Fertility Rates." *PRB*. July 10, 2020. https://www.prb.org/news/population-of-older-adults-increasing-globally.

Prime Minister's Office of Japan. "Hatarakikata kaikaku jikkou keikaku" [Workstyle reform implementation plan]. Updated March 28, 2017. https://www.kantei.go.jp/jp/headline/pdf/20170328/01.pdf.

Quillian, Lincoln. "New Approaches to Understanding Racial Prejudice and Discrimination." *Annual Review of Sociology* 32 (2006): 299–328. https://doi.org/10.1146/annurev.soc.32.061604.123132.

Rankin, Andrew. "Recent Trends in Organized Crime in Japan: Yakuza vs the Police, and Foreign Crime Gangs-Part 2." *Asia-Pacific Journal* 10, no. 7 (2012): 1–21. https://apjjf.org/-Andrew-Rankin/3692/article.pdf.

Rebick, Marcus. *The Japanese Employment System: Adapting to a New Economic Environment*. Oxford University Press, 2005.

Recruit. "Gaikokujin ryuugakusei no saiyou shuushoku ni kansuru deeta-shuu" [Collection of data on recruitment and employment of international students]. *Shuushoku Mirai*. Updated July 3, 2017. https://shushokumirai.recruit.co.jp/wp-content/uploads/2017/11/data_foreign201706.pdf.

Reischauer, Edwin O. *The Japanese Today: Change and Continuity*. Belknap, 1988.

Reskin, Barbara F., and Patricia A. Roos. *Job Queues, Gender Queues*. Temple University Press, 1995.

Reuters. "Japan to Delay 'Womenomics' Target for Female Leaders by up to a Decade." June 30, 2020. https://www.reuters.com/article/us-japan-politics-women-idUSKBN2410MA.

Reuters. "Roitaa kigyou chousa: Josei kanrishoku 10-paasento miman ga 9wari mokuhyou 3wari touku" [Reuters survey: 90 percent of respondents have less than 10 percent female managers, far from the 30 percent target]. Updated September 13, 2018. https://jp.reuters.com/article/female-manager-idJPKCN1LT3HN.

Ridgeway, Cecilia L. *Status: Why Is It Everywhere? Why Does It Matter?* Russell Sage Foundation, 2019.

Ridgeway, Cecilia L., and Hazel Rose Markus. "The Significance of Status: What It Is and How It Shapes Inequality." *RSF: The Russell Sage Foundation Journal of the Social Sciences* 8, no. 7 (2022): 1–25. https://doi.org/10.7758/RSF.2022.8.7.01.

Rivera, Lauren A. *Pedigree: How Elite Students Get Jobs*. Princeton University Press, 2015.

Rivers, Damian J. "Cultural Essentialism and Foreigner-as-Criminal Discourse." In *Cultural Essentialism in Intercultural Relations*, edited by Fred Dervin and Regis Machart, 15–41. Palgrave Macmillan UK, 2015.

Roberts, Glenda S. "An Immigration Policy by Any Other Name: Semantics of Immigration to Japan." *Social Science Japan Journal* 21, no. 1 (2018): 89–102. https://doi-org.proxyiub.uits.iu.edu/10.1093/ssjj/jyx033.

Roberts, Glenda S. "Leaning Out for the Long Span: What Holds Women Back from Promotion in Japan?" *Japan Forum* 32, no. 4 (2020): 555–76. https://doi.org/10.1080/09555803.2019.1664619.

Rohlen, Thomas P. *For Harmony and Strength: Japanese White-Collar Organization in Anthropological Perspective.* University of California Press, 1974.

Rosenberg, Qiaoyan Li. "Labor-for-Citizenship Exchange in Japan: A Three-Step Pathway to Permanent Residence, and Precarious Labor for All." Unpublished manuscript, February 12, 2024.

Rosenberg, Qiaoyan Li. "A Semi-Skilled Guest Worker Regime: Specified Skilled Workers (SSW) in Japan." Panel presentation, American Sociological Association Annual Meeting, Philadelphia, PA, August 19, 2023.

Rubinstein, Rachel S., Lee Jussim, and Sean T. Stevens. "Reliance on Individuating Information and Stereotypes in Implicit and Explicit Person Perception." *Journal of Experimental Social Psychology* 75 (2018): 54–70. https://doi.org/10.1016/j.jesp.2017.11.009.

Saitou, Takeshi. "Gaikokujin ryuugakusei ga shuukatsu no raibaru ni? Fueru nihon kigyou he no shuushoku" [Are foreign students becoming rivals in the job hunt? An increasing number find employment in Japanese firms]. *Benesse.* Updated on August 31, 2015. https://benesse.jp/kyouiku/201508/20150831-1.html.

Sakanaka, Hidenori. *Japan as an Immigration Nation: Demographic Change, Economic Necessity, and the Human Community Concept.* Translated by Robert D. Eldridge and Graham B. Leonard. Lexington, 2020.

Sam, David L. "Acculturation: Conceptual Background and Core Components." In *The Cambridge Handbook of Acculturation Psychology,* edited by David L. Sam and John W. Berry, 11–26. Cambridge University Press, 2006.

Sato, Hiroki. "Expanding Work Opportunities for Women and Support for Work-Life Balance: The Roles of Managers." *Social Science Japan* 50 (March 2014): 23–28.

Scacco, Alexandra, and Shana S. Warren. "Can Social Contact Reduce Prejudice and Discrimination? Evidence from a Field Experiment in Nigeria." *American Political Science Review* 112, no. 3 (2018): 654–77. https://doi.org/10.1017/S0003055418000151.

Schachter, Ariela. "From 'Different' to 'Similar': An Experimental Approach to Understanding Assimilation." *American Sociological Review* 81, no. 5 (2016): 981–1013. https://doi.org/10.1177/0003122416659248.

Schaede, Ulrike. *The Business Reinvention of Japan: How to Make Sense of the New Japan and Why It Matters.* Stanford Business Books, 2020.

Schoppa, Leonard. "The Policy Response to Declining Fertility Rates in Japan: Relying on Logic and Hope over Evidence." *Social Science Japan Journal* 23, no. 1 (2020): 3–21. https://doi.org/10.1093/ssjj/jyz046.

Schoppa, Leonard. *Race for the Exits: The Unraveling of Japan's System of Social Protection.* Cornell University Press, 2006.

Sears, David O., and P. J. Henry. "Over Thirty Years Later: A Contemporary Look at Symbolic Racism." *Advances in Experimental Social Psychology* 37 (2005): 95–150.

Shams, Safi, and Donald Tomaskovic-Devey. "Racial and Gender Trends and Trajectories in Access to Managerial Jobs." *Social Science Research* 80 (2019): 15–29. https://doi.org/10.1016/j.ssresearch.2018.12.020.

Shipper, Apichai W. *Fighting for Foreigners: Immigration and Its Impact on Japanese Democracy.* Cornell University Press, 2008.

Small and Medium Enterprise Agency. "Koyou no doukou" [Employment trends]. Updated June 22, 2021. https://www.chusho.meti.go.jp/pamflet/hakusyo/2021/shokibo/b1_1_3.html.

Starich, Megan L. "The 2006 Revisions to Japan's Equal Opportunity Employment Law: A Narrow Approach to a Pervasive Problem." *Pacific Rim Law and Policy Journal* 16, no. 2 (2007): 551–78.

Steel, Gill. "Introduction: Changing Women's and Men's Lives in Japan." In *Beyond the Gender Gap in Japan*, edited by Gill Steel, 1–24. University of Michigan Press, 2019,

Steel, Gill. "Women's Work at Home and in the Workplace." In *Beyond the Gender Gap in Japan*, edited by Gill Steel, 25–49. University of Michigan Press, 2019.

Strausz, Michael. *Help (Not) Wanted: Immigration Politics in Japan.* SUNY Press, 2019.

Struck, Doug. "In Japan, U.S. Expat Fights the Yankee Way." *Washington Post*, July 5, 2003. https://www.washingtonpost.com/archive/lifestyle/2003/07/05/in-japan-us -expat-fights-the-yankee-way/0d7870b7-7730-499c-ac43-c65c770a859e.

Survey Research Center. "Guidelines for Best Practice in Cross-Cultural Surveys." Ann Arbor: Survey Research Center, Institute for Social Research, University of Michigan. Updated 2016. http://ccsg.isr.umich.edu.

Suzuki, Kazuko. *Divided Fates: The State, Race, and Korean Immigrants' Adaptation in Japan and the United States.* Lexington, 2016.

Taka, Fumiaki. "Nihongo Twitter yuuzaa no chuugokujin ni tsuite no gensetsu no kei-ryou-teki bunseki: Korian ni tsuite no gensetsu to no hikaku" [A quantitative analysis of Japanese Twitter users' public opinions of Chinese people: A comparison with their opinions of Korean people]. *Shinbungaku kenkyuu*, no. 53 (2015): 73–85. http://human.kanagawa-u.ac.jp/kenkyu/publ/pdf/syoho/no53/5305.pdf.

Taka, Fumiaki. "Nihongo Twitter yuuzaa no korian ni tsuite no gensetsu no keiryou-teki bunseki" [A quantitative analysis of Japanese Twitter users' public opinions of Koreans]. *Shinbun kenkyuu* no. 183 (2014): 131–53. http://human.kanagawa-u .ac.jp/gakkai/publ/pdf/no183/18305.pdf.

Takeda, Hiroko. "Between Reproduction and Production: Womenomics and the Japanese Government's Approach to Women and Gender Policies." *Journal of Gender Studies* 21 (2018): 49–70. http://www2.igs.ocha.ac.jp/wp-content/uploads/2018/07 /gender-21.pdf#page=49.

Takenaka, Ayumi, Kenji Ishida, and Makiko Nakamuro. "Negative Assimilation: How Immigrants Experience Economic Mobility in Japan." *International Migration Review* 50, no. 2 (2016): 506–33. https://doi.org/10.1111/imre.12129.

Takenoshita, Hirohisa. "The Differential Incorporation into Japanese Labor Market: A Comparative Study of Japanese Brazilians and Professional Chinese Migrants." *Japanese Journal of Population* 4, no. 1 (2006): 56–77. https://www.ipss.go.jp /webj-ad/WebJournal.files/population/2006_3/takenoshita.pdf.

Teikoku Databank. "Tokubetsu kikaku: Josei touyou ni taisuru kigyou no ishiki chosa (2018 nen)" [Special Project: Survey of companies' attitudes about promoting women (2018)]. Updated August 14, 2018. https://www.tdb.co.jp/report/watching /press/pdf/p180805.pdf.

Tian, Yunchen. "Workers by Any Other Name: Comparing Co-Ethnics and 'Interns' as Labour Migrants to Japan." *Journal of Ethnic and Migration Studies* 45, no. 9 (2019): 1496–514.

Tokyo Bengoshikai Gaikokujin no Kenri ni Kansuru Iinkai. "2021nendo gaikoku ni ruutsu wo motsu hito ni taisuru shokumu shitsumon (reisharu purofairingu) ni kansuru ankeeto chousa shaishuu houkokusho" [Final report on the 2021 survey on police questioning (racial profiling) of persons with roots in foreign countries]. Updated September 19, 2022. https://www.toben.or.jp/know/iinkai/foreigner /26a6af6c6f033511cccf887e39fb794e_2.pdf.

Törngren, Sayaka Osanami, and Hilary J. Holbrow. 2017. "Comparing the Experiences of Highly Skilled Labor Migrants in Sweden and Japan: Barriers and Doors to

Long-Term Settlement." *International Journal of Japanese Sociology* 26 (1): 67–82. https://doi.org/10.1111/ijjs.12054.

Toro, Francisco. "Japan Is a Trumpian Paradise of Low Immigration Rates. It's also a Dying Country." *Washington Post*, August 29, 2019. https://www.washingtonpost.com/opinions/2019/08/29/japan-is-trumpian-paradise-low-immigration-rates-its-also-dying-country.

Transtructure. "Sou roudou jikan no suii" [Trends in total working hours]. Updated January 17, 2024. https://www.transtructure.com/hr-data-analysys/search/hr-analysis-report/p7281.

Tseng, Yen-Fen. "Becoming Global Talent? Taiwanese White-Collar Migrants in Japan." *Journal of Ethnic and Migration Studies* 47, no. 10 (2021): 2288–304. https://doi.org/10.1080/1369183X.2020.1731986.

Tsu, Timothy Yun Hui. "Japan's 'Yellow Peril': The Chinese in Imperial Japan and Colonial Korea." *Japanese Studies* 30, no. 2 (2010): 161–83. https://doi.org/10.1080/10371397.2010.485553.

Tsuda, Takeyuki. "Reluctant Hosts: The Future of Japan as a Country of Immigration." U.C. Davis Research and Seminars. https://migration.ucdavis.edu/rs/more.php?id=39.

Tsuda, Takeyuki. "Racism Without Racial Difference? Co-Ethnic Racism and National Hierarchies Among Nikkeijin Ethnic Return Migrants in Japan." *Ethnic and Racial Studies* 45, no. 4 (2022): 595–615. https://doi.org/10.1080/01419870.2021.1993296.

Tsukasaki, Yuko. *Gaikokujin senmonshoku gijutsushoku no koyou mondai: shokugyou kyaria no shiten kara* [Employment problems of professional and technical foreign workers: from the perspective of occupations and careers]. Akashi Shoten, 2008.

Ueno, Chizuko. "Why Do Japanese Women Suffer from the Low Status? The Impact of Neo-Liberalist Reform on Gender." *Japanese Political Economy* 47, no. 1 (2021): 9–26. https://doi.org/10.1080/2329194x.2021.1892496.

Umakoshi, Toru. "Internationalization of Japanese Higher Education in the 1980's and Early 1990's." *Higher Education* 34 (1997): 259–73. https://doi-org.proxyiub.uits.iu.edu/10.1023/A:1003049301267.

United Nations. "Total Population (Both Sexes Combined) by Broad Age Group, Region, Subregion and Country, 1950–2100 (Thousands)." Updated August 27, 2019. https://population.un.org/wpp2019/Download/Files/1_Indicators%20(Standard)/EXCEL_FILES/1_Population/WPP2019_POP_F08_1_TOTAL_POPULATION_BY_BROAD_AGE_GROUP_BOTH_SEXES.xlsx.

UN News. "Japanese Leader Advocates 'Womenomics' in Address to UN General Assembly." United Nations. Updated September 26, 2013. https://news.un.org/en/story/2013/09/450912.

Valentino, Nicholas A., Stuart N. Soroka, Shanto Iyengar, Toril Aalberg, Raymond Duch, Marta Fraile, Kyu S. Hahn, Kasper M. Hansen, Allison Harell, Marc Helbling, Simon D. Jackman, and Tetsuro Kobayashi. "Economic and Cultural Drivers of Immigrant Support Worldwide." *British Journal of Political Science* 49, no. 4 (2019): 1201–26. https://doi.org/10.1017/S000712341700031X.

Various Authors. "Do Western Men Have It Bad Here in Japan?" *Japan Times*, April 8, 2015. https://www.japantimes.co.jp/community/2015/04/08/voices/western-men-bad-japan-readers-discuss/.

Villarreal, Andrés, and Christopher R. Tamborini. "Immigrants' Economic Assimilation: Evidence from Longitudinal Earnings Records." *American Sociological Review* 83, no. 4 (2018): 686–715. https://doi.org/10.1177/0003122418780366.

Vogel, Steven K. "Japan's Labor Regime in Transition: Rethinking Work for a Shrinking Nation." *Journal of Japanese Studies* 44, no. 2 (2018): 257–92. https://doi.org /10.1353/jjs.2018.0039.

Wagatsuma, Hiroshi. "The Social Perception of Skin Color in Japan." *Daedalus* 96, no. 2 (1967): 407–43. http://www.jstor.org/stable/20027045.

Wakisaka, Daisuke. "Unraveling Migration Policy-Making in the Land of 'No Immigrants': Japanese Bureaucracy and the Discursive Gap." *International Migration Review* 58, no. 3 (2023): 1507–31. https://doi.org/10.1177/01979183231171557.

Weathers, Charles, Shinji Kojima, and Scott North. "Litigating Equal Pay for Equal Work in Japan, 2012–2020." *Journal of Contemporary Asia* 54, no. 3 (2023): 432–52. https://doi.org/10.1080/00472336.2023.2183140.

Weiner, Michael. "Koreans in the Aftermath of the Kanto Earthquake of 1923." *Immigrants and Minorities* 2, no. 1 (1983): 5–32. https://doi.org/10.1080/02619288.1983 .9974536.

Williams, Joan C., Mary Blair-Loy, and Jennifer L. Berdahl. "Cultural Schemas, Social Class, and the Flexibility Stigma." *Journal of Social Issues* 69, no. 2 (2013): 209–34. https://doi.org/10.1111/josi.12012.

World Bank. "Labor Force Participation Rate, Female (% of Female Population Ages 15–64)." Updated April 25, 2023. https://data.worldbank.org/indicator/SL.TLF .ACTI.FE.ZS?locations=JP-US-DE-GB-FR-AU-KR.

World Economic Forum. *Global Gender Gap Report 2021*. Updated March 30, 2021. https://www3.weforum.org/docs/WEF_GGGR_2021.pdf.

World Economic Forum. *Global Gender Gap Report 2023*. Updated July 11, 2023. https://www3.weforum.org/docs/WEF_GGGR_2023.pdf.

Wu, Kaidi. 2021. "Invisibility of Social Privilege to Those Who Have It." *Academy of Management Proceedings* 2021, no. 1 (2021). https://doi.org/10.5465/AMBPP .2021.27.

Yagi, Kaoru. "Josei katsuyaku wo habamu ankonshasu baiasu 2: henken wo norikoeru niwa" [Unconscious bias hindering women's empowerment 2: how to overcome prejudice]. *Lightworks*. Updated January 18, 2022. https://research.lightworks .co.jp/get-out-of-unconscious-bias#thosya_profile.

Yamaguchi, Kazuo. *Gender Inequalities in the Japanese Workplace and Employment*. Springer Singapore, 2019.

Yamaguchi, Mari. "Japan Records Steepest Population Decline While Number of Foreign Residents Hits New High." *AP News*. Updated July 26, 2023. https:// apnews.com/article/japan-population-decline-foreign-low-births-d047ea6136a5 c66ffc45508cb824d5f1.

Yamaguchi, Tomomi. "Xenophobia in Action: Ultranationalism, Hate Speech, and the Internet in Japan." *Radical History Review*, no. 117 (2013): 98–118. https://doi .org/10.1215/01636545-2210617.

Yamamoto, Chika. "Kishida Sets Goal of 400,000 International Students In 2033." *Asahi Shimbun*. April 2, 2023. https://www.asahi.com/ajw/articles/14873637.

Yamamoto, Ryoko. "Migrants as a Crime Problem: The Construction of Foreign Criminality Discourse in Contemporary Japan." *International Journal of Comparative and Applied Criminal Justice* 34, no. 2 (2010): 301–30. https://doi.org/10.1080 /01924036.2010.9678831.

Yamashiro, Jane H. *Redefining Japaneseness: Japanese Americans in the Ancestral Homeland*. Rutgers University Press, 2017.

Yanase, Kazuo, Yohei Matsuo, Eugene Lang, and Eri Sugiura. "The New Population Bomb: For the First Time, Humanity Is on the Verge of Long-Term Decline."

Nikkei Asia, September 22, 2021. https://asia.nikkei.com/Spotlight/The-Big-Story/The-new-population-bomb.

Yeung, Jessie, and Gawaon Bae. "South Korea Reports Population Drop, with More Deaths Than Births for First Time." *CNN*, January 4, 2021. https://www.cnn.com/2021/01/04/asia/south-korea-2020-births-intl-hnk-scli/index.html.

Zorko, Špela Drnovšek, and Miloš Debnár. "Comparing the Racialization of Central-East European Migrants in Japan and the UK." *Comparative Migration Studies* 9, no. 30 (2021). https://doi.org/10.1186/s40878-021-00239-z.

Index

Abe, Shinzo, 100, 104, 187
acculturation, 112–15, 136–40
  benefits of, 123–25
  and career success, 121–23
  and comparison of Asian and Japanese
    workers, 125–26
  demands in sample firms, 117–21
  and earnings, 131–36, 189
  and exclusions of Westerners in economic
    sphere, 167
  imperfect, 141
  in Japan's migration policy, 116–17
  and performance evaluations, 114, 122, 127–29
  and professional networks, 114, 122–23, 125,
    129–31
  region of origin and pressures regarding,
    171–73, 183–84
  research on, 69–70, 115–16
  as resolution to perceived problems of
    immigrant integration, 137–38
after-work socializing. *See* off-hours socializing
age
  and earnings, 31–34, 52–53
  and promotion, 32–34, 75
  wages by, among Asian men, 77–78
  wages by, among Asian women, 78–79
  wages by, among Western men, 80–81
  and women's earnings, 49
  women's labor force participation rates by,
    88, 89*f*
alienation, 115–16, 140, 165, 171
ambition
  of foreign workers, 145, 159
  gender gaps in, 94
  and gender inequality, 79
  and outcomes of Asian versus Japanese
    women, 125
anti-Asian biases, 141–43, 158–62
  causality in relationship between
    representation and, 156–58
  and criminality discourse in contemporary
    Japan, 143–44
  following Great Kanto Earthquake, 235n8
  reasons for absence of, in white-collar firms,
    147–48

  and representation, 151–56
  survey experimental examination of, 148–51,
    152–56, 211–14
  in white-collar firms, 144–47
  See also criminality discourse;
    discrimination; ethnoracial bias;
    ethnoracial stereotypes; racism;
    xenophobia
artificial intelligence (AI), 199
Asian criminality. *See* criminality discourse
Asian men
  acculturation and comparison of Japanese
    workers and, 125–26
  and acculturation and earnings, 131–36
  acculturation and performance of, 128
  and acculturation and professional networks,
    129–31
  acculturation standards for, 114
  continued progress toward equality with
    Japanese men, 12–13, 200–201
  as managers, 75
  optimism for future trajectories of, 159, 162
  reasons for parity with Japanese men,
    191–92
  and region of origin and pressure to
    acculturate, 171–72
  and regression of human capital on earnings,
    75–76, 77
  in research on employment in Japan, 70–71
  self-assessed promotion chances of, 67, 68
  and stratification by gender and region of
    origin, 74
  wages by age among, 77–78
  See also anti-Asian biases; criminality
    discourse
Asian women
  acculturation and comparison of Japanese
    workers and, 125–26
  and acculturation and earnings, 131–36
  acculturation and performance of, 128–29
  and acculturation and professional networks,
    129–31
  acculturation standards for, 114
  and anti-Asian bias, 152
  disadvantage of, 67, 70

www.ingramcontent.com/pod-product-compliance
Lightning Source LLC
Chambersburg PA
CBHW020610050326
40680CB00006B/539